APPROACHES TO ART THERAPY

APPROACHES TO ART THERAPY

Theory and Technique
Second Edition

edited by
Judith Aron Rubin

BRUNNER-ROUTLEDGE

Taylor & Francis Group

Published by
Brunner-Routledge
29 West 35th Street
New York, NY 10001

Published in Great Britain
Brunner-Routledge
11 New Fetter Lane
London EC4P 4EE

APPROACHES TO ART THERAPY: Theory and Technique, Second Edition

7 8 9 0

Printed by Sheridan Books, Ann Arbor, MI, 2001.
Cover design by Robert Williams.

A CIP catalog record for this book is available from the British Library.
   The paper in this publication meets the requirements of the ANSI Standard Z39.48-1984 (Permanence of Paper).

Library of Congress Cataloging-in-Publication Data

Approaches to art therapy : theory & technique / edited by
   Judith Aron Rubin. —2nd ed.
      p.   cm.
   Includes bibliographical references and index.
   ISBN 1-58391-070-0 (hbk. : alk. paper)
   1. Art therapy.   I. Rubin, Judith Aron.

   RC489.A7 A67   2001
   616.89′1656—dc21

                                        2001025120

ISBN 1 58391 070 0 (case)

CONTENTS

ACKNOWLEDGMENTS

There are always many who have helped directly and indirectly with a project as complex as this book. The first edition was my only attempt at an edited volume, and it turned out to be surprisingly free from stress. The same has been true of the second edition, which has also benefited from the availability of a computer and email, greatly speeding up the process.

My colleagues have been prompt and agreeable, even when the changes I suggested in their first drafts were more than minimal. My deepest thanks, then, to each and every one, for writing a chapter or a commentary, and for making my editorial job so pleasant and rewarding.

Special thanks go to the late Elinor Ulman, publisher and executive editor of the *American Journal of Art Therapy*, for permission to reprint all or part of Chapters 2, 3, 8, and 17. I am grateful to the authors of the original chapters or their heirs, who were able to find illustrations as needed; and to photographers Lynn Johnson and Jim Burke for their contributions. Thanks, too, to colleagues who graciously sent me copies of relevant talks, articles, or illustrations: Mimi Farrelly-Hansen, Michael Franklin, Irene Jakab, Frances Kaplan, Ann Mills, Marcia Rosal, Irene Rosner-David, and Elizabeth Stone.

Sadly, many of those who contributed to the first edition are no longer alive. Since they were all true pioneers, I am very pleased that they are represented in this new edition, so that their wisdom can be available to art therapists of this and future generations.

Finally, my deepest thanks to my husband, children, and grandchildren, whose patience and understanding allowed me to complete this work.

CONTRIBUTORS

Susan Aach-Feldman, M.Ed., ATR*

Expressive Arts Therapist, Western Pennsylvania School for Blind Children; Adjunct Faculty, Art Therapy Program, Carlow College, Pittsburgh, PA; Consultant, Arts in Special Education Project of Pennsylvania.

Pat B. Allen, Ph.D., ATR

Cofounder and former Codirector, Open Studio Project, Chicago, IL; Director, Studio Pardes, Oak Park, IL; Adjunct Professor, School of the Art Institute of Chicago; Author, *Art is a Way of Knowing* (1995).

Frances E. Anderson, Ed.D., ATR-BC, HLM

Distinguished Professor of Art and Director, Graduate Art Therapy Program, Illinois State University, Normal, IL; Author, *Art for All the Children* (1978/1992) and *Art-Centered Education & Therapy for Children with Disabilities* (1994).

Robert E. Ault, M.F.A., ATR-BC, HLM

Director, Ault's Academy of Art; Art Therapist in private practice, Topeka, KS; former Art Therapist and Psychotherapist, Menninger Foundation, Topeka, KS; former Director, Art Therapy Program, Emporia State University, Emporia, KS.

Mala G. Betensky, Ph.D., ATR*

Psychologist and Art Therapist in private practice, Washington, DC; Author, *Self-Discovery Through Self-Expression* (1973) and *What do You See?* (1995).

Michael Edwards, RATh., H.L.M.

Jungian Analyst and Art Therapist in private practice, Cornwall, England; former Director, Graduate Art Therapy Program, Concordia University, Montreal, Canada; former Honorary Curator, The C. G. Jung Picture Archives.

Josef E. Garai, Ph.D., ATR*

Professor and Chair, Creative-Expressive Arts Therapies Program, Pratt Institute, Brooklyn, NY; Art Therapist and Psychologist in private practice, NY.

David R. Henley, Ph.D., ATR

Professor and Director, Art Therapy Programs, C. W. Post Campus, Long Island University, Brookville, NY; Author, *Exceptional Children, Exceptional Art* (1992); Clinical Coordinator, Child Therapy Services of the Drs. Hecht, Clinton, NJ.

---

*Deceased.

Eleanor C. Irwin, Ph.D., RDT

Clinical Assistant Professor, Department of Psychiatry, University of Pittsburgh; Faculty, Pittsburgh Psychoanalytic Institute; Drama Therapist and Psychoanalyst in private practice, Pittsburgh, PA.

Edith Kramer, D.A.T. (Honorary), ATR-BC, HLM

Adjunct Professor of Art Therapy, New York University and George Washington University, Washington, DC; Author, *Art Therapy in a Children's Community* (1958), *Art as Therapy with Children* (1971), *Childhood and Art Therapy* (1979), and *Art as Therapy: Collected Papers* (2001).

Carole Kunkle-Miller, Ph.D., ATR

Former Art Therapist, Western Psychiatric Institute and Clinic and the Western Pennsylvania School for Blind Children; Art Therapist and Psychologist in private practice, Pittsburgh, PA; Personal Coach at www.LifelineCoach.com.

Mildred Lachman-Chapin, M.Ed., ATR, CCMHC

Painter, Poet, and Art Therapist in private practice, Sedona, AZ; former Director, Adjunctive Therapies, Barclay and Pritzker Hospitals, Chicago, IL; Author and Illustrator, *Reverberations: Mothers & Daughters* (1995).

Shaun A. McNiff, Ph.D., ATR, HLM

Provost and Dean, Endicott College, Beverly, MA; founder and former Director, Expressive Therapies Program, Lesley College, Cambridge, MA; Author, *The Arts & Psychotherapy* (1981), *Art as Medicine* (1994), *Trust the Process* (1999), *Art-Based Research* (1999), and other books on art and therapy.

Bruce L. Moon, Ph.D., ATR

Director, Graduate Art Therapy Program, Marywood University, Scranton, PA; former Codirector, Clinical Art Therapy Program, and Chief, Adjunctive Therapies, Harding Hospital, Worthington, OH; Author, *Existential Art Therapy* (1990/1995), *Art & Soul* (1997), and other books on art therapy.

Janie Rhyne, Ph.D., ATR-BC, HLM*

Assistant Professor of Art Therapy, Vermont College of Norwich University; Adjunct Professor, Graduate School of Social Work, University of Iowa; private practice, Iowa City, IA; Author, *The Gestalt Art Experience* (1973, 2nd ed. 1996).

Shirley Riley, M.F.T., ATR

Faculty, Phillips Graduate Institute; Art Therapist in private practice, Los Angeles, CA; Author, *Integrative Approaches to Family Art Therapy* and *Supervision & Related Issues* (with Cathy Malchiodi), *Contemporary Art Therapy with Adolescents* (1999), and *Art in Group Therapy* (2001).

Arthur Robbins, Ed.D., ATR, HLM

Professor, Art Therapy, Pratt Institute, Brooklyn, NY; Founding Director, Institute for Expressive Analysis, NY; Faculty, National Psychological Association for Psychoanalysis; private practice of Art Therapy and Psychoanalysis, NY; Author, *The Artist as Therapist* (1987), *A Multi-Modal Approach to Creative Art Therapy* (1994), and other books on art and therapy.

Natalie Rogers, Ph.D., REAT

Artist and Group Facilitator; Founder and former Director, Person-Centered Expressive Therapy Institute, Cotati, CA; Author, *Emerging Woman* (1980) and *The Creative Connection: Expressive Arts as Healing* (1993); Lifetime Achievement Award, International Expressive Arts Therapy Association (1998).

Marcia L. Rosal, Ph.D., ATR-BC

Professor, Florida State University Art Therapy Program; former Distinguished Teaching Professor, Expressive Therapies Program, University of Louisville (KY); Author, *Approaches to Art Therapy with Children* (1996).

Ellen A. Roth, Ph.D., ATR

President, Getting to the Point, Inc., Pittsburgh, PA; former Research Consultant, Western Psychiatric Institute and Clinic, University of Pittsburgh; Editor, *Perspectives on Art Therapy* (1978).

Judith A. Rubin, Ph.D., ATR-BC, HLM

Clinical Assistant Professor of Psychiatry, University of Pittsburgh; Emeritus Faculty, Pittsburgh Psychoanalytic Institute; Art Therapist and Psychoanalyst in private practice, Pittsburgh, PA; Author, *Child Art Therapy* (1978/1984), *The Art of Art Therapy* (1984), and *Art Therapy: An Introduction* (1998).

Joy Schaverien, Ph.D. RATh.

Professor in Art Psychotherapy, University of Sheffield; Jungian Analyst and Art Therapist in private practice, Leicestershire, (UK): Author, *The Revealing Image: Analytical Art Psychotherapy in Theory & Practice* (1991), and *Desire and the Female Therapist* (1995); Coeditor, *Art, Psychotherapy & Psychosis* (1997).

Rawley A. Silver, Ed.D., ATR-BC, HLM

Retired Art Therapist, Sarasota, FL; Recipient, Four Research Awards, AATA; Author, *Developing Cognitive & Creative Skills Through Art* (1978/2000), *Silver Drawing Test of Cognition & Emotion* (1983/1996), *Stimulus Drawings & Techniques* (1989), *Draw a Story* (1993), *Art as Language* (2000).

Barbara S. Sobol, M.A., ATR, LPC

Child and Family Art Therapist, Prince George's County, MD; Clinical Case Coordinator, Montgomery County Department of Health and Human Services, MD; Adjunct Faculty, George Washington University, Washington, DC, Vermont College, New York University; Director, Washington Art Therapy Studio; Consultant, DC Rape Crisis Center.

Elinor Ulman, D.A.T. (Honorary), ATR-BC, HLM*

Founder and former Executive Editor, *American Journal of Art Therapy*; Founder and Adjunct Professor of Art Therapy, George Washington University, Washington, DC; Coeditor, *Art Therapy in Theory and Practice* (1975/1996), *Art Therapy Viewpoints* (1981).

Harriet Wadeson, Ph.D., LCSW, ATR-BC, HLM

Coordinator, Art Therapy Graduate Program, University of Illinois, Chicago, IL; Author, *Art Psychotherapy* (1980), *The Dynamics of Art Psychotherapy* (1987), and *Art Therapy Practice* (2000); Editor, *Advances in Art Therapy* (1989) and *A Guide to Conducting Art Therapy Research* (1992).

Edith Wallace, M.D., Ph.D.

Jungian Analyst and Psychiatrist in private practice, Santa Fe, NM; Workshop Leader, "Opening Channels to the Creative"; Faculty, C. G. Jung Foundation & Institute for Expressive Analysis, NY; Author, *A Queen's Quest* (1990).

Katherine A. Williams, Ph.D., ATR-BC

Former Director, Art Therapy Program, George Washington University, Washington, DC; Graduate, Washington School of Psychiatry Group Training Institute; Art Therapist and Psychologist in private practice, Washington, DC.

Laurie Wilson, Ph.D., ATR-BC

Art Therapist and Psychoanalyst in private practice, New York City; former Director, Graduate Art Therapy Program, New York University; Faculty, NYU Psychoanalytic Institute; Sculptor; Author, *Louise Nevelson's Iconography and Sources* (1980) and *Alberto Giacometti: Myth, Magic, and the Man* (2001).

Key

ATR: Registered Art Therapist, American Art Therapy Association
BC: Board Certified, American Art Therapy Association
HLM: Honorary Life Member, American Art Therapy Association
H.L.M: Honorary Life Member, British Association of Art Therapists
RATh.: Registered Art Therapist, British Association of Art Therapists
REAT: Registered Expressive Arts Therapist, International Expressive Arts Therapy Association
RDT: Registered Drama Therapist, National Association of Drama Therapy

PREFACE

The idea for the first edition of this book was hatched in 1983, as a reaction to a felt need in the field of art therapy. This second edition is a response to the many requests from art therapy educators over the years to add points of view omitted in the first edition. Although I could not include every possibility, I hope that the revisions and additions will be useful.

Only someone who knows and understands a theory well can teach it to others. While this is true for any kind of therapy, it is especially true when the theory must be modified in some way in order to be applied to a specific form of treatment with its own intrinsic qualities, like art therapy, Contributors were asked to introduce the reader to the orientation, note the particular relevance of the theory or concept to art therapy, and to illustrate the approach in practice with one or more brief case examples.

The plan for the book is simple: a series of chapters, each one written by someone who is familiar with the theory involved, and who has worked out a way of integrating it with art therapy. In addition to inviting seven authors to write six new chapters, I have also asked five art therapists who know a particular area to write brief commentaries on the chapters in that section. Finally, I have requested that another colleague write an addendum for a chapter in an area which has undergone especially fertile growth. As a result, this second edition contains the voices of 13 additional art therapists.

In order to make space for the added material while retaining the essence of the earlier writings, most of which are still relevant, it has been necessary to tighten some of the original chapters. In this effort, as in the additions, I have relied heavily on feedback from colleagues who have used the text in teaching over the years. I am also comforted by the knowledge that the first edition is still accessible in libraries, for those who desire to gain access to any material I have omitted.

Since the first edition was published in 1987, I have retired from full-time clinical practice, giving me the necessary time to revise this book. Having been an art therapist for almost 40 years, I remain convinced that the kind of thinking illustrated in this book is essential for anyone who hopes to help people grow through art.

I remind the reader, nevertheless, that the following descriptions—of what is always a heavily nonverbal or paraverbal process—should be understood as mere approximations of therapeutic reality. In fact, because of the limitations of words in describing art therapy, I am currently working on a teaching videotape to accompany a recent overview of the discipline: *Art Therapy: An Introduction* (Rubin, 1998).

As John Locke wrote in his *Essay on Human Understanding*, "We should have a great many fewer disputes in the world if words were taken for what they are, the signs of our ideas only, and not for things themselves." And, as far as I am concerned, the last word on that issue was said by Lewis Carroll in *Through the Looking Glass*:

"The question is," said Alice, "whether you can make words mean so many different things?"

"The question is," said Humpty Dumpty, "which is to be master—that's all."

Hopefully, this book, though far from perfect, will help the reader to be "master" of his or her work as an art therapist . . . "that's all."

Judith Aron Rubin
Pittsburgh, Pennsylvania
July, 2000

INTRODUCTION

Judith Rubin

Some years ago, I described my personal quest for a sound theoretical framework to guide my work as an art therapist, by saying that I, like my chosen field, had been shopping for a theory. Each time I looked for a "goodness of fit," wondering whether I had at last found the "right" theoretical framework for therapeutic growth in and through art. At first, I worked with people on a largely intuitive basis. Later, I looked for ways to understand what was going on and ideas about how best to proceed.

In 1963, art therapy pioneer Margaret Naumburg suggested that, since I was seeing children, I should read Clark Moustakas (1953) on play therapy. I did, and fell in love with his warmth and his respect for the youngsters he saw. For a while, his humanistic approach seemed sufficient, and it was appealingly unintrusive.

Later, however, while working at the Pittsburgh Child Guidance Center (1969–1981), I found that the more disturbed youngsters did not automatically get better just by providing the sort of permissive child-centered atmosphere recommended by Moustakas. I therefore had to look further, and in the course of a search for additional training, I realized that my most helpful supervisors had been those who had a psychoanalytic orientation. Attracted to this framework, largely through those espousing it, I decided to study it in depth.

And, despite Erik Erikson's warning to me in 1964 that I might lose something valuable if I studied analysis, it has been helpful, especially in understanding and working with the dynamics of the more complicated cases that have crossed my path. Nonetheless, Freudian theory has never adequately explained for me all of the richness, mystery, and beauty of the creative process which is at the heart of art therapy.

In search of a theory that could shed more light on that realm, I have delved briefly into Jungian, Gestalt, phenomenological, and humanistic psychotherapy. And I have found that each of these approaches, these different sets of lenses, illuminates slightly different aspects of human personality and growth. I have enjoyed the studying I have done in most theories, usually finding something with which to resonate.

At first, I thought that the solution to my problem would be a kind of patchwork, a mosaic, a collage of different facets from different theories, which together would account for what happens in art therapy. Although this kind of additive eclecticism may yet be the answer, I have doubts about the inevitable inconsistencies of such an attempt. I question the feasibility, in other words, of mixing theoretical apples, oranges, raisins, and nuts.

What seems more probable is that a theory about art therapy will eventually emerge from art therapy itself. It will no doubt partake of elements from other perspectives, but will need to have its own inner integrity in terms of the creative process at its core. Many concepts—from Freudian psychoanalysis and Jungian analytic therapy, from Gestalt psychology and Gestalt therapy, from humanistic and existential thought, from aestheticians like Susanne Langer, from research on creativity by academic psychologists, and from studies of the workings of the brain by neuropsychiatrists—will no doubt prove to be relevant. And no doubt many will not, perhaps even some of those that now seem most appealing. What seems best is to proceed by looking at the experience of art therapy—with an openness that does not categorize or label—until the central themes, issues, constructs, and concepts begin to take shape.

In *The Art of Art Therapy* (Rubin, 1984a), I suggested that "what is needed now is the development of meaningful theoretical constructs from the matrix of art therapy itself" (p. 190) and indeed, I devoted an entire chapter to an awkward initial attempt to do just that. Nevertheless, I also continued to believe in "the possible relevance of theories from other disciplines and their application to our own" (p. 190) despite my "uneasiness about the possibility that we may be forcing art therapy into theoretical molds that do not quite 'fit'" (p. 190).

Also pertinent to this book, "in order to be able to converse and to communicate with students and other professionals, it is necessary to know and understand the similarities and differences between things like Gestalt psychology and Gestalt therapy, or classical psychoanalytic drive theory and the recent developments in object relations" (Rubin, 1984a, p. 190). In other words, if art therapists are to function as sophisticated members of a clinical, educational, medical, or social team, our comprehension of any theoretical stance needs to be as deep and clear as that of others.

It is not only important to know what we are talking about in order to gain the respect of our peers; it is also best for the eventual development of theory in our own discipline. "Being familiar with different theories of how and why people function in general, and particularly in art, cannot but deepen our understanding of the phenomena with which we deal" (Rubin, 1984a, p. 190). I also believe that "it is especially useful, where possible, to read the original (not just someone else's translation of meaning) in order to fully grasp, for example, Freud's (1900) theory of dream formation as well as its technical implications (Altman, 1975)" (Rubin, 1984a, p. 190).

In the chapters and commentaries that comprise this volume, individuals who have studied the original theorists describe the aspects of that theory they find relevant to their work. They then present examples of art therapy conducted according to their understanding of the particular model, so the reader can more easily bridge the gap between the original theory and its possible application to our own discipline. The challenge is "to adapt [any] theory to the special needs of the art therapy situation with as minimal a compromise in the integrity of the theory as possible" (Stone, 1996, p. 1) while making sure that "the art process remains a 'full player' . . . and not just another psychotherapeutic treatment tool" (p. 1).

"Theory is only meaningful and worthwhile if it helps to explain the phenomena with which it deals in a way that enables us to work better with them. To learn . . . theories of personality, psychotherapy, or creativity without actually applying them to real life situations is to grasp neither their meaning nor their significance. Theory and technique should go hand in hand; the one based on and growing out of the other, each constantly modifying the other over time. Although this may sound too intellectual for most art therapists, it may be as important to the continued development of our field as defining the 'basics'" (Rubin, 1984a, pp. 191–192).

That intimate relationship between theory and practice is the main reason why a book like this one is needed. To do things with patients or clients in art therapy without knowing why one does them is simply irresponsible. A good art therapist has some notion of what is "wrong," as well as some ideas about how to facilitate a process of getting "better." Since many different approaches seem to work, it is foolish to debate which is the "correct" one. Rather, it seems most sensible to try to understand each of the common approaches in depth, especially the link between theory and practice.

Professional maturation in any clinical field usually involves "trying on" or experimenting with different approaches, as much to find which one "fits" the therapist as which one "works" with the patient. In fact, I am quite convinced that only if an approach is comfortable for a therapist is it at all useful in his or her hands. As Susan Deri (1984) points out, "one seldom hears acknowledgment that the organizational symbols behind one's outlook are, to some extent, subjectively chosen. We select our conceptual framework not only on the basis of intellectual judgment but also because it is congenial to our way of thinking and because the type of clinical work that follows from it suits our personality" (p. 181).

Reading Deri's (1984) words, I was reminded of a paper I had written for a course many years ago on the connection between my own values and my reactions to different theories of personality and psychotherapy. In it, I talked about how my work as an art therapist was based on certain strongly-held convictions about human beings: that all have genuine creative potential; that most have one or more preferred creative modalities which must be identified in order for each to fulfill that potential; and that all have a natural tendency toward growth, toward actualizing that potential at increasingly mature levels.

I see that growth process as characteristically cyclical—both regressive and progressive—with a tendency toward a kind of homeostasis and order which has both dynamic and static elements. All of these assumptions concern human capacities and positive tendencies—toward creativity, growth, and balance—which seem to be potential in all creatures. It is not surprising, then, that I have often found myself attracted to theories whose picture of man resonates with such optimistic notions—ideas about self-actualization, for example, which form the core of humanistic approaches to personality and psychotherapy.

Despite my conviction that all human beings are internally propelled in the direction of growth, however, providing facilitating conditions for creativity has sometimes been insufficient. Those positive tendencies were often blocked or distorted, and in their stead were destructive or disorderly behaviors. The theory of personality and development which still makes the most sense to me in understanding the blocks and distortions, as well as their genesis, is that derived from Freudian psychoanalysis.

This is especially true of the developmental aspects of psychoanalytic theory, which explain how individuals can be "stuck" at earlier levels, and thus be unable to fulfill their potential. Learning to recognize different adaptive modes and defensive mechanisms for dealing with internal deficits or intrapsychic conflict, has helped me to understand the forms the blocking or distortions take (e.g., "symptoms").

The importance of the symbol, of that powerful form of expression and communication, is also central to my work. To the extent that both Freud and Jung concerned themselves with this aspect of human thought and expression, they have each been helpful.

As we continue, in this new millenium, to struggle toward greater clarity and more coherent theory in the field of art therapy, it is essential that we not abandon the parallel challenge of truly comprehending different theoretical and technical approaches to psychotherapy. It is equally important to continue the debate, and to go on with the attempt to apply ways of thinking about people and change to art therapy, a task begun by the contributors to both editions of this volume.

In 1980 I was asked to review a collection of articles on art therapy that shared a common bias, openly stated by the editors (Ulman & Levy, 1980, p. ix). That volume, like many others in our field, represented a single theoretical point of view. Most had been written by individuals, and were attempts to express the writer's understandings after a period of work as an art therapist. I have written two books of that sort myself, and I think that such personal statements are necessary and understandable in a youthful discipline that is working hard to define its identity for itself as well as for others. In my (unpublished) book review, I noted that there was a crying need in this young and divergent field for a single volume which would clarify and articulate genuinely *different* points of view.

Like a recent overview of the field, *Art Therapy: An Introduction* (Rubin, 1998), the first edition of this book was an attempt to provide a glimpse of different ways of working, and the theories on which they are based. I hope that the chapters in this revised edition will help both students and practitioners to make the leap—from any general theory of personality and psychotherapy to the theory and practice of art therapy.

As for the selection of theories and authors, psychoanalytic theory was dominant in art therapy, as it was in American psychiatry, during the early years of its development (Naumburg, 1947, 1950, 1953; Kramer, 1958). In psychology, there was a heated debate between those espousing psychodynamic approaches and those enamored of behaviorism, which, like analysis, had developed in the beginning of the century.

In response to the determinism inherent in both psychoanalysis and behaviorism, a variety of other approaches were proposed which became known as "humanistic," a "third force" in psychology. Most stressed positive, "self-actualizing" elements in human nature, as well as the ability to take charge of one's fate, and not be at the mercy of either the invisible unconscious or learning experiences.

The first three sections of this book, then, parallel the three major orientations in psychology and psychotherapy: the psychodynamic, the humanistic, and the behavioral (here, psycho-educational). I shall describe the new material in these sections, as well as the two divisions which have been added to this second edition.

There is no new chapter in the psychodynamic section, although this area has been teeming with developments during the past two decades. Because original chapters are still valid, however, I have invited two analytically trained arts therapists to add to what is already there. One, a Freudian, has provided a brief overview of recent developments in an Addendum to the first five chapters. The other, a Jungian, has written an extended Commentary on all seven of the original chapters, with particular attention to their continued relevance and future implications for research.

Although behavioral and cognitive approaches have rapidly grown in popularity among "talking cure" specialists of all disciplines since the time of the first edition, psychodynamic approaches are still widely used by art therapists. Their continuing popularity may be due to the very nature of art, which makes the assumption of a dynamic unconscious intrinsically appealing. Artists often feel as if "inspiration" comes mysteriously from their own depths, and most art therapists are artists themselves, as well as people who work to inspire creativity in others.

As for the humanistic section, I have omitted the Adlerian chapter, largely because it is an approach used by only a small minority of art therapists. Instead, there are two new chapters, one on "person-centered expressive arts therapy." The other, on an "open studio" approach rooted in a spiritual quest, is closely related to "transpersonal" art therapy. Both studio-based and spiritual approaches are of increasing interest to art therapists in recent years. I believe that humanistic approaches continue to be popular, because of the pleasure and possibility of self-actualization inherent in a satisfying creative process, the mysterious healing power of art, and our deep need to connect with something beyond ourselves.

Although still least popular among art therapists, the "stars" of the current psychotherapy scene—behavioral and cognitive approaches—are becoming more widely used. There is a new chapter on cognitive-behavioral art therapy, the orientation where there are the largest number of outcome studies. Since developmental approaches tend to involve more instructional components than either dynamic or humanistic ones, I have included them in the third section of the book, which I have imperfectly renamed "psycho-educational," for want of a better umbrella term.

In addition, there are two new sections in this second edition. One is about systemic approaches to art therapy, that is, working with people as part of an interpersonal and social "system." Although it is possible for an understanding of systems theory to underly individual art therapy, it remains most visible in group and family art therapy. They are the focus of both the new chapter and the commentary, which also deals with the relation of "postmodern" thought to art therapy.

The other new section deals with integrative approaches to art therapy. In it I have included the two original chapters regarding the problem of selection among different theories. I have also added two new ones, dealing from different viewpoints with "intermodal" art therapy, that is, the use of a wide range of expressive arts forms.

Although I could not include all of the many different approaches bubbling on the current scene to this second edition, I have tried to choose those which seem to have settled in somewhat, and which are used by a substantial number of art therapists. My selections have also been guided by my colleagues who train others, and I thank them for their counsel.

Nevertheless, the reader may still wonder at the absence of other approaches included in some textbooks on theories of psychotherapy. Since any selection process is ultimately arbitrary, I apologize to those who feel that important theories have been overlooked or misrepresented. There is, for example, no chapter on feminist or multicultural art therapy, since they represent a sensitivity to aspects of patients' identity which have been neglected in the past, rather than a difference in viewing the process of psychological change. Nor are there chapters on intersubjective, relational, narrative, or solution-focused art therapy, although they are referred to in the added commentaries (cf. Malchiodi, 2001). Should any of them prove to be lasting, they would be possibilities for a third edition. Meanwhile, I have tried to preserve the many still-timely chapters in the first edition, and to add those that seemed most relevant to our field.

The reader may also be concerned that some case examples used by authors to illustrate their approach are relatively long-term by current "managed-care" standards. However, "brief" art therapy can be conducted according to any of the orientations in this book, including psychodynamic ones. Indeed, the basic principles noted in each of the chapters are all applicable to art therapy done under a wide variety of conditions.

In addition, the reader might ask, why so many distinct approaches? The answer is that art therapy is really no different from psychotherapy, in that "the reason why there are so many different definitions ... is that there is lively disagreement about most of the issues central to the therapy process" (Belkin, 1980, p. 1). And, "although therapy is conceived of as a helping process, there is wide disagreement about how the helping is done, and the respective roles of the therapist and patient" (Belkin, 1980, p. 2). Similarly, while all art therapists agree that there is something inherently therapeutic in an authentic creative process, the debate about the nature of that healing element is lively and ongoing, as will be evident.

I was pleased to discover recently that this book's contents represent what most art therapists are thinking as they do their work. As I was about to send the manuscript to the publisher, the latest issue of the American Art Therapy Association journal arrived, with a report of a member survey (Elkins & Stovall, 2000). When asked to identify their main theoretical orientation, approximately 25% chose the "psychodynamic" category (psychodynamic, Jungian, object relations, and psychoanalytic).

The next largest group were the 20% who chose "eclectic," which is related not only to the four chapters on "integrative" approaches, but also to the others incorporating more than one theory (e.g., phenomenological, Gestalt, humanistic, "person-centered," developmental, and systemic). A further indication that art therapists are most comfortable with more than one way of looking at things is the fact that close to 30% of the respondents actually listed more than one theory.

Given the limitations of space, it would be impossible for an author to present a complete scholarly introduction to any of the theories. Rather, each chapter represents one art therapist's sincere attempt to apply what seems relevant from a particular theoretical position to his or her work. You or I might question the selectivity of some authors or the inclusiveness of others. We might also disagree with the way in which an author has interpreted a theory, in terms of the technique described.

What I hope you will gain, however, is an introduction to many different perspectives, and a notion of how one might go about translating theory into technique. If my colleagues and I have accomplished that, we have done at least part of what seems to be needed. If we have also stimulated further theoretical thinking in others, then we have done even more for the future of our discipline.

On a 1979 panel, I said that I hoped that "clinicians would be trained not only to practice well, but also to think clearly; and would be able to begin the hard work of exploring the art therapy process itself, developing a theory with appropriate constructs, the precise shape of which was still a mystery to me at that time. I hoped that we would have the frustration tolerance to sustain us as we struggled towards greater clarity and synthesis. I still believe that we must be willing to take risks, to debate openly, and to continually go back to the data of our clinical work in order to decide how viable—not how attractive—any particular construct seems to be.

Although it would be nice if we were further along in the area of theory development in art therapy at the end of the 20th century, we can take comfort in the knowledge that both art and human beings are wonderfully rich and complex. Thus, it makes sense that our search should be an ongoing and, I suspect, an eternal one. Although there are no easy answers, when art therapists can see the intimate relationship between theory and practice, theory becomes a lively area which can greatly empower our work. This volume, with all its imperfections, is meant to be a contribution to greater thoughtfulness and open-mindedness on the part of those who practice the wonderful work of healing through art.

☐ References

Altman, L. L. (1975). *The dream in psychoanalysis* (2nd ed.). New York: International Universities Press.

Belkin, G. S. (Ed.). (1980). *Contemporary psychotherapies*. Chicago: Rand McNally.

Deri, S. K. (1984). *Symbolization and creativity*. New York: International Universities Press.

Elkins, D. E., & Stovall, K. (2000). American Art Therapy Association Inc: 1998–1999 membership survey report. *Art therapy*, (2000), *17*, (1) 41–46.

Freud, S. (1900/1955). *The interpretation of dreams. Standard edition*, Vol. 4–5. London: Hogarth Press.

Kramer, E. (1958). *Art therapy in a children's community*. Springfield, IL: Charles C Thomas.

Malchiodi, C. A. (Ed.). (2001). *Clinical handbook of art therapy*. New York: Guilford.

Moustakas, C. E. (1953). *Children in play therapy*. New York: Ballantine Books.

Naumburg, M. (1947). Studies of the "free" art expression of behavior problem children and adolescents as a means of diagnosis and therapy. *Nervous & Mental Disease, 71.*

Naumburg, M. (1950). *Schizophrenic art: Its meaning in psychotherapy.* New York: Grune & Stratton.

Naumburg, M. (1953). *Psychoneurotic art: Its function in psychotherapy.* New York: Grune & Stratton.

Rubin, J. A. (1984a). *The art of art therapy.* New York: Brunner/Mazel.

Rubin, J. A. (1984b). *Child art therapy: Understanding and helping children grow through art* (2nd ed.) New York: Wiley. (1st ed. 1978).

Rubin, J. A. (1998). *Art therapy: An introduction.* Philadelphia: Brunner/Mazel.

Stone, E. (1996). The intrapsychic and the interpersonal in art therapy. Paper presented at the 1996 Annual Conference of Art Therapy Italiana, Rome.

Ulman, E., & Levy, C. (Eds.). (1980). *Art therapy viewpoints.* New York: Schocken Books.

PSYCHODYNAMIC APPROACHES

As noted in the Introduction, the chapters in this section reflect the origins as well as many current trends in art therapy. Psychoanalytic theory, contrary to popular prejudice, has never been rigid or static. Its founder was an inquiring explorer whose notions about human beings changed considerably over the course of his many productive years, during which he continually modified his theoretical formulations. Similarly, his followers have continued to question, to debate, and to reformulate ideas about both theory and technique, in both analysis and psychoanalytic psychotherapy (Ellman, Grand, Silvan, & Ellmann, 1998). The first five chapters in this section are all based on Freudian theory, each with a slightly different focus.

Were Margaret Naumburg (1947, 1950, 1953, 1966) alive, she would have been the logical choice to write the first chapter, with its emphasis on Freud's early goal of "making the unconscious conscious," leading eventually to insight ("where id was there shall ego be"). I have written that chapter myself, after considerable internal debate about the propriety of being both editor and author. However, having been trained at an orthodox Freudian institute in classical psychoanalytic technique, which I have tried to apply to art therapy, I felt as well qualified as most of my colleagues to speak as a descendant of our first pioneer.

In the following two chapters, Edith Kramer and Laurie Wilson concentrate on the implications for art therapy of psychoanalytic ego psychology, with particular attention to sublimation and symbolization. Kramer, the originator of one of the earliest theories of art therapy, here further clarifies a position expressed in an impressive list of contributions (1958, 1971, 1979). Wilson has written a stimulating chapter, in which she looks at the clinical phenomena of art therapy, through eyes sharpened by formulations on the development and dynamics of symbolization.

The next two chapters involve still other facets of psychoanalytic theory. Arthur Robbins sees much of value to art therapists in an understanding of object relations, which he elucidates through a vivid clinical example. Mildred Lachman-Chapin then focuses our attention on self-psychology and some possible implications for work in our field (cf. Leibowitz, 1999). Both object relations and self-psychology are areas of lively debate among analysts, discussed in an addendum by Eleanor Irwin, an analytically trained expressive arts therapist.

The other major depth psychologist is Jung, whose popularity among art therapists has always been big in Great Britain (cf. Dalley, 1984), and is rapidly rising among American practitioners. Because Jung himself painted and used art with his patients, those trained in analytical psychology are more likely than Freudians to include creative processes in treatment, such as drawing in the process of "active imagination" or creating imaginary worlds in a tray of sand.

Unable to decide between inviting a Jungian analyst who used art or an art therapist trained in analytic psychology to write the chapter, I resolved my dilemma in a rather cowardly way, but one which I believe turns out well for the reader. I invited both an experienced artist/analyst (Edith Wallace) and an art therapist who is also a Jungian analyst (Michael Edwards), and each has written a fascinating chapter which complement one another quite nicely.

Despite a good deal of literature by Jungians *about* art (Campbell, 1974; Jung, 1950; Neumann, 1959), as well as some on the use of art in analytical psychotherapy (Baynes, 1940; Jung, 1934), these chapters represent a welcome addition to the sole book available at the time of the first edition on the application of Jungian theory to the practice of art therapy (Lyddiatt, 1971). In the interim, a British art therapist and Jungian analyst named Joy Schaverien (1992, 1995) has published some fascinating books about her integration of the two. A scholar familiar with a wide range of analytic literature, she has written a detailed Commentary on this section, a task she has accomplished in a most thoughtful and creative way.

As noted earlier, those depth psychologies which value internal imagery appeal to the artist in every art therapist. The task of trying to comprehend symbolic communication through art is so great that we are constantly challenged to find new and better ways to understand the messages our patients send themselves and us through their images. Psychodynamic approaches, all of which are rooted in the seminal analytic work of Freud and Jung, remain very attractive to many workers in our field. They are, however, only part of the truth for some, and are even aversive to others, as Elinor Ulman acknowledges in her discussion of three Freudian approaches to art therapy, which is found in the last section of the book on integrative approaches.

☐ References

Baynes, H. G. (1940). *Mythology of the soul*. Baltimore: Williams & Wilkins.

Campbell, J. (1974). *The mythic image*. Princeton, NJ: Princeton University Press.

Dalley, T. (Ed.). (1984). *Art as therapy*. New York: Tavistock Publications.

Ellmann, C. S., Grand, S., Silvan, M., & Ellmann, S. J. (Eds.). (1998). *The modern Freudians: Contemporary psychoanalytic technique*. Northvail, NJ: Jason Aronson.

Jung, C. G. (1934/1972). A study in the process of individuation. In *Mandala symbolism*. Princeton, N.J.: Princeton University Press.

Jung, C. G. (1950/1972). Concerning Mandala symbolism. In *Mandala symbolism*. Princeton, N.J.: Princeton University Press.

Kramer, E. (1958). *Art therapy in a children's community*. Springfield, IL: Charles C Thomas.

Kramer, E. (1971). *Art as therapy with children*. New York: Schocken Books.

Kramer, E. (1979). *Childhood and art therapy*. New York: Schocken Books.

Liebowitz, M. (1999). *Interpreting projective drawings: A self psychology approach*. New York: Brunner/Mazel.

Lyddiatt, E. M. (1971). *Spontaneous painting and modelling*. London: Constable & Co.

Naumburg, M. (1947). Studies of the "free" art expression of behavior problem children and adolescents as a means of diagnosis and therapy. *Nervous and Mental Disease Monograph, 71*. (*Introduction to art therapy*. NY: Teachers College Press).

Naumburg, M. (1950). *Schizophrenic art: Its meaning in psychotherapy*. New York: Grune & Stratton.

Naumburg, M. (1953). *Psychoneurotic art: Its function in psychotherapy*. New York: Grune & Stratton.

Naumburg, M. (1966). *Dynamically oriented art therapy: Its principles and practices*. New York: Grune & Stratton.

Neumann, E. (1959). *The archetypal world of Henry Moore*. New York: Pantheon Books.

Schaverien, J. (1992). *The revealing image*. London: Routledge.

Schaverien, J. (1995). *Desire & the Female Therapist*. London: Routledge.

CHAPTER **1**   Judith Rubin

Discovery, Insight, and Art Therapy

☐ Background

Freud recognized early that many of his patients' communications were descriptions of visual images. In fact, at first he actively requested images, using a "concentration" technique to evoke forgotten memories:

> I placed my hand on the patient's forehead or took her head between my hands and said: "You will think of it under the pressure of my hands. At the moment at which I relax my pressure you will see something in front of you or something will come into your head. Catch hold of it. It will be what we are looking for—well, what have you seen or what has occurred to you?" (Freud & Breuer, 1893–1895, p. 110)

Of one of his analysands he wrote: "It was as though she were reading through a lengthy book of pictures" (Freud & Breuer, 1893–1895/1955, p. 193). Even after he abandoned this method in favor of free association, he couched his instructions in visual terms, asking the patient to "act as though you were a traveler sitting next to the window of a railway carriage and describing to someone inside the carriage the changing views which you see outside" (Freud, 1913, p. 135).

Several years later, Freud wrote a passage frequently quoted by pioneer art therapist Margaret Naumburg: "We experience it [a dream] predominantly in visual images.... Part of the difficulty of giving an account of dreams is due to our having to translate these images into words. 'I could draw it,' a dreamer often says to us, 'but I don't know how to say it' " (Freud, 1916–1917, p. 90). As Naumburg was fond of pointing out, Freud did not include drawing as part of classical technique, even though the Wolf-Man did draw a dream during his treatment: "He added a drawing of the tree with the wolves, which confirmed his description" (Freud, 1918/1955, p. 30; see also Freud, 1900).

Freud also reported a drawing by Little Hans—the first child in analysis. After his father drew a picture of a giraffe, Hans made "a short stroke, and then added a bit more to it, remarking 'Its widdler's longer!' " (Freud, 1905/1955, p. 13, Fig. 1). Indeed, drawing and painting were, from the first, well accepted as part of child analytic technique. In the words of Anna Freud, "A further technical aid, which besides the use of dreams and daydreams comes very much to the fore in many of my analyses of children, is drawing; in three of my cases this almost took the place of all other communications for some time" (A. Freud, 1927, p. 30; cf. also Rambert, 1949).

Despite the fact that child analysts were comfortable with art, few who treated adults used drawing or painting, although there were exceptions. Marcinowski "studied dreams of his patients in connection with their pictorial representation" (Bychowski, 1947, p. 34). Pfister tried to "psychoanalyze an artist by means of free association to his own pictures, but had little success in treating this patient" (Naumburg, 1950, p. 12). He wrote enthusiastically, however, of his work with an 18-year-old who "presented a number of oil paintings and drawings which I, in accordance with good analytic procedure, had him at once exhibit and explain to me" (Pfister, 1913/1917, p. 390). In fact, the analysis "dealt almost exclusively with drawings and poems" (Pfister, 1913/1917, p. 399).

In 1925 Nolan D. C. Lewis noted that "the interpretation of the art productions has long been recognized as part of the psychoanalytic technique" (p. 317). Sometimes drawings or paintings were offered spontaneously by the patient and utilized by the analyst (Bychowski, 1947; Hulse, 1949; Liss, 1936; Milner, 1969; Sechehaye, 1951). In other instances, analysts engaged artists to help patients create art, which they then brought to individual (Naumburg, 1966, p. 14; Spitz, 1954) or group analytic sessions (Schilder & Levine, 1942).

Some analysts even asked adults to work with art media in the treatment setting, like Mosse (1940), who encouraged psychotherapy patients to fingerpaint and then associate to the pictures, or Auerbach (1950), who invited patients on the couch to doodle on a pad. Stern (1952) urged patients to paint freely at home and bring the pictures into their analysis. And chances are that many an analyst has asked "a patient [to] draw a dream detail he is having trouble describing" (Slap, 1976, p. 455).

A genuine integration of Freud's insights about unconscious communication through imagery and the use of art in therapy was brought about, however, largely through the efforts of Margaret Naumburg, who began her long and productive career as an educator. In 1914 she founded Walden, a school based on psychoanalytic principles and emphasizing the arts (Naumburg, 1928). One of the first Americans to undergo analysis, Naumburg urged all of her teachers to be analyzed as well.

She began her work during the early Freudian era of "id psychology," when "making the unconscious conscious" was the primary therapeutic goal. The "release" of unconscious imagery through "spontaneous" art expression was therefore central to her approach to education, as well as to her later development of what she called "dynamic art therapy."

Freud's earliest model of the mind was known as the "topographic" theory. As if the human mind were a geological entity, Freud postulated layers or levels of consciousness—from the deepest and most inaccessible (the unconscious), to that which is accessible but not in awareness (the preconscious), to that which is "on one's mind" (consciousness).

He soon added the notion of a "tripartite" division of the mind, with the primitive "Id" as the source of repressed (forbidden) wishes (impulses, ideas) (Freud, 1923). These impulses (the "instinctual drives") constantly strive for discharge (satisfaction) and are expressed in a disguised form, because only in that way can they bypass the "censor" (the force serving to keep unwelcome ideas out of awareness). The "compromise" effected by the "Ego" consists of finding some way to satisfy or discharge the impulse, without offending either the environment (reality) or the individual's moral code

("Superego"). This theory helped Freud explain the compromises found in psychological symptoms, slips of the tongue, and dreams.

The first psychoanalytic therapists modeled their work on Freud's early treatments, in which he strove for "catharsis," and for the "abreaction" of "strangulated affect." Uncovering traumatic events that had been repressed ("making the unconscious conscious") was therefore thought to be the key to recovery from neurotic illness.

Margaret Naumburg, excited by the "spontaneous" art expressions of the children at Walden, also felt liberated by her personal experiences of analysis, which had included making pictures of her dreams and fantasies. She therefore saw "releasing" the repressed (unconscious) through imagery as curative, in a cathartic as well as a communicative sense.

Naumburg shared with many analytic therapists an enthusiasm for the healing potential of symbolic artistic expression, and for the rich projective possibilities of art in assessment. While not alone in her use of art for either diagnosis or therapy, she was unique in stressing its role as a primary agent, rather than an auxiliary tool.

Thanks to a meeting with analyst Nolan Lewis (Naumburg, 1975), she was able to explore using art with youngsters in a psychiatric hospital. Naumburg subsequently published a series of case studies, in which she reviewed the literature on art in diagnosis and therapy and presented her work with the children (1947). These were followed by books on her work with schizophrenic (1950) and neurotic adolescents and adults (1953, 1966).

Naumburg called her approach "dynamically oriented art therapy," based primarily on Freudian understandings. She was also sympathetic to Jung's (1964) notions about universal symbolism ("collective unconscious") and Sullivan's (1953) ideas about "interpersonal psychiatry," both of which she incorporated into her work. As a scholar knowledgeable about many schools of thought regarding symbolism, Naumburg insisted that the only valid meaning of anyone's art came from the person. She was skeptical about simplistic or rigid approaches to decoding symbolic meaning, a position consistent with Freud's teachings about dream analysis.

Most analysts agree that the only valid way to understand the latent meaning of a dream is for the dreamer to associate as freely as possible to it (Altman, 1975). Only such idiosyncratic associations to the manifest content can lead to the hidden significance of the dream, disguised by what Freud called the "dream work" (e.g., symbolization, condensation, displacement, reversal, and other mechanisms of defense). As Freud himself pointed out: "Sometimes a cigar is only a cigar," and all translations of symbolic meaning from manifest content are hypotheses, to be confirmed or refuted by the dreamer's own associations.

Naumburg modeled her approach to the use of art in therapy largely on what the psychoanalysts did. Technically, she attempted to stimulate free association, the method by which Freud made his discoveries. In her role as a therapist who saw the patient's art as a form of "symbolic speech" (Naumburg, 1955), Naumburg remained within the communicative framework of her more verbal model.

In psychoanalysis or analytic therapy the method is, first, for the patient to express him or herself as freely as possible. Then therapist and patient work together toward understanding what is interfering with the patient's ability to function more effectively, that is, internalized conflicts.

Two important tools are the *transference*—the symbolic ways in which the patient perceives and responds to the therapist—and the *countertransference*—the symbolic ways in which the therapist perceives and responds to the patient. The transference helps to identify distorted perceptions, which are assumed to be based on unresolved conflicts from the past. The countertransference is a clue to what is being evoked in the therapist by the patient. Though both were first seen as intereferences, they are now considered invaluable sources of information.

In the course of analytic therapy, the therapist helps the patient to understand and gain control over previously unknown sources of distress through questions, clarifications, confrontations, and other forms of intervention—especially interpretations, in which possible connections may be tactfully proposed. Contrary to the popular caricature of the analytic art therapist arbitrarily imposing meaning on the patient or the art, the method is in fact highly respectful, and the goal is always to help the patient make his or her own discoveries or "interpretations."

Psychoanalytic psychotherapy, then, has as its goals: first, uncovering and thereby discovering repressed material (presumably internalized conflicts that are causing problems), and second, helping the patient to gain insight into the meaning of their behavior in terms of these formerly hidden ideas and feelings. If this process is lived through in a relationship charged with affective as well as cognitive meaning for the patient (the "transference neurosis"), the person can be helped to change considerably, especially when the problem is a neurotic one.

Although I value and utilize other frames of reference in my work, I find the use of art in a uncovering, insight-oriented approach to be the most powerful and exciting kind of art therapy for myself, as well as for most of my patients. The shock of discovering previously unknown and usually unwanted aspects of the self is often visceral. The excitement of not only seeing—but also feeling—connections between what has been known and what has been hidden is equally powerful. "Insight" in good analytic art therapy is no intellectual matter; it is a vivid awareness, which allows all kinds of things that once seemed inexplicable to make sense. When it is deeply felt, grasped, and accepted, the internal shifts which lead to genuine and lasting change can be truly amazing (Shapiro, 1976).

I continue to be stimulated by the developments in ego psychology, object relations, and self-psychology, as described in the other chapters in this section. But the organizing principle for most of my clinical work remains a psychoanalytic understanding of what is going on in the patient, from the point of view of both development (Erikson, 1950; A. Freud, 1965; Colarusso, 1992) and dynamics (McWilliams, 1994). Although few patients today fit a classical neurotic picture, these concepts are still useful, as the following illustrations from art therapy with an adult indicate.

☐ Case Example: Mrs. L.

Some years ago, I had the opportunity to work with a young woman of 27 in individual art therapy. A look at her first art session and a later one may illustrate how a psychoanalytic approach can facilitate both understanding material and making technical decisions. Mrs. L. was invited to choose freely from among the available art media and to create whatever she wished. Like free association, this unstructured approach is designed to help patients to express what troubles them as freely as possible (Rubin, 1984). I made few comments during her spontaneous verbalization, primarily to facilitate a comfortable flow of thought in words, as well as a relaxed process of creating with materials.

I listened to her spontaneous remarks and observed her behavior. I asked only for specific "associations" to the art productions themselves, similar to what analysts often do with dreams. And, in making sense of the material, I thought in terms of the kinds of issues highlighted in an analytic assessment "profile" (A. Freud, 1965; Freud,

Nagera, & Freud, 1965). This first notes the reason for referral, the history, and possible environmental stressors. The referral of Mrs. L. and her 4 1/2-year-old daughter, Lori, had been prompted by Lori's depressive symptoms following her parents' separation. Mrs. L. had become increasingly anxious about her ability to parent either of her two children. The referral for art therapy came after two months of verbal therapy, in which she tended to deny all feelings.

Although Mrs. L.'s depression and anxiety were clearly "reactive" to her situation, her unresolved conflicts and coping mechanisms needed to be understood in order to help her to master the current stress. A psychoanalytic understanding includes not only external "facts," but also the internal "situation" of the patient: the developmental level of functioning (in terms of libidinal and aggressive drive development and object relations), and whether there are any evident fixation points or regressions.

Since psychoanalysis assumes that unresolved conflict is at the root of neurosis, sources of conflict are also noted. Conflict may be with the external world (other people) or "internal" (ambivalence), or "internalized" in a structural sense (between or within one of the metaphorical parts of the mind—id, ego, or superego). To assess a person's capacity for psychoanalytic therapy, one notes frustration tolerance, sublimation potential, attitude to anxiety, and progressive versus regressive tendencies.

A psychoanalytic understanding helps the therapist to know *where* a person is "fixated" (developmentally), *what* is being defended against (feared impulses), and *how* (favored coping and defense mechanisms). We will look at Mrs. L.'s first art session, in order to translate some of this terminology into the clinical "data" of art therapy. As in all dynamic therapy, initial hypotheses need to be continually tested and revised in light of emergent material, as will become apparent when we review a later session.

Mrs. L.'s First Art Session

Mrs. L. nervously selected 12″ × 18″ white drawing paper and thin chalk, and drew a vase filled with flowers of different colors (Figure 1.1). While working, she alternated between voicing concern (confessing that she had practiced drawing the picture at home) and noting that her good grades in art were due to the teacher's clear directions. Though critical, calling the drawing "terrible" and "lopsided," she was able to look at it on the easel and associate to it, in response to my asking "What comes to mind as you look?" She said she loved flowers, loved both growing and arranging them, and that in this interest as in all ways, she was "just like" her mother. Focusing on the red flowers, she said she liked red roses, but that they gave her a sad feeling because they reminded her of a hospital.

Her second drawing was developed from her own "scribble," a "starter" suggested by me because of her intense discomfort about what to do in the time remaining. This (Figure 1.2) reminded her of a "rolled-up wire fence." She tearfully recalled the times she had fenced in her children this past summer. She had to, to do all the chores falling on her shoulders since the separation, like mowing and caring for the lawn. She confessed she had feared my disapproval of the fencing; she was clearly guilty, and worried about having harmed Lori. Mrs. L. was visibly relieved and ready to leave at the end of her first 45-minute art therapy session. She had been controlled throughout, consistent with the referring psychiatrist's feeling that she was highly defended against any threatening feelings and ideas.

A psychoanalytic understanding of the communications (verbal and nonverbal) of anyone, even in the first session, involves the notion of *transference:* the projection by the patient onto the therapist of ideas, feelings, and expectations stemming from unresolved

(text continues on page 22)

Figure 1.1.

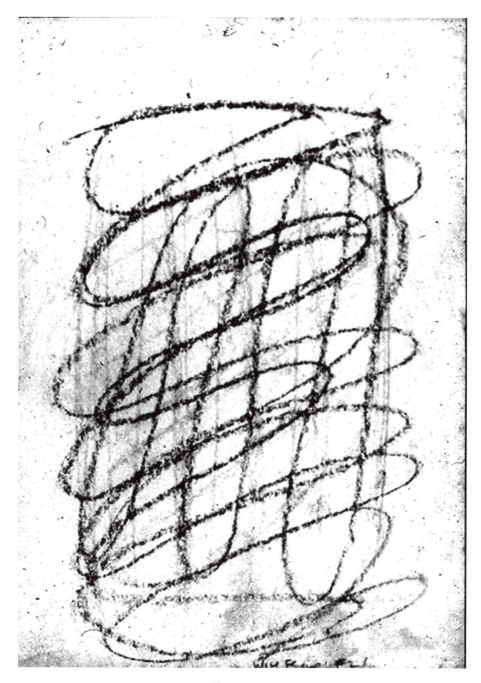

Figure 1.2.

past conflicts. I therefore "heard" Mrs. L.'s comments about the art teacher who gave good directions as a rebuke to me for not telling her what to make and thus making her feel inadequate. She let me know what she wanted from me—clear directions about what to do—and also what she expected—criticism. I heard her critical comments about her art as reflecting little healthy narcissism, as well as an index of a severe, punitive superego.

I also examined my responses to her: the countertransference. While that is partly a reflection of my own internal world, which I had better know about so that it doesn't get in the way of my work; it is also a clue to things about the patient. I found myself feeling critical of her phony, plastic smile, which I realized reminded me of an aunt whose smile was a thin disguise for her hostility. I also felt controlled by her pre-rehearsed picture, even though I was sympathetic to the anxiety it reflected. I wondered how controlling she was of the little girl for whom she had sought treatment.

Mrs. L.'s initial associations to the superficially pleasant manifest content of her drawing—that she "loved" growing and arranging flowers—paralleled her surface presentation of herself as cheerful, in charge, and pleased with life. Her statement that she was "just like" her mother, suggested possible problems with separation and individuation. The theory of the "repetition-compulsion" also led me to assume that her unresolved problems would be replayed in some way with her children.

Manifest art content and initial associations are, like the manifest dream, a deceptive disguise for a less obvious (latent) meaning. Mrs. L.'s subsequent associations—to red roses and the sad feeling they gave her, along with her allusion to a hospital—were her first communications of her own depression. It wasn't clear *who* might be ill. For example, these associations may have indicated anxiety about her health—now that she had been abandoned—or a worried (disguised) hostility toward someone else (mother? husband? children?). Behind the cheerful smile on her face and the colorful stereotyped flowers in the vase lay a good deal of anxiety, suggesting her use of reaction-formation as a defense.

When Mrs. L. blocked, unable to do a second creation, I understood it in terms of "psychic determinism," the analytic notion that any series of behaviors (thoughts, words, actions, art) is linked in some meaningful way. Her blocking was similar to a child's "play disruption" (Erikson, 1950), indicating that the anxiety aroused (presumably by talk of flowers, sadness, and hospitals) was sufficient to interfere with her functioning (e.g., to constitute an unconscious *resistance*).

I therefore suggested a "scribble drawing," which offers the patient his or her own unstructured stimulus upon which to project further imagery, an approach developed independently by a child analyst (Winnicott, 1971) and a therapeutic art teacher (Cane, 1951). Margaret Naumburg welcomed this approach to projection developed by her sister (Cane), since it helped to release imagery dormant in the artist's unconscious (Naumburg, 1966).

Mrs. L. labeled her rapidly drawn image a "Rolled-up Wire Fence." My first thought was of how tightly "wound-up" she herself was, tensely controlling her feelings, which evoked a countertransferential impulse to tickle her. These ideas, surfacing from my "evenly hovering attention," seemed related to her subsequent associations to the fencing in of her children during her summer yard work. Her anxiety about my disapproval, and her fear that she was responsible for Lori's depression, were further indications of a severe superego and a strong sense of guilt. Seeing herself as harmful hinted that her earlier associations—to the roses of sickness and death—may have stemmed from unconscious death wishes toward others, perhaps her mother who she had described as identical to herself. This suggested that she used identification as a defense, a hypothesis confirmed later in therapy in regard to her hostility toward her daughter.

Despite a defensive idealization of me as a "good mother," Mrs. L. was able to use weekly art therapy to explore her feelings of rage and hurt toward both her parents and husband, and to accept her ambivalence toward her children. She soon became able to use her artwork as a valuable source of information about herself. During most sessions, like the one described next, she would work almost casually with the materials—preconsciously it seemed—while telling me the important events of the previous week. Then she would put her picture on the easel and look at it with interest, curiosity, and a desire to learn from it, often regarding it with puzzlement, as if it had come from somewhere else.

Mrs. L.'s Penultimate Art Session
(after 10 months of weekly treatment)

Mrs. L. chose acrylic paints, putting them directly onto a small (9″ × 12″) canvas with a palette knife. Talking of her current concerns, including her sadness about termination, she made a series of oval shapes—some green, some yellow. Regressing to earlier dependent behavior, she asked if it would be "all right to mix the colors together." Reminded that she could do whatever she wished, she mixed them with the palette knife—first slowly, then vigorously—smearing almost the entire surface, creating a large mass of thick yellow-green paint. She finished by painting a solid white border around the mass, effectively "containing" it (Figure 1.3).

As was characteristic by then, Mrs. L. knew she was finished, and placed the painting on the easel where we both regarded it. She first thought of the ocean, titling it *Sea Mist.* Surprised by her association, she went on to say that she doesn't *like* the sea, that she's afraid to go in the water, afraid of fish, a fear she can't seem to conquer.

Figure 1.3.

Figure 1.4.

"Whenever . . . anything brushes my leg, I really, you know, go crazy! Jellyfish, shark—what is it?" Laughing nervously, she described her fear of horses and of being bitten by a dog, recalling that she'd grown up "in a neighborhood with a lot of vicious dogs," and reflected that so many problems go back to her childhood.

She returned to her fear of swimming in the sea and being bitten by a shark. When asked how she felt about her art, she called it "a big round blob," and said—as she often did—"I don't know how it got like that. I didn't *intend* for it to be like that." The painting reminded her of "ripples in the water," and she commented that "it looks kind of *wild*, but I don't think I intended for it to be." She said she was thinking of "something calmer," that "the sea is kind of peaceful," and that she likes wide-open spaces. "I don't like congestion, you know, or being congested or hindered in any way."

Mrs. L. then decided to do another picture, this time using her by-then-favorite medium, thick poster chalk, on a 9″ × 12″ piece of white paper (Figure 1.4). While she drew rapidly, she spoke of her plan to take art classes after termination. Looking at her picture on the easel, she first thought that it looked "like something you'd see under a microscope, like an amoeba. . . . It looks like it might just be a watery mass around it, as if you're taking something out of water and putting it under a microscope, although the water isn't brown, unless it's very muddy water."

Pausing, she seemed blocked, so I asked: "If they were people, who would they be?" She laughed, and said, "Here we go—three again! I always end up with three shapes of some kind. I don't know why that is. I do that very unconsciously, but for some reason or other, it always ends up that way. Oh well, I guess that's me in the middle again. That always seems to be me in the middle." She identified the inside shape as Lori and the one on the left as her son, saying that it looked like she was trying to protect Lori, probably because "she *feels* things more than he does."

Mrs. L. then spoke of Lori as sensitive and fearful, especially at night. She said that last night Lori couldn't sleep, because "she kept visualizing a man crawlin' up on a ladder to her bedroom, or to my bedroom." She named her picture *Mother Love*. She then thought of how Lori would ruminate obsessively about fears, and how she does that too; but "I try to push it out of my mind, like I do anything that I'm afraid of." I wondered if all of this imagery about fear of attack (sharks, dogs, male intruders) was related to the impending termination and her anxiety about being more vulnerable, less "protected" (as she saw herself protecting Lori). Mrs. L. agreed that, although she tends to try to deny or disavow her anxiety, it was heightened by anticipating the separation from her therapist.

Mrs. L.'s artwork in this later session reflects her impulses more than that in the first one—in both the process and her associations. Her surprise in response to pictures and thoughts reflects an enhanced ability to express herself more freely. Her "observing ego" is stronger, enabling her to "see" more frightening imagery; as well as to acknowledge uncomfortable feelings, like sadness and anxiety in response to termination.

Her anger was less accessible to her than in other sessions during this phase, perhaps because hostility toward me was too frightening to contemplate on the next to last session. I had the sense that she was expressing it indirectly through the aggressive smearing of the acrylic paint, which she saw as "breaking" some kind of "rule" (not to mix colors?), as well as in her choice of brown and black chalk for the second picture, first seen as dirty, "muddy water."

Although Mrs. L. rarely worked representationally, she enjoyed projecting images onto her artwork, and was often excited and surprised by what she "saw." This viewing of an image—which she realized came from within herself—had the affectively charged quality of what Kris (1956) called "id insight." Such discoveries of something about the self are critical in psychoanalytic treatment. Although insight alone is not sufficient, its value in conjunction with affective experiences and a sense of conviction is, as noted, extremely powerful.

☐ Conclusion

Having worked in a variety of modes with a variety of patients over the years—including strictly verbal adult analysis, using art in adult analysis, child analysis with art, and psychoanalytic art therapy with adults and children—I am convinced that art can greatly enhance the analytic experience of insight ("seeing in"). This is probably so because art is concrete and visual, in addition to its value in *uncovering* unconscious imagery and *discovering* unconscious fantasies and impulses.

The psychoanalytic approach to art therapy, in the hands of a trained clinician, offers an extremely rich vehicle for change with many patients. My own conviction, shared by those trained in the Freudian tradition, is that classical analysis is neither appropriate nor necessary for most, but that the theory which informs it is still useful in understanding and guiding all therapeutic work, whether the clinician behaves in a supportive/ego-building or in an interpretive/uncovering manner.

In psychoanalytic art therapy, it is often necessary to shift one's stance, sometimes supporting defenses, at other times analyzing them. The shifts are often rapid and the relevant cues subtle, so that it is necessary to be flexible, within certain stable conditions. These have been referred to as the "frame" (Langs, 1979; Milner, 1957) or the "framework for freedom" (Rubin, 1978, 1984). However one conceptualizes that constant, dependable "holding environment" (Winnicott, 1971), it does not mean rigidity.

Rather, in psychoanalytic art therapy, the clinician shifts her stance in accord with what she perceives as most needed by that particular patient at that moment in time.

For example, I try to utilize the "least restrictive" (most facilitating, least intrusive) intervention, as a way of helping a patient who, in some way, indicates a need for the activity of the therapist. For a person who is stuck, like Mrs. L. in her first session, I might suggest a "scribble drawing," or perhaps a series of images, done as freely as possible (Rubin, 1981), thus lending my "auxiliary ego" to the patient's blocked efforts at expression. On the other hand, when a person can handle a more insight-oriented approach, I might wonder what in the previous image or associations could have led to the current "disruption" (e.g., analyzing the resistance).

Similarly, if someone were producing chaotic imagery, I would probably try to find a way to help them sort out and organize the confused images (e.g., supporting defenses). I might suggest framing and viewing one image at a time, or selecting several to put together in a new picture. If the patient was generally able to function at a higher level, and the confusion seemed to be a momentary response to stress, I might ask them to stop and consider what in the preceding images or statements had created tension.

In either case, I would be lending my support where it seemed most critical—either intervening constructively in the creative/expressive process or, where appropriate, inviting the patient's "observing ego" to look with me at what was happening in order to better understand it. In both, I would try to understand the blocking or the regression from an analytic perspective, and would intervene so as to provide what seemed most useful to that patient at that particular moment in time.

In that regard, as in most issues in conducting diagnosis or therapy through art, the psychoanalytic approach to understanding and to intervening has been helpful to me. Although an art therapist cannot possibly behave in the passive, neutral manner of a classical analyst, I have come to feel that in most cases sufficient neutrality for a transference to develop is helpful, whether or not one chooses to analyze it.

Also, as psychoanalysts have stressed, an "alliance" with the patient is absolutely essential to effective therapeutic work, something as true for art therapy as for analysis. As the patient and his art have become less mysterious, the more I have understood of psychoanalytic theory over time. I have no question that the training has made me a better art therapist than I would have been without it.

☐ References

Altman, L. L. (1975). *The dream in psychoanalysis* (2nd ed.). New York: International Universities Press.

Auerbach, J. G. (1950). Psychological observations on "doodling" in neurotics. *Journal of Nervous & Mental Disease*, 304–332.

Bychowski, G. (1947). The rebirth of a woman. *Psychoanalytic Review, 34*, 32–57.

Cane, F. (1951/1983). *The artist in each of us.* Craftsbury Common, VT: Art Therapy.

Colarusso, C. A. (1992). *Child & adult development: A psychoanalytic introduction for clinicians.* New York: Plenum.

Erikson, E. H. (1950). *Childhood and society.* New York: W.W. Norton.

Freud, A. (1965). *Normality and pathology in childhood. Assessments of development.* New York: International Universities Press.

Freud, A. (1927/1974). The methods of child analysis. *The writings of Anna Freud,* Vol. 1 (pp. 19–35). New York: International Universities Press.

Freud, A., Nagera, H., & Freud, W. E. (1965). Metapsychological assessment of the adult personality. *Psychoanalytic Study of the Child, 20*, 9–41.

Freud, S. (1900/1955). *The interpretation of dreams,* Standard ed., Vols. 4–5. London: Hogarth Press.

Freud, S. (1905/1955). *Analysis of a phobia in a five year-old-boy*, Standard ed., Vol. 10, pp. 3–149. London: Hogarth Press.

Freud, S. (1913). *On beginning the treatment*, Standard ed., Vol. 12, pp. 123–144. London: Hogarth Press.

Freud, S. (1916–1917). *Introductory lectures on psycho-analysis*, Standard ed., Vol. 12, London: Hogarth Press.

Freud, S. (1918/1955). *From the history of an infantile neurosis*, Standard ed., Vol. 17, pp. 3–124. London: Hogarth Press.

Freud, S. (1923/1964). *The ego and the id*. Standard edition, Vol. 19, London: Hogarth Press, 1964.

Freud, S., & Breuer, J. (1893–1895/1955). *Studies in hysteria*, Standard ed., Vol. 2, London: Hogarth Press.

Hulse, W. C. (1949). Symbolic painting in psychotherapy. *American Journal of Psychotherapy, 3*, 559–584.

Jung, C. G. (1964). *Man and his symbols*. New York: Doubleday.

Kris, E. (1956). On some vicissitudes of insight in psychoanalysis. *International Journal of Psychoanalysis, 37*, 445–455.

Langs, R. J. (1979). *The therapeutic environment*. New York: Jason Aronson.

Lewis, N. D. C. (1925). The practical value of graphic art in personality studies. *Psychoanalytic Review, 12*, 316–322.

Liss, E. (1936). Play techniques in child analysis. *American Journal of Orthopsychiatry, 6*, 17–22.

McWilliams, N. (1994). *Psychoanalytic diagnosis: Understanding personality structure in the clinical process*. New York: Guilford.

Milner, M. (1957). *On not being able to paint*. New York: International Universities Press.

Milner, M. (1969). *The hands of the living god*. New York: International Universities Press.

Mosse, E. P. (1940). Painting analyses in the treatment of neuroses. *Psychoanalytic Review, 27*, 65–81.

Naumburg, M. (1928). *The child and the world*. New York: Harcourt, Brace.

Naumburg, M. (1947). Studies of the "free" art expression of behavior problem children and adolescents as a means of diagnosis and therapy. *Nervous and Mental Disease Monograph, 17*. (reprinted as *Introduction to art therapy* (1973), NY: Teachers College Press).

Naumburg, M. (1950). *Schizophrenic art: Its meaning in psychotherapy*. New York: Grune & Stratton.

Naumburg, M. (1953). *Psychoneurotic art: Its function in psychotherapy*. New York: Grune & Stratton.

Naumburg, M. (1955). Art as symbolic speech. *Journal of Aesthetics and Art Criticism, 12*, 435–450.

Naumburg, M. (1966). *Dynamically oriented art therapy: Its principles and practices*. New York: Grune & Stratton.

Naumburg, M. (1975). Unpublished transcript, "Interview with Judith Rubin" for film *Art Therapy: Beginnings* (American Art Therapy Association).

Pfister, O. (1913/1917). Analysis of artistic production. In *The psychoanalytic method*. New York: Moffat, Yard.

Rambert, M. (1949). Drawings as a method in child psychoanalysis. In *Children in conflict* (pp. 173–190). New York: International Universities Press.

Rubin, J. A. (1984). *Child art therapy*. New York: Wiley. (2nd Ed., 1978).

Rubin, J. A. (1981). Art and imagery: Free association with art media. In A. E. DiMaria (Ed.), *Art therapy: A bridge between worlds*. Falls Church, VA: American Art Therapy Association.

Schilder, P., & Levine, E. L. (1942). Abstract art as an expression of human problems. *Journal of Nervous & Mental Disease, 95*, 1–10.

Sechehaye, M. (1951). *Symbolic realization*. New York: International Universities Press.

Shapiro, S. L. (1976). *Moments of insight*. New York: International Universities Press.

Slap, J. W. (1976). A note on the drawing of dream details. *Psychoanalytic Quarterly, 45*, 455–456.

Spitz, R. (1954). Review of psychoneurotic art by M. Naumburg. *Psychoanalytic Quarterly, 23*, 279–282.

Stern, M. M. (1952). Free painting as an auxiliary technique in psychoanalysis. In G. Bychowski & L. Despert (Eds.), *Specialized techniques in psychotherapy*. New York: Basic Books.

Sullivan, H. S. (1953). *The interpersonal theory of psychiatry*. New York: W. W. Norton.

Winnicott, D. W. (1971). *Therapeutic consultations in child psychiatry*. New York: Basic Books.

Sublimation and Art Therapy

My understanding of sublimation is based on Freudian psychoanalytic thinking, broadened and confirmed by the findings of ethologists (cf. Lorenz, 1966) and by clinical observations made in the course of my work as an art therapist.

According to Freudian theory, "*sublimation*" designates processes whereby primitive urges, emanating from the id, are transformed by the ego into complex acts that do not serve direct instinctual gratification. In the course of this transformation, primitive behavior, necessarily asocial, gives way to activities that are ego-syntonic and are as a rule *socially productive*, although they may not always be *socially acceptable*. We need only to recall the fate of Socrates, Rembrandt, Freud, and innumerable others, to realize how frequently achievements that undoubtedly came about through processes of sublimation were rejected by society.

Sublimation is no simple mental act; it embraces a multitude of mechanisms. These include displacement, symbolization, neutralization of drive energy, identification, and integration. Always there is a threefold change: of the object upon which interest centers, of the desired goal, and of the kind of energy through which the new goal is attained. Sublimation invariably implies some element of renunciation. Yet sublimation somehow remains so linked to the urges that set the process in motion, that the individual attains through it at least partial gratification and partial relief from the pressure of these libidinal and aggressive drives. Inasmuch as it involves postponement of instinctual gratification and channeling of drive energy, we can perceive sublimation as one of the mechanisms of defense.

Implied in the concept of sublimation is the awareness that man's instincts are in disarray, and can no longer be relied on to safely regulate behavior. We assume that the atrophy of the instinctive programming that regulates the behavior of the lower species occurred as a consequence of the advent of the faculty for conceptual thinking. This enabled man to judge situations on their own merit, rendering the more global do's and don'ts of the ancient instinctual organization obsolete.

Parts of this chapter have been published in a different context in *Art as Therapy with Children* (1971) by Edith Kramer and in *Childhood and Art Therapy: Notes on Theory and Application* (1979) by Edith Kramer in collaboration with Laurie Wilson.

Psychoanalytic psychology also assumes that the dissolution of this mindless (yet exquisitely balanced) organization brought into existence an accumulation of unregulated forces—libidinal and aggressive energies pushing toward immediate discharge— oblivious of time, place, and circumstance, in nonrational, potentially lethal behavior. Man's survival as a species thus depended on the development of a new psychic organization holding the key to all goal-directed behavior, capable of taming and directing drive energy. This new organization, the ego, constitutes man's indispensable organ of survival. Infinitely more flexible and efficient, it is also more fragile and less dependable than the ancient instinctive programming it supplanted.

Sublimation entails establishing a *symbolic linkage* between some primitive need and another more complex cluster of ideas and actions. This presupposes the capacity to evoke ideas and perceive analogies, a faculty involving both primary and secondary process thinking. The ability to perceive analogies belongs to primary process thinking. As secondary process thinking takes over, symbolic representations lose their protean, driven quality and become stable. Imagination replaces fantasy. We must presume that the faculties of primary process and secondary process mental functioning, as well as the capacity for conceptual thinking, evolved simultaneously and interdependently. Evidently, sublimation in the full sense of the word could not occur among any species lacking these mental faculties.

However, we discern among the lower species certain phenomena sufficiently analogous to sublimation to assure us that the process as we conceive of it is not totally without precedent (cf. Lorenz, 1966), and does not constitute a biological impossibility. (See Kramer, 1987, pp. 27–29 for further discussion of these issues.) It is reasonable to postulate that man's subjective experiences can be linked to the physiological process of tension reduction; that actions which are linked only by a long chain of modification to the gratifications of basic urges can have the power to generate emotions of pleasure and pain, and to reduce tension; and that man's biological heritage includes the faculty to channel considerable energies into such processes.

☐ Sublimation in Art Therapy

Sublimation is not limited to the arts. A ubiquitous process, it permeates man's entire life. In this chapter, however, our focus is on sublimation as we observe it in the course of art therapy. We must distinguish sublimation from catharsis, from simple displacement, and from the highly sexualized and/or aggressively charged imagery that we encounter in the art work of psychotics.

Catharsis

When Mrs. Smith, after a day's vacation, found the cottage where she worked as a house parent in an unbelievable mess, she relieved her feelings by covering a white paper entirely with red paint. She then painted a tiny figure with hands upraised in despair on the bottom of the page. After she finished, she had calmed herself sufficiently to resume her duties. Mrs. Smith had found a symbol for her situation: the white sheet of paper upon which she spread the symbol of her all-pervasive rage, the color red. She had experienced the relief that catharsis affords the strong individual who, after such an outburst, is able to return to the task at hand in an invigorated mood.

Failure of Neutralization

When 20-year-old Jim, an ambulatory paranoid psychotic, attempted to draw a tomato using colored pencils, it took on an unmistakably breast-like shape rendered sinister by a dark, blood-red spot that gave the impression of a wound or bruise. The product told of his longing for nurturance, of the pressure of his sexuality, of sadistic perception of the sexual act, and of his anxiety. The picture remained unfinished and appeared misshapen, an unsuccessful attempt at displacement. Sublimation was not attained.

Sublimation Induced and Supported

Sublimation is a complex process requiring a modicum of ego strength and intelligence, yet with some assistance, 18-year-old Jack, an educable retarded man, was able to experience the power of sublimation during a memorable art therapy session. When Jack was informed that his favorite art therapy intern would leave the program before his birthday, he stormed out of the art room in a rage. After a little while he returned and began systematically and angrily to tear up a stack of drawing paper, one by one. Thereupon the chief art therapist took the two halves of a torn sheet and commented, "Now you made two sheets. Will you give me one of them as a present?" Jack was startled. His eyes lit up. He laboriously printed the art therapist's initials on one half of the torn sheet and his initials on the other half, and proffered the half that was inscribed with her initials to the art therapist.

He then began to ask all the people in the room for their initials. He tore paper into even smaller pieces, printed initials onto each of these fragments and proudly went around distributing the many gifts to everyone in sight. His mood had changed dramatically. He had found a way of continuing to give symbolic vent to his pain about being torn from his beloved art therapist. He was still tearing paper; however, he was no longer only destroying it, but was also making more of it. And he was working very hard as the task of remembering the many initials and of forming the letters was taxing his limited intelligence to the utmost. The episode lasted for approximately 20 minutes, until the end of the session. The next day, however, left to himself, Jack broke a number of clay pieces he had made with the intern's help. Without continual support, sublimation could not be maintained.

Sublimation and Other Mechanisms of Defense[1]

Faced with anxiety and emotional turbulence, the ego is likely to mobilize a variety of defenses. Thus, more often than not, sublimation emerges in conjunction with other defensive mechanisms.

Eight-year-old Kenny had sustained second-degree burns on his back, neck, and hands, requiring plastic surgery. A fire had broken out while his mother was away from home for two days, leaving him and his two younger siblings unattended. Kenny's mother was subsequently charged with criminal neglect. After his physical recovery, Kenny was admitted to the child psychiatric ward for observation. An art therapy evaluation session was held as part of the psychological workup.

---

[1]The following case history has been published in somewhat different form in the *American Journal of Art Therapy* (Vol. 23, No. 1) as part of "An Art Therapy Evaluation Session for Children" by Edith Kramer and Jill Scherr.

The session was conducted by the ward's art therapist, whom Kenny had met previously. Also present was an art therapy student, a newcomer. When Kenny perceived a bright-red birthmark on this student's cheek, he was visibly upset and commented on her "ugly scar." When asked to make a drawing, he immediately set out to draw the student's portrait. Observing her intensely, he produced a figure, paying special attention to the detailed rendering of her spectacles and her birthmark. As he drew, he became visibly calmer. Faced with a frightening reminder of his own stigmatized condition, he had at first responded by projection: "Not I, but the *student* is ugly." However, as he began drawing, healthier defenses came into play. Changing passive into active by creating her image, he had also found a way of keeping a watchful eye on this dangerous individual. By keeping himself busy drawing, he managed to look at her without being overwhelmed by anxiety and revulsion. The mature and detailed drawing that resulted testified to considerable ego strength.

However, when Kenny was introduced to clay, he regressed. Smearing and smelling the unfamiliar substance, he dropped it on the floor, yelling: "The floor is bad. It made the doo-doo fall." The intensity and irrationality of his protests signaled the necessity for intervention. Demonstrating that clay had other possibilities, the art therapist attracted Kenny's attention by modeling a clay figure of a little boy. Kenny soon began to play with the figure. Placing him on a clay bed, he declared that the boy was "bad because he peed in bed" (Kenny was enuretic). This led to a discussion of both the clay-boy's and Kenny's own feelings about not being able to control his urination. Hope was expressed that the doctors would be able to help.

The clay-boy safely at rest, Kenny resumed modeling. Pounding out a flat pancake shape and producing a number of clay balls, he discovered that he could make an apple tree by adding a trunk. When he was encourged to paint this tree with tempera paints,[2] he became deeply concerned about the choice of colors. "Apples are red," he mused, "but aren't they brown sometimes?" Kenny asserted that he would have no brown apples because "it would mean they are wormy." Furthermore, he declared that he would use neither brown nor black paint on his tree because they were "bad" colors. He was overjoyed when he discovered that he could make a brilliantly bright green by mixing turquoise blue and yellow, and he initially painted the whole tree including the trunk with this green, while all the apples were painted red. But the result did not satisfy him. He found that black would be a better color for a realistic trunk. He also discovered that he had forgotten to make stems for his apples. He added stems and painted them brown, declaring, "They can be brown but not the apples." The finished work with the stems not attached to the tree resembled a long-handled frying pan holding apples. Kenny was delighted.

The clay brought forth both Kenny's most disturbed and his most mature and healthy functioning. The material's anal connotations led initially to massive regression and loss of reality testing. But when the possibility of forming the clay into symbolic objects was demonstrated, Kenny could respond to the invitation to enact his trouble in symbolic play rather than via delusional behavior. Symbolic play enabled him to ventilate anxiety and obtain reassurance. This sufficed to inspire him to the creation of a good apple tree. Initially, he attempted to rigidly separate good from bad, rejecting brown and black as "bad" colors. He was about to constrict and impoverish his range of action. However, he

---

[2]Ordinarily, children would have to wait until their sculptures have been fired before painting them. But since the choice of color often yields important information about the emotional meaning of the sculpture, an exception is made during the first evaluation session, and the child is encouraged to paint the wet clay.

transcended the inclination to resort to splitting. Instead, he found a way to integrate the colors in a realistic fashion and still create a good apple tree. Sublimation was attained.

The session, however, did not end with this victory, for Kenny was next asked to use the tempera paints to make a picture. Quickly dipping his brush into the black paint, he produced a simple version of his first pencil portrait of the art therapy student and wrote her name above it. But when he used red paint to fill in her scar, he suddenly burst into tears. Covering up her name he replaced it with his own, exclaiming, "I am ugly, my face is ugly, and that's why I want to kill myself." Then, with black paint he added a large stop sign to the picture.

The desperate message naturally required a direct response. Since the art therapist knew of Kenny's ongoing psychotherapy, she could reassure him by reminding him that his doctor was there to help him with his feelings, and by pointing out that he had been able to paint a powerful stop sign, to remind himself that he wanted to get over these dangerous feelings.

The session ended on a hopeful note, as Kenny checked on his apple tree and reassured himself that it would be kept safely—a gesture that confirms that the brief episode of healthy symbolic living had been precious to him, even though sublimation alone had not sufficed to stave off the upsurge of suicidal ideation. Indeed, inasmuch as sublimation tends to reduce the power of rigid defenses, it might have contributed to it. Faced with the full impact of his despair, Kenny had needed to resort to a stark, prohibitive command borrowed from the outside world of law and order. This measure was nevertheless healthier than his initial projection and splitting. Thus, the undisguised communication of his despair opened the way to effective psychotherapy, while the completed apple tree gave hope for continued and fruitful art therapy. More often than not, art therapy and psychotherapy complement each other in such a manner.

Projection, Pornography, and Sublimation

Twelve-year-old Gordon, an ardent and gifted painter, and his friend, John, shared an art therapy session. In the course of the session, the two boys embarked on a bout of so-called "slipping" or "playing the dozens," a ritual of mutual insult where each boy accuses the other's mother and grandmother of every conceivable and inconceivable kind of sexual perversion and promiscuity.

The exchange of vituperation constitutes a conventional social pattern among slum children, whose mothers are in fact promiscuous. It can be embellished with all sorts of colorful inventions, but the crowning insult remains the disdainful declaration "You don't even have no mother." Both partners to the abusive exchange get relief through projection. The child could not possibly accuse his own mother of desertion and immorality, but he can freely accuse another child's mother and have the accusation thrown back at him. Such loaded banter may remain playful among friends, but more often it ends up in a fistfight.

This time peace prevailed. While insults were passed back and forth almost mechanically, Gordon began a large painting of Moby Dick (Figure 2.1; its actual size is 1 1/2 × 4 feet). The subject gave occasion for additional obscenity over the double meaning of the word "dick." One might expect that a painting created while such talk was in the air would at best be crudely obscene. Instead, there emerged a powerful, beautifully executed image of evil, which comes close to embodying the symbolic meaning of Melville's masterpiece.

The white whale is floating on the surface of a light blue sea, spouting a blue jet of water. The sky is indicated by loose blue brush strokes. The whale's body is painted

Figure 2.1.

in subtle shades of gray, with dark-gray accents. The light, silvery atmosphere of the painting contrasts sharply with the whale's evil expression. His mouth is open in a crooked sneer, baring a dark-red cavity surrounded by sharp, white teeth. There is a sly, evil look in his small, black eye. The whole body conveys a feeling of nakedness.

The sexual symbolism of the painting is obvious. We see a composite of male and female elements. The whole whale can be interpreted as one gigantic penis, conceived as a dangerous weapon with teeth. The whale's mouth, on the other hand, can also be interpreted as a vagina dentata, devouring the male organ. The whale as a whole also recalls a woman's body, with the forked tail standing for her thighs and vulva. Most striking are the proportions, roughly 3:8, an unusual, extravagant length suitable for the whale, which indeed fills the paper completely. Equally impressive is the painting's tactile quality. This whale is no decorative symbol; it is a three-dimensional, living creature.

Gordon had been intensely absorbed as he painted the whale's body. Again and again, he brushed over its surface adding more and more subtle shading. Although his way of painting was reminiscent of masturbation, it did not become obsessive or purely repetitive. Gordon never lost command over paint and brush; he knew what he was doing and when to stop. He was proud of the completed painting, and his friend and slipping partner was filled with admiration. The session ended in a spirit of contentment.

If we compare the meaning of the talk that had accompanied the making of Moby Dick with the symbolic meaning of the painting, we find that they both relate to the same painful situation: the boys' unfulfilled longing for mother, their rage over her unfaithfulness, shame over her behavior, and guilt and shame over their own degraded desires and fantasies.

On the surface this all seems to be expressed more directly in the boys talk. "Your mother," it implies, "is promiscuous. She is indeed no mother at all; furthermore, you, her son, are ready to degrade her by attacking her sexually." When we listen closely to the merciless words, we find that the abuse is quite impersonal, uttered so mechanically that it becomes meaningless. Talk circles endlessly around the boys' more profound longing and grief, but it brings no insight or relief. The longing for mother is denied, drowned in the flood of mutual abuse.

When Gordon painted a gigantic image, half fish, half mammal, frightening, fascinating, and unfathomable, he created it out of the same ambivalent feelings, the same fears and pressures that drove him and his schoolmates to relentless vituperation, threats, and fights, but he was no longer obsessed, forced to repeat stereotyped behavior with no will of his own. By finding a symbol that transposed his conflicts from the narrow confines of his life into the wider world of imagination and adventure, he freed himself from meaningless repetition. Painting did not alter the nature of his trouble. He was too deeply injured to make an image of goodness. He could only make a monstrous composite of love and hate, male and female, but in making it he had ceased, at least for the duration of the creative act, to be the helpless victim of his conflicts.

The serendipitous event could not have occurred without the many preceding art therapy sessions during which Gordon discovered his gift and learned to trust himself and to have confidence in the art therapist. During the crucial session the art therapist did not need to intervene. At this juncture her tolerance for the obscene banter and her supportive presence sufficed to establish an atmosphere in which the painting could materialize.

Displacement and Sublimation

In my next example, we can observe the transition from displacement to sublimation. Twelve-year-old Donald, a bright, emotionally troubled child, suffered a psychotic breakdown triggered by a minor operation on his genitals. During one period of his acute illness he developed an obsessive interest in noses. It became his ambition to learn to sculpture "a perfect human nose." During many art therapy sessions he modeled nothing but noses.

Later he tried to sculpture human heads. At first they all looked alike, a huge nose dominating a rudimentary face (Figure 2.2). He became quite distressed by this repetition. He could see very well that people had different faces and noses, but try as he might, he could only make the same nose and the same face over and over again. Finally, he made up his mind to get out of this impasse by devoting himself seriously to making a self-portrait in a more adult manner.

He was taught how to build an armature of wood and plaster and how to apply the clay systematically around this solid core. Built in this manner, the finished sculpture could be cut into halves, detached from its armature, reassembled, fired in a kiln, and finally painted with poster paint. To look at himself, Donald used a shaving mirror with both an enlarging and reducing side. That by simply reversing the sides of the mirror he could get very close to his face or move further away was endlessly fascinating to him. It seemed to help him to establish the right distance from himself and to perceive himself as a whole. When the sculpture had been fired, Donald spent much time carefully mixing the colors for skin, hair, eyes, mouth, and sweatshirt to match his own (Figure 2.3). The sculpture marked a turning point in both his self-perception and his perception of others. He blossomed into a sensitive portraitist able to produce excellent self-portraits in charcoal. This dramatic increase of energy and heightened productivity constitutes one of the hallmarks of sublimation.

Only a short time before, any complex procedure in making sculpture would have been beyond Donald's capacities. He could have used a shaving mirror only for endlessly repetitive play—casting light reflections on walls or making the world larger or smaller at will. It was essential that material, tools, and instruction in using them were available when Donald emerged from his withdrawn and fragmented state. At this juncture the workmanlike logic of building a substantial sculpture in clay paralleled and confirmed the psychic process of reintegration. Moving further away and closer

Figure 2.2.

could be practiced, in order to study detail and totality, with the aim of achieving unity. We see in Donald's story the difference between symptom and sublimation, but we also see how closely linked these two may be and how inextricably they may at times be intertwined.

Sublimation Achieved

The understanding of the process of sublimation is as important in working with adults as it is in art therapy with children. When Carmine Lombardi, a gifted self-taught artist, had conquered his dependency on drugs and alcohol, he became engrossed in sculpting a huge teardrop in marble. Many mishaps occurred. The stone cracked, the shape had to be modified. Somehow the piece resisted completion.

At this juncture art therapist Vera Zilzer suggested that he go out and draw all the trees of his native South Bronx. A large collection of exquisitely composed drawings resulted. They celebrated the impressive ruins of early twentieth century architecture

Figure 2.3.

as it persisted among the rubble and the irrepressive growth of weeds, flowers, and Ailanthus trees (Figure 2.4). Lombardi had neither been encouraged to immerse himself continuously in his grief, nor to escape the tragedy of his environment. Rather, he had been inspired both by works and by example (Vera Zilzer was an excellent artist and thus a suitable object of identification) to integrate his past and present: his inner world and his external situation. Lombardi's work became a source of pride to the community. The process of sublimation initiated in this series of drawings provided energy for artwork of ever-broadening scope.

Figure 2.4.

☐ Conclusion

The art therapist's attitude toward the concept of sublimation must fundamentally influence both practice and theoretical outlook. Art therapists who recognize in it a powerful source of energy will approach their task differently from those who perceive it as little more than icing on the cake. Sublimation cannot be planned or plotted. All we can do is establish an atmosphere wherein the group of processes of which it is born can unfold.

The prototype of this situation has been beautifully described by Winnicott (1965) as one in which the child is in contact with a mother who is benignly available but not at all intrusive. Because the child can be calmly certain of her continued availability, the infant reaches a state of relaxed tension. Experiences belonging to the realm of impulsive, instinctual living, or, to use Winnicott's term, *id experiences*, can occur within the framework of a relationship anchored in the ego, rather than arising from the id, serene rather than passionate. Instead of being overwhelmed, the ego is strengthened by the experience.

Such processes are characterized by a benign contact with the primitive mind that enriches and energizes the ego. Repressions are lifted and older modes of functioning activated. Ideas and memories belonging to the ego's realm are briefly subjected to the mechanisms of primary-process thinking. To be beneficial rather than destructive, this dipping into the domain of the id must occur when the individual is able to resist the pull toward permanent regression, so that even though prelogical primary process thinking prevails and ancient libidinal and aggressive strivings are reactivated, the ego continues to function on a mature level. If all goes well, this brings about new maturational spurts. Ernst Kris, who in 1952 described these processes from a psychoanalytic viewpoint, coined the term "regression in the service of the ego," while Silvano Arieti (1976) suggested the term "tertiary process" for this creative synthesis. However, we must be aware of the risk entailed, for if the ego should be unable to withstand the pressures arising from the id, there may be regression in the pathological sense.

Undoubtedly, the companionable solitude that Winnicott (1965) describes in terms of psychoanalytic understanding constitutes the ideal situation for producing art or for vicariously experiencing it. In the practice of art therapy we must frequently be much more active than the mother Winnicott envisions. At times we must directly participate in the patient's creative efforts. At other times we may be the first to provide the essential catalyst that had been missing in the patients' lives, Kohut's (1966) "gleam in the mother's eye" encouraging ego functioning. As we strive to libidinize the creative process, we must nevertheless maintain a balance between ego support and respect for the patient's need for unmolested introspection. We must remember that only what emerges within an ambience of supportive, but nonintrusive contact can feel real to the person who brings it forth. Enforced productions or information obtained through coercion can rarely be fully assimilated, and have no lasting effect on the individual's life.

Neither intrapsychic conflict nor the conflict between man's drives and the demands of the environment permit final solutions. Sublimation in art remains a continuous task, but one that never becomes stale or empty, as does the repetition born of emotional deadlock. Rather, each new endeavor constitutes a fresh beginning leading to another partial solution so that, if all goes well, each new work becomes more powerful and interesting than the preceding one.

Is there any difference between art and other forms of sublimation? The contemplation of all outstanding feats of sublimation can inspire feelings that are similar to those evoked by works of art. When we admire a bridge, a beautiful carpet, a precision instrument, a heroic deed, a mathematical equation, or any other valuable achievement, it is not only its usefulness that evokes admiration. All of us have experienced the difficulties of taming the instincts, of building ego structure, of becoming human. Therefore, we can experience something of the struggle and of the triumph of sublimation, even when we do not personally benefit from its results and when we have no technical understanding of the specific difficulties that had to be surmounted. Most products of sublimation, however, are in themselves emotionally neutral, even though they arouse aesthetic pleasure or even inspire awe.

Art, on the other hand, retells the story of transformation; it offers primarily the pleasure of witnessing the process. Art's value to society consists in stimulating sublimation and influencing its direction. Artist and audience travel together in two directions, from the primitive source of the creative impulse toward its final form, and again from the contemplation of form to the depth of complex, contradictory, and primitive emotions. In this adventure conscious, preconscious, and unconscious processes complement each other. It is thus probable that affect, which is contained but not neutralized, is essential to art, whereas other forms of sublimation would be disrupted by similar quantities of raw libidinal or aggressive drive energies.

The art therapist who sees in sublimation a process essential to emotional health will want to shield it from untimely interference, and this will influence the nature and timing of therapeutic intervention. In work with the severely disturbed and the retarded, much depends on the art therapist's perception of the boundaries of sublimation and of the role of precursory activities. The theoretical orientation presented in this chapter encourages a search for the vestiges of sublimation even where, in the full sense, it is out of reach.

As we recognize its powers we must guard against any starry-eyed belief in salvation through sublimation, and we must avoid oversimplification. We must remember that art and sublimation are not identical. Art serves a great many purposes, both in the life of individuals and in the cultural and practical lives of peoples, and all of them are likely to become the art therapist's concern. Kenny's story is a good example of the many functions art therapy may serve within the confines of a single session. Premature insistence on sublimation in the face of other pressing needs can be as destructive as failure to recognize its value.

☐ References

Arieti, S. (1976). *Creativity: The magic synthesis.* New York: Basic Books.

Kohut, H. (1966). Forms and transformations of narcissism. *Journal of the American Psychoanalytic Association, 14,* 243–272.

Kramer, E. (1987). Sublimation and art therapy. In J. A. Rubin (Ed.), *Approaches to Art therapy.* (pp. 26–43). New York: Brunner/Mazel.

Kris, E. (1952). *Psychoanalytic explorations in art.* New York: Schocken Books.

Lorenz, K. (1966). *On aggression.* New York: Harcourt, Brace, Jovanovich.

Winnicott, D. W. (1965). *Maturational processes and the facilitating environment.* New York: International Universities Press.

CHAPTER   Laurie Wilson

Symbolism and Art Therapy

The capacity to form and to use symbols distinguishes man from other species. "Instead of defining man as an animal rationale, we should define him as an animal symbol-icum. By so doing we can designate his specific difference, and we can understand the new way to man—the way to civilization" (Cassirer, 1974, p. 26). Visual imagery—the quintessential stuff of symbolism—is the raw material of art therapy. I shall attempt to demonstrate that, by encouraging production of artwork, we are promoting the development of the capacity to symbolize, and that this capacity is linked to a number of critically important ego functions.

David Beres wrote a number of papers on symbolism from the perspective of ego psychology, and proposed extremely fruitful ideas for art therapists. The psychoanalytic definition differs from the dictionary's, in which symbolism is "something that stands for, represents, or denotes something else (not by exact resemblance, but by vague suggestion, or by some accidental or conventional relation)." This is too broad, says Beres (1965), to be useful in differentiating types of indirect representation.

In his view, something that substitutes for something else and is experienced as equal to the original object is not a symbol. It may serve as a sign or a signal, but a symbol must stand *for* and not stand *in* for the thing it represents. Thus, an infant responding to another nurturing adult as it would to its mother is responding to an equally good *substitute* object, not a *symbolic* object. A time will come when the child has developed the mental capacity to know the difference between mother and a substitute. At about the same time (ca.18 months), the child will also be able to think of or *evoke a representation* of mother in *her absence*. Beres emphasizes that symbolism includes more than an immediate response to a signal. A key part of his definition is that a symbol "is a representational object that can be evoked in the absence of an immediate external stimulus" (1968, p. 509).

The capacity to evoke an absent object requires a level of cognitive functioning that enables the symbol-former to perceive and to hold an image in the mind. Piaget (1951)

Parts of this chapter have been published in somewhat different form in *The American Journal of Art Therapy,* 1985, 23, 79–88; 129–133. (Wilson, 1985a; 1985b) uses the term *"object permanence"* for this capacity to evoke an absent object; it is seen as a necessary step on the way to what psychoanalysts call *"libidinal object constancy"* (Fraiberg, 1969).

In order for both of these capacities to develop, the child must first be able to see that the *substitute object* stands as *equal to* the original object, and that the *symbolic object represents* the original object, but is different from it. Beres also suggests that Winnicott's (1953) concept of the *transitional object* refers to the *transition from substitute to symbolic object.* Thus in the comic strip "Peanuts," Linus' blanket is first experienced as mother's comforting presence, and later serves as a reminder of mother, giving comfort.

☐ Symbol Formation

Beres asserts "that the symbolic process is not present at birth . . . it develops along with the growth of ego functions" (1965, p. 8). Indeed, many ego functions must be sufficiently developed for symbol formation to be possible: perception, memory, learning, conceptualization, and the reality and organizing functions. The earliest symbolic functioning occurs in a syncretic, concrete fashion; only later does it progress to an abstract conceptual mode. Thus, an infant who is trying to open a box may reveal his understanding of openness by opening and closing his mouth; some months later the same infant can replace the concrete, gestural *act* with the *word* "open" (Piaget, 1951; Werner & Kaplan, 1963).

Beres (1960) feels that a hierarchy of perceptual experiences underlie all complex mental functioning, like thinking and fantasizing. At the first level he places *sense data,* which may impinge on the organism both from within the body and from the external environment. At this level sensation is a pre-perceptual neurophysiological phenomenon. At the second level these primary sensations are organized into percepts. Dependent on immediate, direct sensory stimulation, percepts are comparable to signals or cues, and may also be called mental registrations or memory traces. At the third level, perception becomes independent of immediate stimulation, a *mental representation* of something not actually present to the senses.

What does all this have to do with symbolism? Beres says that symbolism is a crucial type of *mental representation,* since it provides the building blocks for other, more complex mental representations: images, fantasies, thoughts, concepts, dreams, hallucinations, symptoms, and language. According to Beres, *the symbol is one of the earliest mental representations of an absent stimulus, internal or external.*

That psychic functioning is mediated through mental representations is a concept fundamental to psychoanalytic psychology. As the child's developing ego functions mature, responses to stimuli are mediated almost exclusively through mental representations. Mental functioning takes on its characteristic and unique human quality—perceptions of the external world and of inner drives and affects, are all registered in the mind by psychic representations; and it is to these representations that the energies of the instinctual drives are directed in a process that psychoanalysis calls "cathexis" (Beres, 1960).

The symbol—defined earlier as "a representational object that can be evoked in the absence of an immediate external stimulus"—is therefore a critical link between the world of reality (as stimulus) and human behavior, thought, and fantasy (as response).

☐ Pathology of the Symbolic Process

Dysfunction in symbol formation characterizes severe disabilities ranging from schizo-phrenia to aphasia. A brief look at some specific forms of pathology can help in un-derstanding the value of making visual images in treating them. Beres (1965) notes three clinical areas in which pathology of the symbolic process may be seen: retarded ego development, schizophrenia, and organic brain disease. In all, "the essential el-ement is a concurrent disturbance of the reality function of the ego" (Beres, 1965, p. 16).

Retarded Ego Development

In retarded ego development the child does not develop the capacity to distinguish the representative object from the real object—Linus' blanket *is* mother. We see this clearly with the mentally retarded, whose crippling incapacity in this area (among others) interferes with the normal development of language, thought processes, and object relations.

Elena, a severely retarded, 22-year-old woman with an IQ of 20, had been living in institutions for 18 years (cf. Wilson, 1977). Her records documented a prolonged fixation at the oral phase. She could not be weaned from a bottle until age five, and shortly thereafter developed a habit of collecting and chewing or swallowing bits of string and buttons. In adolescence Elena still collected such objects, but she no longer put them in her mouth. By age 22 she had abandoned this habit; instead she constantly carried, or wore around her neck on a chain, a ball-like clump of metal jingle bells. Elena herself wove the bells together with wire, and from time to time would increase or decrease the size of the cluster. If the bells were taken from her or she accidentally left them behind, she would cry inconsolably or angrily hit or overturn tables or chairs.

In addition to this fixation, Elena had a repertoire of gestures that included rubbing her hands together, stroking her cheeks, mouth, and nose, and holding and rubbing her breasts. Often she began to make these gestures when distressed, but her pained expres-sion usually gave way to one of pleasure or comfort. Elena appeared to be attempting to comfort herself, with caresses that had in the past been given her by others.

When Elena began art therapy sessions, she was fixated on one image: a circle with a pattern of radial lines imposed on it. She repeated this pattern steadily in her artwork for a year and a half, covering sheet after sheet with numerous examples, almost always using red. Although she willingly varied the medium (using crayon, paint, or chalk), she would rarely alter the image or the color. She was also very clingy, needing constant reassurance and praise.

Over the course of two years, Elena gradually progressed, in both her art expression and general behavior, from an infantile dependency to greater maturity. The key to helping was understanding the psychological meaning of her art. By partially satisfying some of her needs, both artistic and personal, and by leading her toward small, but appropriate changes in these two areas, Elena was gradually able to become more flexible and independent, eventually traveling unassisted to the art room.

Her graphic vocabulary also expanded to include concentric circles, images of bod-ies, squares, and ultimately a rich combination of circles, triangles, squares, and hy-brid shapes that she used to draw full figures, clothing, and ornaments. She was able to modify her radial schema, and to include it in different configurations as eyes (Figure 3.1) and breasts.

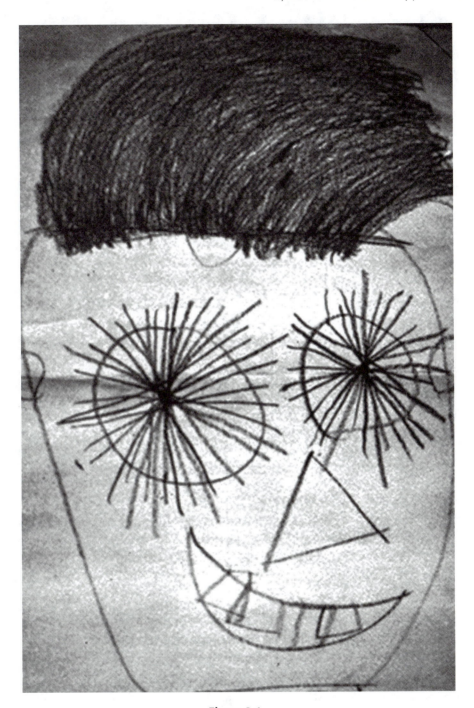

Figure 3.1.

As I realized that Elena's perseverative radial schema stood equally for breast, mother, and bell, I understood the clump of jingle bells to be her transitional object. I now see the desperate attachment to her bells as a *failure of the symbolic function*, since at the start of treatment the bells stood for her as a substitute, not a symbolic object. Elena then developed—through art therapy—a capacity for symbolization, whereby the function of the transitional object shifted from substitute (*standing as equal*) to symbol (*standing as representation*) for the original object—mother.

The persistent making of visual images in art therapy sessions actually seemed to spur the development of her ability to symbolize. As long as the clump of bells and the radial schema functioned as a *substitute* for mother, they were experienced as essential, and could not be given up or altered. When Elena finally developed the capacity to *symbolize* and thereby evoke the absent mother, she was freed to function more flexibly, her security consisting now of symbolic rather than concrete reminders of an absent object. Thus, she was able to leave her bells behind in her room, and to come to sessions unaccompanied either by this transitional object or an actual attendant. We also saw her replace the bells with a pocketbook—another symbolic transformation of the original substitute object.

Schizophrenia

Loss of or problems with reality testing characterize schizophrenia. To Beres, this is a loss of the capacity to recognize and differentiate between the real object and its representation. Making visual images can play a critical role, facilitating an increased capacity for symbolization and associated reality testing. Many art therapists have seen a schizophrenic child or adult regain the capacity to symbolize and increase the sense of reality through the regular production of artwork. Most often, there is repeated expression of key symbols, with a gradual recognition of their meaning, and a consequent ability to differentiate reality from fantasy. The case of Dorothy (Rubin, 1978), in which a schizophrenic girl moved from *being* a bird to *painting* birds—and eventually people—is a typical example of such a process (cf. Wilson, 1985a, pp. 81–84).

Organic Brain Disease

Partial or total loss of the ability to articulate ideas through brain damage is known as *aphasia*. David, a 65-year-old man, was seen in art therapy for three months by Irene Rosner, an art therapist who specializes in work with the physically ill and disabled. He had suffered a stroke, causing paralysis on the right side of his body and an inability to speak intelligibly. Retired for three years from his position as a Social Security examiner, he had maintained a private business in accounting. His wife was disabled with cerebral palsy, as was one of their five children. The family seemed to be supportive and nurturing.

When first admitted to the hospital, David was extremely lethargic. His yes/no responses (head movement) were unreliable, and he was exhausted by any attempts at communication. The psychologist reported that David was only sporadically alert, but when alert did respond to visual stimuli by nodding. Although he seemed to understand some of what was said to him, his attention span was very limited. He emitted a repetitive, grating cry and was demanding.

The treatment plan included daily physical and occupational therapy, speech therapy two or three days a week, and art therapy every other day. Initially art therapy sessions lasted 20 minutes, and were increased to between 45 minutes and an hour as he was able to concentrate longer.

David's first drawings in art therapy were similar to a child's early scribbles. Although his marks looked as if they had been placed randomly on the paper, his drawing process reflected a struggle to gain motor control. The paralysis of his right side meant that David had to use his left hand—not his dominant hand—which had been weakened by a bout with polio in childhood. Nevertheless, he was focused and attentive while he drew. Although incomprehensible to an observer, his drawings seemed to have specific meaning for him. So his art therapist focused on attempting to help him to achieve more recognizable forms.

David's progress in art paralleled the development of drawing in young children. In time, his perseverative vocalization decreased, and he slowly regained the ability to say some words; he then reached the stage of naming his scribbles, although they were still unrecognizable. Like a young child, the name David supplied for a given drawing might shift with the associational current. Thus, at one moment he called an early scribble "ice chips" and at another "fish." At this time the psychologist reported that David was more alert and attentive, was communicating his needs with nonverbal cues, and was responding well to directions.

The next stage in David's development marked an advance in two areas. He began to make recognizable forms, to name them appropriately, and was able to place his marks on the paper in a way that indicated his awareness of the entire page. We can easily pick out the tree in Figure 3.2, titled by David "Fish, Tree, and Amoeba." In contrast to his earlier efforts, David's work now gave evidence of planning and deliberation. He

Figure 3.2.

Figure 3.3.

created numerous intentional enclosures: circles of various sizes, elongated triangles, and irregualr shapes. Because of the shakiness of his hand, the shapes were barely discernible amid the scribbled lines on the same page, as with young children's drawings.

Nevertheless, on close inspection, forms become apparent in David's drawings from this period—in one a face schema, a crude circular shape with two eyes. Soon after, when asked to draw a person, David combined his face scheme with body parts to create Figure 3.3. As he drew, the human figure took on a personal meaning. He began to cry and in response to gentle questioning, said, "My wife—she's short and fat and ugly and wonderful." David had been responding without signs of emotion; now he began to register personal involvement. His reaction, stimulated by his own art, seemed a pivotal event in his psychological recovery. He went on to produce better integrated pictures and to invest them with personal meaning, as well as to make further strides in speech and movement.

In view of all of his therapies, it is impossible to say to what extent his work in art precipitated or merely coincided with a longer attention span, more coherent speech, and appropriate affect. But this moving sequence of events suggests that, just as the development of visual images by young children promotes their capacity to engage in symbolic processes; so brain-damaged adults may be helped to recover symbolic functioning in all areas, including language, through a similar development of visual images.

David seemed to reflect progress first in his drawings, and only later in his language and object relations. With each advancing step of visual symbol formation—scribbles, named scribbles, schemas, recognizable images, and human figure drawing—we can postulate the return of impaired ego functions. Perception, memory, conceptualization, reality function, and the organizing function all unite to once again permit *mental representations—symbols of absent objects*. With the return of this capacity, feelings (affect) and human (object) relations were reinstated—a lost love took on new life.

Conclusion

The lesson to be learned from these two cases is that patients with an impaired symbolic function (and consequent defective ego functioning) can be helped, by the making of visual images, to *develop* the ability to symbolize—a capacity fundamental to almost all civilized activity. Elena's and David's pathologies resulted from developmental irregularities. Elena, a case of arrested development, was able, by making images, to develop the capacity to recall and to relate to an absent object. This step, in turn, promoted increased freedom to explore the world and to function autonomously. Severe regression characterized David's pathology. His production of images promoted higher-level functioning of the capacity to symbolize, and ultimately led to the restoration of object relations.

Language, a shared symbolic system, is central in development and in human experience. When using language is too difficult—or too frightening—practice in symbolizing, by making visual images, can further development. Developmentally impaired patients, like young children, can be helped by exercising the visual-motor function to achieve higher-level functioning—the capacity to symbolize in the form of language. As art therapists learn the particulars of symbol formation and their relationship to developing ego functions, we can arrive at better interventions to promote growth in our patients.

☐ Mental Representation

In order to understand even more fully the part played by symbolism in *psychic functioning*, we return to Beres' (1968) discussion of *mental representation*. The symbol is the *conscious* derivative of the *unconscious* mental representation, what Freud called "psychic reality." There is considerable evidence for the possibility of organized unconscious mental representations, which may be described as "unconscious symbols." Thus, *symbolism gives conscious expression to unconscious mental content*, and serves both adaptation and communication (1968, p. 510).

The concept of mental representation may be better known to art therapists by other names, like *self-representation, body image, memory schema, internal object*, or *representational world*. Beres and Joseph state that "a mental representation is a postulated unconscious psychic organization capable of evocation in consciousness as symbol, image, fantasy, thought, affect, or action" (1970, p. 2). These authors also feel that "mental representations form the unconscious basis for all conscious psychic activity" (Beres & Joseph, 1970, p. 4), and shape our perception of reality.

We respond, not to the external *stimulus* that initiates perception, but to the *mental representation activated by it.* This mental representation is not an exact reproduction of the original stimulus, but is the product of many distorting and mediating forces, including feelings, memories of past experiences, and cognitive states. An individual's "psychic reality" is thus relative and indeterminate, a fact long known to artists. Psychoanalytic clinicians accept this idea, and I suspect most art therapists would agree. It is in the nature of our work to avidly seek the meaning behind or beneath the pictures our patients produce. We accept the notion of hidden feelings, fears, or fantasies revealed by the form and content of the artwork.

Psychic Energy

Another important function of symbolization which is also relevant for art therapy—delay in the response to stimulation. To grasp this we must first understand the psychoanalytic concept of *psychic energy*. Psychic energy is a hypothetical force, derived from the instinctual drives, that impels the mind to activity. "In the human being, stimuli, whether from the external world or from the organs of the body, arouse the instinctual drive forces to the development of a need" (Beres, 1965, p. 13). Beres sees this as a neurophysiological state, before the transformation of the need into a wish, which adds the psychological component.

Drive energies seek discharge through mental or physical activity accompanied by a transfer or flow of psychic energy. The amount of psychic energy invested in a mental process or representation is called its *cathexis*. *Freely mobile* mental energy accompanies the *primary process* and presses for immediate discharge. Energy that accompanies the *secondary process* is generally more or less *bound*. Its discharge can be delayed temporarily or even longer.

The capacity to *bind* psychic energy increases with maturation, and is closely related to the capacity for de-instinctualization or neutralization. With neutralization, energy is deflected from its original pleasure-seeking aims and becomes available for use in ego functioning, as in sublimation. To explain the *delay* of discharge, Beres and Joseph "postulate an unconscious psychic organization that [provides] the basis for binding the energies which otherwise would be immediately discharged"(1970, p. 4). Since cathexes are focused on the mental representation "it follows that mental representations would serve to contain the . . . drive energies, to 'bind' them, . . . to facilitate delay of discharge" (Beres & Joseph, 1970, p. 4).

These mental representations "can be evoked to consciousness as images, fantasies, or thoughts. The building blocks of these conscious manifestations are the symbols. Symbol formation in this sense is an ego function involved in a reciprocal relationship to other ego functions . . . and enters into every manifestation of ego activity" (Beres, 1965, p. 13).

It seems that this partially accounts for the effectiveness of art therapy. By asking our patients to make pictures or sculptures, particularly when they are under pressure to act impulsively, we seek to mediate peremptory drive discharge by interposing visual symbols between stimulus, need, wish, and action. Art therapists can cite many instances of work with impulsive patients, where the promotion of symbol formation encouraged a delayed response to stimulation. The invitation to "put *it* (feeling, idea, impulse) on the paper" or to "express it with the clay,"*instead* of acting it out physically, is a way of taming impulsive drive discharge, and promoting the development of ego functions.

Making the Unconscious Conscious

Symbolism also plays an important role in the relationship of the unconscious to consciousness. Beres says that "the individual who is using the symbol has the *capacity to know* that the symbol is not the original object" (1965, p. 7). This raises the question of consciousness. The symbol itself, which some psychologists call the *vehicle* or that which carries meaning, is understood by Beres to be "a manifest production of which the person is conscious." On the other hand, that which is symbolized, sometimes called the *referent*, may be "conscious; easily available to consciousness that is, preconscious, or repressed and unconscious" (Ibid., p. 8). This is a modification of the early psychoanalytic view (Ferenczi, 1912/1956; Jones, 1916/1920) that true symbolism applies only to symbols whose referents are unconscious. "Only what is repressed is symbolized, only what is repressed needs to be symbolized" (Jones, 1916/1920, p. 158).

Art therapists were long ago introduced to the idea that symbolic activity can facilitate consciousness by Margaret Naumburg, who wrote about it at length in *Schizophrenic Art* (1950), and whose fundamental theories and practices were based on it (1953, 1966). Naumburg's work, and the work of those who follow her theory and method, are based on *making the unconscious conscious*, using the symbolic expression of artwork as a guide and an instrument in the process.

Let us now look briefly at just how art making relates to this process. According to Beres, the symbol is the conscious derivative of the unconscious mental representation. Symbolism therefore serves adaptation and communication, by giving conscious expression to unconscious mental content. It is self-evident, then, that the symbolic vehicle—for art therapists, the artwork—must be conscious.

The *referent* (the idea or thing being symbolized) may, according to Beres, be conscious, preconscious, or unconscious. This, for art therapists, is the crux of the matter. First, how do we determine whether or what part of the symbolic imagery in the art derives from unconscious material? Even if we can answer that one, we are confronted by even more perplexing questions: Is the artist aware of the unconscious referent? Why is it appearing now? Should he be made aware of it? How should this be brought about? What will be the consequences of this awareness?

I shall propose preliminary responses by applying Beres' ideas. It has long been accepted that visual images may reveal the unconscious wishes and conflicts of those who make them. The numerous projective tests using drawings provide evidence of this, and the diagnostic value of this psychic function of symbolism seems indisputable. Through drawing, painting, and sculpture, wishes may be displaced from forbidden objects to their symbolic substitutes. Hence, we find numerous bloody battles in the artwork of young boys, whose aggressive wishes press for expression.

We can say, at the very least, that inner mental representations may be objectified, by being externalized in concrete visual form. But does this externalization change the stage of the referent? Here there are no simple answers. Art history and art therapy reveal numerous examples of artwork, heavily laden with unconscious symbolism, that does not change the awareness of the individuals who produced it. I am certain, for example, that Louise Nevelson did not know her unresolved unconscious conflicts about sexuality and mourning, although she created sculpture that contains many references to them (Wilson, 1981).

Perhaps art is effective in such a case because the external symbolic representation allows distance to be created between the individual and the conflict. Although this does not lead to change, it may be serving a significant defensive purpose. There are many artists whom one feels would suffer great psychic pain if they were deprived of their work. Most art therapists, however, are more ambitious for their patients, and seek ways to encourage or induce change in maladaptive functioning.

But, what if we suppose that, at least sometimes, the externalization accomplished by making a visual image *changes* the unconscious state of the referent—the idea being symbolized—to a preconscious state? This would explain a variety of phenomena seen regularly in art therapy. It has often been observed, for example, that making artwork frees patients who are blocked in verbal expression. To put an idea or feeling into words requires a conscious level of awareness—rather than a preconscious one—and it is common for patients to readily speak about the story or meaning of their art production, after maintaining a stony silence when offered the opportunity simply to speak about themselves and their problems.

Another phenomenon is often observed with patients who are willing to speak, but whose capacity to organize their thoughts and perceptions is gravely impaired—like schizophrenics. There are similar cases where a highly complex fantasy life may be presumed to exist, but conscious communication about it is unobtainable, as with schizoid patients. There, the production of artwork seems to permit the expression, exploration, and organization of the underlying fantasies once they are depicted consciously in concrete visual terms.

Noah, for example, was an extremely intelligent and gifted schizoid, preadolescent boy in day treatment at a special school and treatment center. From early childhood on he had been chronically unhappy, with frequent temper tantrums, during which he broke furniture and hit his mother. And in spite of his 160 IQ, he had always had difficulty in school—not doing homework, crying every day, and without friends.

Noah came to art therapy after several years of psychotherapy, during which he had made fleeting but incoherent references to his science fiction fantasy. In the past year, his psychotherapist discovered that when Noah entered acutely upset and unable to speak, only through drawing was he able to regain internal controls, and to reveal the nature of his distress. It was no surprise, then, that art therapy sessions allowed this extremely withdrawn boy to objectify his fantasy life. Gradually, a narrative tale unfolded through his artwork, depicting a never-ending battle between alien creatures and an intergalactic peace force.

An early clay sculpture called "Imagination" portrayed a nameless planet in the year 7001 populated by odd creatures (Figure 3.4). It seemed to be a symbolic equivalent for

Figure 3.4.

Figure 3.5.

Noah's defensive retreat into fantasy, and the unhappy inner emptiness he was experiencing. During his first year in art therapy, Noah was able to describe the characters in his fantasy, much as he had been able to tell of his daily dilemmas after drawing them for his therapist. He seemed to be externalizing, exploring, and organizing his inner life as he drew and modeled "Legrans" and "Lizardrons," battling for supremacy in their devastated milieu. He spoke about his invented creatures and their battles; I remained within that metaphor. By the end of the first year, his internal conflict over managing his aggressive impulses was appearing in symbolic form in his art.

In the first two sessions of the second year, Noah made a new version of "Imagination" (Figure 3.5). After working silently while finishing the details of this piece, he began to tell the story. He explained that a thin, wedge-shaped missile aimed at earth would destroy the planet in 7103, a year following the date he had assigned to the sculpture. The missile had been sent by Lizardrons, mean bullies who had heard that earth was recovering from a nuclear blast and was becoming habitable again. Noah described the dome-shaped figure at the upper left of the scene as a "cloaked figure, an alien," a species of large beings from far away who could easily move forward and backward into different time frames. He explained that when the aliens discover the cruelty and meanness of the Lizardrons, they fight them and drive them from the galaxy with the warning that if the Lizardrons were to reappear and cause trouble, the aliens would also return to protect the galaxy.

Several months after this session, at about the time he chose to paint the clay sculpture "Imagination II," (Figure 3.6), Noah came to realize some of the meanings embedded in the science fiction fantasy he had depicted. After announcing that imagination comes from inside a person—to which I responded, "like your stories and pictures"—Noah proceeded to identify the Lizardrons as his bad feelings, and the battles he had been portraying as corresponding to an internal emotional struggle.

Though never made explicit, it seemed that the cloaked figure was the art therapist, an interpretation that became inescapable when he painted it the same color blue as

Figure 3.6.

my smock. In retrospect, the idea of aliens as large beings who can move forward and backward at will seemed an excellent metaphor, since I came only once a week and had been away for a long time during the summer break. We can also see the rescuing function Noah had assigned to me in his science fiction fantasy, through the story of aliens driving out the mean Lizardrons.

The act of *painting* this sculpture several months after its original production seemed to serve a number of psychological purposes. First, it brought some of the fantasy material closer to the surface where it could be put into words, and second, it allowed Noah to modify his fantasy. He covered the missile aimed at earth with black paint, so that it seemed to disappear, and announced that it was no longer going to destroy the earth.

What had earlier been inchoate and inexpressible, had begun to take visible shape. An unconscious fantasy, through being given representation, was becoming more accessible to consciousness. In observing this process, I had a feeling I often had in art therapy... that some deeply unconscious material had shifted upward, and had reached a level of preconsciousness by virtue of taking form in the art.

For some patients this may be a sufficient goal, particularly since it may be accompanied by an experience of catharsis. Yet there are other directions that this progress through symbol formation can take. Two of them are well known to art therapists as the Naumburg (1966) and Kramer (1971) approaches. The former uses artwork initially to bring unconscious conflicts to the surface, and ultimately to lead patients to a conscious verbal awareness of these conflicts. The latter aims for a neutralization of the drive energy stimulating the symbolic expression, by guiding that expression toward sublimation in continued production of artwork.

Psychoanalytic ego psychology, with its developmental framework, can be most helpful to art therapists. Applying the theoretical formulations of David Beres on symbolism and mental representation, we can better understand some of the ways art therapy works. One is that making visual images helps patients with defective ego functioning and impaired symbolization develop the capacity to symbolize, an ability fundamental to almost all civilized functioning. Another is that, by understanding some of the roles played by symbolic expression in art, we may become even more effective, and know better how to explain the results of our labors.

☐ References

Beres, D. (1960). Perception, imagination and reality. *International Journal of Psychoanalysis, 41,* 327–334.

Beres, D. (1965). Symbol and object. *Bulletin of the Menninger Clinic, 29,* 3–23.

Beres, D. (1968). The humanness of human beings: Psychoanalytic considerations. *Psychoanalytic Quarterly, 37,* 487–522.

Beres, D., & Joseph, E. (1970). The concept of mental representation in psychoanalysis. *International Journal of Psychoanalysis, 51,* 1–9.

Cassirer, E. (1974). *An essay on man.* New Haven, CT: Yale University Press.

Ferenczi, S. (1912). *Sex in psychoanalysis,* Vol. 1 (pp. 214–237). New York: Dover.

Fraiberg, S. (1969). Libidinal object constancy and mental representation. *Psychoanalytic Study of the Child, 24,* 9–47.

Jones, E. (1920). The theory of symbolism. In *Papers on psychoanalysis* (pp.129–186). London: Balliere, Tindall & Cox. (Original work published 1916).

Kramer, E. (1971). *Art as therapy with children.* New York: Schoken.

Naumburg, M. (1950). *Schizophrenic art: Its meaning in psychotherapy.* New York: Grune & Stratton.

Naumburg, M. (1953). *Psychoneurotic art: Its function in psychotherapy.* New York: Grune & Stratton.

Naumburg, M. (1966). *Dynamically oriented art therapy: Its principles and practice.* New York: Grune & Stratton.

Piaget, J. (1951). *Play, dreams and imitation in childhood.* New York: Dutton.

Rubin, J. A. (1978). *Child art therapy.* New York: Van Nostrand Reinhold.

Werner, H., & Kaplan, B. (1963). *Symbol formation.* New York: Wiley.

Winnicott, D. W. (1953). Transitional objects and transitional phenomena. *International Journal of Psychoanalysis, 34,* 89–97.

Wilson, L. (1977). Theory and practice of art therapy with the mentally retarded. *American Journal of Art Therapy, 16,* 87–97.

Wilson, L. (1981). Louise Nevelson: Personal history and art. *American Journal of Art Therapy, 20,* 79–97.

Wilson, L. (1985a). Symbolism and art therapy: I. Symbolism's role in the development of ego functions. *American Journal of Art Therapy, 23,* 79–88.

Wilson, L. (1985b). Symbolism and art therapy: II. Symbolism's relationship to basic psychic functioning. *American Journal of Art Therapy, 23,* 129–133.

CHAPTER Arthur Robbins

Object Relations and Art Therapy

☐ An Encounter with a Patient's Inner World

A patient comes into my office. I am immediately aware of her eyes, with their sad, liquid emptiness. Her face is expressionless, an occasional smile breaking through. At 47 she is unmarried and very tired. As her story unfolds, I learn that she does not need to work, for she has a small income from her parents' estate. This should allow her some ease, but she busily, even frantically, moves from one task to another. She feels her life rushing by her, becoming increasingly aware that the span of one lifetime is not endless. Paradoxically, she feels younger than her age.

Life has been a series of short and long love affairs for this woman. Some dissolve before they begin; others are filled with pain and remorse. As she talks in a vague poetic way, I am interested and intrigued, but strangely disconnected. There's an ethereal quality about this patient that defies solidity or definition. The one thing that comes through loud and strong is the depth of her loneliness and sense of being lost. I feel the impulse to be warm and protective, even as she eludes me, like sand slipping through my fingers. I'm reminded of an old movie, *Hiroshima Mon Amour*, the story of a young woman's personal disaster as mirrored in an atomic holocaust. For her, eroticism offered a desperate anchor in the midst of a chaotic world.

I ask this woman to draw a picture about herself, with the hope that I will get a more defined picture of the inner world in which she dwells. She protests: "I don't have enough time to do it in the session." So I ask if she would be willing to draw about herself at home. She readily agrees.

Next session she brings me a set of pictures (Figure 4.1), all looking quickly drawn in a monochromatic blue. There is movement in her drawings, but a lack of dimension. Although particularly pleased with one picture (Fig. 4.1C) that she says describes the sensual part of herself, the part that craves contact and needs to be touched, she has nothing else to say about this drawing. She does give some information about the other

Parts of this chapter appear in *The Artist as Therapist* by Arthur Robbins, Human Sciences Press, 1987. Reprinted by permission of the publisher.

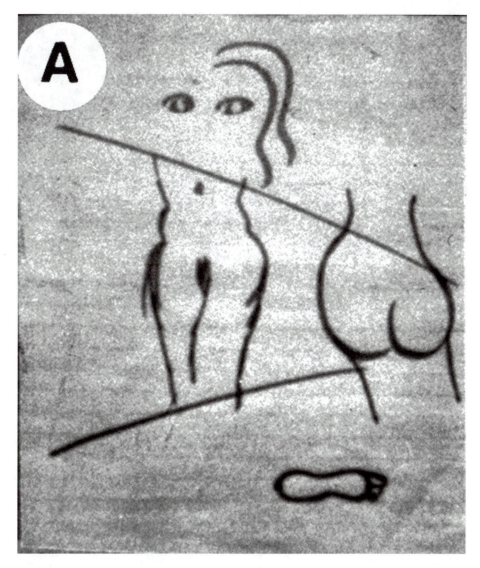

Figure 4.1.

pictures, however. The hands reaching out (Fig. 4.1B) represent the part of herself that needs to be a part of something bigger. In the fourth (Fig. 4.1D), representing the Jewish community she loves, she expands further: "All those people around a big ark in a semicircle meet and are part of something bigger." Again, I am aware of eyes, as those in the picture stare out and search to be taken in. Her drawings are like soft, sensual fragments, reaching out to say "Hold me."

The patient's representations of her body (Fig. 4.1) seem segmented rather than forming a flowing whole, leading me to wonder whether the holding she had received had been given by someone who was disengaged and unrelated. Putting these impressions

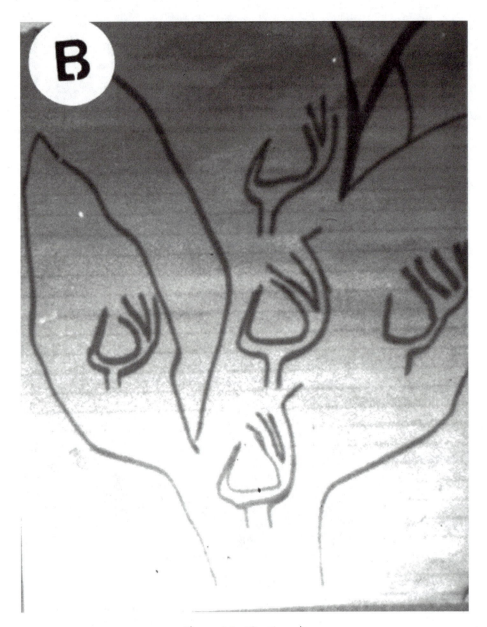

Figure 4.1. (Continued)

together, I see the religious force giving her a feeling of aliveness and superficial cohesion and, along with her eroticism, acting as a compensatory mechanism for her lack of the most basic of connections, that of the mother and child's early resonance.

Although this patient has not spoken of her mother, I sense her presence in the room. She is a brisk, hurried person, easily overwhelming to her child. The child who still dwells within this patient is hungry for contact, while at the same time feeling

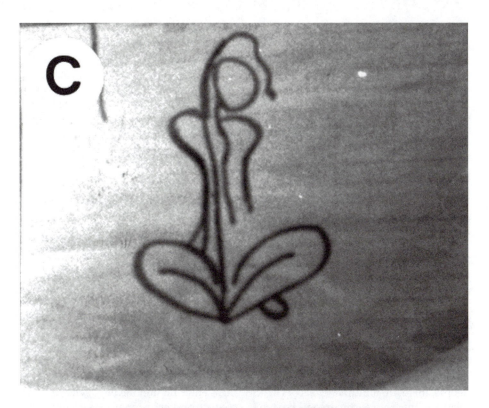

Figure 4.1. (Continued)

frightened of being overwhelmed and controlled, as she was by her mother. These dual pulls cause her to fragment and to become diffuse when intimate contact is offered.

At the same time as images of the mother permeate the atmosphere, a sense of her father crowds into the room with us, in spite of his having gone unmentioned by the patient. I suspect he is the one who supplied physical contact and warmth in a nonverbal way, offering her some semblance of definition.

Discussion

In this brief description, I have attempted to hint at the complex interaction of objective and subjective realities that create a psychological space between two people, from the beginning of therapy. Within this space, past and present merge to create a unique mood and atmosphere. I experience the patient's inner representations of her past expressed in the present. I sense, feel, and see the affects, moods, and attitudes originally connected to her past relationships as they are represented in images and pictures that literally fill my office.

These representations speak of the *me and you* inside each of us that create our individual perceptions of the world, and at the same time induce and shape the social world's response to each of us. The representations within any given patient make contact with the relationships I carry inside me. My internal mother, father, and child touch those of the patient at points of similar experience, perception, and feeling, as we get to know one another. It becomes clear that in any single encounter between two people, there are multiple levels of consciousness entering into the engagement, as the relationships from each person's past make contact, and occasionally lose sight of one another.

Art adds a dimension to this engagement. Sometimes the art mirrors or deepens what is already going on in the relationship. In other instances, the art form may offer something diametrically opposed to the verbal dialogue. This added dimension gives a new perspective on our internal relationships, as it brings us to new levels of consciousness.

It is these early internalized relationships, with their effect on one's current reality, which form the core of object relations theory as I use it in my practice. I am not referring to one unified theory which can be found in a single book, or is espoused by a particular theoretician. My use of this term reflects my own distillation from a body of theory in psychoanalysis.

Going back to its roots in psychoanalytic theory, the "object" in object relations theory refers to the who and what in which a person's libidinal energy is invested. By "libidinal energy" I mean that constitutional reservoir of energy and life that is part sexual, part aggressive, but is more than either. It is the fuel that motivates each of us to reach out and to find relief and contact with the world. Within this framework, human behavior is conceptualized within a tripartite system of id, ego, and superego, which, when unbalanced, creates the conflicts manifesting themselves in the range of defenses and symptoms characteristic of the neuroses.

The id forces, which reflect primitive fantasies, wishes, and so forth, constantly try to make themselves felt and to find satisfaction. Derivatives of these forces are felt throughout life in such forms as dreams and fantasies, and are the stuff of primary process thinking. With maturation, the ego and superego counter and modify the raw id forces: the ego, with its rational, logical, secondary process thinking, working to integrate the demands of outer reality with the inner world; the superego, with its belief system consisting of such notions as the ideal, good, bad, and evil, influencing the ego's reactions to the id. An imbalance among these forces is thought to arise when the oedipal crisis is not successfully resolved.

Psychoanalytic treatment of the neuroses is directed at analyzing defenses, resistances, and the transference, as well as dealing with such issues as shame, guilt, and anxiety. In the neurotic individual, there is a clear sense of an established internal me and you. Much emphasis is placed on making the unconscious conscious, and on bringing primary process material within secondary process organization. The ideal outcome of therapy is modifying the defenses of the ego and prohibitions of the superego, to allow the patient's life space to expand and to tolerate a richer symbolic and imaginative existence.

The patient described in the opening paragraph does not fall within the neurotic category. Like many, she falls into the wide continuum of primitive mental states including— the psychotic, borderline, narcissistic personality, mood disorder, psychopath, and schizoid—all of whom suffer from deficits and problems in the early mother-child relationship. Therapy for these patients cannot be in making the unconscious conscious. That is not possible, as the disparate systems of mental structure lack integration and cohesiveness. The task, therefore, becomes one of building rather than uncovering, and of completing lost dialogues of the early maternal matrix.

Resonance is important in this kind of therapeutic encounter. The therapist "mirrors," or offers emotional responsiveness, which facilitates the process of empathy, crucial in this treatment process. For instance, in the description of the patient in the opening pages, a central theme of treatment would be object loss: the absence of a central figure to give cohesion to the patient's life. The cognitive awareness of this issue by itself would be of little help to her. She would need a relationship in treatment that would both repair the damages of loss, and give her the courage to live through her feelings of pain and abandonment.

As in all treatment where the problems involve inadequate early object relations, there is a paradox. The therapist cannot actually *be* that which the patient lost, yet the therapist's presence and actual living with the patient's problems serve to repair the original damage and problem. In this treatment, we experience patients' early losses and problems, contain and organize their experiences, and hope to give them a climate where trauma, disappointment, and confusion can be reorganized on a higher, more satisfying level. Other issues in dealing with more primitive mental states are loss of boundaries and regression to fusion states, both of which will be tested out and experienced within the treatment relationship.

The Role of Art

Art, in this context, can be a container or organizer that mirrors internal object relations, as well as associated defenses and developmental problems. The relationship offers a safe framework within which to investigate and experience the object world. The expressed art form will exhibit the various levels of definition the relationship creates. Thus, in the opening clinical example, the abstract, but self-contained quality of the art mirrored the quality of the initial therapeutic relationship.

Art therapy offers the possibility for *psychological space*—that which is created through the interactions of two individuals—to be reorganized by mirroring or complementarity (offering opposites). This space has much in common with what Winnicott calls *transitional space* (1971). It is an intermediate area that is neither inside nor outside, but which bridges subjective and objective reality. By extension, dead or *pathological space* can also occur, either in the art form or in the relationship, when expression is weighed down by oppressive defenses. Relationships are experienced and programmed to recreate sterile childhood interactions. Pathological space is one particular dimension of transitional space, and can be experienced on at least two different levels.

In the creative act, the various representations of the patient's world are shaped and reflected through artistic form. This also happens within the interpersonal therapeutic relationship, and can either complement or mirror what is going on in the art expression. The therapist's skill is brought to bear in maintaining a positive, supportive relationship as a background, or structure, in order for the art therapy process to proceed. When pathological space takes over the interaction, it requires ingenuity and creativity to ferret out the hidden object relations and to find the appropriate art form to regenerate psychological space.

Implicit in these notions of transitional and pathological space is the idea that relationships are characterized by different energy systems, which shape and form the space around us. Within each system, there are different levels of openness or closure, completeness or incompleteness. In primitive mental states, the art therapist offers a creative experience to help move the energy system from one level of differentiation to another. Another way of putting it is that we offer the missing link to complete the Gestalt or whole, through mirroring or complementarity.

Art therapy, then, strives to promote new levels of perceptual organization, that involve shifts in energy patterns. The art form offers an added means for working with internalized splits and polarities, and integrating them into new wholes. The representations from our past are expressed through image and symbol, and expand the boundaries of objective reality. Each of these images is shaped by energy, sensation, and color with its own rhythm, volume, and weight. Being nonverbal in nature, these symbols and images are often difficult to express clearly in verbal form, and therefore lend themselves well to art.

This introduces the complex question of the use of words in art therapy. Secondary process thinking, with its foundation in words, must be evoked if the ego is to gain mastery and understanding of primitive material. Although there is secondary process thinking in the logic and judgment used in giving artistic form to a personal image, words are more directly hooked to reality. Changing poetic metaphor into art expression serves as a transition to the world of words, and helps to make sense of the truism that, although verbal material is strongly connected to reality, not all of reality is encompassed by words. From this perspective, different levels of reality can be experienced and understood within the context of nonverbal expression. The art form, then, organizes object relations and mirrors them back to the patient.

☐ Developmental Object Relations

Inherent in the clinical use of object relations theory is a deep-seated understanding of and sensitivity to developmental lines, and how they manifest themselves in adult normality and pathology. Although Freud and his heirs postulated a developmental schema that begins at birth, they believed that the oedipal crisis was so overwhelming that it overrode all that went before. Margaret Mahler incorporated Freud's drive theory, but also saw importance in the first three years of life and the vicissitudes of the mother-child interaction in shaping the personality (Mahler, Pine, & Bergman, 1975). It is here that the foundations of an inside me and you are laid down.

Mahler's (1975) developmental levels begin with the stage of normal *autism*, characterized by a blissful oneness with mother. At about three months the process of attachment begins, with what she calls *symbiosis*. Slowly, out of a nondifferentiated mass, the me and you inside the child become defined. As we trace the stages of symbiosis, where mother and child struggle with separateness and sameness, individuation and differentiation are born, and the child proceeds through the subphases of *hatching, practicing*, and *rapprochement*. The child's growth—from symbiosis to *separation* and *individuation*—culminates in achieving an *identity* and *object constancy*.

At this point, at about two and a half, the child has a firm sense of *self* and differentiated *other*, and can relate to people as wholes, rather than as need-satisfiers. A child can now tolerate ambivalence, having mended the splits of "good" and "bad," and can maintain a narcissistic equilibrium by a form of self-feeding and self-affirmation that is unique to him or herself.

Pathology of Object Relations

Horner (1979) gives a fine outline of some of the problems associated with each developmental period, connecting pathology with issues stemming from faulty early object relations. Problems in the autistic phase form the basis of primary infantile autism, which is characterized by a lack of attachment and organization. Psychopathic personalities are viewed as having had problems in making primitive attachments, although having had a satisfactory initial period of normal autism. Around the fourth and fifth months, when normal symbiosis starts, failures in differentiation create difficulty in discriminating inner and outer reality, seen in psychotic states. Schizoid character formation is seen as stemming from denial of the attachment, which begins in the differentiating phase of symbiosis.

Finally, in the rapprochement stage, occurring somewhere between 12 and 18 months, there are failures in integration and self-cohesion. Problems here result in the borderline and narcissistic personalities. Both types retreat from autonomy, the task of the rapprochement crisis, but they characteristically do so in different ways. The borderline personality tends toward fusion states and a pervasive use of splitting good and bad in the search for the ideal; whereas the narcissistic personality takes refuge in a grandiose self. Although differing in form, there is in both an attempt to return to the perfection of an early state of oneness with mother. The affective disorders are also associated with failures in the rapprochement stage. These patients have not resolved the dilemma of good and bad existing side by side in one space. All that is "good" and nurturing remains on the outside, while their "bad" hunger and greed stay on the inside.

Art Therapy, Creativity, and Play

As just described, each developmental problem generates a particular clinical picture, with its own pain and anxiety, which is recreated in the therapeutic relationship. The art therapist is faced with the challenge of differentiating sometimes similar pictures and reacting appropriately.

Put another way, each requires a complex art frame, to help transform pathological into therapeutic space. Where pathological space lies stagnant, therapeutic space promotes new solutions and new potentialities, with the accompanying sense of a self being reborn. There is room for new relationships and expanded levels of awareness.

The challenge for the art therapist is to provide an art experience that makes this transition possible, and keeps therapeutic space alive. Canned recipes related to each developmental level cannot hope to address issues of such complexity. What is called upon is the art therapist's artistry—in using a conscious symbolic awareness of the patient's artwork and the relationship—to keep the therapeutic process moving.

Winnicott's (1971) conceptualization of creativity and play help tie together the threads of developmental theory, the use of art, and therapeutic technique. Winnicott approaches these relationships from the vantage point of how individuals handle inner and outer space. He begins at the start of life, when the mother's anticipation of her baby's needs allows the infant to maintain the illusion that mother's breast is part of the infant.

> From birth, therefore, the human being is concerned with the problem of the relationship between what is objectively perceived and what is subjectively conceived of, and in the solution of this problem there is no help for the human being who has not been started off well enough by the mother. *The intermediate area to which I am referring is the area that is allowed to the infant between primary creativity and the objective perception based on reality-testing.* The transitional phenomena represent the early stages of the use of illusion, without which there is no meaning for the human being in the idea of relationship with an object as perceived by others as external to that being. (Winnicott, 1971, p. 11)

Creativity, then, is seen within the context of human development. The origins of illusion provide the foundation for the creation of the transitional space of inner and outer reality. In this space, the child at first maintains the illusion that the world is his, and that he can maintain the blissful state of oneness. Only gradually is this illusion of oneness reorganized, to take in the demands of outer reality.

The goal of development, however, is not one of giving up illusion, but of developing the skills and techniques to make our illusions reality. Creativity, within the context of human relationships, permits one's inner imaginative world to become congruent with the outside, so that each person can shape his destiny. The ability to actually *be* the artist of one's social world is contingent on having successfully met the developmental challenges of one's past.

At times, because of the deficiencies and problems of one's past, artistic expression may be a means to rediscover creativity and innovation, although this creativity may not carry over into social relationships. We all know of artists for whom this is true. Art alone, without a supportive therapeutic relationship, will not repair developmental deficits.

In order to recover early creativity and recreate the transitional space so necessary to bridge inner and outer realities, both patient and therapist must be prepared to play, says Winnicott (1971). In fact, he describes treatment as play or, in some cases, as helping the patient to become able to play. If art therapists are to serve this role, they, likewise, must be ready to play. Play, as described by Winnicott, is not aimless activity or simply having fun, although fun may be one of the ingredients. Play in therapy involves the capacity to relax intellectual controls, and to become non-goal-oriented and open-ended, in experiencing and working with psychological space.

In this space, images and symbols move into consciousness with their own logic and organization regarding time and place. Through symbolic play, patients are helped to organize psychological space, both within the art form and within the art relationship. Form and content become one, through a synthesis of primary and secondary processes. This also allows the merging of bound and unbound energy, and balancing between fusion and separateness, and organization and loss of control. Therapeutic play, then, becomes the means by which to create a "holding environment" of relatedness and resonance, within which deficits in early object relations can be repaired, and the potential for creative living can be regenerated.

Approaches for Patients at Different Developmental Levels

It should be noted that problems from each developmental period require a different form of "holding." For instance, in patients who have suffered extreme deficiencies in the normal autistic phase resulting in autistic psychosis, the holding environment in the art form and relationship involves structure, sensory contact, and a capturing of the rhythm in disrhythmic patients.

Patients who have been traumatized in the early stages of symbiosis, when self and other have not been clearly defined, require structure and boundaries, as well as clarity and definition. Because their worlds are so chaotic and disorganized, the holding needs to be gentle, but firm, with words to clarify and to connect the worlds of image and outer reality.

For the psychopathic individual, whose capacity for attachment has been severely impaired, the world of power and games is the language that connects him to people. To be effective, the art therapist must enter this world, and play within its rules. Demonstrating a degree of savvy and alertness to the psychopathic game plan is important. Conversely, "feeding" this kind of patient with materials or love, with the hope of providing and promoting attachment, is a misuse and abuse of the therapeutic relationship. Here, as in all instances, avoiding experiences that are out of synchrony with a patient's object life is the prime diagnostic and therapeutic issue, requiring skill and artistry as well as thought.

Much has been written about the borderline patient, and I refer you to Masterson (1976) and Kernberg (1975) as important resources in this area. Here the patient is stuck in the rapprochement phase of separation-individuation—the "terrible twos"—when a parent often feels he can do nothing right. The child, aware of separateness yet frightened of aloneness, wants to go in two different directions at the same time. The dilemma is to separate while maintaining connection. As he screams, yells, and says "No!" the child's cries for autonomy are enmeshed with the silent need to be held, a need often rejected when the parent tries to come near. In a two-year-old this is understandable. In an adult patient, the picture can be confusing and infuriating. Maintaining a cognitive understanding of these issues is of immeasurable help to the art therapist.

This patient literally consumes both art materials and patience. The task of the art therapist is to keep a very strong and clear perception of what the patient is regressing to, when he or she becomes frightened and "disappears" beneath a cloud of hunger for succor and support. Also, the art therapist must not be taken in by swings between devaluation and overevaluation, and must be sensitive to the ever-present splits of good and bad. This patient is wonderfully adept at splitting a therapeutic team into warring camps. Also part of the picture are such defenses as projective identification (identifying with what we project outward), withdrawal, introjection, and denial. Manifestations of these must be attended to and confronted in the art therapeutic play. Needless to say, a passive approach is not the best holding environment for the borderline patient.

By contrast, the idealization a narcissistic patient offers an art therapist isn't usually defensive in nature. Unlike a neurotic, who idealizes to defend against hostility, idealization is an important developmental step in his treatment process. This patient has not been adequately mirrored or affirmed by a consistent maternal object, so the art therapy interaction can provide a crucial reparative opportunity, offering the long-sought-after mirroring and definition missed in the early family matrix. The interplay of art and the relationship can vary. At times the patient may take in the mirroring of the art in a way that parallels the therapeutic relationship. At others, the patient's ability to deal with the much wanted/feared mirroring is so tenuous that it can only be tolerated nonverbally.

Depressive mood states offer another example of splitting, but one that differs in quality from that used by the borderline personality. Also arrested at the rapprochement level, patients with affective disorders have not been able to integrate the good and bad inside themselves and have held on to strong, hostile introjects while expelling all that is good. Art exercises are directed at helping patients find strength and self-worth, through the discovery of their own artistic expression. The nourishment found in the experience of mastery promotes the discovery of a good self that had been lost, fused with an internal bad object.

The art therapist's assessment of developmental level and his or her ability to experience, organize, and reflect back the inner state of the person provide the environment for the person to reclaim a lost experience, and to find new levels of self-definition and integration.

Again, I cannot emphasize too strongly that growth occurs from the process of going through the pain of an unmet stage of development, rather than from the therapist's gratifying the patient's hunger. I repeat the paradox of treatment: I am with you, but separate; I understand your need, but I cannot take away your pain. To rob a patient of his anger, pain, and despair, no matter how well intentioned, is to do a disservice. What art therapists can offer is a holding environment, which can make pain bearable, and can allow progress and growth to proceed.

Implied in this approach is the notion of duality in our internal psychic structure, a duality that necessitates experiencing at one and the same time softness and hardness, structure and lack of it, distance and closeness, warmth and cold. The resonance art therapists offer patients complements these dualities, so that the aesthetic expression flowing between patient and therapist allows ample room for the complexity of authentic communication. There is a constant possibility of the integration of opposites, as well as a synthesis of primary and secondary process. Room also exists for progression and regression, fusion, and separateness.

☐ Conclusion

Object relations theory as applied to art therapy is but a method to seek out and organize an array of different impressions coming from many levels of awareness. Together, they offer opportunities for the creative use of one's personal resources in responding to therapeutic communications.

An art experience seems to be an ideal form in which to understand the complicated interconnections of creativity development, object relations pathology, and treatment technique. The nonverbal image captures the inexplicable essences of our past relationships, at the same time that it gives them shape and meaning.

As art therapists, our skills in integrating all this offer a special and powerful dimension to a therapeutic team. Our challenge is one of utilizing these concepts from psychiatry and psychoanalysis while maintaining the visions and perceptions we have as artists. Within this perspective, verbal and nonverbal behavior coalesce into a mind/body whole as we, as artists and therapists, give recognition to our respect for continuity and individuation.

☐ References

Horner, A. (1979). *Object relations and the developing ego in therapy*. New York: Jason Aronson.

Kernberg, O. (1975). *Borderline conditions and pathological narcissism*. New York: Jason Aronson.

Mahler, M., Pine, F., & Bergman, A. (1975). *The psychological birth of the human infant: Symbiosis and individuation*. New York: Basic Books.

Masterson, J. (1976). *Psychotherapy of the borderline adult*. New York: Brunner/Mazel.

Winnicott, D. W. (1971). *Playing and reality*. New York: Basic Books.

CHAPTER

Mildred Lachman-Chapin

Self Psychology and Art Therapy

Heinz Kohut, was a training analyst at the Chicago Institute of Psychoanalysis, who was also at one time president of the American Psychoanalytic Association. In 1959 he published a paper in which he identified introspection and empathy as the essential ingredients of psychoanalytic observation. He went on to develop a body of theory known as "Self Psychology" (Kohut, 1971, 1977, 1978, 1984), which has been utilized by many psychoanalytic therapists.

Empathy, or vicarious introspection—knowing what the other person is feeling by acknowledging your own feelings which repeat or reflect his—was not only the key observational tool, but also an essential treatment modality. Kohut developed his theory after observing that some patients with narcissistic features were unresponsive to classical analysis. These clients typically suffered from feelings of inner emptiness, a lack of self-esteem, and difficulties in their social and sexual lives. He questioned their primary relationship to their inner selves, formulating the concept of "self-cohesion," or consolidation of the self. In Kohut's view, failure of empathy on the part of caregivers in the earliest months of life is the main cause of narcissistic personality disorders. And it is through empathic response in the therapeutic situation that cure is achieved.

☐ Narcissistic Development

Kohut (1971) described the earliest stage of narcissistic development, primary narcissism, as one in which equilibrium is inevitably disturbed by the unavoidable short-comings of maternal care. The child replaces the previous perfection by establishing a grandiose, exhibitionistic image of the self—*the archaic grandiose self*—and an admired, omnipotent self-object—*the idealized parent imago* (1971, p. 25). In other words, when the perfection of the original merger with mother begins to fail, the child adopts an "I-am-perfect" (grandiose) view of the self and a "you-are-perfect-and-I-am-part of-you" (idealized) view of the parent. These are the two basic narcissistic configurations.

The editor thanks Sandra Kryder, Ph.D., Social Worker in private practice and Candidate, Pittsburgh Psychoanalytic Institute, for her assistance regarding recent developments in self psychology.

Under optimal conditions, the exhibitionism and grandiosity of the archaic grandiose self are gradually tamed, and the whole structure is ultimately integrated into the adult personality. It supplies the instinctual fuel for our ambitions and purposes, for the enjoyment of our ego-syntonic activities, and for important aspects of our self-esteem. Under similarly favorable circumstances, the idealized parent imago is also integrated into the adult personality. As the ego ideal, it becomes an important component of our superego, holding up to us the guiding leadership of its ideals. If a child, however, suffers severe narcissistic traumas, the grandiose self is retained unaltered, striving for the fulfillment of its archaic aims. If the child has traumatic disappointments in the admired adult, the idealized parent imago is also unchanged (Kohut, 1971, pp. 27–28).

In other words, when development proceeds optimally, the psychic energy that the infant once invested in viewing him or herself as omnipotent and perfect, is gradually made available for use in *doing things* to win attention and admiration. A child who fails to develop properly will not be able to satisfy narcissistic needs through age-appropriate actions. He will persist in expecting to gain attention and admiration while remaining passive, or by engaging in forms of exhibitionism that fail to satisfy the infantile longings. In normal development, the idealized parent imago also undergoes a gradual transformation. Internalized, it takes the form of the conscience and ideals that guide actions. When development is flawed, the child continues to look to the "perfect" other for guidance and leadership.

The archaic grandiose self and the idealized parent imago represent the two poles of narcissism (Kohut referred to the "bipolar self"). Driven by ambition (from the grandiose self) and led by ideals (from the idealized parent imago), the self begins to form. During psychoanalysis special transferences develop, related to each of these. Clients suffering from deficiencies in the area of the grandiose self develop what Kohut called "mirror transferences." They seek the confirmation of their grandiosity that they failed to receive as very young children from the primary or maternal figure. An adult cannot ask for such confirmation without feeling intense shame. And those clients whose need to perceive perfection in a parent figure was unmet in childhood, develop "idealizing transferences."

Kohut placed the "archaic grandiose self," the first stirrings of selfhood, around the end of the symbiotic phase and the beginning of the stage of individuation—the "rap-prochement substage" (Mahler, Pine, & Bergman, 1975) or the toddler stage in the middle of the second year. During this period, failure on the part of the caretaker to mirror the child in an age-appropriate and non-traumatic way, creates deficits in self-structure, which may later result in the failure to develop a cohesive sense of self. If the child is to experience an age-appropriate grandiose self-image, he must feel that exhibitionistic display is safe and effective. The child is assured by the mother's "mirroring," by "the gleam in the mother's eye" (Kohut, 1966). The child's early efforts to exhibit him or herself represent first attempts at individuation, at leaving the symbiotic ties with mother. To be successful, these feats of grandeur and omnipotence must be greeted by the mother with approval and admiration.

Kohut (1984) identifies two other kinds of mirror transferences that can be activated in dealing with the archaic grandiose self. One is a wish for merger, where the patient wants to share in the therapist's perceived magical powers, thereby furthering grandiosity and a sense of omnipotence. The other is a twinship, where the patient feels somewhat separate from but almost identical with the therapist.

As the mirroring proceeds, the goal is to help the grandiose self become less archaic, more appropriate to the patient's age. When the client becomes invested in the product of his or her *own* action—that is, in his or her *own* artwork—this is progress. The sublimatory mechanism can be a "transmuting internalization" which changes archaic responses into more stable psychic structures (i.e., ego building in classical terms).

The longing for an empathic response from the maternal person who is still almost oneself changes into a sense of self-pride in being watched over by "others," real others, as one creates. Real others, then, are objects separate from oneself. Narcissistic investment in an art product helps the client to individuate, to separate from the need to have his exhibitionistic yearnings confirmed in an archaic (infantile) fashion. It is most important that, throughout the mirroring process, therapists hold out the promise of ultimate approval for the real accomplishment; that is, for departure from symbiosis (or the infantile means of achieving satisfaction of narcissistic needs). Mirroring was technically described by Kohut as an empathic responsiveness of the "self-object."

Kohut's self-object is a person or thing valued for its function in enhancing oneself. This differs from a true object, a person who is valued and related to in his or her own right. In the early developmental stages of narcissism, a self-object is needed by the child and is used for the kind of mirroring I have been describing. Failure in empathic response by a self-object can inflict damaging blows to the growing child's sense of self.

With a patient who has a narcissistic personality disorder, the therapist functions as a self-object. The mirror transferences invite the therapist to respond empathically, with a specific kind of nurturing. Ideally, over time, the patient will feel the response, will recognize what he or she is asking of the therapist, will reconstruct some personal history, and—most important—will profit by the reparative empathic experience, by beginning to build a cohesive sense of self.

An example of this process in art therapy is found in the case below, particularly in the therapeutic sequence represented in Figures 5.3, 5.4, and 5.5. In Figure 5.3, Mary sees herself as a devouring and destructive person, whose need for control and almost physical possession of the object is global and omnipotent; the object is seen as something or someone who can and *must* be globally possessable and devourable. I contributed Figure 5.4. She is led to understand her archaic self-object needs from the perspective of an adult looking at a newborn. She then, in producing Figure 5.5, seems to be seeing herself as still "hungry," but within some kind of structured environment.

This translated into an understanding that her hungers could now be looked at in terms of what they actually were in her present reality. She had been fearful of going on a trip with her newfound boyfriend, afraid she would become like the devouring fish in Figure 5.3 and ruin everything. She was able, after this interchange, to actually take the trip and enjoy it. She had modulated her initial response, of *needing* an archaic self-object, to one in which *being with* the self-object seemed more manageable.

In the stage of primary narcissism, the infant has no way to relieve inner tension. Only soothing from a "good-enough mother" (Winnicott, 1971) relieves inner tension. Later, adoption of a transitional object, whereby the absent mother is mentally invoked, allows the child to relieve tension alone. Regulating tension oneself is a basic step in ego structuring.

Kohut, like Winnicott (1971), pointed out that artistic work can be a means of dealing with pain and tension by providing a way of expressing them (rather than keeping them operating *within* the body-mind) and by transforming the tension into a self-regulatory mechanism, like the transitional object. The mechanism can be described in three steps: recall or imaging of an object when it is not there—a crucial first step; the introjection of the object, taking it in but not yet identifying with it; and then identification with the object to the point where it becomes part of the person. Kohut calls this *transmuting internalization,* or structure building. It means the person has achieved a more independent way of relieving tension. Thus, art and creativity are seen as a way not only to relieve tension, but also to build ego strength.

As artists we are drawn to an empathic way of relating to the world. We project our subjective state onto our artwork, which objectifies and expresses our introspection in a form outside ourselves that others can grasp through empathy. We empathically grasp artwork made by others. Thus, we are already attuned to an empathic response; as we help clients to produce expressive works of art, and as we respond to their creations.

We are also very much involved, as artists, in expressing the self. When faced with troubled clients, whatever their pathological label, we may intuitively recognize that these people are troubled in their "selves." Here too, our qualities as artists equip us to function as therapists. It is also likely that certain unresolved grandiose exhibitionistic stirrings are part of our own makeup. Thus, we can not only mirror and empathically accept these archaic strivings in our clients, but can offer to them a solution we ourselves have found. Art can be used as a form of exhibition, as a way to create, to make magic, to be understood, admired, and affirmed.

I also believe that the artwork itself can become a "self-object." The client is helped to shift from considering the therapist as the sole self-object, to the creation of his own self-object. This is a step toward individuation, with the art therapist there to give the longed-for empathic response.

I have also explored another way to provide a kind of mirroring empathic response— by doing art along with the client. After we have dialogued for a while, we each set about drawing, usually not looking at the other's work. I am intensely focused on the client's concerns, but do not plan what I will do. When finished, we first consider the client's work; then mine. After the client has responded to my work, I offer my own comments.

This is a response to the client through my preconscious processes, formed by my artistic skills and informed by my clinical judgment. It is a daring procedure. All good therapists use their unconscious responses, but here there is a *visible* product to be examined by both. It documents the therapist's response. The client becomes vividly aware of the reality of the person he is relating to. The therapist cannot avoid looking at whatever countertransference issues or personal problems appear in the artwork, and must deal with them so as to further the therapeutic relationship. The art therapist has used him- or herself as an artist. The client has received a concrete and vivid empathic response from a real person.

As noted earlier, Kohut's theories dealt with the development of narcissism at the point of the infant's leaving the symbiotic bond with mother. His descriptions of narcissistic transferences refer to unmet needs as the client began to individuate. Kohut was therefore concerned with someone who had traumatic experiences with parental figures, as he or she emerged from what may have been a successful symbiotic relationship.

But what if the first years have not provided the child with a healthy relationship with mother? "The impact of the traumatic environment is felt from the very beginning of life, and distortions of ego development and defects occur in both presymbiotic and symbiotic phases" (Giovacchini, 1984, p. 89). Here, theories of transitional phenomena are extremely useful.

The grandiosity that Kohut discussed becomes a continuation of what Winnicott described as happening during the first year of life, when the *child* takes a transitional object and learns thereby the magic of creating something psychically. Giovacchini (1984) notes the *mother's* grandiosity, that is treating her child as a transitional object, being unwilling to relinquish her omnipotent power over the child. This is another way to look at failure in empathic response to the child's need to individuate.

In the case that follows, Mary had an unmet need for reciprocity, for an empathic response from the external world. I believe this stemmed from her very earliest attempts to bond with her mother. She had not been able to enjoy a healthy symbiosis, where she could learn to soothe herself with the kind of grandiose creativity that Winnicott described. Although this case doesn't fit Kohut's formulations (i.e., a patient needing mainly to individuate), it does highlight the need for a response in terms of the development of *self*, no matter what stage. My technique in art therapy would be the same: an empathic art response to the client's needs *at the level of his needs*. Mary's implicit questions are: What is merging? Is it safe to merge? Will I destroy the person I merge with?

For patients whose need is to try to emerge from a fairly successful symbiosis, the question is: Can I use my omnipotent powers to destroy the bond with mother? Can I destroy mother's hold on me? Can I destroy the merged mother in my mind? Will she admire and encourage and approve my audacities of separation and accomplishment? Will she empathize with my exercised prowess? If I need at times to re-merge, will she let me? If she fails me, will there be someone wise I can be like, separate yet the same?

So, although self psychology is associated with Kohut and his disciples, psychoanalysts and others from many theoretical frameworks have looked at the development of the self, adding their own enriching perspectives. For developments over time, see the annual publications, *Advances in Self-Psychology,* edited by Arnold Goldberg, M.D., as well as his recent writings on the "narcissistic behavior disorders" (1995).

For me, art therapy offers many ways to provide nurturing and empathic responses for the developing self, with the therapist ever aware of the particular step the client is ready and asking for.

☐ Case Example

Mary, a young woman in her early 20's who had been taking drugs since early adolescence, was admitted to a psychiatric hospital after a suicide attempt. She had had a number of drug-related hospitalizations and had been in treatment with several therapists who used interpretation and explanation, not empathic attunement. Her family had given up on her; from their viewpoint, this was to be a final attempt to help her.

As part of the treatment team I provided individual art therapy while she was hospitalized, and continued to see her as an outpatient. She responded very well to the interactive technique I have described, so this was how we worked together most of the time. In the hospital, she would sit in bed, working on a lap board, insisting that the room be dimly lit. I sat beside the bed, using a lap board. When she was an outpatient, we sat at a card table, facing each other. I propped a board up so that she could not see my work, and I rarely looked at hers until she was finished.

Following are two examples of such interchanges, one in the hospital, and one as an outpatient. Figure 5.1, "See Me Sometime," was drawn in the hospital in anticipation of a visit by a former boyfriend, the first visitor since her admission two months earlier. I asked her to do a picture about what she expected, what her thoughts and feelings were about seeing him again. She refused. Instead, working from a scribble, she produced the head of a man "smoking a reefer." He had a stitched-up slit across the side of his face, two frontal eyes on a profile head, and hair that stood on end. The person seemed disoriented, possibly drug induced. I referred to her drug episodes with her boyfriend. She denied this interpretation, said she didn't like the picture, quickly turned it over, and produced Figure 5.1.

Figure 5.1.

She said this picture was like Mae West who said, "Come up and see me sometime." It was "psychedelic" and "fun." She referred to the brightly colored undulating form flowing out of the left side of the female figure as "psychedelic disco lights." She spoke with a kind of tough disdain, "cool," as if she didn't care. The female figure has red arms and shoulders. The border surrounding the figure is a dark and dull blue-black.

My impressions of the image were that she was referring to the sexy, exciting life she'd had with her boyfriend, now compartmentalized and distant. It was a boxed-in memory, suggesting, by its distinct border, a kind of separation from her real self; just as the sexy-looking figure was self-absorbed, sending out "vibes," but connected to no one. It may also have reflected her pronounced feelings of confinement in the hospital, with no visitation or telephone privileges until then. The picture is bleak, brassy, and sad. My associations were of a little girl dressing up in mother's finery, trying to be sexually grown up. I did not voice any of these ideas to her.

Instead I showed her my picture, Figure 5.2. I worked from a scribble, producing a figure which Mary said looked like a nun. She said it was funny to see a nun all naked and feeding a baby. Then she giggled and talked about stories she'd heard of nuns having sexual intercourse. She seemed fascinated by this image, and titled it "The Naked Nun." We talked about babies and mothers, and she repeated her complaints about her own mother, which had been a primary theme of our work all along.

She had described her mother as cold and demanding, expecting too much of her, demanding support from her child instead of the other way around. Mary had had no contact with her for some time before hospitalization, dealing only with her father when family contact was necessary. In the picture the nun-mother is not looking at the baby, not even making the visual connection between mother and child that is so elemental.

Mary was also an adopted child, her mother a diabetic who couldn't have children. Her pictures had many images and references to oral themes. Her psychiatrist described her as "never having found her mouth." She'd never had the symbiotic bond, that is the

Figure 5.2.

precursor to the development of self-soothing capacities. Drug taking was her attempt to soothe herself.

Mary was also fundamentally unattached, as suggested in Figure 5.1, not having formed the first essential bond with mother, thus unable to make genuine attachments in later relationships. The sexuality depicted in this picture is false, an imitation of adult activity, but without relationship to another person. It is frantic, narcissistic, and exhibitionistic.

My picture reflected, I believe, my preconscious sense of her strange relationship to mother and birth. I did not think of the mothering figure as a nun. That was *her* association. As a matter of fact, I don't remember having any conscious thoughts about this picture. But as she developed her associations, it became clear to me that what I had depicted in this picture *for her* was an unnatural mother, someone who wasn't supposed to be sexual and therefore to have a child. It condenses in one image the ideas of coldness, chastity, and mothering. The mother's body, as naked, warm flesh, is forbidden to her and felt as prohibited by the child.

The sexual union that produced the child was also forbidden, illegal. This suggests thoughts about her natural mother, who may have given Mary up for adoption because she was illegitimate. It also implies that sexuality is a remote, illicit activity, magically creating a child but having nothing to do with a relationship, either to the partner or the child. Some of these ideas about sexuality are implicit in her picture of herself (Figure 5.1). My picture presented her with the implications of her own thoughts about her birth, and her fundamental early lack of connection with her mother.

None of this was verbalized between us as interpretations of our pictures. We simply talked about her anger at her mother (in the present) and she made references to lewd nun stories. But, just as my picture had come from my unconscious, mirroring for her what she was saying at a deep level about early, verbally inaccessible experiences; it was, through its image and her associations to it, able to convey to her some of the meaning that I could later articulate for myself.

I believe it was this kind of art dialogue which helped Mary break out of her psychic cocoon in the hospital. She was gradually able to let herself be cared for by various members of the hospital team, to experience some self-soothing, to form some meager relationships, and eventually to leave.

Mary made a remarkably rapid adjustment to life outside the hospital, was able to get and hold a part-time job, and to find a new boyfriend. When that relationship began to deepen, she became afraid. She drew Figure 5.3, "Devouring," after telling me that her boyfriend had invited her to take a trip to visit some of his friends, and that she was fearful. This picture was a response to my asking her to try to draw her fear. She said the large fish at the bottom was herself, that she was about to bite on the hook, and that once she got the hook in her mouth, she would pull down the whole boat with all the people on it and they would all drown. Then she spoke about all the relationships she had ruined, and said she was afraid she would make a mess of this one too.

I showed her my picture, which I had not yet titled (Figure 5.4). Mary described what she saw—a mama bird and some eggs in a nest—but had no other thoughts or associations. I then explained that the eggs in the nest would hatch, and hungry little birds would emerge. I said that for newborn animals (and infants) eating was a life and death matter, that they are blindly voracious, needing and wanting only to fill themselves with food. I explained that this thoughtless, all-consuming greed and need may feel frighteningly destructive to the infant.

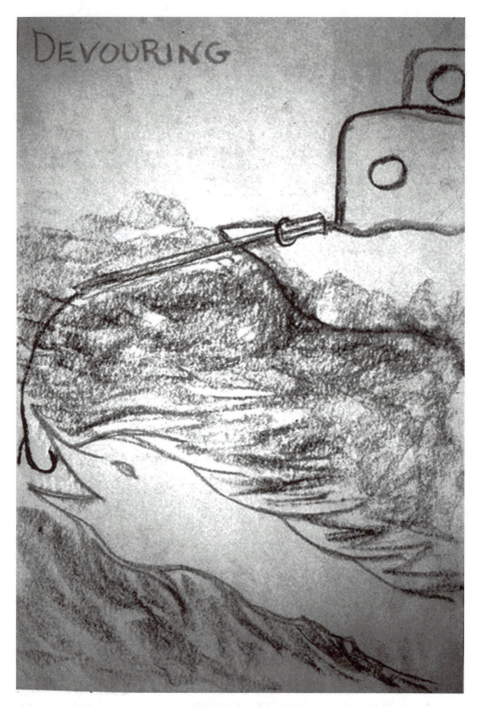

Figure 5.3.

Figure 5.4.

I said that perhaps her present wish to be close to her boyfriend may have that same quality of potentially destructive greed, that sometimes we reexperience later in life the frighteningly devouring nature of this hunger. I suggested that perhaps her own mother bird hadn't brought the worms in a satisfying enough way. She immediately retorted, "So you take it." "Right," I said, "you reach out and devour." She called her picture then "Devouring." I called mine "About to Devour." In this interchange, I had seen the sharp, hungry mouth of the fish that she began her picture with before I started. I thought of a newborn chick, so that my picture of the eggs in the nest was a conscious response to her initial image.

"Wish to Survive" (Figure 5.5), was done by Mary at the next session. She'd clearly continued to think of her devouring hunger, but had begun to see it not as destructive and frightening, but as expressing her own vital needs. She'd gotten in touch with a primitive sense of self which, in itself, began to give her some psychic structure. The geometrical network that forms the environment for this poignant, animal-like figure suggests such structure.

In the first picture dialogue Mary presents herself as a sexual woman having "fun." Sexuality implies intimate physical contact with someone, yet her picture was lonely, self-absorbed, enclosed, sad. My picture was an empathic response to her essential loneliness and lack of truly satisfying intimate contact at a primary, infantile level. As was evident during her hospitalization, this indeed was the level of her pain.

In the second picture dialogue Mary was expressing her fear of the destructiveness of her own insatiable needs. My picture provided a context in which she could understand

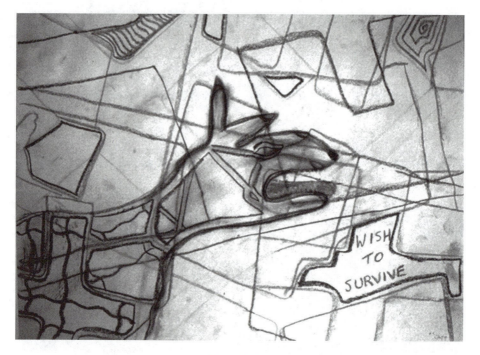

Figure 5.5.

her needs. It was a way of "reframing" for her what she was at last getting in touch with, but was unable to tolerate.

In both dialogues, through empathic response from my artwork, I could acknowledge her grandiosity (being looked at, Figure 5.1, and being powerfully destructive, Figure 5.3) as well as her feeling of disappointment at a failure of empathy in early maternal response (Figure 5.2). I was responding to her very early experiences of the developing self, which cannot be easily expressed in words, having occurred before language. An empathic verbal response may also not be felt as immediately as this kind of artistic imagery.

This does not mean that to be effective, the dialogue must be in representational imagery. These pictures were chosen for ease of presentation and reproduction. There are just as many instances, in this case and in others, of abstract drawings and sculptures by the client and myself. Formal elements of line, color, and shape are also the expressive language of visual/artistic communication, and can be just as powerful as representational pictures or sculptures.

Mary had had a traumatic mothering experience, probably from the beginning of her life. She had not received the kind of maternal empathic responses that provide what Winnicott (1971) called the "holding environment." Thus, vital steps in the development of a cohesive self were missing. For such people, working with an artist in this kind of pictorial dialogue can provide a way of experiencing a primal relationship, where the person can engage more successfully in a mutuality that allows him or her to contribute something—to make reparation, perhaps, for some of the primitive hostility and mortal fears engendered in the infantile dyad.

☐ Relevance to Diagnosis

These treatment approaches are especially indicated for clients with narcissistic or borderline personality disorders. They are also useful with higher-functioning clients whose presenting symptoms are more oedipal in nature. These are people whose continuing difficulties in love and sexual relationships stem in part from a shaky sense of self. Pre-oedipal relationships with mother, especially unresolved grandiosity or overidealization, may be important areas to examine.

Behind the vague, unrewarding, uneven lives of these often worldly and well-functioning individuals, is a need for a more cohesive sense of self and a real separation from internal early mother images. Attuned to signs of such early deficits, the art therapist can respond at some point in treatment with an approach informed by self psychology.

☐ Implications for Treatment and Training

Clearly, art therapists must focus more attention on pre-oedipal development. Verbal psychoanalytic technique, developed largely with and for oedipal conflicts, is not a sufficient model. We should question our use of confrontation and interpretation, determining more clearly to what sectors of an individual's personality we are responding, to make our techniques and responses more fitting and useful. More precisely, there is a need to train ourselves to recognize and respond to the narcissistic components of our patients' psyches, the better to promote healing, through appropriate responses to idealizing and mirror transferences.

Kohut's ideas clarified some of what I had been doing all along in my work as an art therapist. He helped me to better understand what there is in the universal nature of art that makes it work in therapy. My reading of Kohut led me to concentrate on the earliest narcissistic elements of the creative drive, and how best to respond to these strivings. It has meant concentrating my efforts on maintaining an empathic, supportive role, using confrontation or interpretation as options, and then only when a particular situation seemed to justify such techniques.

Not all of our clients are dealing with narcissistic traumas, so our responses must be as varied and finely tuned as the state of our therapeutic skill allows. This means that with some of our patients interpretation and confrontation focused on the resolution of conflict are also in order.

Kohut (1984) postulated the need for self-objects throughout life for everyone. If Kohut is right, as I believe he is, then art in its various forms may be a means of satisfying a lifelong yearning. Art therapists can help people to meet this need. I have found it gratifying that Kohut (1966) and his predecessors (primarily Winnicott), in emphasizing the importance of the development of the self during the earliest stages, made a place for art and the artist in furthering such development.

The art therapist must serve an empathic, nurturing function for clients who lack a cohesive sense of self. This is typical of a great many psychiatric clients, particularly those classified today as borderline or narcissistic personality disorders rather than neurotic. Art and the art therapist can be used by many clients in finding ways to express, *without shame*, those grandiose, exhibitionistic wishes which have not been integrated into the personality and sense of self.

As artists, art therapists are particularly well suited to performing this task because we share, to a greater extent than the average person, our clients' need to exhibit themselves and receive attention, or to meet grandiose expectations of parental figures. But as artists, we have also achieved some success in channeling our narcissistic energy into the creation of age-appropriate (socially valuable), highly cathected products that strengthen the sense of self. Moreover, the nature of our artistic pursuits has sharpened our powers of empathy.

☐ References

Giovacchini, P. L. (1984). The psychoanalytic paradox. *Psychoanalytic Review, 71*, 81–104.

Goldberg, A. (Ed.) (1988–2001). *Advances in self psychology.* New York: International Universities Press.

Goldberg, A. (1995). *The problem of perversion: The view from self psychology.* New Haven: Yale University Press.

Kohut, H. (1959). Introspection, empathy and psychoanalysis. *Journal of the American Psychoanalytic Association, 7*, 459–483.

Kohut, H. (1966). Forms and transformations of narcissism. *Journal of the American Psychoanalytic Association, 14*, 243–272.

Kohut, H. (1971). *The analysis of the self.* New York: International Universities Press.

Kohut, H. (1977). *The restoration of the self.* New York: International Universities Press.

Kohut, H. (1978). *The psychology of the self.* New York: International Universities Press.

Kohut, H. (1984). *How does analysis cure?* Chicago: University of Chicago Press.

Mahler, M., Pine, F., & Bergman, A. (1975). *The psychological birth of the human infant.* New York: Basic Books.

Winnicott, D. W. (1971) *Playing and reality.* New York: Basic Books.

ADDENDUM

Eleanor Irwin

Although there are many recent developments in the fertile field of psychoanalysis (Gedo, 1999), the most dramatic have been in the area of "object relations." Just what does "object relations" mean? While there are many theorists and schools of thought (i.e., interpersonal, intersubjective, social constructivist, relational, etc.), there are also basic points of agreement. Generally, the term "object relations" refers to the ways in which we relate to each other. What distinguishes psychoanalysis from other approaches is its stress on the *internalized* sense (or "representation") of self and other, as noted in the chapters by Wilson, Robbins, and Lachman-Chapin.

The emphasis on object relations in psychoanalytic theory originated with the work of Melanie Klein who, though Freud's faithful disciple in many ways, differed with him in others. One of their disagreements was about the meaning of the word "object." For Freud, an "object" was something (a person, thing, or mental representation) through which a (libidinal or aggressive) drive could be satisfied.

For Klein, on the other hand, an "object" was not some*thing* through which one could be gratified, but some*one* (mother/caretaker) in whom powerful wishes, desires, and rages were invested. Over time, in the child's internalized fantasy relationship with the parents, a sense of being "good" (loved, loving) or "bad" (deprived, hateful) evolved. In stressing the centrality of the child's investment in the caretaker, Klein's writings began a shift of focus in psychoanalytic thinking from the drives to relationships.

The belief that the child was pre-wired for a relationship was echoed and elaborated in the thinking of Fairbairn (1952), Guntrip (1969), Winnicott (1965), and others in the British "independent" group of analysts.

In the United States, a focus on actual relationships was developed by Sullivan (1953) and his colleagues, in what was known as "interpersonal analysis." Into this mix came Kohut, who also stressed the importance of early relationships, and the ways that failures of parental empathy can lead to a fragmented sense of self in the child (cf. Chapter 5). Studies of infant development by analytic researchers like Mahler, Pine, and Bergman (1975), Stern (1965), and others (Beebe & Lachmann, 1992), have demonstrated that children are born with a sense of self that becomes delineated over time, in interaction with caretakers.

From birth onward, the individual "takes in" the external world, forming internal mental representations of the "object" that ultimately become part of the "self" representation as well. Kernberg (1976), who has integrated Freud's drive theory with object relations theory, proposes that in this process of internalization, the self and the object representations are merged, tied together with affect—emotional energy.

Many theorists have seen the infant's first representations as being positive or negative, pleasurable or unpleasurable. Over time, these feelings, with their powerful, cumulative affective charge, coalesce into a sense of gratifed/ungratified or "good me"/"bad me." Similarly, the other (the "object") is seen as "good"(gratifying) or "bad" (ungratifying).

Initially the young child can only take in part of the experience or the person, thus experiencing the other as "part object." With maturity, the individual becomes able to take in all aspects of the other, the gratifying and the ungratifying parts. Able to tolerate the anxiety and ambivalence generated by loving and hating, one can then see the other and the self as whole objects. Only then can a child separate and individuate, because he or she has achieved what analysts call "libidinal object constancy" (Fraiberg, 1954; Mahler et al., 1975). Object relations theory stresses that it is these ongoing experiences with others that form the growing individual's sense of self in the relational world, shaping the personality for better or worse.

In the course of the past several decades, psychoanalysis has shifted from a "one-person" psychology (focus on the patient) to a "two-person" psychology (focus on the interactive process between therapist and patient). This has led to a renewed interest in the area of "attachment" (Bowlby, 1969, 1973, 1980; Cassidy & Shaver, 1999). It also has led to significant modifications of technique, as the therapeutic situation is now seen as an interpersonal, intersubjective matrix within which at least some developmental deficits can be repaired.

Although all of the elements of modern object relations theory were present in Freudian theory, what has changed is their shift to a much more central position (cf. Greenberg & Mitchell, 1983; Mitchell & Aron, 1999; Scharff, 1996). Psychoanalysis in the new milennium is in greater creative ferment than at any other period, with the possible exception of the time of Freud's own formulations. And the majority of the hotly debated issues today relate, in one way or another, to the place of "object (human) relations" in psychological development and in mental health.

☐ References

Beebe, B., & Lachmann, F. (1992). A dyadic systems view of communication. In N. Skolnick & S. Warshaw (Eds.), *Relational perspectives in psycho-analysis*. Hillsdale, NJ: Analytic Press.

Bowlby, J. (1969). *Attachment and loss*, Vols. I (1969), II (1973), III (1980). New York: Basic Books.

Cassidy, J., & Shaver, P. R. (Eds.). (1999). *Handbook of attachment: Theory, research, & clinical applications*. New York: Guilford.

Fairbairn, W. R. D. (1952). *An object-relations theory of the personality*. New York: Basic Books.

Fraiberg, S. (1954). Libidinal object constancy and mental representation. *Psychoanalytic Study of the Child*.

Gedo, J. (1999). *The evolution of psychoanalysis: Contemporary theory & practice*. New York: Other Press.

Greenberg, J. R., & Mitchell, S. A. (1983). *Object relations in psychoanalytic theory*. Cambridge, MA: Harvard University Press.

Guntrip, H. (1969). *Schizoid phenomena, object relations and the self*. New York: International Universities Press.

Kernberg, O. (1976). *Object relations theory in clinical psychoanalysis*. New York: Aronson.

Klein, M. (1964). *Contributions to psychoanalysis 1921–1945*. New York: McGraw Hill.

Mahler, M., Pine, F., & Bergman, A. (1975). *The psychological birth of the human infant*. New York: Basic Books.

Mitchell, S. A., & Aron, L. (Eds.). (1999). *Relational psychoanalysis*. Hillsdale, NJ: The Analytic Press.

Scharff, D. (Ed.). (1996). *Object relations theory and practice*. Northvale, NJ: Aronson.

Stern, D. N. (1965). *The interpersonal world of the infant*. New York: Basic Books.

Sullivan, H. S. (1953). *The interpersonal theory of psychiatry*. New York: Norton.

Winnicott, D. W. (1965). *The maturational processes and the facilitating environment*. New York: International Universities Press.

CHAPTER

Michael Edwards

Jungian Analytic Art Therapy

In his own life and in his approach to analytic treatment, Jung anticipated ideas about using imagery in therapy to which most art therapists would subscribe. Although not a trained artist, Jung was quite a talented amateur landscape painter. However, it was not with landscapes but with inner sources of imagery that Jung was preoccupied (Jaffé, 1979).

In *Memories, Dreams, Reflections* (1963) Jung describes a boyhood of vivid dreams and eidetic fantasy images. At age 10, at a time of stress and personal alienation, he discovered relief in making a secret totemic figure:

> I had in those days a yellow, varnished pencil-case of the kind commonly used by primary-school pupils, with a little lock and the customary ruler. At the end of this ruler I now carved a little manikin, about two inches long, with frock coat, top hat, and shiny black boots. I coloured him black with ink, sawed him off the ruler, and put him in the pencil case, where I made him a little bed. I even made a coat for him out of a bit of wool. In the case I also placed a smooth, oblong blackish stone from the Rhine, which I had painted with water colours to look as though it was divided into an upper and lower half, and had long been carried around in my trouser pocket. This was his stone. All this was a great secret. Secretly I took the case to the forbidden attic at the top of the house . . . and hid it with great satisfaction on one of the beams under the roof . . . I felt safe, and the tormenting sense of being at odds with myself was gone. (p. 34)

Jung later describes how, in 1913, while still feeling disoriented by the trauma of his break with Freud, he found stability by building symbolic structures with stones from the Zürich lakeshore:

> I went on with the building game after the noon meal every day, whenever the weather permitted. As soon as I was through eating, I began playing, and continued to do so until the patients arrived; and if I was finished with my work early enough in the evening, I went back to building. In the course of this activity my thoughts clarified, and I was able to grasp the fantasies whose presence in myself I dimly felt. (Jung, 1963, pp. 168–169)

Throughout his life, particularly at times of personal crisis, Jung drew, painted, and sculpted representations of his inner experiences. This was not a peripheral activity, but a vivid source of personal insight into his situation; informing the development of many of his theories. No other major psychologist attended to his own inner life through imagery in this way. In fact, Jung's ideas can best be understood in the context of the value he attached to the subjective reality of spontaneously generated images.

Freud had led the way in giving recognition and importance to such imagery, especially in dreams, but there is a distinction. Freud treated the dream, the fantasy, or the unconscious factor in a picture as a puzzle to be solved and explained, whereas Jung attempted to relate to the unconscious image as an entity in its own right. In doing so he examined images from a number of perspectives, cultural as well as psychological. His is an open, hermeneutic mode of interpretation, lacking the economy and elegance of Freud's method, but offering instead a reevaluation of traditional ways of understanding inner experience.

Realizing the psychological value that he personally discovered in exploring images from the unconscious, Jung began to encourage his patients to make visual representations of their dream and fantasy material. This began at least as early as 1917, and continued throughout his analytic work. His closest followers worked in a similar way. The paintings and drawings were not generally made during the sessions, but were nevertheless considered integral to the ongoing therapeutic process. From a 1931 paper, "The Aims of Psychotherapy":

> But why do I encourage patients to express themselves at a certain stage of development by means of brush, pencil or pen? . . . At first [the patient] puts on paper what has come to him in fantasy, and thereby gives it the status of a deliberate act. He not only talks about it, but he is actually *doing* something about it. Psychologically speaking, it is one thing for a person to have an interesting conversation with his doctor once a week—the results of which hang somewhere or other in mid-air—and quite another thing to struggle for hours at a time with refractory brush and colours, and to produce in the end something which, at its face value, is perfectly senseless. Were his fantasy *really* senseless to him, the effort to paint it would be so irksome that he could scarcely be brought to perform this exercise a second time. But since his fantasy does not seem to him entirely senseless, his busying himself with it increases its effect upon him. Moreover, the effort to give visible form to the image enforces a study of it in all its parts, so that in this way its effects can be completely experienced. (CW16, 1966a)

Jung does not seem to be describing either catharsis or sublimation, but the idea that the patient enters into a relationship with an unconscious image. Jung (1966a) continues: "It is true, I must add, that the mere execution of the pictures is not all that is required. It is necessary besides to have an intellectual and emotional understanding of them: they must be consciously integrated, made intelligible, and morally assimilated. We must subject them to a process of interpretation."

Jung's early impact on art therapy, as on art education (Read, 1943; Robertson, 1963), was more inspirational than conceptual. His theories were not easily described, but they seemed to liberate the child-centered ideas of both Naumburg and Cane, which were implemented at Walden (Beck, 1958–1959; Cremin, 1961). Jung never published an extended account of his experience with imagery, although he refers often to the technique of active imagination, in which the drawing and painting of images from the unconscious can play a crucial part. *The Archetypes and the Collective Unconscious* (CW9, part 1) and *Alchemical Studies* (CW13) both contain many illustrations of his patients' artwork. *Man and His Symbols* (Jung et al., 1964) was an attempt to make some of his theories more accessible, linking the therapeutic process with archetypal symbolism in mythology, alchemy, religion, fairy tales, and the arts.

Unlike Freud, there is little clinical material to illustrate Jung's use of images in therapy. There are virtually no case histories, and the artwork he shows is accompanied by only the briefest of explanations, which focus on archetypal aspects of the imagery, not on personal associations. Yet it is wrong to infer that he did not elicit such associations. Jung was patient-centered in his methods, and taught that successful interpretations of images can only be made through mutual understanding and insight between patient and therapist, bringing about a synthesis of personal and archetypal material (CW8, 1969, pp. 116–121 and 477). However, as with other dynamic therapies, it is difficult to imagine theory in practice unless one has experienced it or had access to detailed clinical material.

Freud and Jung differed over symbolism. Jung tried to understand symbolic images on their own terms, in a strongly empathic way, rather than as secondary process revisions disguising primary process impulses. This view originated in his research, which convinced him that incest taboos in primitive societies were not, as Freud believed, the result of incestuous practices and desires, but rather were unconscious cultural belief structures, which depended on the *metaphor* of incest for their basis and potency. The totem has blatant sexual connotations, but these serve to focus attention only on its literal rather than metaphoric meaning.

Jung ascribed to symbolic events and images a collective origin, experienced individually, with an added dimension of profound spiritual significance or *numinosity* derived from their deeply unconscious source (Storr, 1983, p. 16). Freud regarded such cultural symbols as products of universally experienced fantasies of childhood, attributing numinous experience solely to the transference. For Jung, the collective unconscious expresses itself through the personal unconscious. As the personal unconscious is structured by the *complexes*, so the collective unconscious is structured by the *archetypes*. Thus Jung linked his earliest studies of word association, which led to the theory of complexes, with later research and clinical findings, which led to the theory of archetypes.

Although Jung maintained that he accepted Freud's model of the personal unconscious, its context and function are greatly changed by the assumption that behind every complex lies an archetype. Jung's symbolic image is neither wholly archetypal nor wholly personal, but derives from and bridges both levels of the psyche. Consciousness may be brought to bear on the unconscious image, giving it visible form and by interpretation, *meaning* which can then be integrated into life (CW6, pp. 442–447).

The symbolic image, for Jung, is its own best explanation; the unconscious does not lie. Only the ego sometimes needs to defend itself against the truth. The image reveals its meaning when it is "accepted" as a projection which virtually speaks for itself, but in a way characteristic of its inherent nature. This acceptance of the unconscious image is not passive; it is treated neither as a symptom nor as a work of art. A relationship is encouraged between the image and its maker, by actively stimulating imaginative inquiry and dialogue, the essence of "active imagination."

Jung's insistence on a fundamental difference between a symbol and a sign is important. He regarded signs as images which refer to discoverable and specific events or fantasies in a person's past—the repressed material of Freudian psychoanalysis. He regarded images as symbolic when they induced strong affects, yet defied complete or precise verbal description. Jung attributed symbolic status to images that Freud would have seen as resistant to interpretation because of unconscious defense mechanisms. Freud confessed himself unable to offer an adequate explanation for the power of art imagery, while Jung gave absolute authenticity to the image, reaffirming archetypal connections between images in therapy and in art.

Jung believed that the deepest levels of the unconscious are already prestructured at birth by the archetypes, psychologically paralleling the biological instincts. Like instincts, archetypes can remain dormant until activated by events in a person's experience. For example, a woman who becomes a mother for the first time discovers in herself an archetypal role of mothering, adequate or otherwise. The archetype gives a particular style to the basic instinct, rather in the same way that a particular species of bird will build a nest in a recognizable way. There are many archetypal possibilities within the human species. The archetypal role is lived out, with and through the raw materials of everyday life, including genetic endowment and environmental conditioning. The archetype works through the complex, also unconscious, and through the living situation of the individual; the bird builds its nest with whatever is available.

Archetypes structure universal events in life, such as the symbiotic attachment to and eventual separation from the mother, making a relationship to the father, passing childhood and adolescent milestones, falling in love, and dealing with birth and death issues. Behind the real parents stand the archetypal parent figures, just as other important people in life are also overshadowed by archetypal projections. These may manifest, in contemporary form, benign and destructive characteristics reminiscent of collective figures: the gods and goddesses and mythological and fairy tale archetypal images, which personify states of affect in the unconscious (Campbell, 1949; Jung et al., 1964; Jung, CW, 13, 1968a; Von Franz, 1982).

The Personified Image in Art Therapy

The therapeutic relationship is both simplified and complicated by the artwork. It is simplified because it does not have to depend solely on confrontation, with transference issues central. Instead, the relationship takes place partly through the artwork, which can variously be described as a buffer, filter, screen, or container. In this triangular situation, the artwork mediates between patient and therapist. Even when resistances are high and the patient produces nothing, the art therapist remains a representative of symbolic communication through art; he or she is "the art person" throughout. Every relationship with a patient in art therapy is somewhat oblique. This allows more freedom to the therapist in terms of transference, but the therapeutic alliance is complicated by factors arising in the minds of both patient and therapist which are born of the marriage—if marriage it is—between art and psychotherapy. It may be helpful to look at some of these factors from a Jungian perspective.

The Experience of Image Making

There is a dynamic in the art therapy setting which is not often discussed. This is the patient's interaction with the medium and with whatever images emerge. It is a dialogue that takes place parallel to, and somewhat independently of, the relationship to the art therapist (Figure 6.1).

Making a mark on paper, or twisting clay into the first shape that suggests itself, begins as an entirely private matter. This act may be preceded by doubt and anxiety about taking the initial step. For the nonartist, the prospect of image making is a heroic undertaking, and at this stage the skill of the art therapist is often directed at reassurance. After the initial shock of beginning, when the decision is taken to enter into a relationship with the medium, what follows can still be fraught with uncertainty. The correspondence

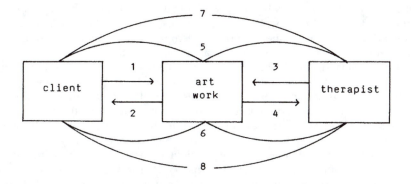

ART WORK	1. Client's Expression
	2. Client's Impression (Visual Feedback)
	3. Therapist's Expectations
	4. Therapist's Perceptions

ART WORK AS MEDIATOR	5. Communication to Therapist Through the Art Work
	6. Communication to Client in Response to Art Work

DIRECT RELATIONSHIP	7. Therapist's Perception of Client
	8. Client's Perception of Therapist

Figure 6.1.

between what is experienced inside and what is expressed outside rarely feels exact, even to a mature artist in good psychological health. For a patient, the connection between inner and outer reality may be bewilderingly absent. This can lead to increased anxiety or a defensive withdrawal of investment in the activity.

From the moment of the first expressive gesture, the subsequent stages of creating do not usually conform to will or expectation. Even a consciously planned and deliberately executed image has a way of seeming to speak back to its creator with a personality of its own. What is more, the personality of the image may not be likable. Often, even usually, it has a quality of "otherness." Yet the image, despite its alien characteristics, belongs to the person who made it. The dialogue now begins between the person and the image the person has made. At the same time, the image itself is still in a process of transformation or resolution. It calls for attention.

The "otherness" of images can be disconcertingly unpredictable. Occasionally, the emerging shapes can be friendly, slipping amazingly into configurations that far exceed intentions or imaginings. When this happens, one can only follow, fearfully, in case the spell is broken. This sometimes happens, and then suddenly the friendly image becomes a betrayer, or is betrayed, leading to immediate disappointment and, worse, the shame of defeat. This can be doubly distressing, because failure seems to belong to the image maker in a way that success rarely does.

Sometimes, too, from the first expressive gesture, it is obvious that progress will be painfully won. The process does not flow; each addition looks vulnerable, awkward, or ineffective. The image maker is reminded of all previous occasions in which there was a sense of artistic inadequacy because, worst of all, it is not clear how to put the matter right or, to put it another way, *to know what the image is asking from its maker*. If there is persistence with a troublesome image in an attempt to bring it under control, or to make it seem more authentic, this can feel like an act of reparation, in the Kleinian sense. If the attempt is abandoned, or the image destroyed, there is a sense of lost opportunity, a real loss. Acting out the literal destruction of an image is rarely a satisfying experience.

In Jungian terms, the above passage is written from the point of view of the patient's ego, based on my own ego recollections of similar struggles with images from the unconscious. All art therapists have techniques for trying to help another through this hazardous journey. I will usually try to convey the idea that the image has a life of its own, and that therefore whatever happens is right. If this works, the individual becomes interested in the unpredictable; the ego learns to watch and relate to the process, rather than seeking to gain control over it. Later, this can develop into recognition that a healing process is taking place by the constellation of a patient-therapist relationship within the patient. This requires, I feel, a parallel therapist-patient internal relationship within the therapist.

Personifying our thoughts and feelings is an ancient tradition (cf. Hillman, 1975). Personified images can become conscious and, better still, can be visually represented. What I refer to as a sense of "otherness" about one's visual images is also an experience of personification. It is from this point that a sense of dialogue with the unconscious can begin.

For the patient, working with images in a spontaneous way almost always seems to call up another side of the personality. The otherness has to be recognized as one's own, and it can be astonishing to discover hidden aspects of the personality confronting the conscious ego. This is why having a sense of dialogue with one's images is so important: if the images are seen by patient or therapist as nothing but the portrayal of a problem, the possibility of a deeper, perhaps more complex meaning is lost. This is where diagnosis through art can be damaging to the healing possibilities in the image, because it often leads to a "good" or "bad" prognosis; this tends to undermine how imagery can carry several meanings at a time.

The image that becomes an actual object confronts its maker with a host of possibilities. If the originating impulse arose from the unconscious, then its expression will be a unique configuration of forms and affects. The image needs to be regarded by both patient and therapist in a variety of ways, from different perspectives, at different times, and in different contexts. The issue should not be, who—client or therapist—does the interpreting. Rather, a severely reductive stance by either may (and probably will) miss subtle overtones and nuances of an image, which need to be responded to with non-judgmental acceptance. It is the therapist's role to establish a therapeutic frame in which the image can be allowed its own authority, without overwhelming the client with its message, but also without being stripped of its iconological power.

For the patient, as the image-making process comes to completion, the dialogue, which until then has been from a close perspective, at times seemingly entirely *within* the image, changes to a more distant perception. The image as separate object allows the maker to stare, to step back, to move across the room. This can be a wholly new experience of the art. If possible, I like to share with a patient the surprise that often comes with seeing the work at a distance. Its otherness has finally established itself.

It is the moment at which the image becomes a part of the outer world; it inhabits the room and exerts its own influence on whoever happens to be there. The completed image, however incomplete, primitive, regressive, or alien, is a new factor in the situation; it is both a statement about and a personification of what was formerly inner experience. What is more, it reminds both patient and therapist that it has an existence independent of its maker. Properly looked after, it may last a lifetime or longer.

It can be surveyed briefly—I will sometimes ask for the transitory first impression, before more developed perceptions begin to take over—casually, out of the corner of an eye, in detail, and at length. A picture can be turned on its side or upside down, discussed animatedly or regarded silently, or compared with other images. Associations may be elicited by both patient and therapist in a hermeneutic style of interpretation. This is very different from using a patient's associations in a reductive way, leading to pathologizing of the image by treating it as a symptom.

Once the first examination of the art is over, subsequent dialogues with the image may take place: tomorrow, in a month, a year, or even 10 years' time. Each time it is likely to have changed less in reality than it seems to have. Whenever we look at the same image, we see it a little differently. As a personified object, the image may demand a particular way of being in the world, at least for a time. Certain images seem to need to be lived with, because their otherness needs to be assimilate gradually.

Since the image can also have an element of *vulnerability*, the assimilation may need to take place in a protected situation, where it will not be exposed to more public viewing than is appropriate. Some images are too powerful or too frightening for assimilation. Then, the therapist must carry an ego role for the patient by taking some responsibility for the image which threatens to overwhelm, by putting it away in a safe place (the symbolism will be apparent), or simply by agreeing to take care of it.

The image is related to by both patient and therapist as if it were an extended part of the person who made it, which, in a metaphoric sense, it is. However, the perception of the image as independent and semi-autonomous must also be preserved, to allow for its personified aspect, and to permit imaginative dialogue with it. Transference feelings are less strongly projected onto the therapist, because they are experienced more objectively through the artwork. The therapist is able to channel counter-transference feelings into caring about, and bringing ideas to, the image.

The notion of the image as, on one level, an extension of the personality and, on another, an independent entity is in keeping with Jung's view of the symbol as having both past and future aspects. It is linked to the past by actual life events, and to the present and future by the archetypal structure inherent in the situation. The therapist's associations and ideas can facilitate bringing archetypal material to consciousness, while offering the client greater flexibility and choice.

This has to be a mutually convincing synthesis of the real-world situation and the imaginal world of metaphor. Archetypal factors are inescapable, but determine behavior negatively only when they remain completely unconscious. By allowing a sense of participation and dialogue with archetypal (and personal) material in personified form, the patient can integrate unacknowledged aspects of personality and, with increased consciousness, come to better terms with life. This might be described as the ability to live *within* one's personal myth rather than be lived *by* it.

I have stressed the nature of a healing role for image making. There is much that I have set aside, including the relation of imagery to the four functions: intuition, sensation, feeling, and thinking; to extraversion and introversion; and to the archetypes themselves. I will not describe the functions or the attitude types, since they are fairly well known (cf. Jung's *Psychological Types:* CW6 (1971). Nor is there space to enter into a discussion of the archetypes (CW9, 1968b) or the complexes (CW7, 1966b). These topics can be touched on only in very general terms.

Jung believed that individuals develop a predisposition toward using one or more of the four functions in everyday life, while other functions remain more or less unconscious. Herbert Read (1943) attempted to show that the function types can be recognized by the style of the art (pp. 143–145, 219–220). However, it is rarely clear whether images come from conscious or unconscious sources. Unconscious aspects can predominate, as with the spontaneous work produced in art therapy. A patient usually functioning as an extraverted thinking/sensation type may experience a less developed form of introverted feeling/intuition in artwork. The "weak" or "inferior" function (Jung, CW6, 1971) can take on a persecutory role or can emerge in a compulsive way. Unconscious factors determine the course of therapy, but the conscious personality is also involved.

In Jungian analytic therapy, certain archetypal themes tend to present themselves in an almost predictable sequence. How it happens varies, but often early stages deal with the *shadow*, the denied and sometimes feared part of the personality, that corresponds to Freud's personal unconscious. The quality of "otherness" may be particularly associated with the shadow, when the art activity or the images are feared or rejected.

At a later stage, the contrasexual figures—the *animus* in the woman and the *anima* in the man—may appear as personifications. At first they may only be experienced by projection; the therapist then helps the patient to recognize these figures as internal in origin, and ultimately to integrate them as much as possible. Archetypal contents, being collective rather than personal, can never be fully assimilated. The goal is learning to trust inner figures, as sources of insight and creative development in individuation.

Although there were times when Jung made a clinical comment about artwork, as in his 1932 paper on Picasso (CW15, 1966c), this is not consistent with his psychology. Jungian therapists sometimes make a kind of diagnosis by noting the dominance of a particular archetypal figure, saying that a patient may have a "negative animus problem" or is in the grip of the "terrible mother." Since the language of such comments is metaphoric, it is difficult to convey the meaning intended. The archetypes contain both positive (creative) and negative (destructive) characteristics and, according to which seem to be surfacing in a patient's life, such archetypal dynamics might be noted diagnostically, as might imagery from the personal unconscious, in a more Freudian sense.

It would be foolish to suggest that any theory should be so open-ended as to undermine its own credibility, yet a considerable virtue of Jungian theory is that it is hermeneutic in its approach to interpretation. It depends on the assumption that unconscious factors can be inferred from psychological clues, like those found in spontaneous imagery. Since Jung developed a multidimensional method of trying to comprehend symbolic images, and since symbols are beyond full intellectual comprehension, any diagnostic or even interpretive comment is both tentative and relative. There are occasions, however, when a reductive interpretation may be used, when there is a need to bring particular issues into focus.

Another major issue is whether the emergence of particular material is favorable or unfavorable to the client. It is often difficult to know whether it is being worked through or is prognostic. Should the therapist be alarmed by self-destructive imagery, or relieved that a previously unconscious impulse is coming to consciousness where it can be drawn into therapeutic work? The answer is that both should be taken into account. The appearance of potentially destructive material should not close the doors to alternatives other than acting out, though that has to be kept in mind. So, too, does the need for a more empathic response and for greater sensitivity and depth, which might be precluded by focusing too narrowly on diagnostic implications in the artwork.

☐ **Theory into Pracice**

My own practice of art therapy has recently included working with adolescents and families in a hospital day treatment program, seeing some private clients, and conducting workshops with students, therapists, and others. My role is very different in each case, but there is some consistency in how I attempt to facilitate peoples' interaction with their own images. In workshops I may also use relaxation, dance movement, or voice improvisation exercises—leading toward, or working out from, the images themselves. Often I will get people to write as a form of active imagination, in response to their images, to amplify meaning. The central focus remains with the art, unlike psychoanalytic free association, where the artwork may serve only as a point of departure. This writing can be in the form of a story or poem; occasionally I will ask an individual to write a letter to the image, telling it how it is experienced; this will often prompt a "reply" from the image, and at times an interchange of "correspondence."

Such an exercise has to be carefully related to the situation and can never be prescriptive. When used successfully, it can facilitate the move from projection to personification. Once the personified affects are experienced as entities, a sense of working with the unconscious begins. This may be uncomfortable, possibly involving shadow personalities or negative aspects of parental archetypes. On the other hand, there may be figures or symbolic images which convey a transcending sense of relating to new energies and depths of meaning. What is important is that such personified figures are related to as inner images, however relevantly they might also be linked with people in the artist's real-life situation.

With a child or a seriously disturbed adult, there is usually little direct interpretation, but rather a sense of mutual involvement in the imagery, a staying with the symbolism. The therapist's ego can act as a guide, while investment in and valuing of the art therapy process is expressed through countertransference to the artwork; or, in Jungian terms, by the therapist trying to maintain contact with the Self (Schwartz-Salant, 1982, p. 14), Jung's term for the archetypal center of the conscious/unconscious psyche.

A therapist in training, or a patient with good ego strength who has reached a sufficient stage of independence, may be encouraged to research the imagery as well as to make personal associations. This hermeneutic process involves searching for meaning, using imagination, and noting what is experienced as authentic. The therapist's countertransference reactions need to be carefully monitored in this approach.

Two contrasting examples may help to illustrate the way a Jungian approach to art therapy can work in practice. In the first, an 18-year-old adolescent, who had been described as "borderline" following several bizarre self-destructive acts, had been in weekly art therapy for about eight months. His recent pictures were almost all produced by squeezing copious amounts of acrylic paint onto the paper, which, after folding, opened into Rorschach-like configurations. My patience felt strained by the apparently defensive nature of this activity, and perhaps by the quantity of expensive paint that was being consumed. This was no simple limit-testing situation, however, nor do I think that it could be adequately described as regression.

He seemed very invested in what was happening, and I derived some comfort from this, as from the information that he was coping better than before in other aspects of his life. The pictures were increasingly used by him as vehicles for projection, and he gave some of them names like "Confusion/Delusion" and "Prehistoric Crustacean." The final picture in this series marked a significant change in our relationship and in his progress (Figure 6.2). This time, we both saw the demon that emerged from the

Figure 6.2.

mess of paint, also a tiny, doll-like figure at the bottom. We sensed a new rapport, and were able to talk about the picture from a similar viewpoint. It seemed as if this was the image he had been "accidentally" trying for, and that my response—authenticating his demon—was what he needed.

The second example is from the journal of a woman in a group. I think these extracts give some idea of dialoguing with imagery in the way that I have described:

> When I left this week's workshop, I was puzzled by the emptiness and "lack of connection" that I was experiencing. . . . My discomfort began during the session when I tried to engage my image in conversation—it was stilted, wouldn't flow and seemed extremely unnatural. My conversation with K.'s work, by contrast, flowed smoothly and easily. There was no *affect* stirred, felt, or expressed during almost the entire session. When I realized this, I tried to follow that feeling, or lack of it, to its source. I recalled that while lying relaxed on the floor I was very aware of my heartbeat and that I had fantasized a responding beat from the depths of the earth.
>
> *Someone* got up from the floor and went to sit at the table—but it was not me. *I* stayed where I was. That someone very deliberately selected an image from the past and decided to paint a version of it. It was an "ego choice," but who was orchestrating things? With which complex did the ego align itself and which one was projected? The image produced was, in itself, split. It showed a woman's body apparently emerging from the earth, as far as just above waist level [Figure 6.3]. In yesterday's image, there is an oddly injured look about the woman's head—a kind of spreading bruise. . . . She has her eyes closed—going inward or shutting out? Neither. It struck me, at about 2:00 A.M., that the reason I had had difficulty in our conversation was that she was, in fact, *dead*.

(text continues on page 92)

Figure 6.3.

Why did I choose a dead issue? Why was it not safe for me to be as I am today? There was a definite regression—not a complete denial—but a portrayal of an earlier version, perhaps, of myself. Why did I choose specifically *that* stage to which to regress? What was forbidden/acceptable then? There was not much play—that much is for sure; everything was very serious. The barriers were up and there were rigid boundaries. It was "safe" for me then, devoid of emotion. Yesterday I reexperienced the affect of that time in terms of no affect: a straightforward denial of feelings. No wonder her head looks bruised. She is a self-battered woman who wouldn't laugh and couldn't cry. She was also very boring—she probably bored herself to death. And yet, as Hillman (1979) says, "We easily lose touch with the subtle kinds of death "(pp. 65–66) . . . ." When we have put our day world notions to sleep "death is the most profoundly radical way of expressing the shift in consciousness" (pp. 65–66).

To conclude . . . who is the woman? This is certainly no whimpering Persephone—this has the appearance, at least, of a woman of purpose, going down of her own free will. For this image to have presented itself in this particular form, at this particular time, even though consciously chosen and based on a previous image, it must live somewhere still. Somewhere in my own psyche there lives, paradoxically, a dead woman.

☐ Comments and Conclusion

Later in the workshop series, this woman experienced a vivid sense of reconnection to her lower body, especially the legs (Figure 6.4). With this came a spontaneous release of affect, which she was able to integrate into her personal life. Thus, a tendency toward dissociative deadness of affect was related to, not simply as a problem, but as an archetypal factor in the psyche. In the case of the adolescent, the archetypal possession—which, in Jungian terms, characterized his borderline life experience—was objectified in the imagery, perceived, and thereby loosened in its grip on the conscious personality. The ego of the individual, in both cases, was able to give up some of its unrealistic striving for autonomy by admitting to—and also relating to—alien figures in the unconscious.

It is the therapist's task to ensure that such a compromise by the ego is made with sensitivity, often putting the therapist into the temporary "holding" role with which art therapists are familiar. In both examples, the therapeutic work consisted in affirming respect for and trust in the imagery—not as romanticized art for art's sake, nor, in these instances, as a source of clinical information, or even as an interesting intellectual adventure into archetypal configurations—but as a symbolic and potentially insight-provoking synthesis of internal and external realities.

As Freud's major contribution to art therapy was in demonstrating the latent content in dreams and fantasies; so Jung's was to treat such images as communications from the psyche, to be understood in their own terms and on many levels. Thus, from a Jungian perspective, the image can never be adequately described, however true certain interpretations may be in some sense. Jung, I believe, restored to the psychotherapeutic view of fantasy and dream images an acknowledgment of their complex and subtle affinity with artistic values and insights—which are, in turn, inevitably shaped by both personal and archetypal determinants in the unconscious.

☐ References

Beck, R. H. (1958–1959). Progressive education and American progressivism: Margaret Naumburg. *Teachers College Record, LX*, 198–208.

Campbell, J. (1949). *The hero with a thousand faces*. New York: Bollingen.

Figure 6.4.

Cremin, L. (1961). *The transformation of the school 1876–1957*. New York: Vintage.

Hillman, J. (1975). *Revisioning psychology*. New York: Harper.

Hillman, J. (1979). *The dream and the underworld*. New York: Harper.

Jaffé, A. (Ed.) (1979). *C. G. Jung: Word and image*. Princeton, NJ: Princeton University Press.

Jung, C. G. (1963). *Memories, dreams, reflections*. A. Jaffé (Ed.). London: Collins and Routledge & Kegan Paul.

Jung, C. G., et al. (1964). *Man and his symbols*. London: Aldus.

Jung, C. G. (1966a). The aims of psychotherapy. In *The practice of psychotherapy, collected works*, Vol. 16. Princeton, NJ: Princeton University Press.

Jung, C. G. (1966b). On the psychology of the unconscious. In *Two essays on analytical psychology, collected works*, Vol. 7. Princeton, NJ: Princeton University Press.

Jung, C. G. (1966c). *The spirit in man, art and literature, collected works*, Vol. 15. Princeton, NJ: Princeton University Press.

Jung, C. G. (1968a). *Alchemical studies, collected works*, Vol. 13. Princeton, NJ: Princeton University Press.

Jung, C. G. (1968b). *The archetypes and the collective unconscious, collected works*, Vol. 9, part I. Princeton, NJ: Princeton University Press.

Jung, C. G. (1969). General aspects of dream psychology, and the transcendent function. In *The structure and dynamics of the psyche, collected works*, Vol. 8. Princeton, NJ: Princeton University Press.

Jung, C. G. (1971). *Psychological types, collected works*, Vol. 6. Princeton, NJ: Princeton University Press.

Read, H. (1943). *Education through art*. London: Faber & Faber.

Robertson, S. (1963). *Rosegarden and labyrinth*. London: Routledge & Kegan Paul.

Schwartz-Salant, N. (1982). *Narcissism and character transformation*. Toronto: Inner City Books.

Storr, A. (1983). *The essential Jung*. Princeton, NJ: Princeton University Press.

Von Franz, M.-L. (1982). *An introduction to the interpretation of fairy tales*. Dallas: Spring.

Edith Wallace

Healing Through the Visual Arts

"If you bring forth that which is within you, what you bring forth will save you. If you do not bring forth what is within you, what you do not bring forth will destroy you." (Gospel of St. Thomas)

History and Description of Active Imagination

To write about the Jungian approach to therapy is a formidable task, and I consider it inadequate because Jung needs to be experienced; this is the reason I originally became involved in art therapy, and it made me realize the importance of Jung's view of the unconscious to art therapy.

I have chosen to use one method—active imagination—which deals with images, and is based on the fact that we must trust such images which arise from the depth of the psyche. This method presupposes that truth resides in the unconscious, not only on a personal, ego level, but as a profound historical truth, and is manifested in archetypal images arising from the collective unconscious. The central archetype which Jung called the "Self" is of special importance in healing. It has a regulating, stabilizing function, compensating for any imbalance that might arise. It could also be called one's inner wisdom and guide; I call it the "creative source."

Thanks to the work of the great trailblazers of depth psychology, we know that anything contained in the unconscious, but not brought to light, will have a life of its own and an influence on consciousness. For Jung, this influence can be beneficent as well as noxious, and we are certainly far from knowing the total depth of the unconscious. In other words, the mystery of life as well as the wish to penetrate it will be with us forever.

Since the image precedes the word, we can, through images (as well as through body movement), evoke unknown aspects of the psyche, and bring them to the light of consciousness; this results in understanding and, often, healing. For healing to take place, however, we must take the consequences of what we have understood, and bring our understanding into the reality of lived life.

When we open ourselves to the unconscious—the irrational—there is danger as well as reward. Jung was well aware of this:

As a result of my experiments I learned how helpful it can be, from the therapeutic point of view, to find the particular images which lie behind emotions. . . . In order to grasp the fantasies which were stirring in me "underground," I knew that I had to let myself plummet down into them, as it were. I felt not only violent resistance to this, but a distinct fear. . . . It was during Advent of the year 1913—December 12, to be exact—that I resolved upon the decisive step. I was sitting at my desk once more, thinking over my fears. Then I let myself drop. Suddenly it was as though the ground literally gave way beneath my feet, and I plunged down into dark depths. I could not fend off a feeling of panic. But then, abruptly, at not too great a depth I landed on my feet. (Jung, 1961, pp. 177–179)

The irrational and what is behind it manifests in emotionality, sometimes uncontrollably so. It is the first sign of a message from the depth, and if we can be detached enough, it can become a dialogue between conscious and unconscious. The progression can then be from (1) emotionality to (2) a specific emotion, which may find expression in (3) an image, which can reduce the violence of the emotion; the image may be explained in (4) words, an articulation necessary for conscious understanding—a message received.

While confronted with certain fantasies that had great emotional impact, Jung knew he would have to step right into them, if he wished to bring understanding to this uncharted territory of the psyche. Before using the method which he later called *"active imagination"* on others and publishing it, he experimented on himself, as related in the above quote from his autobiography. By his own request, these memoirs were not published until his death in 1961. Active imagination is first mentioned in "The Transcendent Function," an essay written by Jung in 1916 but not published until 1957. In 1935 Jung lectured at the Tavistock Clinic in London to a group of doctors. In the discussion he was asked about active imagination, and he gave the following explanation:

A fantasy is more or less your own invention, and remains on the surface of personal things and conscious expectations. But active imagination, as the term denotes, means that the images have a life of their own and that the symbolic events develop according to their own logic—that is, of course, if your conscious reason does not interfere. . . . For instance, if my unconscious should prefer not to give me ideas, I could not proceed with my lecture, because I could not invent the next step. (Jung, 1935/1976, pp. 171–172)

In a commentary on *The Secret of the Golden Flower* (1931/1967), Jung wrote: "in cases of a high degree of inflexibility in the conscious oftentimes the hands alone can fantasy; they model or draw figures that are quite foreign to the conscious" (p. 17).

In the collected correspondence, there is a letter of April 23, 1931 to Count Hermann Keyserling, who had consulted Jung about some experiences that his very rational mind could not fathom. Jung responded: "The unconscious has a different rhythm from consciousness and different goals." He advises Keyserling to subordinate his philosophical skill and descriptive powers to those unknown contents and ask:

"Who or what has come alive . . . who or what has entered my psychic life and created disturbances and wants to be heard?" To this you should add: Let it speak. Then switch off your noisy consciousness and listen quietly inward and look at the images that appear before your inner eye, or hearken to the words which the muscles of your speech apparatus are trying to form. Write down what then comes without criticism. Images should be drawn or painted assiduously, no matter whether you can do it or not. Once you have got at least fragments of these contents, then you may meditate on them *afterwards*. Don't criticize anything away! If any questions arise, put them to the unconscious again the next day. Don't be content with your own explanations no matter how intelligent they are. Remember, your health is seriously at stake and the unconscious has an unknown, far-reaching control over it. Treat any drawings the same way. Meditate on them afterwards and every day go on developing what is unsatisfactory about them. The important thing is to let the unconscious take the lead. You must always be convinced that you have mere afterknowledge and nothing else. In this case, the unconscious really does know better (Adler & Jaffe, 1973).

Jung's simple definition of active imagination (from *Essays on a Science of Mythology*) was: "A method, devised by myself, of introspection for observing the stream of interior images" (1949, p. 228). This, however, is not enough. In *Memories, Dreams, Reflections*, he wrote expressly:

> The images of the unconscious place a great responsibility upon a man. Failure to understand them, or a shirking of ethical responsibility deprives him of his wholeness and imposes a painful fragmentariness on his life. Recognizing the world means creating it. (1961, p. 193)

An example of spontaneous active imagination may clarify. A female patient of mine in a private mental hospital who had suffered from involutional melancholia was coming out of her depression. Had I told her that it was time for her to go home, I might have met with opposition. The hospital was a comfortable place with no obligations, whereas going home meant shouldering her usual responsibilities. Her unconscious came to our aid, though she knew nothing about Jung. One day she came to her session with this story: "You know, doctor," she said, "I had this image: I had been walking in the woods and I was coming out of them and there was the main highway. I told myself, 'Oh no, it cannot be,' and I tried to pull myself back in. But every time I did that I was in the same place again." She understood, she got the message, *and* she went home.

This fulfills all the requirements of active imagination. Marie-Louise von Franz (1983) spelled it out in an essay republished as a supplement to Margaret Keyes' *The Inward Journey*. She breaks down active imagination into four different stages, with which I concur:

1. "First one must empty one's mind from the trains of thought of the ego" (von Franz, 1983, p. 125). She points out that since this is difficult for some, it may be easier to paint. She notes that emptying the mind is similar to meditation, but that the welcoming and dealing with the images is very different.
2. Next we let the image enter our field of attention. This requires a special kind of inner focusing. It is necessary to catch the images without holding on with so much concentration that the very tension of the endeavor could arrest the process. Nor can we allow image after image to pass by with too little focus on our part. If there is no observer, there cannot be any relating either; such people forget that there is a process going on that is happening to *them*.
3. Now is the time to write down what has been seen, to paint or sculpt or dance or write music that was heard, to give outer form to the experience. Since not everything can produce images, active imagination can also start with any medium. It is the step of materializing, which usually means body involvement, and often a body impulse as well as a body understanding.
4. This is when we must take the consequences of messages received, the ethical confrontation Jung speaks about. We must recall that something is happening to us as we are and live in reality, not some evasive fantasy dreamt by an imaginary ego—an attitude that prevents any kind of transformation, as if we were not touched by the whole process. In active imagination we start with picking up messages from the unconscious.

☐ Art and Active Imagination

The difference between active imagination and the dream is that we are fully awake witnesses to what is happening while it is happening. It is one of Jung's ways of using and understanding spontaneously arising manifestations of contents from the unconscious: images, body movement, words, or music; in other words, the arts in psychotherapy.

Jung felt that when we are involved in this process of active imagination through any of the arts, we should not call it "art" (1961, p. 187). I disagree, since the search of any real artist is the same as Jung's search for "the supreme presentiments of consciousness and the loftiest intuitions of the spirit" (cf. Kandinsky, 1947; Klee, 1945). As Van Gogh wrote: "There is something infinite in painting—there are hidden things of harmony or contrast in colours, things which are effective in themselves and which cannot be expressed through any other medium" (1963).

There is magic in both healing and creating. Creating comes and goes and we become its instrument, while making our conscious contribution. If healing means—at least in part—recovery of potential, a certain receptive "emptiness" is essential for the process to occur. The stage needs to be set for listening to that inner voice; to make it heard or visible requires stillness. Images imposed from the outside can be an intrusion and an interference to the arising of inner images. What we must "throw to the winds" to be "empty" in the process of creation (and healing) is that which we have learned, all aspects of conditioning. We must again become like a child who knows and trusts its own powers. There is no need to strive for the genuine, the original, the spontaneous; they are simply there, and often they will surprise us because we have moved so far away from them.

I think that one reason I prefer using brilliant, translucent-colored tissue papers, which often produce beautiful results, is that they encourage confidence—to go on, to stay with the process, to go deeper, and through it to enhance development and growth. The emphasis is on transformation, but there is none without first healing. If the aim is to get to the cellar and the cellar stairs are cluttered, our first task is to take care of the clutter.

☐ Dialogue

One aspect of active imagination that needs to be emphasized is *dialogue*. The aim is that the conscious and the unconscious talk to each other. The dialogue starts with oneself and the many people of one's inner household. As they appear, they can be confronted, we can come to terms with them, and they can turn from opposers to helpers. All this is part of growth, development, and healing; it is a lifetime's work, an ongoing process. *Dialogue* also means confrontation.

This is the inner process, and it goes from more to less irrational. The *process* in a series of dreams, visions, or pictures is a story, the unfolding of the messages needed for growth and development. It can dissolve a complex and integrate those pieces that can be integrated only after the dissolution. This is the healing process. In the growth process it is more a balancing of opposites to make them live peacefully together—a "mysterium conjunctionis"—a coming to terms, often through dialogue.

Continuing use of any art medium can foster this kind of process. In active imagination the initial material is that which arises from the unconscious, from inside. This does not mean that it cannot be stimulated or even started by an outer image, especially if there is a strong emotional response to something. This usually indicates a correspond-ing image on the inside that can and wants to be pursued and brought to the light of day.

I had my first experience with art therapy when I used active imagination in a most unorthodox way. I started work with a group and invited members to use translucent-colored tissue papers for collaging, which seemed helpful for opening up to messages from the unconscious. Working with tissue paper, glue, and brush brought forth freer shapes, which seemed to emerge from a greater depth of the psyche: it acted as an opener and channel builder. Eventually, shapes would emerge that had great impact and meaning. But this could happen only if the work was done playfully, unselfconsciously, like a child, without preconceived ideas, notions, or manipulation. It meant just very seriously enjoying the process of playing while enjoying the colors, sometimes taking pleasure in what emerged, sometimes being surprised, and eventually finding meaning in it.

Images come in a series. Often a story unfolds that wants to be written down. Discov-eries happen sometimes only after the story. However, something has been touched, the person is moved to write a story after having seen the images—the meaning is there. Usually, the person has been touched deeply enough to bring about transformation. It is exciting and absorbing work, often continued for years. The absorption is reminiscent of both child and artist. It is also helpful at those moments in life when nothing seems to want to move, when one is stuck. One of the values of this work consists in opening new channels. The doing is the first step, the first part of the dialogue. The first injunction is: Forget all you know, all preconceived ideas, all known forms or images. Play!

Once this process has unfolded, in all its spontaneity, we then take a very close look at what has appeared. We let it speak to us, and we need to "listen" as we did before, when something wanted to become manifest. Now we need to know *what* has manifested, to catch the message. This is also a dialogue, the injunction being: Let it speak back to you; what does it say to you? This *looking*, to which a good deal of time is given, is a 3-step process. First: *Looking* in the ordinary sense—just simply looking at the object and realizing something has been made. Second: *Noticing* that one can see more things than appeared to be there at first—a different kind of perceiving, but still connected with actual appearance. Third: *Seeing*. This is a true recognition, a revelation: There is more to it than meets the eye. This hits me, it has meaning, it tells me something that I did not know before. I receive a message. I see the world anew. I perceive a truth.

Only this last is a step into depth. The whole process is a far cry from analyzing and diagnosing; these are only surface procedures compared to the third stage, which leads to true understanding. It requires patient, relentless observation; while awakening a different kind of perception from a deliberate analytic procedure. Such messages from the unconscious need constant circumambulation to be understood, and I say "constant" advisedly. We may have only gotten hold of the dog's tail, when it is his face we need to see. This means: Don't let go of the tail, work your way up to the face. If we let go, the dog is likely to run away. All this takes time.

The liberating effect is apparent in every workshop; but it happens only when there is a true letting go. Those who cling to the known cannot reach it, and there are always some who cling ardently because the other mode has been their security. For example, a middle-aged building contractor in one of my workshops made a collage with the mood and feeling of nature in an abstract way, which wasn't "reasonable" order. At the last minute, and quite deliberately, he put a sun in one corner. It was just too unbearable for him otherwise. But another person detected it as a last-minute addition and confronted him: Hadn't he stuck the sun on as an afterthought? He had to admit this was true. Only "when man is capable of being in uncertainties, mysteries, doubts without any irritable reaching after fact and reason" is he capable of creation in the arts.

Letting be, allowing, can best be achieved in a playful way, and the joy of a playful way is felt. We can go by the motto: "All art is meditation." Once one takes brush in hand a calm descends, a concentration ensues, which makes the "listening" possible. Play has been described as a "non-purposive state" (Winnicott, 1971, p. 55). By adulthood we are so conditioned that we have to trick ourselves into being open. One trick is to play, and that means: play seriously and work playfully. We must step aside to allow the depth, the unconditioned, to speak. For Jung, play was a necessity. He states (1923/1971) "It is serious play. . . . It is play from inner necessity. The creative mind plays with the object it loves" (pp. 154–155).

Comparisons to myth or fairy tale or any other age-old manifestation that originated from the depth of the psyche are called "*amplifications*." They help us to understand the symbolic meaning of a present-day image that comes from the same depth. A true "*symbol*" creates a connection between conscious and unconscious. Its form expresses something that cannot be said more clearly, because it is not yet clearly understood. It is, however, a help to understanding what goes on in the depth of the psyche, which leads to self-understanding and self-knowledge—always a force for healing and growth. Once understood, the symbol has done its job; its function fulfilled, it often loses power and meaning.

As far as *diagnosis* is concerned, labels are for the safety of the therapist and to the detriment of the patient. We are presented with an individual with his or her specific mixture of problems. The pieces to the puzzle are all askew. They need to be put together to make the picture which then represents this particular person. For therapeutic purposes we need to see—and that acts as "diagnosis"—where the pieces are askew and how they might be put together. When we see the picture, we see the real person who may find his or her individual story, which characterizes that person, the "individual myth," as Jung has named it. That could be the end result, perhaps the ideal result.

The emphasis is on the *healing* factor of the psyche, not what we as therapists *know*—even though we need to know much. We work with our being, more than with our knowledge. Art therapy, active imagination, and meditation are *methods*, precious ones. They are means of making the psyche speak, bringing to light what was hidden in the dark, either doing damage or left unused. Too much unused potential leads to sickness. Lived potential means psychic health. Art can be an obsession, but it is that driving force which can be our ally in art therapy, and we must engage it.

We may invite images, but find ourselves confronted with emptiness. This can be frustrating, even frightening; it should not be done without a guide. When we hope for manifestations from the unconscious, whether in dreams or in artwork, there comes a moment for a new dimension to break through. We often need to go through a moment of emptiness. This is the time for the "leap in the dark"—the jump—a quantum jump.

The "guide," the therapist, needs to know about the workings of the psyche. Jung speaks of an "individuation process," an "integration of the personality," and that there is a regulating factor in the psyche, a guiding wisdom: the Self. We need to learn to trust our inner wisdom, to know that in the unconscious the truth resides—in a superficial, very personal sense and in the deepest, transpersonal sense.

It The Bubble, is sometimes difficult for people to take images that arise from the unconscious seriously, and we must take them absolutely seriously, but not as absolutes. This is the place where all the resistances and objections arise: "It is only play; I should be doing something more serious, more important!" However, there is nothing more important. I have suggested that we play seriously and work playfully. Any manifestation from the unconscious speaks a symbolic language, says something which—being not yet understood—cannot find a clearer language.

☐ An Example of Active Imagination

Setting the stage for transformation can be a very active pursuit and quite hard work. Following is an interesting illustration of the balance and timing between activity—what we can and must do—and standing still or taking a "leap in the dark," not knowing where it will land us.

It is the story of a young woman—in her late twenties—who, as the first two pictures show (Figures 7.1 and 7.2), was struggling to get out of the protective womb of the mother. She then had some visual images that—characteristically—moved; so there was a process going, a story which she wrote down and later illustrated. This young woman had been working with me for some time, and so was now ready for such a process. Although active imagination can and often needs to be done by the analysand on his or her own, there must be some supervision, and there must be readiness.

Christina's Story

December 29th. I can see only darkness; then I see that there is a lake with faint reflections of light on it. The water leads into a tunnel. I am in a green boat on the lake; I have a pole to push the boat forward. I go into the tunnel (Figure 7.3). The only source of light is a small white light in the distance. It illumines the walls of the tunnel. They are wet and shiny. It is very quiet, the water is motionless. Only the boat makes ripples on the surface as it moves forward. I push the boat until the passage becomes too narrow and I leave the boat and dig. I had expected rock, but there is crumbly earth. I break through and find that I am looking out on a huge vault, like the inside of a huge bowl. I am on the side, about two-thirds up. There are lights in the crevices above, like a firmament, but I know it is all deep under the earth. I must get down to the bottom. I find that I have a sturdy white nylon rope, and I fasten it to something securely and let myself down. The bottom of the vault is pitch dark, and swampy. I manage to move on by stepping on tufts of grass. Then I feel rather than see a huge snake. She is not threatening, but very powerful. I get up on her back and she carries me. We come to a place where I see a blue glow, like an iridescent blue glass bowl. Around it dance flames; they are blue like the inside of candle flames. Around the blue flame sits a circle of dwarflike little men, guarding it. In the middle of the blue is something gleaming white-yellowish; I can't see what it is.

December 30th. Then suddenly I am inside the blue bubble, which now seems as high as a room. It has a round hole in the middle of the bottom; out of the hole shoots up a jet of water, and it balances a luminous white large pearl—the white thing I saw from afar. As I look at the shimmering pearl dancing on the water, I know that I shall fall into the hole if I take it. I hesitate, stretch out my hand, withdraw it. Then I take heart and take it. I fall, and am on a meadow with spring flowers (Figure 7.4). I look at the pearl in my hand. It feels soft, gelatinous. It is now a small object of the form of a child, but all covered with the gelatinous substance, so that I can't see its limbs or its features. I know I must protect it from drying out. I find some huge green leaves, and I pluck some and carefully wrap the child into them.

(text continues on page 105)

Figure 7.1.

Figure 7.2.

Figure 7.3.

Figure 7.4.

January 1st. I take my leaf-wrapped bundle and go into the forest. It is a spruce forest, no undergrowth, all dark and quiet. An animal comes toward me on the path, a wolf with yellow eyes. He quietly tugs on the bundle; I understand he wants me to come along. We go to the left into the forest, off the path, and go until we reach a freer space and a brook. We follow it back up to its source. It comes out of a little pool, very clear, but so deep that one can't see to the bottom. On the water is a big strong leaf, shaped like a receptacle for my bundle. I put my bundle into this leaflike bowl and am just about to take my hands off when I see the edges curl together and the water begins to move, in a churning and downward-sucking motion. I snatch the bundle back. I have it safely, but now the water recedes when I try to catch some in my hands to moisten the bundle. The wolf has watched all this; now he looks at me inscrutably, turns and vanishes into the forest. I begin to worry; where shall I get water so that the bundle doesn't dry out? Then it starts to rain gently; I go back down alongside the brook until I come to the edge of the forest. Night has fallen. There is a moon, and some misty clouds.

I have come to a pasture. I see a cow and walk toward her (Figure 7.5). I see that the leaves of my bundle have wilted and take the top leaf off to look at the child. The cow starts licking it, and slowly there emerges a boy-child with black hair and blue eyes.

January 5th. I need milk for it. I am thinking about milking the cow, and then I see she has vanished. In front of me stands a young woman. She has bared breasts, she is beautiful. I know she is a whore; I also know that she is the one who has abundant milk for the baby.

Figure 7.5.

Discussion

This is a transformation story, a new birth, a change from daughter to mother, from being carried and protected to being responsible for carrying and protecting a precious child, that was behind the luminous pearl which she acquired through her own effort and trust. At first she has to be active: (1) she pushes the boat with a pole; when she gets stuck (2) she digs; (3) after finding a rope, she fastens it and lets herself down on it; (4) she moves on by carefully stepping on tufts of grass to avoid the swamp; (5) she climbs on the back of a huge snake who carries her; all along knowing she wants to get to the bottom of it, though she is already deep down under the earth.

The encounter with the snake is an important moment in the story (Figure 7.6). The huge snake is an elemental creature who now carries her, and is female according to her own statement. Her wish to be carried is also a need, not to be expected from her own mother or any substitute, but from an elemental archetypal force in nature, also in her nature.

Then comes the "leap" for the pearl, and after that decisive step there is a change. The light quality, the very atmosphere—as the illustration shows—has changed. This is reminiscent of the Grimm story of "Mother Holle." A girl who lost her spindle while spinning by a well is sent by her wicked stepmother to bring back the spindle. In despair she jumps into the well where the spindle was lost, and finds herself on the same kind of sunlit, flower-strewn meadow as in Figure 7.4. She shows the same courage and fortitude, and tasks also await her, as well as a reward. Christina is now concerned for

Figure 7.6.

the child in need of her care—she becomes the caring, carrying, protecting mother also looking for nourishment.

In the gnostic "Hymn of the Pearl," in which a young man is sent by his father to retrieve a lost pearl, the pearl represents the soul. The young hero at first forgets all about his mission and gets into bad company, but finally, in real distress, he remembers and returns home with the pearl, the soul regained. The dwarflike figures in Christina's vision are guardians of the pearl, those underground helpers we all have, the "cabiroi" of whom Goethe in *Faust* (Part 2) says: "Small in length, mighty in strength."

There is one more crucial moment in Christina's story. Guided and challenged by a wolf, she comes to a source of water where she can wet her bundle which needs to be kept moist (given life). She is ready to take her hands off the bundle when she notices that the water recedes "in a churning, downward-sucking motion." Now, and this is crucial, she is alert enough to snatch the bundle, to prevent this newborn child from disappearing into the unconscious, where all the work would have been lost. At this moment the wolf leaves, as if he had been sent to test her.

Now help comes in the form of rain—from above, in contrast to the pool of water— from the earth. The cow, who has appeared in the moonlit landscape, is not the one to provide milk to nourish this new-found spirit, represented by a boy-child. Nourishment must now come from a human being, a young woman who knows how to relate to men, even though, as a whore, she is not the best representative of a fulfilling, intimate relationship. The transformation is from a child, protected and carried by the mother, to an adult who knows how to care for her own soul, and how to protect and find nourishment for her new-found spirit.

The consequence she had to accept was to move away from the mother world; for one thing, it was now time for her to work with a male analyst. This also helped her to withdraw projections, like expectations with negative feelings for her mother. The Great Mother—earth, snake—had come to her aid, and had made her courageous actions possible. Such archetypal forces reside in all of us, often strong and driving.

Although Jung did not do "art therapy," the use and understanding of images are of utmost importance in Jungian work. The aim is not to produce art, but to use that which comes from hidden sources—which can be brought to light through art media— to promote consciousness, understanding, growth, and transformation. It is always a process, whether for the artist, the "patient," or the healer. Through highlighting and illustrating what Jung meant by "active imagination," I hope I have clarified what may be of use in art therapy, a process that accelerates both healing and creative potential— which are synonymous in my mind. If we do not live our potential—or at least part thereof—we become sick. Living our potential means health and wholeness.

☐ References

Adler, G., & Jaffé, A. (Eds.). (1973). *C. G. Jung letters.* Vol. I. Princeton, NJ: Princeton University Press.

Jung, C. G. (1949). *Essays on a science of mythology, collected works,* Vol. 9. Princeton, NJ: Princeton University Press.

Jung, C. G. (1961). *Memories, dreams, reflections.* New York: Vintage Books.

Jung, C. G. (1967). Commentary on *The secret of the golden flower, collected works,* Vol. 13. Princeton, NJ: Princeton University Press. (Original work published 1931)

Jung, C. G. (1971). *Psychological types, collected works,* Vol. 6, Princeton, NJ: Princeton University Press. (Original work published 1923)

Jung, C. G. (1976). The Tavistock lectures. *Analytical psychology: Its theory and practice, Collected Works*, Vol. 18. Princeton, NJ: Princeton University Press. (Original work published 1935)

Kandinsky, W. (1947). *Concerning the spiritual in art*. New York: Wittenborn.

Klee, P. (1945). *On modern art*. London: Faber and Faber.

Van Gogh, V. (Roskill, M., Ed.). (1963). *The letters of Vincent Van Gogh*. New York: Atheneum.

von Franz, M.-L. (1983). Introduction. In M. F. Keyes, *The inward journey*. La Salle, IL: Open Court.

Winnicott, D. W. (1971). *Playing and reality*. New York: Basic Books.

☐ Recommended Readings

Edinger, E. F. (1973). *Ego and archetype*. Baltimore, MD: Pelican Books.

Hannah, B. (1981). *Encounters with the soul: Active imagination as developed by C. G. Jung*. Santa Monica, CA: Sigo Press.

Harding, M. E. (1958). What makes the symbol effective as a healing agent in analytical psychology *International Record of Medicine, 171*(12), 732–736.

Hull, C. F. (1971). Bibliographical notes on active imagination in the works of C. G. Jung. *Spring* (a yearly publication), pp. 115–120.

Jacobi, J. (1955). Pictures from the unconscious. *Journal of Projective Techniques, 19*(3).

Jacobi, J. (1969). *Vom Bilderreich der Seele: Wege and Umwege zu sich selbst*. Freiburg: Walter-Verlag.

Jung, C. G. (1964). *Man and his symbols*. New York: Doubleday.

Jung, C. G. (1966). *The spirit in man, art and literature, Collected Works, Vol. 15*. Princeton, NJ: Princeton University Press.

Jung, C. G. (1968). *Analytical psychology: Its theory and practice*. New York: Pantheon.

Kalff, D. M. (1980). *Sandplay*. Santa Monica, CA: Sigo Press.

Keyes, M. F. (1983). *The inward journey: Art as therapy for you*. La Salle, IL: Open Court.

Neumann, E. (1959). *Art and the creative unconscious*. New York: Pantheon.

Neumann, E. (1979). *Creative man*. Princeton, NJ: Princeton University Press.

Perry, J. W. (1953). *The self in the psychotic process*. (Foreword by C. G. Jung.) Berkeley, CA: University of California Press.

Perry, J. W. (1974). *The far side of madness*. Englewood Cliffs, NJ: Prentice-Hall.

Sandplay studies: Origins, theory and practice. San Francisco: C. G. Jung Institute, 1981.

Wallace, E. (1975). Creativity and Jungian thought. *Art Psychotherapy, 2*, 181–187.

Wallace, E. (1980). Establishing connections between two worlds. In I. Baker (Ed.), *Treatment in analytical psychology*. Felbach: Adolph Bonz.

Weaver, R. (1964). *The old wise woman: A study of active imagination*. London: Vincent Stuart.

Weinrib, E. (1983). *Images of the self: The sandplay theory*. Boston, MA: Sigo Press.

COMMENTARY: POSTSCRIPT 2000

Joy Schaverien

It was inspired of Judith Rubin back in 1987 to envision a book revealing the interplay between the variety of theoretical stances that informed art therapy practice. In the 14 years since *Approaches to Art Therapy* was first published, art therapy has developed, and there is now a rich body of literature specific to the profession. In 1987 the scene was very different and *Approaches* was a timely contribution, revealing as it did the state of practice at that time. In this commentary for a new edition at the beginning of a new century, consideration of its continuing relevance for clinical practice seems appropriate. It is also worth considering the future, and where these ideas might lead in terms of research.

Rubin invited contributions from established art therapists whose personal quests had led each of them to link their practice with a different set of theories. As the reader knows, the chapters draw on diverse psychological approaches, and give a rich sense of differences and similarities between the practitioners. The illustrations are the linking thread in each contribution. In the psychodynamic section, which I will discuss, the writers stick closely to their psychoanalytic mentors, but all propose ways of adapting these theories in relation to the specifics of art therapy. In this brief postscript it is my intention to draw out the points which seem relevant as a foundation for future development. In order to do this, I attempt to apply the concepts discussed to pictures made in clinical practice. First, though, a few thoughts on the two main threads of this section of the book—art and psychoanalysis.

Art therapists come from a variety of backgrounds but most, if not all, are artists in one form or another. Thus, first a reminder of the art materials seems to be in order. For me, and I suspect for others too, it is only necessary to recall the texture of paint to be reminded of the sensual pleasure in art. Consider color applied with a brush dipped in the thick creamy mix of pigments and oil, or the thin wash of watercolor staining a blank sheet of paper. There is liberation in the rather messy, active process. It engages touch and the sense of smell, as well as vision.

Then there is language; the words used to describe colors evoke in the mind's eye subtle distinctions between them that engender far more than the generic terms red, blue, or green. Imagine, for example, cadmium red, vermillion, scarlet lake, rose madder; notice how each evokes its own tints and reverberations. Place these next to the complementary greens—viridian, jade, or emerald—and notice how each is subtly altered by the presence of the other. Thus a figure/ground relationship is established where first one color is dominant and then the other; there is a visual interplay between them as their priority alters. This play with color is part of the potentially rich experience that

109

we offer to those who present themselves in our art therapy studios. It is these and other physical materials, offered when someone embarks on this depth psychological project, which distinguishes art therapy from other forms of therapy.

Psychoanalysis, that influential model for understanding the twentieth century mind, may also be considered, metaphorically speaking, as a figure/ground relationship—characterized, not by the interaction of complementary colors, but by the interplay between conscious and unconscious. There is a perceptual shift between that which is consciously known, and that which was previously unconscious. Very often this is evoked through the transference, when feelings belonging to the past become activated in the present, opening up a possibility for change.

Although it is not made explicit here, in my view it is the emphasis on the transference that distinguishes psychoanalytic from humanistic and behavioral approaches. Regarding the priority of the transference in different forms of art therapy, I have suggested (1992, 1995) that, in some cases, the artwork is the figure, the main focus of attention. Here, the therapeutic relationship forms the background from which it emerges.

However, in other cases, the therapeutic relationship is the figure, with the transference as the central focus of attention, while the art provides a ground which illustrates the relationship. There are times when the interplay between the two is equally balanced; priority shifts from one to the other. Although not stated in these terms, this book addresses many of these similarities and differences in practice. The topic of this psychodynamic section seems to be the search for a balance in theory and clinical practice, and between art and psychoanalysis.

In Chapter 1, Rubin considers the historical perspective of Freudian psychoanalytic theory, which influences her own work. An analyst herself, she reminds us of pioneer art therapist Margaret Naumburg, and shows, through a case, the way in which her own psychoanalytic training informs her interventions. The difference between art therapy and psychoanalysis is evident; ten months of weekly sessions are not psychoanalysis, yet this chapter shows a psychoanalytically informed stance in action. Rubin expresses her view that classical psychoanalysis is neither appropriate nor necessary for most, but that "the theory which informs it is useful in understanding and guiding all therapeutic work." (p. 25). It seems to me that one of the guiding principles of this section is an open consideration of the contribution psychoanalysis can make to art therapy theory.

The proof of the efficacy of theory is in its clinical application. In order to demonstrate that the theoretical base of this section continues to be relevant in clinical practice, I am going to draw out some of the main points in relation to clinical material of my own, using two pictures extracted from a series. They are taken from the detailed case study in *Desire and the Female Therapist* (Schaverien, 1995). The first is "The Bubble" (1995, Figure 4.4, p. 71); the second "The Hero" (1995, Color Plate 10, opposite p. 65). The aim is to demonstrate the clinical application of the theoretical observations of the writers in the psychodynamic section of *Approaches to Art Therapy*.

In order to give substance to the discussion, a brief background to the case is necessary. Carlos, as I have called him, was a young man, suffering from anorexia, who was an in-patient in a psychiatric unit. "The Bubble" (Figure CI.1) was made at the beginning of his stay in the hospital when he was confined to bed rest, due to his very low body weight.

Figure C1-1, The Bubble, is a faint pencil drawing that shows the atrophied physical and psychological state of the anorexic patient on admission. He lay curled up on his bed most of the day, and he drew this picture at that time. We see a deathly embryonic figure encased in a bubble/womb. It has no genitals, and the world is seen as separate and a long way away from him. Although we could not predict it, he was to stay in this room

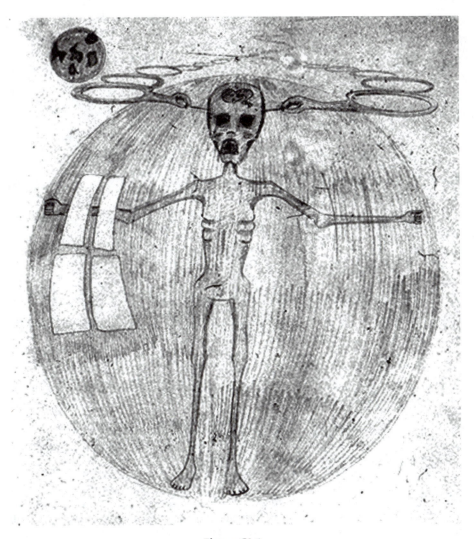

Figure CI.1.

for nine months until his agreed target weight was attained. Clearly nine months is significant in terms of his regressed state, and the bubble picture seems to emphasise this with its womblike, circular, containing shape.

The second picture, "The Hero" a painting (Figure CI.2), was made when he was nearing the end of his stay in hospital ten months after Figure CI.1 was made. The agreed target weight had been achieved and, no longer on bed rest, Carlos was due to be discharged from the hospital. A figure, painted in orange, stands on top of a central mound of grass. His back to the viewer, he faces a huge sun whose rays spread across the picture. The way the figure stands on the mound of grass seems to suggest a sort of rebirth from the earth. This is emphasized if we regard the womblike nature of the other picture. A black bird flies towards the sun and, on the right hand side, the figure holds a bloody sword aloft with both his hands. Balls or bubbles float in the atmosphere.

Figure CI.2.

Let us turn now to each of the chapters, and see what light they might shed on our understanding of the pictures.

Kramer's book on "art as therapy" was published in 1971 (Kramer, 1971), the year that I began to work as an art therapist, and I remember how helpful it was to read an art therapist who was giving some form to the experience that I intuitively knew worked. Although this case is from many years later in my career, I turn to the question of how we might view these two pictures in terms of sublimation. Kramer, referring to Freud writes that: "'*sublimation*' designates processes whereby primitive urges, emanating from the id, are transformed by the ego into complex acts that do not serve direct instinctual gratification. In the course of this transformation, primitive behavior, necessarily asocial, gives way to activities that are ego-syntonic and are as a rule socially productive" (p. 28).

Her discussion shows how art in therapy can be a form of sublimation, through which this process of transformation can take place. Kramer stresses the need for optimal conditions, and writes that: "Sublimation cannot be planned or plotted. All we can do is establish an atmosphere wherein the group of processes of which it is born can unfold" (p. 38).

Providing the circumstances where such transformation can take place is the task of the art therapist. Containment and holding were certainly a significant aspect of the work with Carlos. For a patient presenting with anorexia, control is a significant issue, and art is a particularly helpful offering as it does, as a means of autonomous self-motivated exploration. In art therapy the therapist may observe without being experienced as intrusive; thus she "establishes an atmosphere where this [transformation] begins to unfold."

Regarding the two pictures, I suggest that sublimation can be seen to have been taking place. If we regard "The Bubble" (Figure CI.1) we see a deathly figure that has no autonomy; it seems to be without motivation, or libido, as is emphasised by the lack of genitals, an impression added to by the tentative use of art materials. If we turn to "The Hero" (Figure CI.2), we see a huge movement has taken place. This is evident both in the use of paint, and in the imagery. The sword, for example, can be seen in many different ways. First it is a sword dripping with drops of blood and can be seen as symbolic of aggression. This fits with his own interpretation of the picture.

In the early days of his treatment Carlos was depressed, regressed, and unaware of his anger. Now, ten months later, he was very aware of it and he had, so to speak, taken up the sword and done battle with his inner world oppressors. His psychological understanding had developed, and he emerges from the deathly womb in which the figure had been trapped. We might understand that his anger has been transformed into a positive force for life. Libido is evident in many aspects of the picture; in the sword and in the way the sun seems to flood the whole scene. Further, if the sword is viewed as the penis of the artist, we see that his previous impotence is now transformed into a potent state. He holds his sex aloft. If we consider Kramer's view that as the transformation takes place "primitive behavior . . . gives way to activities that are ego-syntonic" (p. 28). then we could describe this process, in part, in terms of sublimation.

In her discussion of symbolism (Chapter 3), Laurie Wilson focuses on the importance of the ability to symbolize in healthy development. She argues that those patients with "an impaired symbolic function . . . can be helped by the making of visual images" (p. 47). In Wilson's case material she gives examples of the movement achieved first through art, and then through the gradually attained conscious awareness of the meaning of the art works. I concur with her findings (see Killick & Schaverien, 1997). The impairment of symbolic functioning is an integral aspect of anorexia, as evidenced by the concrete manner in which unconscious psychological problems become focused on food. Food becomes a central concern, masking the underlying psychological issues.

I have suggested that, as a *transactional object*, the artwork may offer a means of transition from the concrete obsession with food to a more symbolic form of relating. This seems to be a similar movement to that which Wilson discusses. She proposes that art offers a means of transformation in the psychological state. In association with the last example in her chapter, she writes that she felt "that some deeply unconscious material had shifted upward and had reached a level of preconsciousness by virtue of taking form in the art" (p. 52).

This helps in understanding the process with Carlos, as we can see that, by the time he made "The Hero," something that had previously been unconscious (in "The Bubble") was now nearer to consciousness. The fact that the sword is turned outward seems to point to this, as well as the fact that it is held to the right hand side, which, in classical Jungian terms, could be understood to be the conscious side of the figure. This was confirmed when, regarding this picture, Carlos pointed at the sword and said "Previously this would have been turned inward."

The object relations discussed by Arthur Robbins (Chapter 4) reveal the creative process in action. His patient comes to life as a person, and conveys an integration of object relations theory and art therapy. Robbins writes "Art therapy. . . strives to promote new levels of perceptual organization, that involve shifts in energy patterns" (p. 60). This change in energy can be observed in the contrast between Carlos' two pictures. Robbins writes that "the borderline personality tends toward fusion states and a pervasive use of splitting good and bad in his search for the ideal; the narcissistic personality takes refuge in a grandiose self" (p. 61).

Anorexia is a borderline state, and the splitting Robbins discusses was evident in the early stages, where all the good was outside of Carlos and the bad was within him. In

Figure CI.1 the deathly consequences of tarrying too long with the desire for fusion with a longed for maternal shelter, are all too apparent. The later picture (Figure CI.2) could be seen as evidence of a rather grandiose phase, and indeed Carlos was quite high at that stage, but the triumph is also in attaining separation. The important thing is that such states are recognized and mediated via the therapeutic relationship. Robbins concludes: "our challenge is one of utilizing these concepts from psychiatry and psychoanalysis while maintaining the visions and perceptions we have as artists" (p. 64). It seems to me that this is still a very important project for art therapy.

In Chapter 5, Mildred Lachman-Chapin discusses two rather different forms of mirroring: the artwork as mirror, and the mirroring function of the art therapist. Influenced by Kohut's self psychology, she proposes that certain forms of narcissistic disturbance respond to the mirroring of the art form. She writes of two developmental configurations of narcissism, when the first, and assumed, merger of the infant with the mother begins to fail. At this point the child adopts an "'I am perfect" view of the self. The second is the "you are perfect and I am part of you" view of the parent. These defensive positions protect the self from loss and are, as she points out, age appropriate aspects of the development of the self. Problems arise when these become the fixed means of relating, which we sometimes meet in adult clients. During this stage, affirmation by the mother could be understood to be a form of mirroring. In normal development the mother signals her approval of the child in all sorts of ways.

Lachman-Chapin suggests that there is a similar form of affirmation for the client who "becomes invested in the product of his or her *own* action—that is, in his or her *own* artwork" (p. 67). Thus her point is, as I understand it, that there is affirmation first in making the artwork, and secondly, in the response from the therapist as she watches the client at work. The therapist holds out "the promise of ultimate approval for the real accomplishment; that is, for departure from symbiosis" (p. 68).

With Carlos, both of these forms of mirroring were significant. His pictures mirrored back to him, affirming his state; while my interest and attention, as his therapist, encouraged and affirmed that what he was doing was worthwhile. The "Bubble" picture (Figure CI.1) seemed to confirm his state to him, bringing home to him just how emaciated he was. At the time he wrote: "I feel very embryo/baby like and also very old and deathly." A very different sense of self was mirrored in "The Hero" picture. Here his self-confidence in his separate state was affirmed by seeing the picture. Then, when he showed this picture to me, I shared his pleasure in his new state, which also could be understood to be a form of positive mirroring.

A different form of mirroring discussed by Lachman-Chapin is more controversial. She writes that our qualities as artists equip us to function in particular ways, one of which is making art alongside the client. She argues that this can be understood as a form of mirroring. Whether or not this approach is deemed appropriate depends on the client and the setting. The problem, as I see it, is that it introduces complex transference material. For example, the client may envy the therapist's artistic ability, and so feel inhibited in attempting to begin. Perhaps the therapist may not engage in her own art for real because, if she did, she might get too engrossed in her own work and her attention is then taken from the client. Thus, the affirmation of the first form of mirroring is forfeited. However, in reading the chapter, I was convinced that this approach worked with the client described by Lachman-Chapin. Therefore, I think its application needs careful consideration and may be helpful with certain clients.

Michael Edwards' chapter integrates the history and theory of Jungian practice. He sets Jung's historical relationship to art therapy in context, and then presents ways in which the artwork operates as mediator within the therapeutic relationship. The artwork mediates between patient and therapist. Even when resistances are high and the patient produces nothing, the art therapist remains a representative of symbolic communication through art ... "Making a mark on paper or twisting clay into the first shape that suggests itself, begins as an entirely private matter" (p. 84). This privacy was a very important aspect of the process for Carlos, who needed to be able to make his first marks in privacy. Only later did he choose to show the pictures to me.

Edwards discusses the personification of images. He writes of "a sense of *otherness* about one's own visual images [which] is also a sense of personification and that from this point ... a dialogue with the unconscious can begin" (p. 86). This dialogue with the image is a very Jungian approach, yet it is used by many art therapists without really understanding from whence the idea first came. Again, the theory fits my example. Carlos did engage in dialogue with his images, and he also wrote about them. In this way their meanings became embellished, and led to further realizations.

Edwards writes graphically of the influence and effects of such imagery, and I would like to extract a few lines, which I think say a great deal about the very special qualities offered by art in therapy: "the moment at which the image becomes a part of the outer world; it inhabits the room and exerts its own influence on whoever happens to be there. The completed image, however incomplete, primitive, regressive, or alien, is a new factor in the situation; it is both a statement about and a personification of what was formerly an inner experience" (pp. 86–87).

As indicated in Rubin's introduction, the chapters by Edwards and Wallace are complementary; the one flowing easily from the other. Edith Wallace describes active imagination as an approach, which takes the image's journey forward through dialogue. In a way, it offers a background to all the chapters in this psychodynamic section of the book. Active imagination underlies many art therapy approaches, but it is often taken for granted. This is true, even though not all art therapists who apply this method have read Jung.

Active imagination is rarely so well described and explained as it is here. The distinction is made between dreams where the dreamer is asleep and active imagination, which takes place when the protagonist is awake. Active imagination becomes manifest through art and through writing, as long as the censor of the conscious mind can be, so to speak, placed in neutral. Wallace demonstrates through a very moving case example how the psyche, given the right conditions, will lead and show the way.

For a final time I turn again to the case of Carlos. His pictures, and the record he kept of his associations to them, were a form of active imagination. The series, from which the two pictures shown here are extracted, reveals a journey which was itself a form of active imagination. Carlos' body was safely held in the bed in the hospital ward and he was taken care of. This left him free to embark on a psychological journey and, a bit like snapshots taken on the way, his pictures give a sense of the road that he traveled. The "Bubble" picture was his starting place, and the "Hero" shows where his journey had arrived at the end of his treatment.

So having, I hope, shown that I am convinced by the theoretical contributions of this section of this book, I return to the questions with which I began. Is this still relevant for practice today? I certainly think so, and hope that my commentary has shown this to be the case. The second question is—where might this lead in terms of future research?

Art therapists, trained in art, used to lack confidence in the validity of their own aesthetic tradition, but this book shows that this is not the case any more. Gone are the days when the art person was seen as the deferential handmaiden of the psychiatrist. Since those early days, art therapists are able to speak with the weight of authority of the understanding of their own practice. Much of this is due to books like this one, and to the increasing investment of time and money in art therapy research. Since 1987 when the first edition of this book was written there has been a significant increase in art therapy research. This is an immense help in developing a grounded professional identity.

Art therapists still work with colleagues trained in scientific disciplines, and this does offer the potential for interesting dialogue as well as professional jealousies. Colleagues whose formative experiences lie in the area of science are sometimes puzzled; simultaneously envying the alchemy of the art materials and yet fearing its power. In order to authenticate practice, art therapists may need to use medical terminology when discussing clinical work. We, the artists, learn the language of science and to speak of pathology, of structures of the mind, of the workings of the synapses of the brain.

Then, turning to the developmental models of psychoanalysis, which seems to offer a more compatible companion for art in psychotherapy, we use the theories of Freud and his followers. Still, caution is required if we are not to pathologize the image—that life force of the imagination. Diagnosis and interpretation are important, but if we are not inadvertently to extinguish the vitality of the client's relationship to the artwork, we must wait for the image to interpret itself, to reveal its multiple layered meanings. More art therapy research is needed, but using methods and language that do not distort the process to fit some scientific norm. Genuine inquiry is required, and the combination of art and psychoanalysis is one area for further investigation.

Wherever they are working, art therapists offer their clients the opportunity to fashion otherwise inexpressible patterns of psyche and present them in a physical form. As the chapters in this book show, this is an autonomous form of experience, which sometimes reveals far more than was previously known. The common factor, in the diverse chapters in this section, is the conviction of the healing potential of art. Art can offer a spark in the "dark night of the soul," but analytic understanding mediates.

☐ References

Killick, K. & Schaverien, J. (Eds.). (1997). *Art, psychotherapy and psychosis.* London: Routledge.

Kramer, E. (1971). *Art as therapy with children.* New York: Schocken Books.

Schaverien, Joy (1992). *The revealing image: Analytical art psychotherapy in theory & practice.* London: Routledge.

Schaverien, J. (1995). *Desire and the female therapist: Engendered gazes in art therapy and psychotherapy.* London: Routledge.

HUMANISTIC
APPROACHES

HUMANISTIC
APPROACHES

The chapters in this section do not derive from a shared theoretical framework like those in the first, where all acknowledge a debt to either Freud or Jung. What they have in common is an optimistic view of human nature and of the human condition, seeing people in a process of growth and development, with the capacity to take responsibility for their fate. Those initiating "third-force" movements in psychology did so partly in reaction to the analytic idea of "psychic determinism," that humans are at the mercy of unconscious dynamics, which must be known to be in charge.

Indeed, many art therapists cite the shortcomings of psychoanalytic theory as one of their reasons for turning to other frameworks (e.g., chapter authors Garai, Betensky, Allen, and Rogers); and Janie Rhyne's teacher, Fritz Perls, was a disillusioned analyst. Jung's ideas, in contrast, are felt by many to be more compatible with humanistic approaches (cf. Garai, Rogers, and Allen).

Each of the approaches in this section tends to be assertively open-minded and anti-doctrinaire. There is no "classical" technique in either humanistic or transpersonal psychotherapy. Indeed, such a notion is quite out of synchrony with the individualistic thrust of both the founders and the followers of these orientations.

One humanistic approach not included in the first edition of this book was that known as "person-centered" (formerly "client-centered"), developed by psychologist Carl Rogers. In the interim, his daughter Natalie published *The Creative Connection*, using multiple modalities in a person-centered context. Like Shaun McNiff (Part V, Chapter 20), she calls her work "expressive arts therapy" rather than "art therapy;" though for both art is central. More than one art form is also used by Garai, Allen, as well as by Rhyne, especially in her book (1973/1996).

This does not mean that offering many expressive modalities is limited to humanistic art therapists. In this book alone, examples are found in the chapters on Jungian, developmental, and integrative approaches (e.g., McNiff and Henley). Other contributors have written elsewhere about their use of movement, drama, music, and poetry along with art; including myself, Lachman-Chapin, Moon, Robbins, and Wadeson.

It is probably no accident that "intermodal" ways of working are especially appealing to therapists for whom spirituality is important, since religious rituals have always made use of the evocative power of all of the arts—music, dance, drama, and many visual forms: face and body decoration, masks, costumes, sand painting, fetishes, etc.

Currently, there is a growing popularity among art therapists of what are sometimes called "fourth force" or "transpersonal" (spiritual) approaches. Developed within humanistic psychology, they are a logical extension of focus from the individual to his or her place in the larger community, in the world, and in the universe (cf. Farrelly-Hansen, 2000; Franklin, 2000; Horovitz-Darby, 1994: Moon, 1997; Myers, 1999).

Although psychodynamic approaches still dominate art therapy, it would seem that humanistic ones continue to increase in popularity, especially among those defining their orientation as "eclectic."

☐ References

Farrelly-Hansen, M. (Ed.). (2001). *Spirituality & art therapy: Living the connection*. Philadelphia: Jessica Kingsley.

Franklin, M. (2000). Art practice/psychotherapy practice/contemplative practice: Sitting on the dove's tail. *Guidance & Counseling, 15*(3), 18–22.

Horovitz-Darby, E. G. (1994). *Spiritual art therapy*. Springfield, IL: Charles C. Thomas.

Moon, B. (1997). *Art & soul*. Springfield, IL: Charles C. Thomas.

Myers, T. (Ed.). (1999). *The soul of creativity*. Novato, CA: New World Library.

Rhyne, J. (1973/1996). *Gestalt art experience*. Chicago, IL: Magnolia Street Publishers.

Rogers, N. (1993). *The creative connection*. Palo Alto, CA: Science & Behavior Books.

CHAPTER

Mala Betensky

Phenomenological Art Therapy

The term *phenomenology*, known since the middle of the 18th century, has been elaborated on by a number of philosophers. Husserl (1913/1976) gave it a new meaning as the Science of Consciousness, a study of phenomena (things, objects) as they present themselves in consciousness as immediate experiences. A phenomenon (a verbal noun, from the Greek verb "to appear") can be perceived and observed with our senses and our minds. Phenomena include visible, touchable, and audible things in the world around us, as well as all that belongs in the realm of mental experience. Through the study of consciousness, Husserl tried to reduce the perception of phenomena to their essence.

Phenomenology grew into a movement in Western Europe, reached the United States mid-century, and was introduced into philosophy and psychology. Phenomenology also influenced psychotherapies, particularly humanistic ones, with a call to turn "to the things themselves," and to an investigation of the fullness of subjective experiencing of "things," away from preconceived or inferred theories about them.

I became acquainted with philosophical phenomenology as a student. Its interest in a qualitative exploration of the human experience, and its opposition to restricting psychology to behavior or to reductionist views in the study of man, was what I was looking for. I had already arrived at a synthesis of my background and interest in psychology, psychotherapy, the history of ideas, and art. But I was searching for a method that I could use, and phenomenology seemed to answer my quest.

By then, art had become central in my therapeutic work, and both phenomenological theory and method felt appropriate for art therapy (Betensky, 1976, 1978; Betensky & Nucho, 1979). Since theory is essential to art therapy, which is empirically oriented, I shall first explain a basic concept of phenomenology: intentionality (Husserl, 1913/1976).

Man in the World—The Subject of Intentionality

Art has to do with man and his very being. In art therapy, we often meet overburdened man, preoccupied with his own world and its stresses. At times he is compelled to flee

Dr. Betensky's first book, *Self-discovery through Self-Expression*, was published in 1973. In 1995 she published her second book, *What do you see?* in which she describes her phenomenological approach in greater detail.

from the burden—into pathology. His art-therapeutic work may become a source not only of immediate release, but also a *pre-intentional* record of his experience of stress and flight. Guided by a therapist into the *intentional* perception and study of his art, truly seeing his own painting or sculpture may open new possibilities for him.

The act of *seeing* is vital. Perhaps this is one of art therapy's most important contributions to psychotherapy and to phenomenology, because art therapy pays attention to authentic experience in a twofold way. First, clients in art therapy produce a work that is a direct experience. Then, they see its appearance in their eyes and in their immediate consciousness, and this is a second direct experience. In this, they need some help in learning how to look, in order to see all that can be seen in the art production.

When I succeeded in suspending all my *a priori* judgments and all acquired notions about what I was supposed to see, when I trained my eyes to look with openness and with intention at the art object, I began to see things in that object that I had not seen before. I began to understand the truth in Merleau-Ponty's statement that "to look at an object is to inhabit it and from this habitation to grasp all things" (1962, p. 168). This is a phenomenologist's way of looking in order to see—with intentionality.

Intentionality and Meaning

Intentionality means that I am intent on what I am looking at. With my intent look, I make it appear to my consciousness more clearly than before. The object of my attention begins to exist for me more than it did before. It is becoming important to me. Now it *means* something to me. At times, a meaning becomes vital to my existence, to my being. Man is an intentional being, with an intentional consciousness that makes the world actual to him. Intentionality may even help to invent new worlds, and to make the invisible visible, as in the arts and sciences.

Intentionality as Relatedness

Intentionality also means that our consciousness always relates to somebody or to something, which means that it is always directed to reality. A client of mine, overburdened and withdrawn, persisted in drawing tables, stools, airplanes on the ground, and other still objects. Cautious about making contact with the world, he was trying to direct his intentionality first to inanimate objects. He was not simply hiding his feelings. On the contrary, he was turning toward real objects and was trying to get to know them in the *lebenswelt*, the everyday life. Hence, his production of stools and tables in many positions. He was starting to return from an escape from being in the world.

Intentionality and Body

Intentionality of consciousness resides in the body, which explains man's orientation to the world. We are born into a world that is already there; our body meets the world. With our senses developing along with the body and with consciousness, we discern things in the world. Nor do we go about it piecemeal, appropriating each activity to its own sense organ alone. When our eyes see and our ears hear, it is not a function of the eyes or ears alone; it is the whole body that is conscious of what the eye sees and what the ear hears in the visible/sonorous world.

The famous art teacher Nicolaides (1941) expressed it well when he taught his students how to look at a model. He said that "what the eye sees, i.e., the various parts of the body, actions and directions, is but the result of the inner impulse, and to understand that one must use something more than the eyes." When we run or rush, our whole body is in motion, intent on the purpose and destination of our running. Thus, our body is permeated with intentionality within the wider unity of the body.

Unity of Body

The wider unity of the body includes sexuality. Merleau-Ponty (1962) studied the phenomenological nature of sexuality, in contrast to the psychoanalytic view of artistic symbols (cf. Arnheim, 1972a). He saw sexuality as finding its expression in many behavioral ways that are not explicitly sexual. Phenomenologically seen, sexuality is not a force by itself. It transcends itself, along with other human forces, and merges with them, so that we cannot pinpoint exactly which force makes us do what. Together, these forces characterize our body in a subjectively unique unity.

Unity of Emotion and Unity of Expression

The same intentionality permeates emotion, in contrast to a dualistic view. In Strasser's (1977) philosophy of feeling, emotion is a "determinate mode of man's gradually accustoming himself to the world," characterized by *motus* or movement. This explains the animation or excitement of the whole person in anticipation of an emotional experience. *Motus* is also evident in many manifestations of expressivity characterized by the unity of body-consciousness-feeling. The experience of *motus* is known to artists and inventors. Art therapists, too, notice the rising *motus* in the subtle, but observable transition in their clients' art processes, from pleasurable play with art materials to more serious art expression.

Established by Klages (1936) as the principle of the *unity of expression*, it was submerged in American psychology by the impact of Freudian psychology and the wave of behaviorism. But it has reappeared in more elaborate form in Strasser's (1977) work, and in the writings of Kwant (1978), who studies expression as a creative disclosure of being. Strasser places emotion *within* intentionality, and identifies three phases accompanying expression. The pre-intentional phase is a vague state experienced as some pressure generated from an impression, ever so slight, of an unidentified object in the field of vision. The vagueness becomes intentional in the second phase, where it connects with the identified object. It turns meta-intentional in the third phase, when the object is fully perceived and felt as part of one's existence.

Meaning

With this crescendo of intentionality of emotion in relation to the object—like a client's art expression—an additional factor emerges: meaning (Frankl, 1969). Meaning appears early in life when the baby busies its eyes with a visual area, in an effort to structure a bit of the surrounding reality. This is the child's movement toward the world, a first expressive activity, on a preconscious and pre-intentional level. In the process of growth, it becomes conscious, emotion-laden, and meaningful, when the child interacts with the world. Then, the child organizes the visual field so that a certain object in that field becomes visible, and thereby begins to exist more than other things in that field of vision. It then takes on some importance, and thus becomes meaningful.

I often observe a similar structuring and emergence of meaning in my clients' discoveries as they look at their art expressions. I also find that the emergence of meanings, even small ones, as when a line or a color suddenly becomes visible, enables clients to see unrealized possibilities or untapped potencies. This may have some bearing on the question of the unconscious in phenomenological thinking about art therapy.

Phenomenology of the Unconscious

The vagueness of stirrings toward an object yet to be identified in a visual field, classified in phenomenology as preconscious and pre-intentional, is the closest meeting point between psychoanalysis and phenomenology. The study of consciousness was not well known at the time that Freud formulated his brilliant conceptions, nor were the founders of phenomenology interested in psychoanalysis. Much the same could be said about Gestalt psychology in its beginnings. The lack of contact among these orientations is easily understood, as a result of each school's total focusing on the challenge of its own early endeavors.

Later, however, phenomenologists did write about the unconscious, Husserl stating that it "is anything but a phenomenological nothing, but itself is a marginal mode *(Grenzmodus)* of consciousness" (Spiegelberg, 1972, p. 236). Heidegger (1960) comes somewhat closer in his concept of *Dasein* (being-in-the-world). There are, he says, two dimensions of being: the one that does not show itself (ontological), which is intimately interwoven with the one that does show itself (ontic). Phenomenology can reveal the concealed dimension of being. Thus, unconscious processes are hidden in the ontological dimension of *Dasein*, which phenomenology can reveal (Richardson, 1965). Yet Heidegger is also convinced that beyond the phenomena of phenomenology there is "nothing else."

It seems to me that art therapy comes closest to fulfilling the task that Heidegger assigned to phenomenology: revealing the hidden aspects of man's being as phenomena accessible to consciousness and to conscious investigation. Art therapy can best achieve this aim phenomenologically by means of a free expressive process, with art materials freely chosen by the client, along with a method in which the client views his art production as a phenomenon within a structured field of vision.

☐ Special Features of the Approach

From studies in the psychology of art (Kreitler & Kreitler, 1972), we learn that the structural components of art carry and convey expressive qualities. In my own research, round and oval lines in pastel colors conveyed warm emotions; strong reds and some other basic colors indicated strong, aggressive, but also loving feelings; zigzag lines with pointed angles were related to violence; and upward or downward lines expressed corresponding moods and modes of being. While touching on universal meanings in the fine arts, in art therapy these convey mostly subjective meanings about the overburdened self, though occasionally they approach universal truths in their untrained simplicity.

The Gestalt psychology of art also contributes much to art therapy, with its concepts of a Gestalt—its inner relationships and "whole" qualities—and the importance of seeing (Arnheim, 1969, 1972b). Gestalt psychology also contributes its theory of *isomorphism*, which gains more clarity in light of the phenomenological unity and intentionality of body.

Clinical psychology (particularly the Rorschach examination and some drawing tests) is capable of enriching art therapy, if we know how to use such aspects as color, form, and movement, and can skillfully relate them to the appropriate elements of clients' art expressions. On the Rorschach, *form* is the shape of a blot visually perceived as fixed in its outline; *color* responses are determined by color and form as well as by color alone; and *movement* responses are influenced by subjects' visual memories of movement observed, experienced, or imagined in relation to form or to parts of it. From experience and observation in art therapy we know that areas, even daubs, of color can define form; that in some productions areas of color merge in ways that defy form; that in others form dominates color; and that in still others color is omitted in parts or details of an otherwise-chromatic painting. We also see movement in patient art, and stillness in the absence of movement; and we can distinguish inward and outward kinds of movement.

#13

The following example shows similarities and differences between Rorschach responses, formally structured in a perceptive process, and spontaneous art expression, informally based on a creative process.

The Rorschach and Mrs. N.

On the Rorschach, Mrs. N. scored outstanding sharpness of form visualization in many tiny areas of the blots. She gave no color responses, even on the most colorful cards, and had only one response with color as a second determinant. Good, original, and miniscule form was her dominant response. Her protocol was that of an intelligent person in stabilized depression.

Reluctant to use art materials, she agreed to "play" with paint and pastels. In all of her seven productions on large (18″ × 24″) paper, the entire surface was covered with light grays, dark grays, blue-grays, and gray-browns, which spread over a few daubs of red and yellow crowded together in the bottom right corner. No form was directly visible, nor did the colors define form. Yet her involvement was visibly growing and intriguing to me. When the productions were mounted for the "What do you see?" procedure, I was amazed to see—among the light and dark shadings of the flowing colors—tiny clear figures and faces with large eyes, as I followed her finger tracing the outlines of the now-visible forms.

Her art productions, springing from the creative process, concurred with the statistically calculated Rorschach diagnosis. On the Rorschach she perceived and reported depression. In her artwork she painted the depression spreading over her emotions. Sharpness of minute form perception, along with a scarcity of color responses, is, indeed, a symptom of profound depression. Thus, an art therapist may notice indications of depression in a client's use of color and form, even without a Rorschach. The concurrence of my client's painting with her Rorschach responses and diagnosis helped me not only to better understand her difficulties, but also to decide about the direction of art therapy with her.

#13

#5

The House-Tree-Person (H-T-P) Drawing Test

The H-T-P test (Buck, 1948) is popularly, but often inappropriately, used by art therapists as a "technique." It can be very beneficial to clients when properly used, not when taken out of its intended context, but as a diagnostic and therapeutic method. During my internship in child psychotherapy at a mental health clinic in the late 50's, I asked the children to use color in the H-T-P, first as an experiment, then routinely as a sequel to the original pencil-and-paper version, for diagnostic purposes.

#5

For therapeutic purposes, I mount the two sets of products vertically. There are then two parallel columns of pictures that can be examined silently, horizontally as well

#5,
#18

as vertically, by the clients. This viewing is followed by description and unfolding according to the phenomenological method. This therapeutic application of the H-T-P test has proved to be most fruitful as a source of clients' self-discovery, particularly in regard to how they feel about themselves in the present, how they felt about themselves in the past, and how they feel about the world they live in.

Art Materials

Another essential feature is art materials. Several sizes and textures of paper, other surfaces for painting or drawing, pastels, poster paints, water colors, collage materials, soft wood, earth clay, and the appropriate tools should all be available. These materials are active participants in the client's artwork. They challenge sight and touch. They stimulate emotional arousal and consciousness. Being themselves bits of the world, these materials contribute to the client's getting back in touch with the world. Thus, there is an ongoing dynamic process between material and art maker. It is of special interest to notice which of the materials evokes the most expressiveness (Betensky, 1982).

Before the Artwork Process

Informal experimentation with art materials is most helpful—like mixing paints, or dropping a drop of one color into another to watch how the color spreads, and then reversing the sequence. Such "experiments" serve not only as a "warmup," but also as a pleasurable way of creating new possibilities and taking small, safe risks.

Words

The phenomenological approach does use speech, because words are expression, just as art is; because consciousness, thought, and speech are one; and because in phenomenology we intend to articulate, and that is the job of words. In this method, however, words have a special role at an appropriate time, as specified in the following discussion.

The Art Therapist

The therapist's task is to watch the client at work, in addition to giving active guidance or participating in other ways. It is largely a silent task, but the therapist as participant-observer is far from passive. He or she is busy unobtrusively observing the client's facial and bodily expressions of moods, and modes of choosing and using art materials during the creative process. Sensing to what extent the client needs the art therapist's physical closeness or other support is another aspect of the task, and noticing one's own visceral and emotional reactions to what the client does is yet another.

☐ The Phenomenological Method of Art Therapy

Table 8.1 is a general outline, applicable to individual sessions as well as to the overall process of therapy. The first two sequences were dealt with earlier. Its uniqueness lies in sequences three and four.

TABLE 8.1. The phenomenological method of art therapy

Sequence 1:	Pre-art play with art materials
	Direct experiencing
Sequence 2:	The process of artwork—Creating a phenomenon
Sequence 3:	Phenomenological intuiting
	***Phase 1*: Perceiving**
	1. Visual display
	2. Distancing
	3. Intentional looking
	***Phase 2*: What-do-you-see procedure**
	1. Phenomenological description
	2. Phenomenological unfolding
Sequence 4:	Phenomenological integration

#20

Sequence 3: Phenomenological Intuiting

This deals with the client's direct experience of his production, in two phases. Phase 1, *Perceiving* facilitates its perception in three steps. The first step is *Visual Display* of the art expression. When the client indicates to the therapist that the artwork is completed, both place the sculpture or tape the picture where it can be conveniently viewed.

The next step is *Distancing:* The therapist suggests that both of them step back or move their chairs back to gain perspective. The art product is now a phenomenon with an existence of its own. It is now a part of the world, separate from its maker, with its own properties. It can now be examined objectively, from a distance, and without preconceived notions. The powerful emotions contained in the visual product can now be viewed with a certain measure of detachment.

The third step is the process of *Intentional Looking* at the art expression. The therapist now asks the client to take a long look at the picture, sculpture, or collage. She may say something like, "Now take a good look at it. First study it and see what you can observe. When the picture is right in front of your eyes, you don't always notice things that you can see later when you have gained some distance from your picture. So, take a long look and try to see everything that can be seen in your art."

The client now concentrates and looks, without distractions. He is in communication with the phenomenon he has produced. The art maker becomes the receiver of messages deposited, half-knowingly, in the artwork. Now, as beholder, the client receives the messages embedded in the art expression, which has become the phenomenal field. Awareness is now deepened and enriched by new observations, which seem like discoveries.

It is important for the therapist to realize that a great deal of this activity may be taking place in silence. It is therefore essential that the client be given sufficient time to examine the artwork and, most important, that the therapist learn the importance of silence, develop the ease to bear it, and guard against casual comments that might distract the client.

#7

In Phase 2, *What do you see?*, the therapist invites the client to share the results of the three earlier steps: Visual Display, Distancing, and Intentional Looking. The therapist asks, "*What do you see?*" This simple question contains two fundamental aspects of the phenomenological approach. One is the importance of individual perception and meaning—what do *you* see? You, the creator, do not need to see the picture the way others do. *Your* way of seeing is essential, and is what we are now interested in. This question underscores the rightness and value of subjective reality. According to the phenomenological view, each person's inner reality is a fact of paramount importance.

The other notion contained in the question "What do you see?" deals with phenomenological evidence. All that can be *seen* is seen in the art expression itself, not surmised or thought out from a pre-established theory. This is achieved by guiding the client to notice specific structural components in the artwork and the feelings they convey; how certain components relate to one or more others; whether they clash, complement, or coexist; what the organization is; whether the components of the content may be grouped in any way; what these groupings share in common; and whether that is seen in the art itself. Vague feelings slowly reach awareness, and a new ability to identify and name them appears.

Phenomenological Description. Phenomenological seeing is getting the self in touch with the art expression in a very precise way. This is possible by virtue of a kinship and an ongoing interaction between the self and the outer world, the art expression serving as the center. In answer to "What do you see?" the client-turned-beholder gives a *description*, as precisely as he can, of what is in the picture. The art therapist's guidance may be needed in naming the elements of the art.

Phenomenological Unfolding. The phenomenological discussion of the art expression is the second step. The therapist helps the client to unfold, as it were, the private meanings contained on various levels in the visual product. As in the previous phase, the therapist merely indicates points for discussion, addressing components and objects *in* the art.

The following excerpt from a 12-year-old girl's *description* of her picture (Figure. 8.1) shows how the art therapist's initiatives are limited to guidance in the naming of elements, and addressing points for discussion about components and objects in the art.

Therapist: *What do you see, J?*

J: *I see a girl playing with her ball in the park.*

T: *Playing with her ball.*

J: *Can I say something else I just saw?*

T: *Of course, just say it.*

J: *Well, now I see that she doesn't really care to play with the ball.*

T: *Mmm . . . I was wondering about that. What else do you see?*

J: *Nothing, really. Oh, over there is her dad, in the back, kind of behind.*

T: *Mm hmm. Her dad.*

J: *Yeah. And he doesn't care to walk. [sounds angry]*

T: *What else can you see on your picture?*

J: *[pointing far up] Oh, oh, see that house? That's our house, and see my mom? She goes back into the house? See, she told my dad to take me to the park and . . . and now I don't see anything else. [abruptly, cries, then quiet]*

T: *[handing a tissue to J] Well, I remember, when I had tears in my eyes I couldn't see well at all, so I will see for you right now. And what I see on your picture has lots of bright colors and is very pleasant to look at.*

J: *You mean the sun and the trees? The sun, I made it setting. It makes everything in the park so pretty.*

Figure 8.1.

T: *Yes, that is what I see, and you put it all in the picture. Now, what would you call all these things at sunset on your picture—things that are not people, but that make people feel what you just described? Find a word for it, can you?*

J: *You mean, the whole park and the sky and the sun? Something like what's around? Or background?*

T: *That's it, you just said it, background. Now let's go back to the people in the foreground.*

J: *The girl and her dad.*

T: *Mm hmm. What on the picture shows us that she doesn't really care to play with the ball, and that Dad doesn't really care to walk? Can you take another look and tell us?*

J: *Well, see, the ball is rolling away, almost to the end of the paper, and she doesn't run after it. She just walks, and her face is, kind of, worried? The mouth . . . oh, I don't know how to draw what a mouth . . . looks like. [grimaces]*

T: *What about the mouth on the picture?*

J: *It's just a straight line, looks like mad or something.*

T: *And the father?*

J: *Oh, he looks like he wasn't there. See, he didn't want to go. He was mad with me. And, oh look, I forgot to fill in his blazer. And I didn't hardly make him a face.*

Answers to the question "What do you see?" often act as catalysts, drawing out the essence of the existential dilemma as simply as a client is able to state it. A withdrawn adolescent boy who produced a picture of a fish in a net responded to this question with a reality-oriented description: "I see a fish . . . caught in a net." He went on to say, with growing tension in his voice, that the fish "feels sad and mad."

In the next session the *description* continued, when the boy was able to point to the lines in the picture that conveyed the "stiffness" of the fish and its immobility in contrast to the brilliant colors "decorating" the fish. In reply to the therapist's wonderment about this contrast, the boy said that the fish was "mad . . . because *he* couldn't show his colors to all the other fishes in the water." The pronoun "he" served as a transition to the boy's subsequent ability to refer directly to himself. This is an example of a process of self-discovery in *becoming*: the pre-intentional level of identifying himself with the fish was becoming intentional.

An adolescent girl responded to the question about her picture (Figure 8.2): "Well, I see a group of people. They are sort of standing around and they look sort of distressed, and everything." These first statements are then discussed and further specified, and the girl's often-used "and everything," for which she had no clear concept (though it meant something to her), is gradually clarified and understood by both client and therapist, as the discussion of the artwork proceeds. The therapist must be a good listener to pick up vague clues from a client's slow and laborious verbal reflections about art expressions.

The unfolding of the ideas and feelings contained in the art usually proceeds along one of two lines. One starts with the client, and deals with subject matter. The other emphasizes structural properties and the relationships among them. The therapist will usually listen to the client's description of content and will then turn to structure. With the adolescent girl, the therapist tried to find out: Who might the people be? Why are they all huddled together. Are they trying to protect themselves from the cold or, perhaps, from something else? What is happening to them right now? What might happen in a moment? As much as this approach yields in the client's interesting observations about subject matter, it is not all.

Figure 8.2.

From a phenomenological perspective, discussions of content are less fruitful than the possibilities offered by the structural components of the artwork. With their ability to convey emotional meanings, they represent the inner reality of the client more accurately and more acutely than the content, which is on a somewhat more disguised level of symbolization.

#7

The following dialogue and picture are part of the author's videotaped art therapy session, "Making a Scribble" (Nucho, 1977).

T: *Now let's take a look at the placement of the figures. Which figures are placed where on the sheet of paper?*

Cl: *Well, the people are all sorta huddled together, and um . . . they seem like they are all sorta huddled together in little groups . . .*

T: *Which groups are huddled together? Can you make some groupings there?*

Cl: *This group right here and these three figures . . . and these three right here and those two . . . and that one up there . . .*

In a later session, "that one up there" became the center of self-discovery: the girl recognized herself.

Sequence 4: Phenomenological Integration

The last sequence is phenomenological integration, which includes three aspects of self-discovery. The first consists of the client's reflections on the development of the artwork. The person may comment on the original intentions and on the actual outcomes of those intentions, as seen in the completed work. Although some components of the completed product may have been decided upon and executed deliberately, others may have arisen perchance or as if on their own, without a conscious decision or even with no awareness on the part of the art maker. Here is an example:

Cl: *It looks like this person right here . . . ummm . . . is not worried as all the others.*
T: *Which one?*
Cl: *This one right here.*
T: *The one in yellow?*
Cl: *Uh-huh.*
T: *Is not worried as the others? Uh, huh, uh huh. [long pause] Were you aware of that while you were drawing it? Or do you see it now?*
Cl: *No, I see it now.*

The second aspect of phenomenological integration is the search for similarities and differences in a client's artwork over time. By looking at current art with previous work, the client discovers certain recurrent components or themes (Betensky, 1973). The adolescent girl noticed how the sense of "heaviness" present in two pictures she selected was handled differently in each. This intra-series comparison leads to a discernment of patterns, first in one's art, and then in one's responses to situations in life. Developing an ability to see patterns in the art expressions leads the client to a further recognition of patterns in behavior. A questioning of such patterns by the client then follows, and that eventually leads to change.

The third aspect of phenomenological integration flows naturally: the search for parallels between the client's struggles with the process of art expression and efforts to cope with real-life experiences. From a discussion of the changes she had made "here on the paper" in an art therapy session, the adolescent proceeded to comment that she was now more able to choose and to make friends, and also to schedule her classes at school—two of her major recent difficulties in life situations.

☐ Conclusion

Through the act of looking at their own art expressions, new facets of themselves become apparent to the art makers, and new communication takes place between the art expression and the subjective experience of the client-turned-beholder. Clients learn to perceive more clearly and more articulately the phenomena of the formal components and their interaction in the artwork. They then connect them with their inner psychological forces, and apply the newly acquired art of looking to phenomena outside and around themselves, in their own world and in that of others.

As they discover facets of themselves in their interactions with others, something else happens: they transcend their self-centeredness and become members of the world, literally, in their everyday life. They assume responsibility for their artwork from the start, and actively participate in the intellectual and artistic process of working through the difficulties that have arisen in interactions between themselves and others. This is the special contribution of the phenomenological approach to art therapy—arrived at by creating art and the subsequent treatment of its organization—from pre-intentional functioning to fully intentional living.

☐ References

Arnheim, R. (1969). *Visual thinking.* Berkeley, CA: University of California Press.

Arnheim, R. (1972a). Artistic symbols—Freudian and otherwise. In *Toward a psychology of art.* Berkeley, CA: University of California Press.

Arnheim, R. (1972b). *Toward a psychology of art.* Berkeley, CA: University of California Press.

Betensky, M. (1973). Patterns of visual expression in art psychotherapy. *Art Psychotherapy, 1,* 121–129.

Betensky, M. (1976). The phenomenological approach to art expression and art therapy. *Art Psychotherapy, 4,* 173–179.

Betensky, M. (1978). Phenomenology of self-expression in theory and practice. *Confinia Psychiatrica, 21,* 31–36.

Betensky, M. (1982). Media potential: Its use and misuse in art therapy. *Proceedings, 13th Annual Conference* (pp. 111–113). Baltimore, MD: AATA.

Betensky, M. (1995). *What do you see?* London: Jessica Kingsley.

Betensky, M., & Nucho, A. O. (1979). The phenomenological approach to art therapy. *Proceedings, 10th Annual Conference.* Baltimore, MD: AATA.

Buck, J. N. (1948). The H-T-P test. *Journal of Clinical Psychology, 4,* 151–159.

Frankl, V. E. (1969). *Man's search for meaning.* Boston: Beacon.

Heidegger, M. (1960). *Sein und zeit.* Tubingen, Germany: Neimeyer.

Husserl, E. (1976). *Ideas.* NJ: Humanities Press. (Original work published 1913) (cf. also *Husserliana,* microfilm, New School for Social Research, New York).

Klages, L. (1936). *Grundlege der wissenschaft vom ausdruck.* Leipzig, Germany: Foundation for the Science of Expression.

Kreitler, H., & Kreitler, S. (1972). *Psychology of the arts.* Durham, NC: Duke University Press.

Kwant, R. C. (1978). *Phenomenology of expression.* Atlantic Highlands, NJ: Humanities Press.

Merleau-Ponty, M. (1962). *Phenomenology of perception.* London: Routledge.

Nicolaides, K. (1941). *The natural way to draw.* Boston: Houghton Mifflin.

Nucho, A. (1977). *Making a scribble.* Baltimore, MD: University of Maryland School of Social Work.

Richardson, W. J. (1965). The place of the unconscious in Heidegger. *Review of Existential Psychology and Psychiatry, 5,* 265–290.

Spiegelberg, H. (1972). *Phenomenology in psychology and psychiatry.* Evanston, IL: Northwestern University Press.

Strasser, S. (1977). *Phenomenology of feeling.* Pittsburgh, PA: Duquesne University Press.

CHAPTER **9**

Janie Rhyne

Gestalt Art Therapy

Like most approaches in our field, Gestalt art therapy has developed in alignment with theories and practices underlying broader-based disciplines. Gestalt art therapy grew out of two very different movements. The first, Gestalt psychology, developed from laboratory research in perception and learning; the second, Gestalt therapy, evolved from applications in psychotherapeutic practice. Gestalt psychologists have earned respected places in academia, but do not extend their concepts to clinical applications. Gestalt therapists base much of their practice on some theories of Gestalt psychology, but have adapted them to support therapeutic interventions. Gestalt art experience incorporates ideas from both, aiming for their integration in a Gestalt approach to art therapy.

From Gestalt Psychology to Gestalt Therapy

Gestalt perception and its implications were investigated in laboratory experiments by German psychologists in the early 1900's. They were interested in how organisms make sense of what they perceive in the world around them. Wertheimer, Kohler, and Koffka, fleeing from Nazi Germany, brought Gestalt psychology to the United States. Lewin and Goldstein, also emigrating in the 1930's, were influenced by Gestalt principles. Lewin, a social psychologist, was known for his "field theories," especially as applied in group dynamics. Goldstein, a neuropsychiatrist, was the leading exponent of "organismic theory," stressing the unity, integration, consistency, and coherence of a normal person, and that pathological disorganization was the result of an oppressive environment.

Fritz Perls came to New York in 1947, also in flight from Nazi Germany, but with an in-between decade of living in South Africa, where he and his wife Laura practiced psychoanalysis. Laura had studied Gestalt psychology in her training, and Fritz dedicated an early book to Gestalt psychologist Max Wertheimer. In New York Fritz and Laura met writer Paul Goodman, who, from their incomplete manuscript, elaborated and made comprehensible the theoretical base of Gestalt therapy in *Gestalt Therapy: Growth and Excitement in the Human Personality* (Perls, Hefferline, & Goodman, 1951).

Laura stayed in New York and Fritz wandered, eventually finding his place in 1963 at Esalen Institute in California. From that time, he was hailed as the founder of Gestalt therapy; he was then 70 years old. From a lifetime of wandering, both geographically and ideologically, Fritz brought to his way of working a rich mixture of personal and theoretical ideas. As a practitioner he demonstrated his rebelliousness, his early fascination with theater, his education as a psychoanalyst, his training analysis with Wilhelm Reich, his pragmatic use of some findings by Gestalt psychologists, and his courage in challenging "phoniness"—in himself as well as in others. He also acted as a director of improvisational theater with patients, with the group members and himself enacting personal dramas in the interest of an awareness of human complexity (cf. Perls, 1969).

Fritz invented therapeutic techniques, too; he experimented with them, continuously exploring how he could use them to be more effective. Unfortunately, many of his techniques have been popularized as "rules and games," that some may use as a substitute for personal effectiveness as a therapist. Fritz decried this reduction of his creative methods to mere "gimmickry." Though he basked in the image of himself as a great performer and often played the clown, he took his therapeutic task quite seriously and was dedicated to authenticity as a psychotherapist.

Though Gestalt therapy focuses on "organismic" functioning, other humanistic therapies also assume "wholeness;" some stressing an explicitly "holistic" approach. Which approaches are defined as "humanistic" depends on the context. Since the sixties, new psychotherapies have sprung up like plants in the rainfall after a dry season. In the midst of this proliferation, roots and branches get intertwined; it is not easy to see what they sprouted from, what directions they are growing in, or which will thrive.

The approach that I developed and called "Gestalt Art Experience" is humanistically oriented. From the rich soil of California in the 1960's, it sprouted and grew like a weed, natural and indigenous. Innovative therapeutic approaches were growing rampant there and then; Gestalt art experience was one of them. Workshops with Fritz Perls and training at the Gestalt Institute of San Francisco fostered its growth, as did dialogue with other humanistic therapists. I brought to my training in Gestalt therapy education and experience as a professional artist. Also, for some years I had worked with people using art as an expressive language. And I was intrigued by how implications of Gestalt psychology supported my own understanding of art as communication. So I brought with me some seedlings that I had gathered in other times and places.

☐ Gestalt Assumptions and Applications

The basic assumption of Gestalt therapy is that individuals can deal effectively with their life problems. The central task of the therapist is to help clients fully experience their being in the here-and-now, by becoming aware of how they prevent themselves from feeling and experiencing in the present. The approach is basically noninterpretive, and clients carry out their own therapy as much as possible. They make their own interpretations, create their own direct statements, and find their own meanings. Finally, clients are encouraged to experience directly in the present their struggles with "unfinished business" from the past. By experiencing their conflicts, instead of merely talking about them, they gradually expand their own level of awareness, and integrate the fragmented and unknown part of their personality" (Corey, 1982, p. 98).

Rooted in existential philosophy and phenomenology, Gestalt stresses assumptions of personal responsibility for the course of one's life. Gestalt therapists challenge clients toward growth and the development of their innate potential. In keeping with other existential psychotherapies, the therapist maintains genuine contact with the client. Believing that no one can be other than subjective in any relationship, existential-minded

Gestaltists aim for authenticity rather than objectivity. The therapist enters into the relationship mutually with the client, accepting that the therapeutic process will change both. Transference is not encouraged; it is seen as avoidance of the present-centered, person-to-person relationship.

Gestalt work with dreams is similar to how a Gestalt art therapist evokes clients' awareness of meanings expressed in their visual imagery. Dreams are assumed to represent existential messages that reflect current ways of being in the world. Clients recognize that the dream configuration is their own creation. They are asked to "work through" their self-created images by "taking the part" of each person and thing in the dream. For Gestalt art therapists, this is an effective way to elicit more awareness of personal meanings made graphic through art media.

☐ Art and Gestalt Approaches

Several years ago I wrote about how the linkage between Gestalt psychology and Gestalt therapy was easily observable in the activity of art therapy (Rhyne, 1980). Theories which are difficult to explain in the abstract can be immediately comprehended when they are applied to understanding concrete referents in the forms of art. In an expressive art therapy process, the concepts are transposed into vivid percepts.

> In my work as an art therapist, patients, clients, students and I communicate verbally, of course, but we do so mostly in reference to some representations they have created in non-verbal media. So we have the concrete artifact present among us; its presence allows us to experience and express immediate perceptions and awareness. We do not have to talk *about* configurations, figure/ground relationships, dynamic movement, contact/boundaries, coherence and fragmentation in the abstract; rather we speak *of* these phenomena in the very act of perceiving and becoming aware of what is obviously there. Though we can't be sure of how directly the *content* of expressive forms portrays the ideas and actions of the image-maker, we presume that humanly created forms show similarity in *structure* with human behavior. So instead of talking about isomorphism, we are observing the sense of the theory as we apply it. (Rhyne, 1980, p. 77)

We contact each other through the presence of the drawing, seeing the interplay of lines, shapes, and forms within the wholeness of it as a Gestalt. Morover, enactment of the forms, through sounds, gestures, and movements, brings into play kinesthetic and other sensory, immediate perceptions. Without pushing for interpretations, we explore the dimensions of the drawing and elaborate its impact, through active, present experiencing. Personal meanings may or may not emerge in the course of discovering; the client's expressive process is directed toward an expanded awareness of what makes sense in his or her own life. "No matter what direction we take, we will still be relating what we do to premises gathered from Gestalt psychologists: though we need not ever mention their theories or use their vocabularies, my client and I have applied their tenets in the kind of Gestalt therapy I like to do" (Rhyne, 1980, p. 78).

Other Gestalt therapists incorporate art, in keeping with their own ways of working with clients. Among these, Joseph Zinker (1977) stands out as an articulate proponent of the *Creative Process in Gestalt Therapy*. In the chapter, "Art in Gestalt Therapy," he writes:

> The reason drawing or painting may be "therapeutic" is that, when experienced as a process, it allows the artist to know himself as a whole person within a relatively short period of time. He not only becomes aware of internal movement toward experiential wholeness, but he also receives visual confirmation . . . from the drawings he produces. (p. 236)

Zinker is a painter as well as a practicing therapist, and he believes that "all creative activity begins with movement." He designs "Gestalt art workshops" so that the participants begin literally moving their physical bodies in space, responding to the rhythms of accompanying music. "They start drawing only after they have been enabled to "ground their bodies and locate their energy" (Zinker, 1977, p. 242).

> Participants are asked to get into their mobility by concentrating their energy on moving from inner activity outward. Music facilitates this process. Participants are encouraged to move at their own pace and in their own idiosyncratic way. All movement is good. All spontaneous activity is nurtured and supported. (Zinker, 1977, p. 242)

Celia Thompson-Taupin, a registered art therapist active with the Gestalt Institute of San Francisco, also leads Gestalt art groups. In "Where Do Your Lines Lead?" (1976) she tells how she involves groups in making and enacting their own experiences.

> The line game is played by tacking a large sheet of paper on the wall, and having on hand a basket of crayons or pieces of chalk of various colors. One person at a time is "it." That person comes up to the paper and is told, "Select a color and draw a line or a shape." That being done, he is told, "Now another, with a different color." I usually ask the person to make the sound and movement of each line or shape. Other group members are encouraged to mimic and get into the spirit of how each line feels to the person who is "it." At this point, many choices are open. One possibility is the "gestalting" of the two lines or shapes by "it." Another . . . is to say to "it," "Now use people in the group to be your lines and dramatize what is going on. You are the director of the play for the next few minutes—and you can also be one of the characters. It's your show." What happens from this moment on is rarely dull and often involving for the whole group. (p. 113)

Violet Oaklander, in *Windows to Our Children* (1978), tells of her Gestalt work with children and adolescents. She encourages them to express their feelings with art media, dream work, role playing, storytelling, creative dramatics, and other kinds of enactment. She writes that her "goal" is to help the child "become aware of herself and her existence in the world." Dr. Oaklander is a certified member of the Los Angeles Gestalt Therapy Institute and uses Gestalt in her practice of marriage, family, and child counseling. Increasingly, other therapists and counselors are including Gestalt art experience in their repertoire of therapeutic modalities, synthesizing ideas from many sources, as they apply them in ways appropriate to their own specializations.[1]

For many years I have led Gestalt art experience groups, sometimes in weekend or five-day workshops, and sometimes ongoing, continuing for weeks or months. I find group art experience invigorating for me and for those who join. They are lively and exciting; participants stimulate, support, and challenge each other—and me. There are slow times, too, and desperate struggles to break through deadening layers of "unfinished business" that get in the way of savoring present awareness and contacts. In many ways the groups are therapeutic, directed toward encouraging people to shed neurotic patterns and get on with living fuller, more constructive lives. I still lead such groups and still find them exhilarating.

During the years, I have also worked with clients in one-to-one sessions, in longer-term, quieter, and more individualized ways. With some clients, I find that a Gestalt approach which is supportive as well as challenging can strengthen them, as they seek

---

[1]While Janie Rhyne was trained by Fritz Perls in San Francisco, Elaine Rapp was trained by Laura Perls in New York and developed her own approach to Gestalt art therapy in groups (Rapp, 1980).

to take charge of and change the course of their troubled lives. I describe and illustrate one way in which a client and I are currently working through her present problems.

☐ Structured Gestalt Approach with a Client: Wendy

This way of working through visual/verbal perceptions illustrates visual thinking in action; it demonstrates how "thinking with the senses" can be part of a therapeutic process. Rudolf Arnheim (1969) has insisted that physical and psychological phenomena are isomorphic—their forms are similarly structured. In this kind of Gestalt art therapy I assume that the clients' created images are isomorphic with their behavioral patterns. Thus, the dynamics of perceived structures in drawings can be transposed into a recognition of behavioral patterns, and then into an expansion of clients' awareness of how they can bring about changes in their existence.

Clients are asked to make sequential abstract drawings representing their responses to a series of words naming emotionally laden experiences. The whole series is a Gestalt—a configuration created by the clients. Each drawing is a part of the sequence; each drawing is also a Gestalt itself. So when we discuss the drawings, we arrange them so we can see them all at once, and so we can also pick up any one for selective study.

In observing the drawings, we focus on structure and form as content; we pay attention to implied directional movements in the lines and shapes; we are interested in interrelationships among forms, and in perceiving how these imply dynamic tensions. We are especially observant of figure/ground relationships; we identify forms that seem to demand attention. We ask how these visual images may be related to present concerns in the client's actual living. We scan all the drawings together, looking for visual patternings that make sense in terms of the client's actual behaviors. We pool our resources and our perceptions in order to foster the client's healthy growth and integration.

A client, whom I call Wendy, is making her way through troubled times; she has been in therapy with me for almost a year. She is a very attractive 25-year-old woman. Only recently has she discovered that she is also very perceptive and intelligent. Now she wants to actively develop her capabilities in real life. This is not easy for her. As her history shows, Wendy has rebelled against what she doesn't want, but has not yet found out what sort of life she does want and can create responsibly.

Wendy was born and bred in a town big enough to have a country club, a gathering showplace for upper-middle-class success, solidarity, and privilege. Wendy's family "belongs;" in their immaculate home the prime values are godliness, cleanliness, propriety, orderliness, rationality, and conformity. Within this value system, the family has prospered. Wendy has defied their values, and has no sense of belonging anywhere.

Wendy has three brothers and no sisters. She remembers that even as a small child, "running away" from her family was her way of finding her "spot." Sometimes she literally ran into the woods, refusing to be found; at others she climbed a favorite tree and hid in its branches, or nested herself in the vines covering an old stile crossing a fence that bounded the family land. Wendy also has vivid memories of intense excitement in discovering how brightly she could cover things with color; she loved leaves and grasses and bits of bark collected on "little walks in the woods." She felt an affinity for small things and enjoyed "getting lost" in fantasies where she felt free to "be the air" or "a leaf floating in a breeze." Wendy still has fearful dreams of being very little, trying to get away from being "choked" or "belted" by large parental figures who attempt to curb her wanderings.

During high school, Wendy went even more into her inner world of fantasizing. After two years away at art school, she found friends who also questioned, but she didn't accept their answers. Back in her hometown, she fell in love with an artistic young man who seemed to know what he wanted. Wendy went with him to the university to go on with her art. The young man soon left her, and Wendy became pregnant in a rebound affair with another man she barely knew. She gave birth to a daughter, but refused to marry the baby's father. Wendy's frustrated family angrily disowned her. On Aid for Dependent Children for the last three years, Wendy has lived alone in a trailer park, with her little girl as her companion in fairy tale fantasies that the "world out there" was not worth confronting.

But, as time passed, Wendy began going to bars at night, meeting and getting involved with men, wanting relationships. Her dependency needs led her into too-close, too-fast sexual affairs; her needs for independence kept her out of any relationship that might lead to marriage. Wendy's family wanted to "re-own" her while dictating the terms—get married or get a job. They knew nothing of her "sleazy" life at a local bar for "derelicts." She visited her parents' home, agreed to accompany them to the country club, but her mother had hysterics when Wendy donned a "sweatshirt" dress for the occasion. Furious at her family's demands, she still longed for their acceptance. Alternately defiant and ashamed, Wendy doubted the existence of God, but felt she was surely going to hell.

Wendy came into therapy with me, paying my reduced fee with money she earned as a cleaning lady. She described her life as being like that of a rabbit, scuttling around in underground burrows connected by long, dark tunnels. She poked her head out in the light of reality with real fear that she would be destroyed. Now she is venturing out more. Her old conflicts with her mother are now out in the open, and there are fierce confrontations. Her mother still slams doors in her anger, and Wendy is left alone, but now she no longer runs away and hides.

At night, in the security of her trailer, she sometimes paints large, sloppy pictures of her frustration. At other times she writes in a journal, questioning and wondering about religious beliefs broader than those of her parents. She battles with men, too, not wanting to settle for "sex for sex's sake." Wendy's drawings and paintings are full of activity. They reflect her determination to take an active role in directing her movements in her own life space—sometimes underground in her introspective times, and sometimes out in the open, fighting to make a place for herself and her daughter. Her lifestyle is rather "schizzy," with rapidly shifting figure/ground relationships, polarities, conflicts, and frequent ambiguities.

Wendy is aware of what she is experiencing; she is frightened and concerned. She is also showing her courage in dealing with the choices and decisions she must make. She says, with sadness and fortitude, "Nobody else can do it for me; it's all up to me." Wendy's present concerns are with the transition from childhood dependency to adult independence. Her difficulties in maturation, however, involve problems that were not dealt with in her past. As a child, Wendy's natural development was thwarted by her family's imposition of a rearing that ignored her individuality.

In working with Wendy, as with other clients, I am guided by my own beliefs about human nature, and my personal constructs of how individuals can maximize their fullest maturation. I believe that from their psycho-evolutionary history, human organisms are naturally endowed with innate urges for survival, and for the actualization of inherent potentials. These are the prime motivations for all behavior. Human beings strive toward growth, selecting from their environments whatever resources are available for assimilation. Human beings try to change incompatible circumstances; what they cannot change they adapt to, and they come to terms with environmental realities.

Thus, innate "urges" toward self-realization and existential "musts" toward autonomy direct all of us toward a sense of unity within ourselves, and toward an appreciation of differences in contact with others.

Wendy expressed her natural creativity early in her life, but it was neither appreciated nor even recognized by her family or the nuns charged with her education. They tried to force her into a mold where she didn't fit. Wendy responded by creating a private world where she felt at home. Her innate urge for actualization of her own potentials was and still is, healthy and intact. She has not yet realized that she must also come to terms with what she cannot change in her environment. Her existential struggle is with her conflicting directions: of moving out into more contact with outer actualities and, at the same time, staying with the further exploration of inner resources available to her as she makes her own choices.

The drawings shown here are taken from a series of those done by Wendy during the last few months. As with other clients, I initially asked her to make simple abstract drawings of her experience of eight primary emotions: (1) fear, (2) anger, (3) joy, (4) sadness, (5) disgust, (6) acceptance, (7) anticipation, and (8) surprise. Sometimes I also ask for drawings of "being sane" and "going crazy." We spend at least one session looking at the drawings together and tape-recording their descriptions, associations, and sometimes personal interpretations of their visual messages. I ask the clients to compare the drawings in terms of similarities and differences, and to verbalize any recognitions of figures that emerge, and of patterns of which they are aware. The clients do most of the talking; they express in words whatever the experience evokes in response to their creations.

Afterward, I suggest that they do drawings of other experiences that seem important—to develop and elaborate the themes that pattern their lives. We continue this process of letting one drawing lead to the making of another; sometimes I suggest the topics, sometimes the clients do. Between us, we keep ourselves up to date, using drawings made between sessions to enhance our awareness of current happenings in their lives.

I will use some of Wendy's drawings and some of her words to demonstrate some of how clients and I work together, how we use these graphic representations as guidelines to direct the therapeutic process in times of transition. I have chosen six drawings from a fuller series made initially by Wendy and kept up to date with others created by her from time to time. I have chosen to illustrate how Wendy expresses (1) anger and fear, (2) anticipation and surprise, (3) acceptance, and (4) present state.

I based my choice on my observation that how people express these emotions reflects their openness to initiate changes. I perceive *anger* and *fear* as being emotionally loaded with past-oriented, deeply enmeshed habitual "fight-or-flight" reactive behavior. *Anticipation* and *surprise* are more future-oriented. Self-fulfilling prophecies show up in the guise of *anticipation*. Willingness to open up to novel experience is suggested in *surprise*. *Acceptance* is present-oriented, indicating readiness to "come to terms" with others and the environment. *Present states* are expressions of what is figural in the person's here-and-now experience.

To our first five sessions Wendy brought paintings she had made during the past few years, as well as those she was presently working on in her trailer. We used these as references, while she described the events and processes in her life. For her sixth session, I assigned the homework of doing drawings of commonly experienced states of mind. Wendy made the drawings of *anger, fear, anticipation,* and *surprise,* and we explored what they meant to her during the following three sessions. Wendy's words, as I quote them here, were taken from tape recordings made while she was describing the drawings of

Figure 9.1.

emotions I had assigned to her as homework during the months of June, November, and the following January.

Anger (Figure 9.1) "is coming down from the top . . . those white pointed shapes are coming down into the gray . . . the anger eats the gray . . . I mean it overpowers that and it cuts through . . . [the black squares and rectangles] come out from the side . . . they are rational . . . they are over the white shapes [anger]. The squares [rationality] move around the triangles [anger] . . . the crosshatching is whatever I am angry at . . . another person, outside world . . . noises that happen."

Fear (Figure 9.2) "is a vertical rectangle on the left side . . . two thick vertical lines . . . a nose is coming out and this is what it's looking at . . . all this white space . . . and there's absolutely nothing in that white space 'cause there's nothing to fear. Inside the rectangle there are all the things . . . I'm thinking to fear about . . . a strong black line is a kind of block that keeps fear in check . . . just like the square black line keeps surprise in check."

Anticipation (Figure 9.3) "is a nice thing to feel . . . an exciting thing. When I anticipate something, that takes up my total thought so that's why the background is black. This

Figure 9.2.

white shape coming down from the top is almost like a fish jumping into a pond and he hasn't touched the pond yet. He's just about there. A fish knows that he wants water but he doesn't know what the next hole is going to be like."

Surprise (Figure 9.4): "inside the square is an organismic shape . . . and inside the organism is a little-bitty black square . . . that's the point of surprise . . . and the squiggling lines that are spreading out . . . that's my reaction to surprise . . . it's a shock, sometimes . . . but the outer square, done with the heavy black lines, sort of keeps the surprise in check."

Our weekly sessions continued for three months. Then, Wendy began canceling and postponing sessions, phoning and saying, "Something came up and I can't come." Her voice would trail off when I asked for reasons. After six weeks of no sessions, Wendy called for an appointment. Although she kept it, she spent the time avoiding contact with me or with her own problems.

I then asked her to make drawings of some emotions named by me; *Acceptance* (Figure 9.5) was made at that time. Wendy spoke of it in rather impersonal terms. *Acceptance* . . . "was the hardest to draw . . . another person is on the top . . . shapes like

Figure 9.3.

black teeth ... and I'm the white teeth on the bottom ... the part in between is the out-side world ... all those black dots ... thoughts and different people, everything else ... the up-and-down lines are the interactions between two people ... they're roots ... mine are going up to the other person ... the horizontal lines are the uniqueness of each person ... I'm the black line at the bottom ... with wavy distrust lines between me and my teeth. I'm rejecting two thin black lines from the other person that come down in the center ... but I am accepting one that has come down through my teeth and my distrust line and other obstacles to get into the heart of mores and values."

For the next week's session, I suggested that Wendy do drawings of emotions that she was experiencing, and name the ones she considered important. She did a series of figurative drawings, depicting herself as a child. Then, after another week's absence, she brought in a drawing that she named *Contempt* (Figure 9.6). "My face toward me ... eyes and a striped beak, a large and a powerful being looking down on a small embry-onic being that can't help itself ... at first I identified with that little being and then I saw myself turning into the monster...." While describing it, she confessed that in the

Figure 9.4.

last few months she had "fallen in love," gotten pregnant, had an abortion, and was desperately confused about her own "evil and sin." We stopped taping; Wendy was sad and crying for the "little embryonic being," but she was also ready to begin working through her conflicting perceptions and directions in moving into the world.

In *Anger* (Figure 9.1) she had dramatized coming down into the "outside noisiness" of "whatever"; the force of her "white anger" is interrupted by "rational squares" that move across, getting in the way of her movement. She uses heavy black lines as boundaries around her sharp angry thrusts. She keeps *Fear* (Figure 9.2) and *Surprise* (Figure 9.4) "in check" with heavy black lines, but there is a lot of activity going on inside and between the boundaries. Wendy *Anticipates* (Figure 9.3) with pleasure and excitement and considers *Acceptance* (Figure 9.5) with distrust, but also with a willingness to let someone reach into the heart of her private space. Wendy's labeling of the present as *Contempt* (Figure 9.6) allowed her to face both her helplessness and her power. In the months following, Wendy always kept her weekly appointments, bringing with her drawings and paintings that emerged from her deepening sense of her own values and goals.

Figure 9.5.

Working through these polarities has not been easy for her. She has become more aware of how her message relates to feeling helpless in her family of origin, having an abortion, thus using her power to take away life, and being a mother, who is now responsible for making a way for herself and her child in the outside world.

Wendy's visual language, in many drawings not shown here, includes a heavy black line as a boundary between inner and outer realities. She also frequently uses irregularly shaped dots to describe the outside world. In *Anticipation* (Figure 9.3) no boundaries or outsiders are involved. In *Contempt* (Figure 9.6) Wendy does not include either the outer world or any boundaries between the two related figures. She now knows that both of these are aspects of her personality, and that she must own and integrate them into her awareness if she is to function effectively.

Though the kind of structured activity I have described with Wendy is quite different from the spontaneous enactments often used in Gestalt art therapy with groups and individuals, the same principles apply here as in the freer approach. The simple abstract drawings are considered as a part of a larger whole; qualities and properties are interactive within the field; the client describes and interprets her own drawings in visual/verbal language; I keep in contact with the client through the presence of her

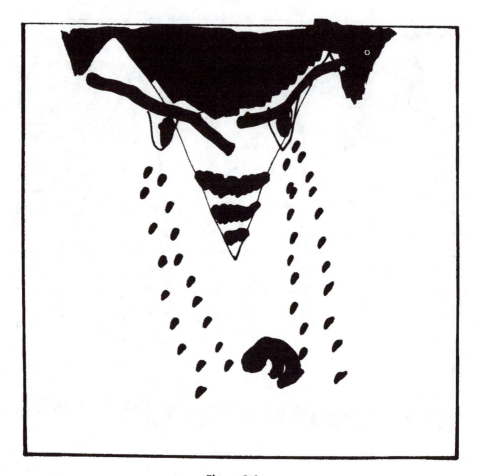

Figure 9.6.

drawings; and, most important to me, we are working together with the existential aim of facilitating the client's awareness that she is responsible for choice-making and for self-direction in living her own life.

☐ Summary

Gestalt art therapy deals with the whole configuration of personal expressiveness in visual messages, in voice tone, in body language, and in verbal content as well. Gestalt art therapy is aimed toward encouraging—even insisting on—responsible, honest, direct communication between client and therapist. Contact between them can be the mutual exploration of visual statements and can also involve enactment in movement, vocalization, and other active manipulation of persons and materials in space and time. This is done in such a way that the therapist can observe—and sometimes enter into—the art drama being created by the client.

Theoretical backing for this sometimes rowdy behavior comes from the Gestalt concept that human activity, like any other organic activity, is that of an organism contacting and interacting within the configuration that is our environment. Through our senses we become aware, we perceive, we gain insight about the nature of the world and of our place in it, by contacting what's "out there" directly with our innate organismic perceptual system. Thus, Gestaltists encourage experimentation and exploration through sensorimotor activation, believing that this often facilitates the recognition and clarification of problems.

In a therapy session the therapist is also a part of the configuration—another organism who naturally perceives and actively responds. A Gestalt art therapist is also likely to focus on the active movement in the art done by clients. She interests clients in the forms and patterns of their visual message. She encourages clients to actively perceive what is going on in lines, shapes, textures, colors, and movements. She wants clients to experience their created forms, and to make this experience a part of their organismic awareness. She aims to evoke in clients a sensing of how their forms can express personally involving meanings.

Gestalt art therapists are more likely to give workshops than to present papers. Like other practitioners, we have our bags of tricks and even games and gimmicks that we can write about, demonstrate, and sometimes teach to others. But the theories of both academic Gestalt psychology and applied Gestalt therapy, still require eliciting from intelligent, human organisms their own awareness and insight.

Gestalt art therapy is not for everybody, neither for all art therapists nor for all clients. It is surely not the only kind of good therapy. It doesn't always work; some patients are not able to mobilize themselves, much less manipulate their environments. Insight seems to be unavailable to some patients; holding them responsible for their perceptions is too much to ask.

Though many of us have advocated "lose your mind and come to your senses," we know that "use your senses and come to your mind" is what we aim for. Gestalt art therapy demands that clients must "do the work," not only of creating the representations, but also of recognizing their own self-configurations. Despite all the emphasis on the experiential in Gestalt art therapy, the theoretical background and actual practice involve therapist and client in a highly cognitive activity. Rudolf Arnheim says that those who practice the arts are "thinking with their senses" (1969, p. v.).

That's a premise underlying the work of all Gestalt art therapists; the theories of Gestalt psychology are based on this respect for human nature's ability to recognize the forms that balance and satisfy. Gestalt art therapists work toward activating in all clients their potential for perceiving—in their own visual messages—their needs and their resources. Like other Gestalt therapists, we work very hard not to get in the clients' way when they gain the true insight that they, on some level of awareness, can sense and then use their own resources for activating growth and excitement in their unique human personalities.

☐ References

Arnheim, R. (1969). *Visual thinking*. Berkeley, CA: University of California Press.

Corey, G. (1982). *Theory and practice of counseling and psychotherapy, Rev. Ed.* Monterey, CA: Brooks/Cole.

Oaklander, V. (1978). *Windows to our children*. Lafayette, CA: Real People Press.

Perls, F., Hefferline, R. F., & Goodman, P. (1951). *Gestalt therapy: Growth and excitement in the human personality*. New York: Dell.

Rapp, E. (1980). Gestalt art therapy in groups. In B. Feder & R. Ronall (Eds.), *Beyond the hot seat*, pp. 86–104. New York: Brunner/Mazel.

Rhyne, J. (1973/1996). *Gestalt art experience*. Chicago, IL: Magnolia Street Publishers.

Rhyne, J. (1980). Gestalt psychology/Gestalt therapy: Forms/contexts. *A Festschrift for Laura Perls— The Gestalt Journal, 8*(1), 77–78.

Thompson-Taupin, C. (1976). Where do your lines lead? Gestalt art groups. In J. Downing (Ed.), *Gestalt awareness*. New York: Harper and Row.

Zinker, J. (1977). *Creative process in Gestalt therapy*. New York: Brunner/Mazel.

☐ Recommended Readings

Perls, F. S. (1969a). *Ego, hunger and aggression*. New York: Vintage Books. (Original work published 1947)

Perls, F. S. (1969b). *Gestalt therapy verbatim*. Lafayette, CA: Real People Press.

For an enjoyable experience, which is also truly informative: *Gestalt Therapy Integrated* by Erving and Miriam Polster. New York: Vintage Books, 1973.

For a number of varied approaches used in Gestalt therapy: *Gestalt Therapy Now*, edited by Joen Fagan & Irma Lee Shepherd, New York: Harper/Colophon Books, 1970.

Another collection of articles is: *The Handbook of Gestalt Therapy* edited by Chris Hatcher and Philip Himelstein, New York: Jacob Aronson, 1976.

The *Gestalt Journal*, published semiannually (Box 990, Highland Park, NY 12528) includes new ideas and arguments from Gestalt therapists and has given Laura Perls the attention she deserves.

CHAPTER Josef E. Garai

Humanistic Art Therapy

The basic principles and assumptions of humanistic psychology are summarized in Table 10.1. The humanistic approach to art therapy is based on three assumptions. First, people are not seen as "mentally ill," but rather as encountering specific problems in their efforts to cope with life—as a result of intrapsychically or environmentally caused conflicts. Treatment is directed toward reinforcing the will to live, and developing the ability to find meaning and identity in as fully creative a lifestyle as possible.

Second, the inability to cope successfully with life's vicissitudes or to find satisfactory avenues for self-actualization, meaning, and identity is a common phenomenon, affecting most people to a greater or lesser extent. The so-called "identity crisis" is not a one-stage phenomenon adolescents go through to reach "maturity." Identity crises may occur at any life stage, when a transition toward some new kind of lifestyle is required. Instead of waiting to "cure" people during periods of tension, a humanistic art therapist helps people to integrate the various "identity crises" into creative-expressive lifestyles, and to move toward further experiences of change. This preventive care is based on promoting life experiences that enhance curiosity, excitement, self-expression, and intimacy.

Third, *self-actualization* resulting from lifestyles of genuine self-disclosure and honesty remains basically sterile, unless the person can formulate a *self-transcendent* goal that makes life more meaningful by adding a "spiritual" dimension to it (Frankl, 1963, 1973). This requires a commitment to relate one's own needs to those of the community at large, through genuine intimacy and honest openness in relations with others.

These three principles can be summarized as: (1) emphasis on life problem solving, (2) encouragement of self-actualization through creative expression, and (3) emphasis on relating self-actualization to intimacy and trust in personal relations, and the search for self-transcendent life goals.

In humanistic art therapy, patient and therapist embark together on a journey of exploration of inner images, fantasies, dreams, and archetypes. This adventure into the depths of the psyche enables patients to crystallize blocked or unexplored facets of inner experience, in order to increase an awareness of deep feelings, anxieties, and

Parts of this chapter have already been published in the *American Journal of Art Therapy*, 1974, 13(2), 151–164.

TABLE 10.1. Basic principles of humanistic psychology (Bühler, 1971)

1. A person must be studied as a whole.
2. A person's life must be studied as a whole, i.e., on a developmental basis interrelating all the stages from birth to death.
3. Self-realization and fulfillment, rather than adjustment and absence of tension, are the basic goals of human beings that provide meaning and identity.
4. There are three basic life tendencies: the need for pleasure, characterized by personal satisfaction in sex, love and ego recognition; the need to belong and find security through self-limiting adaptation to society; and the need for creative accomplishments.
5. Each individual has a deep need to integrate these three basic needs in a pattern that is characteristic of his or her identity.
6. Each individual faces the need to balance conflicting tendencies or polarities within his or her psyche.
7. Guilt and anxiety are not the exclusive result of superego prohibitions, but are caused equally often by the failure to utilize one's own inherent creative potential or to create a meaningful lifestyle.
8. Identity is fluid and yet stable throughout a person's life, requiring continued attempts to reintegrate and to reconcile polar tendencies and different needs.

hopes. Humanistic art therapy can become the royal road to the emergence of *creative man*, no longer alienated from the inexhaustible wellsprings of his vital inner energies. My theory of humanistic art therapy is greatly influenced by Otto Rank, whose *Art and Artist* (1932) takes readers on a journey of discovery through the realms of creation. It encourages them to be "artists in life," shaping their own existence by tapping the depth of inner experiences. The goal is a balanced individual, who can establish a rhythmical flow between such polarities as love and anger, weakness and strength, privacy and intimacy, cooperation and competition, dependency and independence, dominance and submission, and hope and despair.

The humanistic art therapist attempts to create a nonjudgmental atmosphere, suggesting that man can be both good *and* bad, strong *and* weak, loving *and* angry, and dependent *and* independent. Once people are aware of these polarities, they can give up perfectionistic standards of performance and behavior. They can proceed toward self-actualizing choices and commitments, rather than self-destructive ones.

The different modalities represented by art, dance, music, poetry, and drama therapy replace the traditional emphasis in healing on "illness" and symptoms, with a concentration on unfulfilled creative potential. The goal of therapy is not getting rid of fear, unhappiness, and anxiety. It is to transform these feelings into honest expressions in some modality, in order to experience the exhilaration flowing from accomplishing authentic expression. Instead of seeking to avoid sickness, the individual seeks the exceptional well-being described by many (Houston, 1982; Jacobi, 1965: Maslow, 1975; Moustakas, 1977; Muller, 1982).

I have outlined the application of humanistic-holistic principles to art therapy in a series of papers (Garai, 1975, 1976, 1979) and in a training manual, "Holistic Healing Through Creative Expression" (1984). I believe that holistic integration aims at a harmonious cooperation between body and mind, body and spirit, and mind and spirit;

and that a person must seek such integration not only within himself, but also with the environment.

☐ **Art Exercises**

To show how humanistic principles can be explored in art therapy, I describe an exercise designed to achieve awareness of *individuation*. Individuation might be described as the attainment of authenticity, autonomy, and actualization of the self. The most important step is to accomplish the developmental task of learning to be a separate person, able to take charge of one's own life. This requires completing the process of separation from the parents. This then leads to genuine individuation, providing the basis for autonomy. The autonomous person is able to take full charge of his or her own life. He can enjoy the state of aloneness, without experiencing feelings of loneliness and despair; and has the courage to stand alone, without feeling lost or abandoned.

People are first asked to draw or model feelings of intolerable loneliness caused by the absence or unavailability of a close and cherished person. Then, they are asked to draw or model an aloneness that permits separate space, freedom from intrusion, and the ability to select any activity without concern about the judgment or criticism of others. A comparison of the drawings or modelings from both provides insights into the way individuals handle problems of loss, and how they attempt to move toward constructive aloneness. Indeed, every creative person knows how important it is to preserve one's own individual space and freedom of choice; and how these basic needs require the temporary exclusion of even the closest friends and lovers, as when one is engaged in creation.

Another art exercise is designed to achieve an awareness of holistic personality *integration*. Each person is given two pieces of colored plasticine modeling clay, two sheets of sketching paper, and an assortment of crayons. The instructions are: "Take a piece of clay, close your eyes, and model the clay with your eyes closed. Imagine that you are fragmenting and splitting yourself, that you engage in activities or thoughts that cut off your body from your mind, your mind from your spirit, and yourself from your natural environment. Try to impart these splitting tendencies to the piece of clay you are modeling." After 12 minutes the instructions are: "Now wait until I count from 1 to 3. When you hear the number 3, open your eyes and place the clay of your self-fragmentation next to the first sheet of paper. Then draw the experience of your self-splitting, in any way you desire."

The second part of this exercise begins with these instructions: "Now take another piece of clay, close your eyes, and model it with your eyes closed. Let images come to your mind, showing how you attempt to integrate your body, mind, and spirit harmoniously, so as to satisfy your basic needs and feel whole within yourself and in your environment." After 12 minutes the instructions are: "Wait until I count from 1 to 3. When you hear the number 3 open your eyes, place the clay figure of your self-integration next to the second sheet of paper, and draw the experience of your harmonious self-integration in any way you wish."

In a group, a comparison of drawings or clay models of the two conditions can be made by the participants first in dyads, then in groups of four, and finally by the whole group with the assistance of the leader. The goal is to clarify the movements of individuals from fragmentation to self-integration, as reflected by their interpretations of the symbolic meanings of their clay models and crayon drawings. It is a simple, yet powerful method of helping people achieve an awareness of holistic integration.

Humanistic Definitions of Creativity

Humanistic definitions differ from those that define creativity as a secondary phenomenon, rather than as an innate human drive. These theories may be called "deficiency compensation theories." They include traditional psychoanalytic theory, which postulates that creativity results from the sublimation of libido, that is, the channeling of sexual energy (libido) into substitute forms of socially acceptable behavior. Freud (1958) believed that the great achievements of civilization arose from the sublimation of libido. The idea that Leonardo da Vinci created his sublime paintings, Michelangelo his immortal sculptures, Shakespeare his plays and sonnets, and Beethoven his symphonies because of some frustration of their sexual drive seems untenable to humanistic psychologists.

Other theories that deny the primacy of creativity as an innate human striving are also unsatisfactory. These include modifications of the Freudian position, such as Kris' (1952) suggestion that creativity requires a "regression in the service of the ego." Adler felt that creativity stems from man's need to achieve superiority and perfection, to overcome basic feelings of inferiority. Rank (1932, 1973) suggested that creativity is the result of man's struggle between the life fear and the death fear; that it represents an attempt to overcome the death fear by gaining immortality, through the act of creating something that outlasts its creator (Meerloo, 1968). All of these are "deficiency compensation theories" and are unacceptable to humanistic psychologists, because they reject the assumption of creativity as an independent and innate human drive.

Humanistic psychologists and therapists are drawn to dynamic-holistic theories of creativity. These include Jung's ideas, which assume the presence of a "collective unconscious" encompassing the experiences and memories of the human race. The *collective unconscious* evokes *archetypes* and *symbols*, which constitute the reservoir of creative ideas possessed by everyone, including artists. Jung also postulates an innate creative drive as common to all human beings (Jacobi, 1965).

May's theory (1953, 1976) states that authentic creativity is the process of bringing something new into being. Creative people—artists, poets, scientists; composers—are the ones who, according to Plato, express *being* itself. They are the ones who enlarge human consciousness. The symbols they use require, as a response, a basic change in the life of the observer. The creative process is an encounter between the creator and the environment. The painter encounters the landscape. The intensity of the encounter, the absorption in the creative act, and the transformation of both environment and self, determine the quality of the creative process.

Moustakas (1977) posits that creativity involves personal growth, self-renewal, and self-actualization. He shows that significant gains in awareness and self-knowledge are kindled from within, rather than from external sources. Moustakas claims that all human beings have the ability to be creative and to relate authentically to others, while maintaining their uniqueness. This potential is, however, threatened by pressures toward conformity exerted by society, and by movements toward material gain, superficial communication, and safe, conventional relationships. He stresses the significance of honesty and freedom in human relationships, within a framework of ethical responsibility and high moral standards.

Moustakas (1977) believes that crises precipitate periods of self-doubt, that move the person toward new awareness, resolution, and changes in the self. He clarifies the difference between neurotic and healthy anger, and shows how the honest expression of feelings can be used for growth, when it releases tension and paves the way for deeper ties and greater honesty between those involved. Moustakas uses vivid sensory images and stresses the meaningfulness of silence, self-dialogue, and meditation in creative discovery. He states that creativity, inherent in each human being from birth, requires the expression of each person's uniqueness. Each individual has his or her unique style of creative expression, which, like a fingerprint, is characteristic only of that person.

Langer (1967, 1970) proceeds from the assumption that the concept of symbolism is the characteristically *human* element in cognition, and that *symbolic* expression and understanding have brought about the great departure from animal mentality. She defines art as the symbolic expression of an artist's knowledge of feeling, which is quite different from symptomatic expressions of currently felt emotions. Like Jung, May, and Moustakas, she stresses the importance of individuation and identity formation, resulting from involvement in the creative process. Langer's theory is closely related to the need to express symbolic meaning as proposed by others (Garai, 1977/1978; Singer & Pope, 1978).

Humanistic art therapists have also been influenced by the findings of brain research. Some have devised specific techniques to reinforce intuition, empathy, and spatial discrimination, dominant characteristics of the right hemisphere; in order to achieve harmonious coordination with the dominant characteristics of the left hemisphere: logical reasoning and rational thinking. In our society, the emphasis on logical thinking, reasoning, and rationality in the educational system has led to diminished training in empathy, intuition, and imagination, which are indispensable for problem solving and innovative decision making.

Genuine creativity is characterized by intense awareness, a heightened state of consciousness, and joy at the moment of execution. Creativity involves the whole person, the unconscious acting in unity with consciousness. It is therefore not irrational, but rather supra-rational. It is a mystical experience in which the individual merges with the cosmos, and in which total unity alternates with vast diversity.

☐ Further Applications of Humanistic Theories

Humanistic art therapists also use dream interpretation, to help their clients get in touch with important messages from the personal and collective unconscious. Interpreting dreams using art has been described by several workers (Ahsen, 1973; Garai, 1976, 1984; Von Franz, 1972). Whereas Freud believed that dreams are symbolic expressions of infantile wishes, revealing repressed libidinal strivings, humanistic therapists, tend to regard dreams, like Jung, as symbolic messages from the deepest layers of the unconscious. They may relate to unfulfilled creative aspirations and aspects of autonomy and identity that require conscious attention to find resolution. Dreams can actually lead to solving problems.

This is evident in the dreams of Niels Bohr, the Swedish physicist, who won the Nobel Prize for solving the mystery of the composition of the atom (Garai, 1976). In his dream, Bohr saw a huge sun with fiery flames radiating in rays away from the center. Then he saw little suns radiating similar flames, arranged in an elliptical orbit intersecting with the large sun. Then he saw another elliptical orbit with little suns and flares intersecting the first two orbits, and finally, a third elliptical orbit with little flares also intersecting with all other orbits. After he awoke, he wrote it down and began to meditate on its meaning.

After two days, he postulated his theory: The atom is composed of a nuclear core, which is intersected by three elliptical orbits of protons, electrons, and neutrons. The large sun symbolized the core, the first elliptical orbit the protons, the second the electrons, and the third the neutrons. Bohr had been preoccupied during his waking hours with his explorations of the atom, but his dream enabled him to find the imagery that enabled him to put the various strands of the theory together.

Humanistic art therapists use dream interpretation in a variety of ways. I have used mental imagery to help people remember a recent or recurrent dream. They are then asked to draw or model the dream. The dreams are interpreted as messages from the collective unconscious, and their specific significance for the dreamer at this time is explored. The dreamer is encouraged to define his or her unfulfilled desires for growth, self-actualization, and individuation through archetypes (Jung, 1959) and eidetic imagery (Ahsen, 1973).

Humanistic art therapists are also aware of the importance of *mental imagery* in the healing process. Simonton (1980) uses imagery to help patients with advanced cancer. He asks the patient during laser beam therapy to imagine that the laser beam is attacking the cancer cells by being directed to the site of the cancer. Then he asks the patient to imagine that his own healthy cancer-fighting cells are forming a powerful rear guard, joining the frontal attack of the laser beam to conquer the cancer. Simonton found that by imagining this scenario, the patient's own immunological defenses were enhanced, accelerating the cure.

Imagery is frequently employed in holistic healing. I have sometimes encouraged my clients—instead of taking pain-killing drugs—to imagine their pain, how heavy it feels, and how it affects specific parts or organs of their bodies. Then, they are asked to draw a picture of the pain. Next, they are asked to imagine that the pain is gradually leaving the body, that the muscles begin to relax, and that it is no longer bothering them. When invited to draw the pain leaving the body, they sometimes experience a similar, but longer-lasting effect than that derived from drugs.

Another use of guided imagery invites a client who is unable to solve an important problem to imagine that he is relaxing on a quiet beach or near a mountain pond, thinking about ways to solve the dilemma. If this seems difficult and the client feels "stuck," he can call on the "inner adviser," tell that person about the problem, and through dialogue move toward solution. The art therapist may ask the client to draw the dialogue, to ascertain the symbolic meanings of the messages received. Many believe that healing and transformation are determined mainly by the individual's ability to listen to the messages emanating from his or her own mind (Feldenkrais, 1973; King, 1981; Naisbitt, 1982; Walsh & Shapiro, 1983).

☐ Case Material

How the humanistic art therapist approaches diagnosis and treatment is described in case histories and drawings in "Reflections of the Struggle for Identity in Art Therapy" (Garai, 1973). The comprehension of symbolic meaning, the sharing of prelogical, paralogical, mythological, magical, and allegoric symbols, images, and thought processes, can circumvent the treacherous duplicity of verbal communication. It may also create an immediate emotional bond between therapist and client.

In order to establish such a relationship, the art therapist must constantly check back with the client to see if she is attuned to that person's symbolic messages. The therapist must never jump to premature conclusions about their meaning, derived from the "universal" symbolism of psychoanalytic or mythological theories. She must keep in mind the specific symbolic meaning of the message for this client at this particular stage of life, in the context of his or her life history and experience.

Thus, for instance, a young business executive, who drew a picture of himself trying to climb up a very *high* flagpole and falling off just below the summit, at first accepted the art therapist's interpretation that he seemed to fear the loss of his sexual potency. When he revealed that his sex drive had become stronger and been satisfied more often than ever before, the traditional psychoanalytic explanation was disproved. The flagpole was really a symbol of his desire to reach the top of the ladder of success in his company. His fear of being unable to reach the top position had been aroused by the remark of a competitor on the previous day, to the effect that he had better try to go more slowly in his efforts to reach the top, in order not to attract the envy and retribution of his peers.

☐ Therapeutic Process

The following excerpt[1] from a case history further illustrates the humanistic approach to art therapy:

Ken, an art student, entered psychotherapy at age 21 because of a psychotic episode after using marijuana. He was a tall, well-built young man whose deep-set, penetrating eyes usually looked suspicious. At the beginning of therapy, he was unable to complete his artwork for graduation, had broken up with his girlfriend, had quarreled with his mother, and was afraid of "going crazy."

The only child of parents who divorced when he was five, Ken was still greatly attached to his overprotective, seductive, rejecting mother whose love he had sought to gain as a child by playing the "cute clown" and by intellectual precocity. He harbored deep resentment against his father, who had remarried and who had never acknowledged him as an artist.

Ken suffered from severe depression and guilt. There were paranoid projections, hysterical symptoms, and various psychosomatic complaints. He vacillated between impulsive acting out and withdrawal into dreamlike states. He was diagnosed as an inadequate personality with passive-aggressive dependency strivings and sexual confusion.

In a series of self-portraits and paintings of his dreams, Ken was able to resolve his identity conflicts and move toward self-actualization, first in individual and then in group art therapy. In the first painting he brought to group (Figure 10.1), his expression is defiant. Ken said, "This is me as the 'monkey' performing to please my mother . . . I act like a helpless clown."

In Figure 10.2, he is framed by a playing card. His feelings about this painting fluctuated between depression and elation. He said: "Life is a game of chance. My game is that of the king on the throne clad in a sailor's jacket. The throne gives me power and authority. Yet the sailor's jacket promises me free-roaming self-direction in a kind of happy-go-lucky frame of mind . . . I guess it's the conflict between the father and the child

---

[1]A more complete account of this case study appeared as an article, "The Use of Painting to Resolve an Artist's Identity Conflicts," in the *American Journal of Art Therapy*, 1974, *13*, 151–164.

Figure 10.1.

Figure 10.2.

in me. . . . I have the wings of the bumblebee, which permit me to gather the honey of life in free flight . . . yet my hands and feet feel like heavy solid stones holding me down. . . . I feel that I am always held back by some pool of water from flying into the open air."

At this moment in his life, Ken was simultaneously experiencing the thrill of success and the fear of failure. He had found a warm, responsive woman who had moved into his apartment, and he had sold one of his paintings for an unexpectedly high price. These new experiences of success led to exhilaration, on the one hand, and to the reawakening of his old fears of failure and insignificance on the other. The conflict between his desire to move out into the world and enjoy life, and the desire to cling to his familiar pattern of immobility, withdrawal, and helplessness is poignantly expressed in this painting. The therapist was able to help Ken relate this conflict to his past overdependency on maternal guidance, and his still uncharted future. This reinforced Ken's tendency to move away from excessive dependency on his mother, and helped him begin to work through his guilt about self-actualization.

His dependency was expressed in a series of paintings. Figure 10.3 had been created shortly before starting therapy. It depicts a dream scene, which he described: "I am the black man in a crowd in the city. . . . I am the gorilla in the red shirt. . . . I'm really a 'dumb fuck' taking care of the queen. She is my mother with a crown on her head and an anxious look on her face . . . worried about being raped by the brute. On my head is

Figure 10.3.

a figure, half bird and half woman . . . the bird is clawing my head. It's a symbol of my mother not letting go of me." This painting contains three archetypal maternal figures—the queen mother, the witch mother, and the prostitute mother—the latter lying prone at the right of the gorilla, who has turned away from her toward the mother queen. #19 Ken sees women as simultaneously alluring seductresses, devouring and oppressive witches, and demanding queens. His black face, white arm, and red shirt reflect inner conflict between purity and sin, goodness and badness, pleasure and pain, virginity

Figure 10.4.

and promiscuity, and depression and joy—themes that emerge in various guises in the work of many creative artists.

Several months later, Ken brought in a painting of another dream, from which he remembered awakening in a state of joyful relief (Figure 10.4). He explained it: "My mother is finally dead . . . buried in the rocktomb. Her head is cut off and she breathes her last gasp. . . . The monkeys are glad and dancing around the grave. The green guy [bottom left] is me getting rid of my anger and laughing. The blue fellow [bottom right] represents my more serious self that grieves about her death and wants to contemplate the newly won freedom." Two group members pointed to a yellowish penis on the "serious self," with a strong erection. Ken eventually acknowledged it, and then explained that imagining his mother's symbolic death permitted him to enjoy his sexuality and potency without further guilt feelings.

Polar conflicts constitute a rich source of productivity in the creative expression of many artists. I believe that such conflicts are not neurotic, but rather are the very essence of human existence. Ken's paintings are not merely a weapon in his struggle to deal with his neurotic problems. They also demonstrate the artist's ability to probe the depths of the primary process, and to emerge with ever-new perspectives.

☐ Conclusion

The humanistic art therapist is deeply concerned about the future of the world and the challenges mankind will face as we move into the third millennium. I believe that we are entering the *age of the person* (Roszak, 1979). For the first time in the history of mankind, each person's right to the fullest development of his or her unique personhood and identity is the sacred trust and shared goal of society.

For the first time, people are relying on their own inner changes in their attempts to change society. In the past, we believed that fundamental changes in the structure or system of society would bring about changes in personality and lifestyles. The socialistic society was supposed to produce the idealized "socialistic man," and the democratic society the idealized "democrat." The *Aquarian conspirators* (Ferguson, 1980) believe that only profound inner transformations in the lives of many people can lead to a fundamental societal transformation.

The following five principles have been espoused by many humanistic psychologists and therapists (Houston, 1982; Hubbard, 1982) and are common to all humanistic approaches. They state that:

1. Each individual has the right to the fullest development of his or her unique identity, personhood, and lifestyle.
2. Each individual has the right to expect respect for his or her unique personhood, identity, and integrity or wholeness from all other people.
3. Each individual is encouraged to associate him or herself with any other individuals on the basis of shared common goals, interests, ideas, handicaps, and lifestyles as he or she sees fit.
4. Each individual has the right to challenge any authority or institution to respond positively to his or her need for recognition of his or her unique personhood and identity.
5. Each individual is encouraged to seek both internal wholeness, that is, a harmonious balance between body, mind, and spirit, and external wholeness, a wholesome connectedness with other people in the microcosmic and the macrocosmic environment (Garai, 1984).

In the humanistic-holistic approach to art therapy, the ancient principle *mens sana in corpore sano in spiritu sano in mundo sano* is a good metaphor, since the goal is *a healthy mind in a healthy body in a healthy spirit in a healthy world*. I believe that the person who genuinely experiences his wholeness also respects the integrity, identity, individuation, and idealism (the 4 I's) of both himself and every other human being. Such a holistic philosophy leads to a way of life of care, compassion, and concern (the 3 C's), which flows organically from the integration of authenticity, autonomy, and actualization of self (the 3 A's).

The humanistic-holistic art therapist believes that the attainment of this way of living constitutes a goal that is within the reach of every single human being. Therefore, she is engaged in a lifelong journey, together with her clients. This basic credo will inspire him or her with the "courage to create," which Rollo May so eloquently described (1976). This credo will also inspire her with the "courage to heal," since the original meaning of the word "healing" conveys the sense of "making whole." The truly dedicated healer is a healed or whole individual, who heals or makes whole those whose sacred trust rests in him as the healer who, in healing himself, is healing others.

☐ References

Ahsen, A. (1973). *Basic concepts of eidetic psychotherapy*. New York: Brandon House.

Bühler, C. (1971). Basic theoretical concepts of humanistic psychology. *American Psychologist, 24,* 378–386.

Feldenkrais, M. (1973). *Body and mature behavior*. New York: International University Press.

Ferguson, M. (1980). *The Aquarian conspiracy: Personal and social transformation in the 1980's.* Los Angeles: J. P. Tarcher.

Frankl, V. E. (1963). *Man's search for meaning*. New York: Pocket Books.

Frankl, V. E. (1973). *The doctor and the soul*. New York: Random House.

Freud, S. (1958). *On creativity and the unconscious*. New York: Harper & Row.

Garai, J. E. (1973). Reflections on the struggle for identity in art therapy. *Art Psychotherapy, 1,* 261–275.

Garai, J. E. (1975). The humanistic approach to art therapy and creativity development. *New-ways, 1*(2), 2, 8, 19.

Garai, J. E. (1976). New vistas in the exploration of inner and outer space through art therapy. *Art Psychotherapy, 3,* 157–167.

Garai, J. E. (1977/1978). The will and empathy in art therapy. *Journal of the Otto Rank Association, 12*(2), 32–53.

Garai, J. E. (1979). New horizons of the humanistic approach to expressive therapies and creativity development. *Art Psychotherapy, 6,* 177–183.

Garai, J. E. (1984). Holistic healing through creative expression: A training manual in holistic healing for creative-expressive arts therapists. *Art Therapy, 1*(2), 76–82.

Houston, J. (1982). *The possible human: A course in enhancing your physical, mental, and creative abilities.* Los Angeles: J. P. Tarcher.

Hubbard, B. M. (1982). *The evolutionary journey: A personal guide to a positive future*. San Francisco: Evolutionary.

Jacobi, J. (1965). *The way of individuation*. London: Hodder & Stoughton.

Jung, G. C. (1959). *Four archetypes: Mother/rebirth/spirit/trickster*. Princeton, NJ: Princeton University Press.

King, G. (1981). *Imagineering for health: Self-healing through the use of your mind*. Wheaten, IL: Theosophical.

Kris, E. (1952). *Psychoanalytic explorations in art*. New York: Schocken.

Langer, S. K. (1967). *Mind: An essay on human feeling*, Vol. I. Baltimore, MD: Johns Hopkins University Press.

Langer, S. K. (1970). *Mind: An essay on human feeling*, Vol. II. Baltimore, MD: John Hopkins University Press.

Maslow, A. H. (1975). *The farther reaches of human nature*. New York: Viking.

May, R. (1953). *Man's search for himself*. New York: Delta Dell.

May, R. (1976). *The courage to create*. New York: Bantam.

Meerloo, J. A. M. (1968). *Creativity and eternization*. New York: Humanities Press.

Moustakas, C. E. (1977). *Creative life*. New York: Van Nostrand Reinhold.

Muller, R. (1982). *New genesis: Shaping a global spirituality*. Garden City, NY: Doubleday.

Naisbitt, J. (1982). *Megatrends: Ten new directions transforming our lives*. New York: Warner.

Rank, O. (1932). *Art and artist: Creative urge and personality development*. New York: Knopf.

Rank, O. (1973). *The trauma of birth*. New York: Harper & Row.

Roszak, T. (1979). *Person/planet: The creative disintegration of industrial society*. Garden City, NY: Doubleday.

Simonton, C. (1980). *Getting well again*. New York: Bantam.

Singer, J. L., & Pope, K. S. (1978). *The power of human imagination: New methods in psychotherapy*. New York: Plenum.

Von Franz, M.-L. (1972). *Creation myths: Patterns of creativity in creation myths*. New York: Spring.

Walsh, R., & Shapiro, D. H. (1983). *Beyond health and normality: Explorations of exceptional psychological well-being*. New York: Van Nostrand Reinhold.

CHAPTER 11

Natalie Rogers

Person-Centered Expressive Arts Therapy: A Path to Wholeness

From the very nature of the inner conditions of creativity it is clear that they cannot be forced, but must be permitted to emerge. (Carl Rogers)

Part of the psychotherapeutic process is to awaken the creative life-force energy. Thus, creativity and therapy overlap. What is creative is frequently therapeutic. What is therapeutic is frequently a creative process. My own integration of the arts into therapeutic practice is called "person-centered expressive arts therapy." The terms "expressive therapy" or "expressive arts therapy" generally include dance, art, and music therapies; as well as journal writing, poetry, imagery, meditation, and improvisational drama. Using the expressive arts to foster emotional healing, resolve inner conflict, and awaken individual creativity is a relatively new, expanding field.

☐ What is Expressive Arts Therapy?

Expressive arts therapy is an integrative multi-modal therapy with the emphasis on the healing aspects of the creative process. Movement, drawing, painting, sculpting, music, writing, sound, and improvisation are used in a supportive, client-centered setting to experience and express feelings. All art that comes from an emotional depth provides a process of self-discovery and insight. We express inner feelings by creating outer forms. When we express these feelings in visible forms, we are using art as a language to communicate our inner truths.

In the therapeutic world based on *humanistic* principles, the term "expressive therapy" has been reserved for nonverbal and/or metaphoric expression. Humanistic expressive arts therapy differs from an analytic or medical model of art therapy in which

This chapter weaves together and expands many quotes and images from two sources: Natalie Rogers' (1993) book, *The Creative Connection: Expressive Art as Healing,* and her chapter (1999) in *Foundations of Expressive Arts Therapy,* edited by Stephen and Ellen Levine. Reproduced with permission of the publishers.

art is used to diagnose, analyze and treat people. Rather, we believe in the ability of individuals to find appropriate self-direction, if the psychological climate is empathic, honest, and caring. Our tradition draws from many humanistic psychologists—notably Carl Rogers, Abraham Maslow, Rollo May, and Clark Moustakas. These pioneers defied the authoritarian medical model and created a relationship model of personal growth in which the therapist respects the client's dignity, worth, and capacity for self-direction.

Using the arts expressively means going into our inner realms to discover feelings and to express them through visual art, movement, sound, writing, or drama, without concern about the beauty of the art, the grammar and style of the writing, or the harmonic flow of the sounds. Although interesting and sometimes dramatic products often emerge, we leave the aesthetics and the craftsmanship to those who wish to pursue the arts professionally.

We use the arts to let go, to express, and to release. Expressive art therapists are aware that involving the mind, the body, and the emotions brings forth intuitive, imaginative abilities as well as logical, linear thought. Since emotional states are seldom logical, the use of imagery and nonverbal modes allows the client an alternate path for self-exploration and communication.

The creative process itself is a powerful integrative force. Verbal therapy usually focuses on emotional disturbances and inappropriate behavior. Like verbal therapy, the expressive arts move the client into the world of emotions, yet add a further dimension—a way to use the free-spirited parts of the personality. Therapy can include joyful, lively learning on many levels: sensory, kinesthetic, conceptual, emotional, and mythic. Clients report that the expressive arts help them to go beyond their problems, to find a new sense of soul or spirit, and to envision themselves taking constructive action in the world.

☐ **What is Person-Centered?**

The client-centered or person-centered philosophy of my father, Carl Rogers, is the foundation on which my mode of expressive arts therapy rests. This approach requires the therapist to be empathic, open, honest, congruent, and caring, as she listens in depth, and facilitates the growth of an individual or a group. Central is the belief that every person has worth, dignity, the capacity for self-direction, and an inherent impulse toward growth.

I base my approach to expressive arts therapy on this very deep faith in the innate ability of each person to reach toward full potential. Just as Carl veered away from psychoanalysis and interpretation, so, too, have I rejected analytic and interpretive forms of art and movement therapy. In terms of methodology, this means I follow the client's lead as he discusses his art, movement, or writing. The words of my father are always with me:

> Empathic understanding means that the therapist senses accurately the feelings and personal meanings that the client is experiencing and communicates this acceptant understanding to the client. When functioning best, the therapist is so much inside the private world of the other that he/she can clarify not only the meanings of which the client is aware but even those just below the level of awareness. Listening of this very special, active kind, is one of the most potent forces for change that I know. (Kirschenbaum & Henderson, 1989, p. 136)

I want to emphasize the words "communicates this acceptant understanding to the client." It is a rare experience to feel accepted and understood when you are feeling fear, rage, grief, or jealousy. Yet, this empathic response heals.

As friends and therapists, we frequently think we must have an answer or give advice. However, this overlooks a very basic truth. By genuinely hearing the depth of the emotional pain and respecting the individual's ability to find his or her own answer, we are giving clients an opportunity to empower themselves and discover their unique potential. Empathic listening also encourages peeling the layers of denial and defense, which allows clients to feel safe to try the expressive arts as a path to becoming whole.

☐ The Creative Connection™

I have coined the term, "the creative connection," to describe a process in which one art form stimulates and fosters creativity in another art form, linking all of the arts to our essential nature.

Using the client-centered roots of my psychological training as well as training in movement and art therapy, I made some personal discoveries. I found that when I danced a sad or angry feeling in the presence of an empathic, nonjudgmental witness, my feelings and perceptions shifted dramatically. When I drew the images after moving, the art became more spontaneous, expressive, and revealing. If I followed the art with free writing, I plunged further into guarded feelings and thoughts. Thus, I realized that the empathic witness to art, movement, and journal writing is similar to a client-centered therapist.

#17

I also conceptualized the notion that using the arts in sequence evokes inner truths which are often revealed with new depth and meaning. Movement unlocks our creative energy, which gets expressed in visual art. Expressing the self through visual art fosters poetry or spontaneous writing. As we take risks and experiment, we are capitalizing on the brain's right hemisphere and its capacity for nonverbal, nonlinear experience. Inner healing takes place because of this "creative connection" (See Figure 11.1, "The Individual Creative Force").

The creative connection process that I have developed stimulates a form of self-exploration which is similar to the unfolding petals of a lotus blossom on a summer day. In the warm, accepting environment, the petals open to reveal the flower's inner essence. As our feelings are tapped, they become a resource for further self-understanding and creativity. We gently allow ourselves to bring forth what has been denied to awareness— that which rests in our unconscious. Simply put, we cannot integrate all aspects of self without involving all aspects of self. We reawaken our creativity by engaging in the process of creativity.

☐ Using Expressive Arts with Clients

Traditional psychotherapy is verbal, and the verbal process will always be important. Although offering the arts as another means of expression is a departure from the way my father worked, I am respectful of the integrity and self-direction of the client, and try to empathetically enter his or her frame of reference. Yet I have discovered that using the arts as another language brings me even closer to the client's world. The I-thou relationship is enhanced as I listen to clients' exploration of their movements, images, or sounds. Even more amazing is the fact that in creating the art, clients' feelings shift.

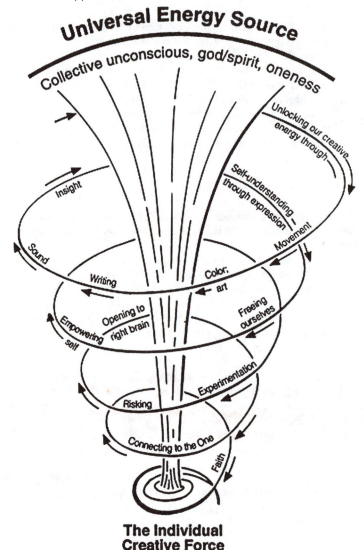

Universal Energy Source

Collective unconscious, god/spirit, oneness

Unlocking our creative energy through

Self-understanding through expression

Insight

Sound

Movement

Writing

Color; art

Opening to right brain

Empowering self

Freeing ourselves

Experimentation

Risking

Connecting to the One

Faith

The Individual Creative Force

The Creative Connection Process: By moving from art form to art form, we release layers of inhibitions, bringing us to our center—our individual creative force. This center opens us to the universal energy source, bringing us vitality and a sense of oneness.

Figure 11.1.

Incorporating movement, sound, art, journal writing, and guided imagery enhances the therapeutic relationship in many ways. Using the expressive arts helps clients to identify and be in touch with feelings, explore unconscious material, release energy, gain insight, solve problems, and discover the intuitive and spiritual dimensions of the self.

People ask me how I introduce the expressive arts in a counseling session. Some time during the first three sessions, I describe the client-centered philosophy and the expressive arts process in the following manner:

> As an expressive arts therapist I have training in the use of movement, art, and guided imagery to help you to explore—to go on your inner journey—through symbolic, nonverbal modes. At times, I will offer these methods to you. Often a healing process occurs by using this type of spontaneous, free expression. We need not be concerned about the artistic quality of the product. However, the product can give you new information about yourself. I do not use art to diagnose you or to interpret you. The art and movement processes are available to you as another avenue of self-exploration and healing. The arts can also be another language to use to communicate with me.

At this point, I ask for some reaction from the client. Some people are eager to use the materials. Others say, "I can't draw," or "I'm not a creative person," or "I've got two left feet and can't dance." I reassure them that it is not a test of their creativity, or drawing or dancing ability, but a method of self-discovery. Those who are fearful usually lose that sense, if they decide to take the risk and try some form of art expression.

I also assure clients that when I offer them the opportunity to express themselves nonverbally, they always have the option to say "No." I might say, "I will make suggestions and encourage you, but the decision is up to you. I will respect it." I may hear a sigh of relief from the client, yet I often find that many are eager to use the expressive arts modalities.

☐ Trusting the Client's Path

People who observe me in a demonstration counseling session often ask, "How did you know whether to suggest art or movement or sound with that client?" I don't know, in the sense that there is a right or wrong art form to offer. I use clues from the client and, most importantly, I trust the client to tell me the appropriate path. I always give a choice.

People also ask, "At what point do you offer the opportunity to use an art process?" There are many possible entrees to choosing art as a language. When a client is expressing strong emotion, for example, I often ask "Would you like to explore that in color or movement as well?" The client may say "No, I need to talk some more." That is perfectly acceptable to me. If she says "Yes, that seems like something that would help me discover more about this feeling," I will then ask, "Would you like to draw, or move, or make sounds?" I follow the client's lead. If a client chooses visual art, I sit silently as an empathic witness.

Then I ask the client to tell me what the experience was like as she created the piece. We look at it together and I encourage the client to describe it and give it any meaning. She is allowing me to enter her world of imagery and imagination. If the client wants to move or dance the picture, that furthers the journey. I constantly check: "Does this feel right to you? Do you wish to explore more? Am I understanding you correctly? Do I get your real meaning here?"

Here the reader might ask, "Why is the person-centered approach to expressive art therapy so important to you, Natalie? Why do you create this non-judgmental, permissive, accepting environment? Why do you insist that the therapist not interpret the art or movement? Don't you believe these art forms tell volumes about the client?"

These are valid questions. I do believe the arts express many lost or undiscovered aspects of Self. I also realize I cannot possibly understand the real meaning of the art as the client experiences it unless I listen deeply, asking the client the type of questions that can help her explore these meanings. It would be arrogant on my part to think I know better than the client (no matter how much training I have had) what she is trying to portray, or what an image or movement means.

I always treat a client with the same kind of respect that I would want from a therapist. I have had experiences where people have looked at my art, and have immediately told me what I am feeling or what the art means. To be misunderstood after revealing a very personal and private part of myself leads me to mistrust the person who interpreted the art. My reaction is, "I don't think I will ever show him another piece of my art!"

Our art is extremely personal. To gain someone's trust I believe we must honor their experience. To do otherwise may close down the client's creativity or break the rapport between client and therapist. If the client happens to like the therapist's interpretation of the art, then he or she will return again and again to find the meaning from the authority figure—the therapist—rather than develop the ability to find meaning for him- or herself.

Also, we know that the creative bud is very delicate. Dozens—no hundreds—of people have told me they stopped painting, dancing, writing, or singing, because they were judged, graded, or put down as a child. Teachers flunk children in art class, tell students to mouth the words of a song, or ridicule their dancing. One degrading evaluation can stop a person from ever again picking up a paintbrush, singing with friends, or expressing themselves through dance. When we work with clients, we need to remember that creativity has to be nourished and supported by honoring and respecting their courage in sharing it with us.

How do I help a client process their art? First, I ask them to explain what the process was like. "What were you feeling as you were painting (or moving)?" Another inquiry would be "What do you feel when you look at your picture (or sculpture or collage)?" Here are some other suggestions which help the client find meaning in their art:

- "Let the image speak to you. What message does it have for you?"
- "Have a dialogue with the image. Write the dialogue in your journal."
- "Tell a story in the third person about this image, starting with 'Once upon a time.'
- "Try putting a title on your artwork as a way to enhance its meaning."
- "If there is a section of the drawing or painting that is vague or seems incomplete, try another picture expanding on that part."
- "Find the section that is most troublesome. Do another painting that will explore that section."

In all of this, I am a companion on the client's path of self-exploration. I am not leading the way. I do not know the final destination. I can only hold the lantern while the client blazes the trail.

I might suggest using movement and/or sound to express the line, rhythm, or color in a painting, which helps a person to embody their art. Movement is also a way to expand feelings by putting them into kinesthetic form. It is a potent avenue for self-awareness, insight, and healing. When a client expresses fear, for example, the therapist might say:

> Would you be interested in exploring that feeling through movement? Find your space, close your eyes, and let the feeling express itself through your body. You could take a pose, showing your fear. Put sound to the pose, if you wish. Then let that posture shift. Take a pose of how you would like to feel in that situation. Notice the kinesthetic shift it takes to get from the first pose to the second. Try it again. What are you learning about yourself?

☐ The Creative Connection Group Process

To involve people deeply in this creative connection process, we designed a program where group participants spend many hours each day in a sequence of art experiences that lead them into their inner realms.

Each step of the way, feelings are given artistic expression. We might start with some "authentic movement," moving with eyes closed and letting the body speak while inviting participants to put sounds to those movements.

After 20 minutes of turning inward yet expressing outwardly through moving, people silently express themselves in paint, pastels, clay, or collage. By now the sacred space for creativity has been created through the collective, side-by-side inner experiencing. The art comes out of a felt body experience. It might be abstract colors splashed on the page with abandon, or carefully constructed collages; it doesn't matter. Each person feels safe to be free in his or her style and expression.

Next, participants write for ten minutes without stopping, censoring, or being concerned about the logic of what emerges, so that they can access their free associations or stories. The writing does not have to pertain specifically to the movement or visual art. This is a time to use a free-floating form of writing, in order to let the subconscious emerge.

Following this sequence, there is a time to share verbally. Talking about the process with an empathic listener helps people to understand the experience. This can also be a time to explore the meaning of the image by giving it a voice, or to experience the colors or the flow of the lines by letting them suggest movement and sound. Perhaps the writing suggests a dramatization. This spiral of activities continually peels off layers of inhibition, dropping us into the core of our being.

Finding one's center makes it possible to be open to the universal energy source, bringing vitality and a sense of oneness.

☐ The Healing Power of Person-Centered Expressive Arts

It is difficult to convey in words the depth and power of the expressive arts process. I hope that in sharing the following personal episode, you will vicariously experience my process of growth through movement, art, and journal writing in an accepting environment.

The months after my father's death were an emotional roller coaster for me. The loss felt huge, yet there was also a sense that I had been released. I felt that his passing had opened a psychic door for me, as well as having brought great sorrow. Expressive arts served me well during that time of mourning.

A friend invited me to spend a week at a cottage on a bay. I painted one black picture after another. Every time I became bored with such dark images, I would start another painting. It, too, became moody and bleak. Although my friend is primarily an artist, her therapeutic training and ability to accept my emotional state gave me permission to be authentic.

I also went to a weekend workshop taught by another friend, an artist/therapist. I spent my time sculpting and painting. This time the theme was tidal waves and again, I drew black pictures. In my grief, I felt overwhelmed. Painting the black tidal waves

Figure 11.2.

over and over expressed my sense of helplessness (see Figure 11.2., "Black Wave"). One clay piece portrayed a head peeking out of the underside of a huge wave.

The details of emptying my parents' home, making decisions about my father's belongings, and responding to the hundreds of people who loved him was taking its toll. Once again, my artwork gave free reign to my feelings, and yielded a sense of relief. Being encouraged by my friend to use the art experience to express and understand

Figure 11.3.

my inner process was another big step. I thought I should be over my grief in a month, but these two women gave me permission to continue expressing my river of sadness. That year my expressive art reflected my continuing sense of loss, as well as showing an opening to new horizons.

As is often true when someone feels deep suffering, there is also an opening to spiritual realms. Three months after my father's death, I flew to Switzerland to co-facilitate a training group. It was a time when I had a heightened sense of being connected to people, nature, and my dreams. I experienced synchronicities, special messages, and remarkable images. One night I found myself awakened by what seemed to be the beating of many large wings in my room. The next morning I drew the experience as best I could (Figure 11.3, "White Wings").

One afternoon I led our group in a movement activity called "Melting and Growing." The group divided into pairs, and each partner took turns observing the other dancing "melting," and then "growing." My cofacilitator and I participated in this activity together. He was witnessing me as I slowly melted from being very tall to collapsing completely on the floor. Later I wrote in my journal:

> I loved the opportunity to melt, to let go completely. When I melted into the floor I felt myself totally relax. I surrendered! Instantaneously I experienced being struck by incredible light. Although my eyes were closed, all was radiant. Astonished, I lay quietly for a moment, then slowly started to "grow," bringing myself to full height.

My heart had cracked open, leaving me both vulnerable and with great inner strength and light. A few days later, another wave picture emerged. This time bright blue-green water was illumined by pink-gold sky (Figure 11.4, "Blue-Green Wave").

Figure 11.4.

I share these vignettes for two reasons: first, I wish to illustrate the transformative power of the expressive arts. Second, I want to point out that person-centered expressive arts therapy is based on humanistic principles. For instance, it was extremely important that I was with people who allowed me to be in my grief and tears, rather than patting me on the shoulder and telling me everything would be all right. I knew that if I had something to say, I would be heard and understood. None of my colleagues interpreted my art or gave me advice on how to grieve.

☐ My Humanistic, Person-Centered Credo

People often ask me how my theory and counseling differ from my father's. People who view the two videotapes where I demonstrate counseling (Rogers, 1988, 1997) or who witness me in person, tell me they perceive my deep connection to my father's way of being. Like Carl, I usually go into an altered state of consciousness as I enter the frame of reference of the client. I try to be intuitively in tune with the feelings, as well as some of the unspoken messages. I call this "listening to the music as well as the words." I continually respond so that the client knows she is understood. Together, we adjust any misunderstandings. Clients can be our best teachers.

Each of us has our own set of values. The credo I have developed over twenty-five years as a psychotherapist summarizes, in a very personal way, my person-centered expressive arts philosophy:

> I am aware that going on one's inner journey can be a frightening, exhilarating, exhausting adventure.
> I will be present for you but not intrusive.
> I have faith that you know how to take care of yourself. I won't be responsible for you or take away your power.
> Nor will I abandon you.
> I will respect you and your decisions for yourself. I have faith in your ability.
> I will support you and encourage you on your inner journey.
> I may challenge you and your belief system, at times, but I will always respect you and your truth.
> I will encourage you to try new things, to take risks into the unknown of your inner world, but I will never push you.
> I will offer you expressive arts media to help you open up to your innate creativity and discover your inner essence. You are free not to use these media.
> At times I will give you my opinions and feedback but will always check it out to see if it is meaningful to you.
> I will honor my own boundaries and yours to the best of my ability.
> I will share my value system and beliefs with you so that you know why I am saying and doing what I say and do.
> I am open to learning from you at all times.
> I make mistakes, do things I'm not pleased with, and am misguided at times. In such instances, I will say so. I am able to say, "I'm sorry."

☐ Transcending Inner Polarities

When I work with groups we often spend time brainstorming our "inner polarities" and come up with long lists: love/hate, strength/weakness, close/distant, introvert/

extrovert, happy/sad, peaceful/violent, and so on. Although the opposites may appear to be "good" or "bad" characteristics, it is not that simple. While people in denial may need to acknowledge and accept their grief, other individuals may need to allow themselves feelings of delight or optimism.

In Jungian terms, the "shadow" is that aspect of the self that is unknown or that lives in the realm of the unconscious. The parts of the self we have rejected, denied, or repressed are frequently thought of as destructive or evil impulses. The shadow parts take emotional and physical energy to keep in check. To know, accept, express, and release the dark side in not-hurtful ways is essential in preventing these powerful forces from being acted out in violent forms.

However, we can also relegate to the realm of the unconscious our creativity, strength, rebelliousness, sensuality, sexuality, and willingness to love. So, when we risk exploring the depths of the unconscious, we may find many lost treasures. Discovering our unknown parts allows them to become allies: long-lost sub-personalities that we need in order to be complete. We become more whole, energized, compassionate people.

The expressive arts are powerful tools to help us uncover anger, fear, shame, loneliness, apathy, and the deep well of depression. I have been present while many clients or group participants have used movement and art to express their fear of death, of going insane, or of staying forever in the deep dark pit of depression. When given a voice, an image, a sound, a dance, the fears can become forces for change. When accepted for exactly what they are, they can help us on our road to recovery.

Accepting our shadow may be less difficult than embracing the light. When we talk about embracing the light, we are talking about opening to our spirituality, our ability to experience love, compassion, and all-encompassing states of consciousness. Many of my personal expressive art pieces convey my sense of the spiritual (see Figure 11.5, "Feminine").

In my years as a therapist and group facilitator, I have found that people are often uncomfortable acknowledging and feeling love. They readily accept negative thoughts about themselves and others, but find themselves fending off compliments, caring, and affection. We tend to armor ourselves against receiving love. Being able to give and receive, whether from another person, animals, or a universal energy source, may be the prerequisite for being able to offer unconditional love.

☐ The Path to Wholeness

Since not all psychotherapists agree with the principles embodied in this chapter, it is important to state them clearly:

> All people have an innate ability to be creative.
> The creative process is healing. The expressive product supplies important messages to the individual. However, it is the process of creation that is profoundly transformative.
> Personal growth and higher states of consciousness are achieved through self-awareness, self-understanding, and insight.
> Self-awareness, self-understanding, and insight are achieved by delving into our emotions. The feelings of grief, anger, pain, fear, joy, and ecstasy are the tunnel through which we must pass to get to the other side: to self-awareness, understanding, and wholeness.

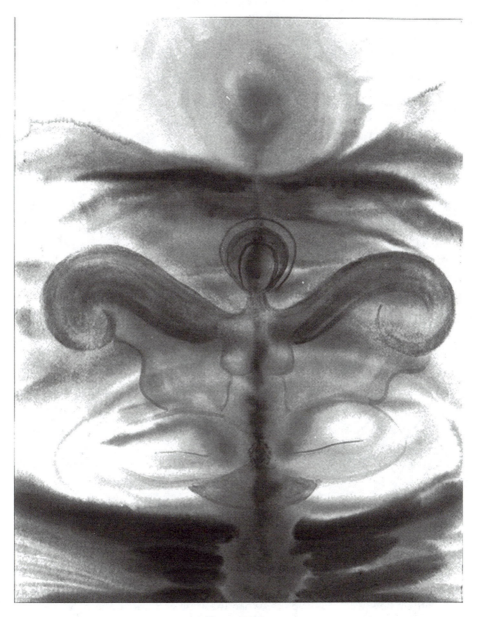

Figure 11.5.

Our feelings and emotions are an energy source. That energy can be channeled into the expressive arts to be released and transformed.

The expressive arts—including movement, art, writing, sound, music, meditation, and imagery—lead us into the unconscious. This often allows us to express previously unknown facets of ourselves, thus bringing to light new information and awareness.

Universal Energy Source

Universe

World

Connecting to the world, being aware of nature, other cultures, history

Community

Collaborative & cocreative endeavors, mutual caring, higher purpose

Compassion

Connecting to one other person in an empathic & supportive environment

Relationship

Becoming aware of new aspects of self

Insight, self-understanding empowerment

Self

Inner Journey through expressive arts process

Going into unknown/unconscious

Allowing the inner impulse (the creative life force) to come forth

Myth & ritual

Being "heard" & "listening"/witnessing

Connecting with community

We are all ONE

Figure 11.6.

Art modes interrelate in what I call "the creative connection." When we move, it affects how we write or paint. When we write or paint, it affects how we feel and think. During the creative connection process, one art form stimulates and nurtures the other, bringing us to an inner core or essence, which is our life energy. A connection exists between our life force—our inner core, or soul—and the essence of all beings. Therefore, as we journey inward to discover our essence or whole-ness, we discover our relatedness to the outer world. Inner and outer become one.

There are many discoveries to be made with this work: finding spirit, soul, the ability to laugh at oneself, new wisdom, or the knowledge that with each struggle in life there are major lessons to be learned.

In our goal to become whole people, more fully actualized and empowered, awareness is always the first step. Without awareness, we have no choices. Personal integration is part of the natural flow of events when we use symbolic and expressive media. Once we uncover unknown aspects of self, the process includes letting these parts find their rightful places in our psyches. Then we are more able to experience the ecstatic universal oneness, a sense of being connected to all life forms (see Figure 11.6, "We Are One").

☐ References

Kirschenbaum, H., & Henderson, V. (Eds.). (1989). *The Carl Rogers reader*. Boston: Houghton Mifflin.

Levine, S. K., & Levine., E. G. (Eds.). (1999). *Foundations of expressive arts therapy*. London: Jessica Kingsley.

Rogers, C. R. (1951). *Client-centered therapy: Its current practices, implications, and theory*. New York: Houghton Mifflin.

Rogers, C. R. (1961). *On becoming a person*. Boston: Houghton Mifflin.

Rogers, C. R. (1977). *Carl Rogers on personal power: Inner strength and its revolutionary impact*. New York: Delacorte.

Rogers, C. R. (1980). *A way of being*. Boston: Houghton Mifflin.

Rogers, N. (1988). *The creative connection: Self-expression as a path to personal empowerment*. [Video]. (Available from Person-Centered Expressive Therapy Institute, Cotati, CA, and from www.nrogers.com)

Rogers, N. (1993). *The creative connection: Expressive arts as healing*. Palo Alto, CA: Science and Behavior Books.

Rogers, N. (1997). Psychotherapy with the experts: Person-centered therapy with Dr. Natalie Rogers [Video]. (Available from Allyn & Bacon)

CHAPTER

Pat Allen

Art Making as Spiritual Path: The Open Studio Process as a Way to Practice Art Therapy

The primary contribution of a spiritual approach to art making is the opportunity to experientially dissolve dualism. Spiritual practice is undertaken out of the belief in the existence of a force, power, energy, or reality greater than the individual self, and the related belief that it is possible and desirable to experience our relationship with this reality. This force or energy can be called God, the Universe, Nature, or Creativity, among other names. In the words of William James (1902/1961) in *The Varieties of Religious Experience*, there is a "belief that there is an unseen order, and that our supreme good lies in harmoniously adjusting ourselves thereto" (p. 59). Making art can become a means to perform this adjustment, as it creates a path to that unseen force which is easily traveled by way of image making.

The idea of a cosmic unity is found at the heart of all traditions. As Seymour Boorstein (1966) states in *Transpersonal Psychotherapy* "the ultimate goal of the spiritual quest is the experience of oneness with the universe" (1966, p. 5). The practical value of experiencing oneness with the universe is that it leads in a very natural way to compassion for others and the will to do no harm. Typically, laws and rules are relied upon to achieve civilized humane behavior.

All of the world's wisdom traditions, in addition to providing a creation story and offering some notion of what awaits us after death, also challenge the duality generally experienced in life by holding out mystery teachings. The more esoteric aspects of these traditions were not, however, usually available to the general populace. The Kabbalah in Judaism, for example, could traditionally be studied only by married men over the age of 40 who were already deeply learned in the laws, precepts, and observances of the religion. Historically, only a few individuals in any society were involved in such a spiritual quest. The hermits, mystics, and sadhas lived apart from everyday life.

For ordinary people there was religion, a practical, daily, or once-a-week dose of uplifting or moralizing teaching from a professional. The meaning of life was defined by one's tradition, and important life passages such as births, marriages, and deaths, were served by participating in a community ritual handed down for generations. Just as therapy was originally only available to an educated elite and now occurs in many variations across all social strata, from psychoanalysis to self-revelation on television talk shows, spirituality has also become more egalitarian.

One of the most significant factors in bringing spiritual ideas into mainstream culture has been the arrival of teachers from the East. Over the objections of his monks, Soyen Shaku became the first Zen priest to visit the United States in 1893 to attend the World Parliament of Religions. In the early 1960's, Japanese teachers began developing Zen centers in the United States, and by the mid-70s had trained a uniquely American generation of Zen teachers. Tibetan Buddhist Chogyam Trungpa (1984, 1996) came to North America in 1970, and eventually founded the Naropa Institute in Boulder, Colorado, which currently houses a Transpersonal Art Therapy training program (Franklin, Farrelly-Hansen, Marek, Swan-Foster, & Wallingford, 1999; Franklin, 1999, 2000).

Early students of Eastern philosophy were artists, poets, and great thinkers of the era, like Allen Ginsburg, Jack Kerouac, Thomas Merton, Arnold Toynbee, and psychoanalysts Erich Fromm and Karen Horney (Tworkov, 1994). Suzuki made Zen teachings widely available through his accessible English writings. The ideas and practices associated with many forms of Eastern thought became common currency, especially on the West coast, and by the mid-70's psychotherapy was being influenced as well.

Therapists, seekers of another kind, began to see a relationship between spiritual and psychological well-being. A spiritual quest, however, is only truly meaningful within the context of an engaged life. It is necessary to be able to travel back and forth between the poles of existence: activity and rest, individual and universal, personal and communal, a sense of interior self and a feeling of connection to the web of life. As individual therapists became influenced by their own practice of Eastern spiritual paths, their ideas about the goals of treatment or the expanse of human existence changed to include experiences that extend beyond the self, called the *transpersonal* dimension (Walsh & Vaughan, 1996). Aided by thinkers like Ken Wilber (1997), whose work has mapped a unified theory of the evolution of consciousness, therapists began to define *transpersonal psychology*, and its approach to psychotherapy.

The major differences in practice that grow out of the transpersonal approach are described by Walsh and Vaughan (1996) as an *evolution* in psychology. In psychoanalytic models, therapists put aside their own feelings, offering themselves as blank screens for a client's projections. Humanistic-existential therapists redefined the therapeutic relationship by saying that the therapist ideally opens herself fully to the client's and her own reactions. "To this human participation, transpersonal orientation adds another perspective: the therapist may serve the client best by viewing the relationship as a karma yoga to foster his own personal growth through consciously serving the client. . . . The therapist's openness and willingness to view therapy as a process of learning and service can provide useful modeling for the client" (1996, p. 23). Rather than being an expert, the therapist is a fellow traveler, learning from the client as they learn from experiences leading to a greater awareness of the larger movements of consciousness that affect both. The therapist seeks points of connection and works on the issues mirrored to him by the client, aiming to expand his own consciousness and, as a result, be of greater service to the client.

As practitioners continue their own journeys they attempt to integrate their transformative experiences into their work with others. There is a recognition that this approach is not for everyone, that pitfalls, such as ego-inflation, can occur when there is confusion over what is personal and what is transpersonal. Like every aspect of knowledge, spiritual ideas can be used for good but also for harm. Calling something spiritual can make it seem a noble refuge when it is merely a garden variety avoidance of everyday responsibilities.

☐ The Place of Art

This is why art therapy offers something uniquely valuable for those of us who are concerned with transpersonal or spiritual dimensions. For it gives us a way to bring these dimensions directly into the work we do with others. Rather than focusing primarily on expanding consciousness, like meditation, art making offers a practical path—for the making of images is in itself a *practice*, a *discipline* that offers a grounding in everyday reality.

Practice, here defined as mindful engagement in a discipline on a regular basis, is needed in order to learn how to traverse any spiritual path. Art making offers unique possibilities as a method of spiritual practice, because of its ability to travel back and forth between any of the pairs of opposites that comprise our experience of duality in a general sense, while simultaneously allowing personal lessons to emerge for an individual. Guidance about everyday life is as available as cosmic insights about the workings of the universe. The connection between these two can become manifest through making art, allowing what Carl Jung called the "union of opposites" to occur within the individual. Jung, in fact, was one of the first to employ art making in this manner and for this purpose.

Throughout a significant period of his life, Jung engaged in making images and dialoguing with those images. They were created privately as a "self-experiment . . . trying to understand the fantasies and other contents that surfaced from his unconscious and to come to terms with them" (Jaffe, 1979, p. 66). Of enormous significance was an image of an old man called Philemon with whom Jung shared long dialogues. "Psychologically, Philemon represented superior insight. . . . To me he was what the Indians call a guru. . . . Philemon represented a force which was not myself" (Jaffe, 1979, p. 68). After six years of engaging in the practice of art and writing, Jung transcribed his insights in his *Red Notebook*, which in fact became the sourcebook for all his subsequent theoretical writings.

This work drew him to studies of Eastern philosophy, to the study and painting of mandalas, and to the suggestion to his patients that they take up painting as part of their analysis. Jung came to understand that "Everything living dreams of individuation, for everything strives towards its own wholeness" (Jaffe, 1979, p. 78). He noticed that the form of the mandala, which became prevalent in his art work, was also found in nature from the most minute scale, as in the formation of crystals, to the unfathomably large image of the sun or moon, or the vibrational image of sound when spoken in such a way as to record a visual image (Jaffe, 1979, pp. 78–79). Jung found, through his personal explorations, that the unfolding of individual psychology is intricately connected with an innate capacity to know the divine. Art and writing constituted his ladder between the individual and the universal, revealing the divine in everyday life.

Florence Cane (1951/1983), author of *The Artist in Each of Us*, clearly understood that art making can be a spiritual practice. She felt that through creating art the individual progressed naturally in his or her personality integration. Her teaching methods echo many spiritual practices, in her focus on breath, rhythmic movement, and chanting mantric sounds. "It is as if movement, feeling and thought represented three dimensions, and in learning to use all three, the child were permitted to glimpse the fourth dimension, spiritual awakening" (1951/1983, p. 35). Cane was aware that while engaging in a disciplined practice of art making, one's problem areas arose naturally, and that the demands of creating art provided reparative opportunities. Like Jung, she saw the unfolding of the individual into unique wholeness as a natural process that needs support far more than intervention. She found the art studio an ideal home in which this process could unfold. Later, Shaun McNiff (1989) carried forward this trend in his painting studios, and in the inclusion of all of the expressive arts in his work and the training of students.

More recently, Michael Franklin, Director of art therapy training in the program founded by Mimi Farrelly in 1992 at Naropa Institute, helps students integrate personal spiritual practice with their training in clinical and studio art therapy (cf. Franklin, 1999; Franklin, Farrelly-Hansen, Marek, Swan-Foster, & Wallingford, 1999). Embedded in Naropa's tradition of transpersonal psychology, the program maintains the art-based tradition in art therapy that traces its roots to Edith Kramer (1958, 1971). As committed practitioners of diverse spiritual traditions, Franklin and his colleagues are carefully articulating how art therapists on personal spiritual paths can practice art therapy in the world. Students are clinically trained and able to sit for the counselor's licensing exam, and at the same time are required to engage in regular spiritual disciplines that will support and inform their work.

Art Therapy and Spirituality: The Open Studio Approach

I had been deeply inspired by both Jung and Cane in my choice of a career as an art therapist. However, my real-life mentor was Margaret Naumburg, and it was from her that I and many other art therapists took our cue. Naumburg had taken a different path, where the same techniques that her sister Florence Cane had employed toward spiritual awakening, were instead harnessed for psychological insight. Rather than a natural unfolding of the human personality, a dynamic process was imagined, in which the individual struggled against conflicts within the self for mental health. The element of involved art making as practice was lost when, perhaps as a sign of the times, one of the strongest claims made for art in therapy was that it "speeded up" the process of gaining insight. And it was insight, rather than a harmonious alignment of mind, body, and spirit that was considered the therapeutic goal.

Acquiring insight in a speedy manner is not as compatible with making art as it is with making signs and symbols. The premature search for meaning seems to circumvent the creative process, by short-circuiting the energy needed to stay engaged with an image. As in nature, processes of growth and change unfold quite simply on their own timetable and with the right conditions. It is the understanding and providing of the right conditions that makes the art therapist most helpful in work with others.

After many years of clinical work in the mid-70's and 80's, I found that, for me, working psycho-therapeutically with others impaired and inhibited my own art making and sense of connection to the creative force. It also seemed that, except for a few champions of the soul like Shaun McNiff (1989, 1992), art therapy as a profession had somehow left the bright thread of spirit out of the weave, as it struggled to achieve self-definition as well as recognition and parity with mental health disciplines.

Going back to my own art in search of the answer to my dispirited condition, I tried to systematically strip away whatever seemed superfluous from art therapy as I had learned and practiced it so far. I was trying to locate once again the healing spirit of art. The three key principles that I rediscovered about art as a spiritual practice are:

Intention, Attention, and *Witness* (Allen, 1995a). It is, however, one thing to develop a personal approach to art making that answers one's own spiritual needs and quite another to determine whether it has relevance to anyone else.

In 1995, after several years of discussion and experimentation with ourselves and others, Dayna Block, Deborah Gadiel, and I set out to discover whether it is possible to make one's own art alongside others and be of service at the same time. This intention guided our development of the *Open Studio Project,* an art studio located in a Chicago storefront, which became a laboratory for these ideas (Allen, 1995b). Over the past eight years we have refined and developed a process that owes a great deal to traditional art therapy but offers a different way to do it. The Open Studio Process is founded on these elements: *intention, attention to art making,* and *witness through writing and reading.* This method is available to art therapists as one way of working, but it demands that any facilitator be honestly engaged in the process every time he or she provides it to others.

While transpersonal psychology offers us many useful concepts with which to craft ideas about the larger dimensions of human consciousness, it remains, as all talk therapies do, a largely intellectual enterprise. The Open Studio Process serves the manifestation of spiritual ideas in tangible ways, while at the same time minimizing some of the traps of both transpersonal and art therapy that remain as vestiges of their origins. Where transpersonal psychology adds modeling karma as a new concept to the practice of art therapy, art therapy can, through the Open Studio Process, manifest these ideas in very concrete ways. By engaging in one's own art making alongside another person, the therapist models in actuality what faith in a force larger than oneself looks like—the process of risk and openness to the unseen.

This approach places certain demands on the art therapist and reorders typical priorities. The basic premise is that "Creativity" is another name for the life force energy, and that art making is one means to receive and cultivate this energy. Just as one would hardly seek a Tai Chi instructor who has only watched videos or observed others practice the movements, or who has refused to show by his own example his commitment to the discipline, only an art therapist with a personal understanding of making art can truly work in this way. Living in the moment with fear and wonder is the very essence of creating, and is a necessary condition for this kind of work.

Similarly, concepts such as diagnosis and treatment are given up, as in other humanistic approaches, in favor of the practice of intention and witness. *Intention* in this model is a statement, composed by each person for him or herself, directed toward the universe, acknowledging what it is that the participant wishes to receive from engaging in the process of art making. The art therapist, too, makes an intention for herself. She might address her role as facilitator, but it must be one of non-interference and doing no harm. In other words, an appropriate intention for an art therapist could be: "I am open to my own learning, and I do no harm to others as I facilitate this experience." It would be incorrect to say "I help others gain insight" or "I facilitate the learning of others." There is a recognition that the primary relationship is between each individual and the creative force, and that those present form a community of service to this force and to each other through their personal honesty in their own process, rather than in covert attempts to "help" one another.

For this reason, no comments about the art or the witness writing are allowed. This is perhaps the greatest difference between traditional art therapy of any orientation and the Open Studio Process. While there may be conversation during art making, the rule against comments about art work is observed. Following the art making time, usually two hours long, each person sits before his or her art and looks at it, noticing body sensations, judgments, and reactions.

Then writing begins. Participants are encouraged to write as freely as possible, without regard for grammar, syntax, or sense, adding anything that comes to mind, including judgments or self-observations, without censorship. Beginners are especially encouraged to describe their work in order to really see it. Dialogue with the image is another way to engage deeply. By addressing a question to the image and inviting it to speak, the artist affirms its autonomous existence as the guise of soul, as well as a willingness to engage with its wisdom. This takes five to twenty minutes.   #4

Then, whoever wishes is invited to point out her art work and to read aloud her intention, witness, or any portion of these. The others wait in silence until the next person chooses to read. While there are sometimes sighs, laughter, and even tears, which may be said to constitute commentary, the rule against verbal comments is strictly held and adhered to by all, participants and facilitator alike. Even caretaking behaviors and supportive comments are discouraged during the witness reading. During this time the group members serve as the embodiment of "witness consciousness" (Franklin, 1999), that spacious expanse of no judgments where anything can be held and let go of.

Depending on the facilitator and the nature of the experience, the group may close at that point, or if time remains, a chime is rung and a brief centering meditation or a physical exercise is offered. After formal closure, members sometimes chat socially for a while; and if an individual feels a need for a slower transition to life outside the studio, he or she is invited to help wash brushes or participate in other aspects of cleanup as a grounding experience.

What takes place in this experience? Can it be considered a form of art therapy? Let's consider each element of the process and the theory behind it:

Intention #18   #6

Intention acknowledges that each individual is responsible for deciding what he or she wants to understand, change, or accept about him or herself. There is neither the responsibility nor the right to evaluate or set goals for another person. The setting of an intention may be highly personal and specific one day and more global the next. At any given time in a group, the intentions of participants will span the gamut. Some examples of intentions are:

> I connect to my creativity and allow it to lead me.
> I am open to my learning.
> I understand how to intervene in my family issues without doing harm to myself or others.
> I release my judgments about _____.
> I understand what is behind this feeling of anxiety, depression, helplessness.
> I gain insight into how to facilitate positive change in my life, in my workplace, in my community.

We learn from each other and from simply considering what it really is that we intend toward ourselves, others, and the world. However, we also come to see, as Rabbi David Cooper (1997) points out:

> It is important to understand that an intention behind an act does not ensure its results. #10
> Intention must be balanced by awareness. The greater the awareness, the greater the probability that something good will come out. The denser the awareness, even though one's intentions may be good, the greater the risk that things will not turn out so well. We could

do something kind hearted for someone without realizing that this could bring enormous grief into his or her life. (p. 141)

Learning about intention and the discernment required occurs through modeling and sharing among group members. For example, one participant went through a phase where she was setting intentions for her husband and child rather than for herself. Soon, through her own images and witness dialogues, she recognized the futility of this approach, allowing us all to become conscious of how we often seek to change others rather than ourselves.

Art Making #18

Making art is one of the primary ways to refine one's awareness. The making of images, as any art therapist knows, often unearths the hidden complexities of our lives and feelings. The Open Studio Process encourages engagement with simple materials, but in an involved and sustained way. Participants are encouraged to begin spontaneously and then allow the energy of the image to lead. We follow the image by paying close attention to our physical state. A sense of pleasure or flow is a sign that we are serving the image well. Time may fly or seem endless; other concerns may drop away. If there is music playing in the studio we may not hear it, or it may carry us to a deep place. Boredom, physical discomfort, or a feeling of being stuck and not knowing what to do next, signal that we are off track. When we notice these sensations, it is time to ask the image for help and guidance.

Stepping back and addressing the image directly by asking, "What do you want?" can sometimes be enough. Otherwise, a brief interval of witness writing can serve to let us know how or why we are resisting the flow of energy of the creative force through the image and back again to ourselves. Often, we discover fear. We may have created an aesthetically pleasing image, but the image wants more and we resist "messing it up." Sometimes an image becomes dark, and we fear that something threatening will emerge. We try to stay with the image. If it is too difficult to keep working, we might just sit and look. Writing and dialoguing is an excellent way to move through any impasse.

The experience of pleasure in art making is one of its crucial values. Experiencing genuine pleasure creates a sense of trust. Like having a guide on a mountain climbing or scuba diving adventure, our trust in the image as guide allows us to travel deeper and higher into the complex dimensions of life.

Witness Writing #18

This is a key component of the Open Studio Process, in which we simply record all that we experience. Often beginning with a description of the piece is helpful, just to train ourselves in the crucial act of paying attention to what is before us. We can describe the image as a way of appreciating it: "You are so bright and full of color." "I like the way that black line snakes around the top of the page." We are also free to say what we don't like and to note ways in which the image is different from what we expected. It is important to examine our judgments as a valuable form of information. If there is something in the image that makes us uncomfortable, it is worth reflecting on. We recognize that the image has a life of its own. Its opinions and wishes may be quite different from ours. Our overriding intention is to serve the image as a manifestation of the creative force.

Therefore, we address the image to learn what it requires. When we ask the image "What do you want?" the answer is usually very clear: "Brighten my background, define my features more clearly, add an owl to the picture." We may also ask the image what it has to say to us. Direct guidance is almost always forthcoming. It may have to do with the art process or not. The image may tell us to rest, to hold our tongue in a particular situation, to create an image in a particular medium, or to do nothing. The witness writing is a way to practice listening to the inner voice of wisdom, and has proved remarkably useful in illuminating and developing the relationship of the image to the person who made it. In every case, we hear from the image a unique wisdom that enriches not only the writer, but all who are present.

After writing, each person has the opportunity to read their writing aloud. Hearing the words and dialogues is powerful, and often reveals yet another level of meaning or impact, both to the one who reads and those who listen. As we sit and listen to one another, the sounds of struggle, joy, resistance, acceptance, anguish, and humor ring with truth. Because we make no comments, we must each sit with the feelings aroused in us by our own truth and that of others.

This self-restraint is a crucial part of the process and trains us to become mindful of what we say, why we say it, and how little of what we say is either necessary or helpful. We see our judgments of others shift and change, as we hear their images speak. The being with others in this respectful way, owning our own reactions, creates a space for profound empathy among individuals and for the overall human condition. We learn to tolerate strong emotions, rather than to suppress them or act them out through blurted platitudes.

In a sense, the overall process is an action metaphor for the values described by the Dalai Lama: "Spirituality I take to be concerned with those qualities of the human spirit—such as love and compassion, patience, tolerance, forgiveness, contentment, a sense of responsibility, a sense of harmony—which bring happiness to self and others" (1999, p. 22). Images, emotions, words, rise and are seen, and fade as the group itself serves as the witness consciousness sought in meditation. The truth that we are unique yet profoundly connected individuals is felt and experienced over and over. A sacred space is created where truth in all its forms is welcome.

While the Open Studio Process can be practiced by individuals alone, the energy of the group has a compelling part to play. As we hear our own thoughts and feelings echoed by others, or at times hear a counterpart to some emotion that balances our own, we are reminded again and again of the depth and variety of the human condition, and feel ourselves an integral part of the human family. At the close of a group, participants often express feeling nourished and deeply satisfied. The hunger for meaning and connection seems indeed to be met by this humble process.

#12

☐ The Story of Janet

Try to imagine that alongside Janet are perhaps half a dozen others deeply engaged on any given day in painting a tiny watercolor with intense concentration, arranging the beaded covering on a sculpture of a female figure, standing and drawing abstract strokes on a huge sheet of kraft paper taped to the wall, etc. In the background a Celtic harp tape plays, and outside the plate glass window of the storefront studio, commuters walk purposively toward the train, latte in hand, occasionally glancing in, and perhaps wondering why grownups are engaged in what appears to be play during business hours.

Janet's Dog

Janet, an organizational consultant, has a fascinating professional life. As an independent consultant to nonprofits, she helps design and organize large-scale fund raising events. She is adept at helping organizations see their strengths and capitalize on them to fuel their mission and keep their work going. The nature of her work is feast or famine, periods of huge effort and then down time, big payoffs at the end of a project and lean months in between. Janet has to provide her own structure, and the skill of discernment is crucial to keeping balance in life as well as in her checkbook.

While recovering from bronchitis, Janet formed the intention to nurture herself and to give caring to herself, tapping into and leveraging her own strengths. Her intention read in part:

> It means not living for the moment, not buying expensive things, not thinking I'm rich because I get a big contract. It means focus and control. It's a different lifestyle—not running all over the country to visit friends, but following my dream of buying a house . . . I need enough nurturing—I need more nurturing—images of nurturing.

The image that came to Janet was a dog. He took shape over a number of months. For Janet, who likes to work fast and get things done, creating a sculpture of the dog was a new experience. If she worked too fast, he wouldn't be strong enough; he had to be built up of many layers and finally covered with plaster gauze. Then, when he was all built, his ears didn't look quite right to her and his neck wasn't strong enough. In her witness writing the dog asked to have these parts fixed. Janet did the extra work and the dog approved (Figure 12.1).

Figure 12.1.

Janet: *How did I do?*

Dog: *Good. You bit the bullet, ripped me apart, or performed surgery, and put me back together—better. Just like the house and mortgage process. Take a look, do something, see results, take the next step, regroup, try again to shape it.*

Janet worked on other pieces as well during this time, but the dog presented many challenges, technical as well as personal. He wanted a stand, to look both earthbound and flying, to have both a strong foundation and a launching pad. His heart was a matter of great concern and care. Sometimes his advice was simple, yet profound.

Janet: *Dog, anything else?*

Dog: *Walk the dog.*

Janet: *What does that mean?*

Dog: *First literally—all the dogs in your life—walk them whenever you can. Second, get out yourself and get air and exercise. Third, keep practicing!*

The dog finally came close to being finished, but continued to advise Janet and remind her of her goals. From her witness writing:

> The dog is lustery and smooth—wild circles are under the surface yet can be seen—especially underneath. I like him—he's solid, substantial, sturdy, yet sleek and shiny. You can see his bumps, bruises and irregularities (like mine), but they are part of the whole. You can see the glitter stripes, but they are like lines of a past life, scars, sentiments of the future. Looks doughy and determined, but strong enough to get where he's going—running.

Janet: *Want to speak?*

Dog: *You did good. Your dogged determination is paying off. You are walking the dog. But remember, we dogs need walking every day. Once a week doesn't do it!*

Janet: *What else?*

Dog: *Finish me up, glue me down, put a removable bottom on. Wrap up the hearts and dog—the little one—and find a place for me.*

> The dog, like the tree, is rooted in the earth—in life, in trust . . . I really did create something here—extremely satisfying. Paint "Walk the Dog" somewhere on it. Make plans to come back.

☐ Reflections

Janet's dog (see Figure 12.1) was created during weekly groups where five to seven participants gather to engage in the process together. Each person's work speaks not only to its maker but to the group as well. Many of us resonated with the advice Janet received from her dog. Janet continues to use the Open Studio Process as a means to gain pleasure in using materials, to slow down and figure out what she needs in the moment, as well as to explore issues in her life. She is getting married soon and organized an event about weddings, where she gathered all sorts of images, hung them up in the studio, and invited guests to witness the images.

This sort of deepening of any aspect of life is a natural outgrowth of the process, where eventually life itself becomes an amazing, ongoing work of art that we can continually witness and learn from, delight in, and become curious about. Our particular feelings, like anxiety or anger, become like the colors we paint with, and we can decide to tone them down, or eliminate them from our palette for awhile, and see how the overall work is shaping up with fresh colors.

The overall outcome of engagement in this process as a spiritual practice is a subtle transformation of personality, as the individual accesses the meaning and purpose of his or her life. Along the way insights are gained, struggles are resolved, and perceptions are sharpened. A larger lens grows through which to view life, putting one's particular faults and failings and those of others into a perspective of lessons to be learned, for the benefit of the world at large as well as for the self.

In the usual practice of therapy the therapist puts her faith in and seeks her guidance from a theoretical point of view. The client puts his faith in the therapist. In the Open Studio Process, it is assumed that there is an intelligence, a force, of which we are a part, that seeks to manifest itself through us; and that if we make the effort, through disciplined practice, to align ourselves with this force, we will be guided to truth and right action. Each of us has something unique to bring to life and to share with each other. "It is in the telling and retelling, as truthfully as we can, and in the genuine witnessing of all the stories of all people that we heal ourselves and the world" (Allen, 1995a, p. 199).

☐ References

Allen, P. B. (1995a). *Art is a way of knowing*. Boston: Shambhala.

Allen, P. B. (1995b). Coyote comes in from the cold: The evolution of the open studio concept. *Art Therapy, 12*, 161–166.

Beals, J. (2000). *Dog stories: Witness writings from the Open Studio*.

Boorstein, S. (Ed.). (1996). *Transpersonal psychotherapy*. Albany: State University of New York Press.

Cane, F. (1983). *The artist in each of us*. Craftsbury Common, VT: Art Therapy Publications. (Original work published 1951)

Cooper, D. (1997). *God is a verb: Kabbalah and the practice of mystical Judaism*. New York: Riverhead.

Dalai Lama. (1999). *Ethics for a new millennium*. New York: Riverhead.

Franklin, M. (1999). Becoming a student of oneself: Activating the witness in meditation, art, and supervision. *American Journal of Art Therapy, 38*, 2–13.

Franklin, M., Farrelly-Hansen, M., Marek, B., Swan-Foster, N., & Wallingford, S. (November, 1999). *Transpersonal Art Therapy Education*. Panel presentation, AATA Annual Conference, Orlando, FL.

Jaffe, A. (Ed.). (1979). *C. G. Jung: Word and image*. Princeton, NJ: Princeton University Press.

James, W. (1902). *The varieties of religious experience*. New York: Collier MacMillan. (Orginal work published 1902)

Kramer, E. (1958). *Art therapy in a children's community*. Springfield, IL: Charles C. Thomas.

Kramer, E. (1971). *Art as therapy with children*. New York: Schocken Books.

McNiff, S. (1989). *Depth psychology of art*. Springfield, IL: Charles C. Thomas.

McNiff, S. (1992). *Art as medicine*. Boston: Shambhala.

Trungpa, C. (1984). *Shambhala: The sacred path of the warrior*. New York: Bantam.

Trungpa, C. (1996). *Dharma art*. Boston: Shambhala.

Tworkov, H. (1994). *Zen in America*. New York: Kodansha International.

Walsh, R., & Vaughan, F. (1996). Comparative models of the person in psychotherapy. In S. Boorstein (Ed.), *Transpersonal psychotherapy*. Albany, NY: State University of New York.

Wilber, K. (1997). *The spectrum of consciousness*. Wheaton, IL: Quest Books.

COMMENTARY

Bruce Moon

The chapters in this section emerge from the authors' commonly held belief in the inner wisdom and resilience of human beings. Betensky, Rhyne, Garai, Rogers, and Allen offer their own unique visions of art therapy, under the larger umbrella of humanistic approaches. These authors share a deep conviction that individuals long for, and strive to create, meaning in their lives. Despite changes—in health care delivery systems stressing short-term therapy, and in literary forms emphasizing gender-inclusive language—in the time since the first publication of this text, the earlier contributions hold up remarkably well. Perhaps this is a testament to the unchanging core issues of human existence.

The new chapters by Rogers and Allen are significant additions to the humanistic literature of the discipline. Their image of the expressive art therapist as a fellow traveler is clearly in synchrony with the offerings of the earlier contributors, while being closely aligned with ideas advanced by McNiff (1992, 1998), Moon (1994), and others.

My endeavors (Moon, 1995) as an existential art therapist have led me into countless encounters with clients' artworks, as well as with my own images. In our common search to understand the meaning of these many artistic works—through mutual self-exploration, self-revelation, and responsive art making—I have witnessed exhilarating breakthroughs by suffering people who were determined to make changes in their lives.

I have come to value artistic processes that support both spontaneous expression and disciplined mastery of materials. I especially admire humanistic methodologies that open channels of self-expression and self-awareness, through artistic activities that enable people to explore their own hopes and visions about how they want to live their lives. Broadly speaking, humanistic methodologies engage art therapists and their clients in tasks that encourage openness, and honor whatever psychic material emerges in the artwork. An art therapist's sensitive alertness to the inner villains and heroes of individual consciousness is greatly enhanced by looking—lovingly—at the image metaphors created by clients.

Betensky, Rhyne, Garai, Rogers, and Allen have all developed humanistic approaches to helping troubled clients looking for safe haven in the supportive milieu of art therapy. As Moustakas (1994) notes, "Again and again I have witnessed the natural tendency of people to share their stories openly and freely when the climate of learning fosters and encourages self-disclosure" (p. 2).

Each of the approaches to art therapy presented in this section emphasizes the importance of "being" in the context of relationships with others, with images, and with the world. Humanistic models embrace the significance of creativity, self-direction, potential, and meaning in all human interactions. These models do not regard human beings from the viewpoint of those looking for pathologies and symptoms, but rather as creatures who are illuminating, self-creating, and self-disclosing.

In humanistic approaches to art therapy the focus is on whatever emerges in the individual's artistic expressions, and whatever leads toward new, healthy possibilities for life. These approaches offer the potential for the person in therapy to move toward a self-fulfilling and meaningful life through artistic engagement.

The contributions in this section remind the reader that the human being who has entered therapy is the central focus of decision-making and action. As Moustakas notes, "The person-in-therapy retains control over his or her own destiny" (1994, p. 6). These respectful and caring humanistic art therapists intervene in the client's world in such a way as to inspire a search for meaning. The creative search, or journey, is one that is shared by client and therapist. Whatever malady afflicts one's life, the possibility is always present for resolution of conflict and creation of meaning—through artistic processes in the context of art therapy relationships.

☐ References

McNiff, S. (1992). *Art as medicine*. Boston: Shambhala.

McNiff, S. (1998). *Trust the process*. Boston: Shambhala.

Moon, B. (1994). *Introduction to art therapy: Faith in the process*. Springfield, IL: Charles C. Thomas.

Moon, B. (1995). *Existential art therapy: The canvas mirror*. Springfield, IL: Charles C. Thomas.

Moustakas, C. (1994). *Existential psychotherapy and the interpretation of dreams*. New York: Jason Aronson.

III

PSYCHO-EDUCATIONAL APPROACHES

PSYCHO-EDUCATIONAL APPROACHES

The approaches in this section all share an emphasis on learning, and actively design the therapeutic situation to facilitate the client's acquisition of a new skill or behavior. For this reason, I have grouped them together and renamed the section "psycho-educational." Frances Anderson, whose Adaptive approach has much in common with those in this chapter, notes in her Commentary that all of the authors refer to the research findings on which their work is based. This is another feature which sets these approaches apart from most of the others in this book and one which is consistent with the essential pragmatism they have in common.

Behavioral, cognitive, and cognitive-behavioral approaches have been extremely popular for several decades among talk therapists. Because of the specificity of their goals, they lend themselves to precise evaluation in both research and treatment. Although brief therapy can be conducted using psychodynamic or humanistic frameworks, the approaches in this section are those most often used in short-term treatment. The fact that outcomes can be more easily measured also makes these methods especially attractive to funding sources, in this era of cost containment.

In Ellen Roth's chapter on the application of behavioral techniques to the practice of art therapy, she describes her models, as well as her own invention: "reality shaping." Her sensitive implementation of what could otherwise be quite mechanistic, should help to allay the anxieties of many art therapists about the dangers of what may at first seem an intrinsically anticreative mode.

In Marcia Rosal's chapter on cognitive-behavioral art therapy, she describes a great variety of ways in which art therapists have used that approach in their work. She then details her own clinical work with a depressed woman, using "mind-state drawings" and other cognitively-based interventions.

In the chapter on a developmental approach, Susan Aach-Feldman and Carole Kunkle-Miller describe a way of working that uses various theories of development as their frame of reference. The authors draw from theoreticians as diverse as Mahler and Piaget, in order to construct an art therapy that facilitates growth for individuals in whom it is gravely impaired. Their creative interventions are similarly broad-based, from multi-modal expressive activities to behavioral techniques.

From philosophers' explanations of what man expresses in art (Langer, 1957), to psychologists' studies of creative thinking (Arnheim, 1969; Barron, 1972; Gardner, 1982), using art activities to promote cognitive growth has had a natural evolution. Rawley Silver's chapter describes her own unique methods, which depend on assessing and developing cognitive abilities through art activities (Silver, 1978).

Although it would be possible to employ a developmental, behavioral, or cognitive approach with patients whose only problems are emotional, it is probably not accidental that most of the authors in this section developed their theory and technique in the course of work with the disabled. Silver first worked with the hearing impaired, later extending her work to those with learning disabilities, cognitive impairments, and other conditions which interfere with language. Roth, Aach-Feldman, and Kunkle-Miller served children with severe intellectual and sensory deficits, as well as social and emotional problems. And even though cognitive-behavioral therapy is applicable to intelligent patients of all ages, it is especially helpful for those who are disabled.

The potential applications of behavioral, cognitive, developmental, and cognitive-behavioral approaches to art therapy are multiple, and I believe that most have not yet been explored or articulated. I hope that the reader will be inspired to think of yet additional ways of utilizing the kind of thinking reflected in this section, some of which are noted in Frances Anderson's forward-looking Commentary at the end.

☐ References

Arnheim, R. (1969). *Visual thinking*. Berkeley, CA: University of California Press.

Barron, F. (1972). *Artists in the making*. New York: Seminar Press.

Gardner, H. (1982). *Art, mind and brain: A cognitive approach to creativity*. New York: Basic Books.

Langer, S. (1957). *Problems of art*. New York: Charles Scribner.

Silver, R. A. (1978). *Developing cognitive and creative skills in art*. Baltimore, MD: University Park Press.

Ellen Roth

Behavioral Art Therapy

Behavior therapy is a technique designed to treat directly observable undesirable behavior, what psychodynamic therapy calls "symptoms." Behavior therapy rejects the notion that problematic behavior is a symptom of underlying conflicts maintained by unconscious dynamic processes. Rather, behaviorists view aberrant behavior as a learned phenomenon, which is maintained by environmental and situational determinants. Their model of treatment is to first assess behavior, and then to alter it through procedures that modify old behavior or that teach new behaviors (e.g., conditioning techniques, systematic desensitization, modeling, etc.). Desired changes are defined and demonstrated empirically, and are evaluated throughout treatment.

"Behavioral influence in therapy has evolved in two directions, one based on Pavlovian concepts of learning, with a major focus on emotional learning; and Skinnerian methodology, with an emphasis on observable behavior and change through contingent reinforcement. The former has developed in the outpatient setting, is usually a one-to-one therapy regimen, and is applicable to neurotic problems; while the latter has developed in inpatient settings.... The former ... has come to be identified as "behavior therapy" while the Skinnerian applications are most often referred to as "behavior modification" (Goldstein, 1973, p. 207).

Although its roots may be traced to Pavlov, a Russian physiologist, behavioral psychology has emerged over the past 40 years as an American theory (Hall & Lindzey, 1975). The principle of *classical conditioning* investigated by Pavlov (1927) with dogs is that, when an unconditioned stimulus (food) is repeatedly paired with a neutral stimulus (the sound of a metronome), the neutral stimulus will eventually elicit the unconditioned reflex response (salivation) in the absence of the unconditioned stimulus (food). In this case, the sound of the metronome becomes a conditioned stimulus, and salivating to the sound a conditioned response.

Watson and Raynor (1920) showed that fears are learned, by using classical conditioning techniques to induce fear reactions to rats, rabbits, and other furry objects in an infant. Wolpe (1958), who originated *systematic desensitization*, treated anxious patients by pairing deep-muscle relaxation and hypnosis with a hierarchy of anxiety-evoking stimuli. The person imagines anxiety-provoking scenes, from least to most disturbing, in a "psychophysiological state that inhibits anxiety" (Brady, 1975, p. 1825). The effect is achieved by *counterconditioning*.

Skinner (1953) advanced the principles of *operant conditioning* first studied by Thorndike (1911/1965). In operant conditioning, behaviors are controlled (strengthened or weakened) by the events that follow them. Positive *reinforcement*, with primary (e.g., food), social (e.g., praise), or generalized (e.g., money) reinforcers, increases the likelihood of a particular behavior recurring; *punishment* (e.g., disapproval) is likely to decrease its recurrence; and cessation of reinforcement (e.g., ignoring) leads to *extinction*. Operant conditioning techniques include *shaping*, which involves bringing someone closer to a desired behavior by reinforcing small steps that gradually lead to it. This is done by reinforcing *successive approximations*, which include responses that either "resemble the final response or which include components of that response" (Kazdin, 1975, p. 37). Like shaping, *chaining* involves a sequence of behaviors.

In shaping behavior, there are two major reinforcement schedules: *interval* and *ratio* reinforcements. *Continuous* reinforcement means that a behavior is reinforced each time it occurs. Once a behavior occurs consistently, it can be maintained on an *intermittent* reinforcement schedule. Lutzker, McGimsey-McRae, and McGimsey (1983) note that "behaviors that are reinforced on an intermittent schedule are more resistant to extinction (i.e., they continue to be performed in the absence of reinforcement) because the individual performing the behavior has become accustomed to not having each performance of the behavior reinforced" (p. 33). Shaping and chaining behavior are facilitated by *prompts*, which include "cues, instructions, gestures, directions, examples, and models to initiate a response" (Kazdin, 1975, p. 41). Their gradual removal is called *fading*.

Another important component of the operant paradigm is the concept of *generalization*. Learned behavior may be generalized or transferred to other settings (stimulus generalization), or changes in a behavior may be associated with changes in related behaviors (response generalization).

Learning theories developed in the laboratory are also applicable to the study of personality and social behavior. Dollard and Miller's (1950) *stimulus response theory* of personality embraces analytic theory, translating psychoanalytic formulations into principles of learning. They postulate that all behavior, including neurotic behavior, is learned. Learned behavior is acquired as a function of four fundamental principles: drive, cue, response, and reinforcement. "If neurotic behavior is learned, it should be unlearned by some combination of the same principles by which it was taught. We believe this to be the case. Psychotherapy establishes a set of conditions by which neurotic habits may be unlearned and non-neurotic habits learned. Therefore, we view the therapist as a kind of teacher and the patient as a learner" (Dollard & Miller, 1950, pp. 7–8).

Bandura and Walters' (1963) *social learning theory* is concerned with observational learning and imitation; for example, "the tendency for a person to reproduce the actions, attitudes, or emotional responses exhibited by real-life or symbolized models" (1963, p. 89). New behavioral responses are learned, or existing behaviors are modified, by observing the behavior of others. Thus, exposure to *models*, can influence behavior negatively or positively. Additional behavioral *strategies* include role playing, assertiveness training, flooding, and aversive techniques (Goldstein, 1973).

Behaviorists define *neurosis* as "persistent unadaptive behaviors which have developed through learning or the deficit of adaptive behaviors due to insufficient learning" (Goldstein, 1973, p. 217). The goal is "to reverse unadaptive learning and furnish learning experiences where appropriate responses have not been learned" (Goldstein, 1973, p. 220).

The behavioral approach to treatment begins by identifying a specific complaint (*target behavior*) that requires modification. A *history* is taken to learn the cause-and-effect relationships of the problem behavior. The therapist and client develop a trusting working relationship in which the goal of therapy is mutually agreed upon. *Treatment goals* are clearly stated, and the target behavior is carefully described. As noted by Kazdin, "the target behaviors have to be defined explicitly so that they can actually be observed, measured and agreed upon" (1975, p. 66). In strict behavior modification programs, the *frequency* of occurrence of the target behavior is also first objectively assessed, which establishes a *baseline* rate of performance. Appropriate techniques are administered that will change behavior to the desired goal, with continuous monitoring to evaluate change.

☐ Behavior Theory and Art Therapy: Common Ground

The behavioral approach to art therapy presented in this chapter involves the application of behavior modification techniques (operant conditioning and modeling procedures) to the practice of art therapy (with emotionally disturbed, mentally retarded children). At first, the idea of a behavioral approach to art therapy may appear antithetical. Behavioral techniques, however, are used by all art therapists. For example, encouraging a blocked or inhibited patient to make a scribble in order to involve them with media, then praising the individual for participating, is a behavioral approach (e.g., reinforcement).

I have found behavioral techniques to be especially useful in doing art therapy with emotionally disturbed, mentally retarded children (Roth, 1978, 1979, 1983; Roth & Barrett, 1980). This is a group with whom behavior therapy is known to improve adaptive behavior (Keogh & Whitman, 1983; Thompson & Grabowski, 1972; Whitman, Sciback, & Reid, 1983). Behavioral art therapy not only helps disturbed retarded children with their behavior, but addresses their emotional needs as well.

A behavioral approach to art therapy has also been demonstrated to be effective with severely anxious children (DeFrancisco, 1983) and aggressive adults (van Sickle & Acker, 1975). Others who might benefit are those who are neither highly verbal nor intellectually sophisticated.

☐ Reality Shaping: A Behavioral Approach

An art therapy approach of special utility for emotionally disturbed, mentally retarded children is what I call "reality shaping." (Roth, 1978). It combines traditional art therapy techniques with behavior modification principles; it involves education during the process of therapy. Reality shaping begins by identifying a concept that is poorly conveyed in the child's art productions. This concept is then developed into representational form through the construction—first by the art therapist and then by the child—of increasingly complex two- and three-dimensional models. This structured technique gives concrete form to vague concepts that may be related to a child's pathology.

☐ Case Illustrations

Following are three cases illustrating the technique of *reality shaping* with disturbed retarded children. These children were hospitalized in the John Merck Program for

Emotionally Disturbed-Mentally Retarded Children, which provided a multidisciplinary approach to treatment and education in a therapeutic milieu.

The Case of Larry

This case concerns a mildly retarded 6-year-old named Larry. Larry exhibited a severe speech delay, hyperactivity, and a history of destructive behavior. Repeated dangerous acts included playing with knives, gas jets, and the kitchen stove. He had swallowed pills (he was hospitalized three times to have his stomach pumped), and he showed constant disruptive attention-seeking. The event precipitating hospitalization was setting fire to his family's home, using a cigarette lighter he found in his mother's purse. He ignited a lampshade, and then stood outside the house watching it burn, while laughing and hysterically screaming, "Burn house, burn house!" No one was hurt during the fire, but Larry's bedroom was badly damaged. Serious injury to family members could have occurred, had the father not awakened and ushered everyone out of the house.

Larry's art therapy evaluation occurred soon after his admission. He was free to choose whatever materials he wished to use. His first works were a series of paintings in which all the colors were smeared together, suggesting a high degree of anxiety expressed through regression. No verbal comments accompanied these paintings. A month after admission, he began to participate in weekly half-hour art therapy sessions. By this time, his paintings consisted of separate, distinct areas of color distributed around the paper; that is, the colors were no longer smeared together.

Larry took an interest in small wooden craft sticks. He began by gluing the pieces of wood to a sheet of paper and then painting over them. For six weeks, his art products consisted mainly of groups of sticks glued vertically to the paper and then painted. Each of these wood formations was identified as "a house." In painting these structures, the color red was used selectively. For example, one red stick would appear in the center of the paper, surrounded by sticks that were blue, green, and black.

It was clear from his products that he had difficulty conceptualizing a house. At this point in therapy, I switched from using a nondirective approach to employing *reality shaping*, which incorporates behavior modification principles. The *goal* or *target behavior* was for Larry to represent a recognizable house on a two-dimensional surface. To help him to properly conceptualize a house, I prepared a simple outline of a house made of pieces of wood, and glued the sticks to a sheet of paper (Figure 13.1). The same materials with which he had been working and with which he felt comfortable, were used to create the house schema.

This model was the first step in *shaping* his understanding of how to make a house. We talked about the various parts of the house. Larry could identify the roof and the windows, for which he was *positively reinforced* with praise. When he was not able to label the walls, chimney, or door, I identified these parts for him. Larry became physically involved with the model by painting over each section of the house as we talked about it. This also reinforced his understanding of how the parts were connected. The color red was still used selectively, on one upstairs window and the door.

The second step took place in the next session. Larry was invited to construct the outline of a house with sticks on paper, while referring to the *model* that we had made the previous week. He was encouraged to imitate the model. He was able to do this with *prompts* in the form of verbal instructions and physical guidance. Each time that he put a craft stick in an appropriate placement, he was praised (*continuous reinforcement*).

After he successfully made an outline of a house on a flat surface, the next step was the construction of a three-dimensional house (Figure 13.2). This house (10" × 10" × 10"),

(text continues on page 201)

Figure 13.1.

Figure 13.2.

which took 16 sessions to complete, was made out of the same wooden sticks with which he had had a series of successful two-dimensional experiences. I facilitated his construction of the foundation of the house with verbal and physical *prompts*, as well as positive *reinforcement*. Once the foundation, which established the basic shape of the house, was laid, however, the prompts were *faded* out, and continuous reinforcement was replaced by *intermittent reinforcement*.

Larry was very protective of this house, always wanting reassurance that no one else would touch it. When the house was completed, he took it home. His mother reported that he had slowly and deliberately taken the house apart, and that he kept the pieces in a drawer in his room. First, Larry had damaged his family's home. Now, by destroying his miniature house, he had perhaps symbolically mastered the situation.

Two months after the three-dimensional house was built, Larry spontaneously began to make x-ray paintings of a house. These paintings were very different from his earlier ones of random shapes of color. They were characterized by a large rectangular shape (house), derived from an understanding of "houseness," based on the construction of his earlier houses. Various forms within the house were identified as household items, such as a couch, a window, etc. His paintings now possessed a sense of geometry and order, indicating that his ability to represent a house was beginning to generalize or transfer to another medium.

Larry next spontaneously made another three-dimensional house. It was prefabricated out of cardboard, and hence put together much more quickly than the first house. It was also painted. This house represented a synthesis of his previous work. It combined the exterior of the first three-dimensional house with the interior of his recent two-dimensional paintings. The interior of the cardboard house was divided in half. The partitioned area represented Larry's bedroom, to which he had set fire. It had a red window. This bedroom was his first concrete reference to the scene of the fire, although he had referred to fire in numerous sessions.

Three weeks later, Larry created another house, a primitive structure made out of clay, with both exterior and interior. The interior contained a partitioned area with two beds. He stated that one bed was his, and that the other one was for me. I inferred from our relationship and the context of the session, that my presence in the bedroom meant that the bedroom would be a safe place to be in if I were there. Larry took this house home.

A few weeks later, Larry made a clearly recognizable drawing of a house, consisting of a rectangular base with a triangular roof. There was also a door and two windows. It was very similar to the first model of a house he had made by gluing pieces of wood to paper. It was clear that the *target behavior* of representing a recognizable house on a two-dimensional surface had been successfully achieved.

Simultaneously, symbolic material associated with houses continued to emerge at an accelerated pace. For example, this recognizable house, which had generalized from three to two dimensions, was also enclosed within a red and orange border identified as "a road." This border reflected ambivalent feelings concerning the house. It seemed to be a protective line, intended to shield the house from destruction. But the use of red also suggested a house surrounded by the threat of fire.

The following week, Larry began to make another three-dimensional house out of small matched pieces of wood. It consisted only of an exterior. While adding the chimney, he commented that his own home did not have a fireplace. Larry worked on it for six weeks, while also using other media.

Two paintings from this period were of special interest. One was an x-ray painting of a house. Next to the house was a figure identified as "Ellen," who was "coming to visit." This was the first human figure that Larry had represented in a year of art therapy. The second painting was of a "fire truck" going to a fire, also the first image of its kind.

During the next three months, Larry's art products focused on objects in his environment that were clearly identifiable, such as stoplights and parking garages, in addition to occasional houses. That he could at any time return to drawing the image of a house was evidence that the learned behavior was *maintained* over time.

In contrast to these carefully delineated paintings of objects, a painting emerged one day in which the colors were smeared together, called "Fire." I commented that it was "a picture of fire." Larry immediately responded, "I saw a real fire!" He recounted in detail the scene of the fire in his bedroom, though he did not make any reference to how the fire had begun. From this time, Larry was able to deal more directly and openly with the subject of the fire in his home. He also made gains behaviorally and conceptually, as well as in his ability to graphically represent real objects.

Discussion.   Behavior modification techniques were successful in teaching Larry how to represent a recognizable house. The construction of houses was meaningful to him on three levels. First, developing the concept of a house into representational form was an achievement in which he experienced pleasure and the pride of accomplishment, serving to raise his self-esteem. Second, through the construction of three-dimensional houses, he was able to represent in concrete form the main structural aspects of a house. These miniature houses served to clarify and organize his concept of a house, which initially was extremely vague.

Third, making two- and three-dimensional creations that actually resembled houses enabled Larry to bring into focus the reality of the fire-setting incident that had been so traumatic. The houses facilitated his eventual ability to talk about fires, houses being burned, and other related anxiety-provoking subjects. It was an opportunity for Larry to work through his conflicts within a supportive environment. By building miniature houses, he was also able to symbolically undo the harm he had caused by burning his own home, and thereby assuage his guilt.

The Case of Paul

Paul was an 8-year-old, moderately retarded boy, admitted to inpatient psychiatric hospitalization with the parents' complaint that he was unmanageable at home. His behavior was described as stubborn, defiant, irritable, and destructive of property. He had temper tantrums, was unresponsive, and was difficult to comfort. At times, he appeared disoriented; he was afraid to be alone. He tormented his siblings, showed both active and passive aggression toward his parents, and was aggressive toward peers. In unfamiliar situations, he was withdrawn.

During his art evaluation, Paul made eight paintings, each a large mass of smeared colors and dribbles, which were not identified. For the first two months of weekly art therapy, his preferred medium was paint, and his work was similar to that of his first session. These paintings, however, were consistently identified as "trees." After two months of Paul naming masses of smeared colors "trees," I decided to use the technique of *reality shaping* to help him to properly conceptualize a tree. The goal was for Paul to be able to represent a recognizable image of a tree on a flat surface.

To *shape* his understanding of what a tree looked like on paper, as opposed to in a natural environment, I prepared a three-dimensional model of a tree by attaching a small branch with leaves to a piece of wood. I taped it to a sheet of paper, and painted the wooden trunk. Paul and I talked about the parts of a tree, first differentiating the tree-top and trunk. After reviewing these parts, I gave Paul the same three-dimensional materials I had used. Together, we made a similar model of a tree.

The next step involved transferring the three-dimensional form to a flat surface. The following week, we talked about the parts of a tree while referring to the three-dimensional models. With verbal guidance (*prompts*) Paul was able to paint a recognizable tree, differentiating the tree-top (i.e., green mass) from the tree-trunk (i.e., linear brown brushstrokes extending downward from the tree-top). During this activity, he was *continuously reinforced* with praise for his mastery of the task.

Having successfully represented the general form of a tree, the next step involved further *differentiating* the tree-top, by making forms like branches. With verbal cues and manual assistance, Paul was shown how to paint individual lines at the top of the trunk, which represented branches. Next, he painted a similar model on his own. At this point, I had some concern that I had guided Paul into a very narrow and sterile conception of a tree. My fears, however, were soon relieved.

Two weeks later, he painted a series of trees, incorporating the forms that we had been developing, but adding his own personal color scheme. The trees that he painted were not green and brown, but appeared in the full array of autumn tones (red, yellow, orange, purple). The target behavior, representing a tree on a two-dimensional surface, was achieved. The development just described evolved over a period of five weeks.

Once Paul had mastered the schema, his art work no longer focused exclusively on trees. He began to incorporate other themes into his artwork as well (e.g., faces). During the following year, Paul occasionally painted a tree or group of trees, which incorporated the general form that differentiated the top from the trunk; evidence that Paul had internalized the tree schema, and that his learned behavior was maintained over time.

Discussion.   The use of reality shaping was an effective means of teaching Paul how to paint a recognizable tree. Initially, his art work focused on smeared forms identified as "trees." His concept of a tree was given an appropriate schema through the use of two- and three-dimensional models. Although it is unclear exactly what trees meant to this child, it is clear that the image was an important one. Once he had mastered the tree, he was very pleased with himself. The activity served to raise his self-esteem, bolster his confidence, and expand his cognitive capacity—by creating a visual link between an object in the real world and his concept of that object. Mastering trees gave him a bridge to the world of people, as he began making other objects, like faces.

The Case of Kelly

Kelly, a 7-year-old, mentally retarded girl, had developmental delays in motor, language, perceptual, and conceptual functioning. Performance in these areas was uneven, with her mental ability and social skills ranging from two to four years. At the time of admission, Kelly exhibited inappropriate behaviors: frequent temper tantrums, poor frustration tolerance, inability to interact with peers, and speech that was largely echolalic.

During her diagnostic art evaluation, Kelly exhibited very dependent behavior, requiring physical contact to maintain graphic control. For example, when she placed my hand on hers, she could draw a circle. I did not control her drawing, but simply let her sweep my hand along with her own. As long as our hands were touching, her marks were linear and controlled. When I withdrew my hand, she scribbled randomly.

Figure 13.3.

Kelly began to participate in regular art therapy sessions four months after her initial session. By this time, she no longer sought physical assistance when drawing or painting. Her response to my request to draw a person was a web of circular scribbles and random lines (Figure 13.3). As she made this drawing, she named numerous body parts and pointed to these parts on her own body. Nevertheless, they appear only as named scribbles.

In addition to drawing and painting, Kelly often used plasticine. Her performance with this three-dimensional medium was more advanced than with two-dimensional materials. She made numerous types of foods, and we pretended to eat them. This suggested that a more deliberate use of three-dimensional media might promote developmental gains.

The *goal of reality shaping* was for Kelly to draw a person, an image she had been unable to create. I began by helping her to conceptualize a face. First, I made a model of a face by putting plasticine features on a plastic egg, creating a kind of Humpty-Dumpty. Second, we made a similar model using the first as a reference. Without prompting, Kelly's first face was a lump of plasticine stuck onto an egg. But with verbal *prompts*, physical *guidance*, and *continuous positive reinforcement*, she learned where to place facial features. In making these faces (Figure 13.4), she acknowledged as physical references her facial features and mine too. She was encouraged to comment, with the placement of each feature, that they did not touch one another. Thus, she learned separation of parts.

Once Kelly had mastered a three-dimensional egg face, I drew an egg shape on a piece of paper, suggested that she place pieces of plasticine within it where facial features belonged, and then trace around them (Figure 13.5). With *guidance*, she was able to do

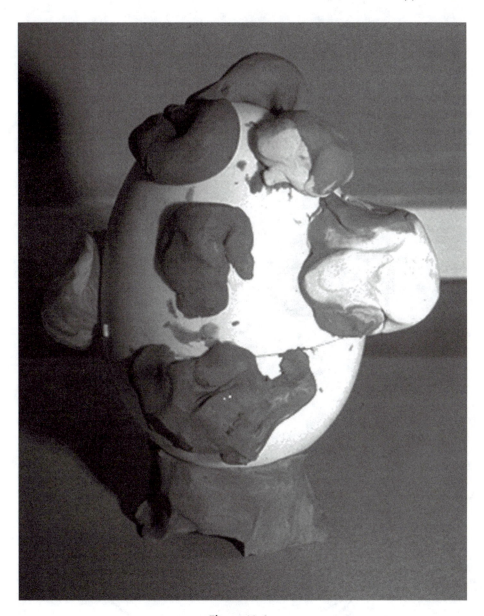

Figure 13.4.

this. In helping her to conceptualize a face schema on paper using her favorite materials, the three-dimensional use of plasticine was transferred to a two-dimensional surface.

Four weeks later, Kelly spontaneously drew a face on a sheet of paper, accurately placing the features (Figure 13.6). She had internalized a facial schema, and she was able to represent it two-dimensionally. During the same session, she also made a finger painting of a face, indicating that she was able to *generalize* the schema to other media.

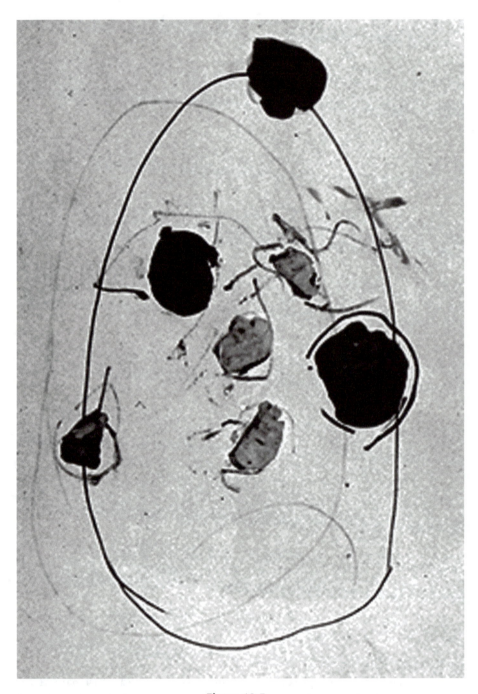

Figure 13.5.

Figure 13.6.

After Kelly had demonstrated that she could accurately draw a face, I went back to the three-dimensional model, using the plastic eggs and plasticine to help her to conceptualize a more complete figure. Humpty-Dumpty was expanded to include a body, arms, and legs.

The same process used for teaching Kelly to draw a face was applied to drawing a human figure. Plasticine features and appendages were added to a sheet of paper already containing the outline of a head and body. Kelly traced around the appendages to get a sense of their forms, as well as where they existed in relationship to other body parts. The next step involved my drawing circular forms representing a head and a body with Kelly drawing the arms and legs. Four months later, she was able to draw, by herself, a human figure incorporating all the body parts we had focused on. The *target behavior* of learning to draw a person was achieved.

Discussion.   During a little over a year of art therapy, Kelly's artwork underwent significant changes. She became able to make controlled marks without external support. By means of *reality shaping*, this ability was channeled into making a human figure, using three-dimensional and two-dimensional *models*. We also talked about and pointed to her own facial features and body parts. Eventually, she was able to internalize a facial schema, and to represent it on paper without reference to a physical model. The representation of additional body parts followed.

Reality shaping focused on developing Kelly's drawing skills, teaching new behaviors, and expanding her cognitive ability. It served as a means of orienting her to reality in terms of her body image. Kelly became aware of her body parts and the interrelatedness of her physical structure.

☐ Concluding Comments

Reality shaping involves the use of behavior modification techniques and models to systematically teach new behavior and to develop concepts not fully understood by the child. Through operant conditioning (prompting, shaping, and positive reinforcement) and modeling, the child learns new behavior which is maintained over time. The technique provides a consistent approach that allows the child to build on learned behavior. Two- and three-dimensional models serve as conceptual references and promote modeling behavior.

Reality shaping is not directed at assessing internal psychological variables or biological conditions. While the child is learning new behaviors and acquiring new behavioral skills, other gains may also occur. For example, this technique may facilitate the child's ability to express images that are disturbing, like Larry's house on fire. Disturbing ideas or fantasies that may underlie the child's pathology can then be explored, using more traditional art therapy approaches.

Concepts that are not disturbing, but which are important to the child's sense of reality, can also be developed. A diminished capacity to think abstractly is a notable feature of retardation (Cytryn & Lourie, 1975). Through the sequential use of simple concrete models, the child can attain an increased level of abstraction. A behavioral approach in art therapy can therefore be an effective means of treating both the emotional disturbance and some of the cognitive effects of retardation.

☐ References

Bandura, A., & Walters, R. H. (1963). *Social learning and personality development*. New York: Holt, Rinehart, & Winston.

Brady, J. P. (1975). Behavior therapy. In A. Freedman, H. Kaplan, & B. Sadock (Eds.), *Comprehensive textbook of psychiatry/II* (Vol. 2) (pp. 1824–1831). Baltimore: Williams & Wilkins.

Cytryn, L., & Lourie, R. (1975). Mental retardation. In A. Freedman, H. Kaplan, & B. Sadock (Eds.), *Comprehensive textbook of psychiatry/II* (Vol. 1) (pp. 1158–1197). Baltimore: Williams & Wilkins.

DeFrancisco, J. (1983). Implosive art therapy: A learning-theory-based, psychodynamic approach. In L. Gantt & S. Whitman (Eds.). *The fine art of therapy* (pp. 74–79). Alexandria, VA: American Art Therapy Association.

Dollard, J., & Miller, N. E. (1950). *Personality and psychotherapy*. New York: McGraw Hill.

Goldstein, A. (1973). Behavior therapy. In R. Corsini (Ed.), *Current psychotherapies* (pp. 207–249). Itasca, IL: F. E. Peacock.

Hall, C. S., & Lindzey, G. (1975). *Theories of personality*, 2nd ed. New York: John Wiley.

Kazdin, A. E. (1975). *Behavior modification in applied settings*. Homewood, IL: The Dorsey Press.

Keogh, D., & Whitman, T. (1983). Mental retardation in children. In M. Hersen, V. B. Van Hasselt, & J. L. Matson (Eds.), *Behavior therapy for the developmentally and physically disabled* (pp. 205–246). New York: Academic.

Lutzker, J. R., McGimsey-McRae, S., & McGimsey, J. F. (1983). General description of behavioral approaches. In M. Hersen, V. B. Van Hasselt, & J. L. Matson (Eds.), *Behavior therapy for the developmentally and physically disabled* (pp. 25–56). New York: Academic.

Pavlov, I. P. (1927). *Conditioned reflexes*. G. V. Anrep (Trans. and Ed.). London: Oxford University Press.

Roth, E. A. (1978). Art therapy with emotionally disturbed-mentally retarded children: A technique of reality shaping. In B. K. Mandel et al. (Eds.), *The dynamics of creativity* (pp. 168–172). Baltimore: American Art Therapy Association.

Roth, E. A. (1979). Choosing an appropriate candidate for art therapy among emotionally disturbed-mentally retarded children. In L. Gantt et al. (Eds.), *Art therapy: Expanding horizons.* (pp. 48–55). Baltimore: American Art Therapy Association.

Roth, E. A. (1983). Art therapy to promote ego development in disturbed retarded children. In L. Gantt & S. Whitman (Eds.), *The fine art of therapy* (pp. 13–19). Alexandria, VA: American Art Therapy Association.

Roth, E., & Barrett, R. (1980). Parallels in art and play therapy with a disturbed retarded child. *The Arts in Psychotherapy, 7,* 19–26.

Skinner, B. F. (1953). *Science and human behavior*. New York: The Free Press.

Thompson, T., & Grabowski, J. (Eds.). (1972). *Behavior modification of the mentally retarded*. London: Oxford University Press.

Thorndike, F. L. (1965). *Animal intelligence*. New York: Hafner. (Original work published 1911)

van Sickle, K. G., & Acker, L. E. (1975). Modification of an adult's problem behavior in an art therapy setting. *American Journal of Art Therapy, 14,* 117–120.

Watson, J. B., & Raynor, R. (1920). Conditioned emotional reactions. *Journal of Experimental Psychology, 3*(1), 1–14.

Whitman, T. L., Sciback, J. W., & Reid, D. H. (Eds.). (1983). *Behavior modification with the severely and profoundly retarded*. New York: Academic Press.

Wolpe, J. (1958). *Psychotherapy by reciprocal inhibition*. Stanford, CA: Stanford University Press.

CHAPTER

Marcia Rosal

Cognitive-Behavioral Art Therapy

What a man thinks of himself that it is which determines
or rather indicates, his fate. (Henry David Thoreau)

Professionals interested in the inner workings of the mind are infinitely fascinated by just how much of our behavior reflects the way we think and feel. Based on current research about the antecedents of human behavior, cognitive-behavioral therapists use knowledge about the thoughts and feelings of their clients to discuss, understand, and ultimately to change behavior. In this theoretical model, thoughts and feelings are referred to as "higher cognitive processes," and clients are asked to learn about, identify, and access patterns and modes of thinking and perceiving. Once they understand their cognitive patterns, clients are exposed to a series of techniques designed to change cognitive processes that may be detrimental to mental, emotional, and physical health.

This chapter presents an overview of how cognitive-behavior therapy (CBT) principles and art therapy intersect. A short history of the cognitive revolution is presented, followed by an outline of the cognitive-behavioral therapy model. How art therapists have integrated CBT principles in their work with clients is then the focus of this chapter. Finally, a case example will illustrate how art therapy can have a cognitive-behavioral base.

☐ Development of Cognitive-Behavior Therapy

The "cognitive revolution in psychology" (Baars, 1986) took place in the 1970's but its roots were older. During the early part of the twentieth century, pure behaviorism was dominant. It was based on research which demonstrated that new behaviors were learned from the stimulus-response connection. In this model, behaviors could either be learned or eliminated through the use of reinforcements. If a new behavior was the goal, the reinforcement was usually an external reward. If decreasing a specific behavior was the targeted outcome, then reinforcements were withheld when the behavior was exhibited.

Behaviorism was a break from traditional psychological modes of understanding human behavior. Psychologists working early in the twentieth century were troubled by the lack of objective data supporting widely-held psychological principles. Thus, from about 1913 to about 1960, many social scientists studied only overt, observable phenomena. During this period, behaviorism—understanding how behaviors were learned and eliminated—was hailed as the metatheoretical base of psychology and understanding human behavior (Baars, 1986).

However, psychologists trying to grasp how human behavior differs from that of the rest of the animal world realized that the human capacity to think, to ponder, and to use language and mental images greatly affected the learning process. Indeed, it was found that reinforcement itself could be an internal process. Many of us have observed ourselves using "inner speech"—whether self-deprecating: "I'm stupid," "I'm unfit to hold this job," "I'm incapable of caring,"or grandiose: "I'm ready for anything!" The theory that evolved to explain the profound impact of internal messages on human behavior is called "cognitive psychology."

Cognitive psychology is a descendant of "social learning theory." One of the first explanations of the human capacity to use higher mental processes as mediators of behavior was Miller and Dollard's 1941 book, *Social Learning and Imitation*. They identified two levels of learned behavior. The first level behaviors, simple stimulus-response behaviors, included automatic habits and all behaviors that were a direct response to both environmental cues and internal drives. The second level behaviors such as language, imagery, thinking, and affect were used for problem-solving. These cognitive operations mediate and facilitate the generation of solutions to a wide variety of problems that people face every day. Miller and Dollard acknowledged that many actions were a complex blend of both types of behaviors, and that human beings have a huge capacity for the second type, called "higher mental processes" (p. 48).

Another social learning theorist, Bandura, wrote in 1969 about how we are "continually engage[d] in self-evaluative and self-reinforcing behavior" (p. 32). Although Miller and Dollard (1941) felt that social learning theory confirmed some psychoanalytic principles, Bandura saw clear differences between the two theoretical models:

> Social learning theory approaches treat internal processes that are manipulable and measurable. These mediating principles are extensively controlled by external stimulus events and they regulate overt responsiveness. By contrast, psychodynamic theories tend to regard internal events as relatively autonomous. These hypothetical causal agents generally bear only a tenuous relationship to external stimuli, or even to the symptoms that they supposedly produce. (Bandura, 1969, pp. 10–11)

Whereas Miller and Dollard (1941) agreed with psychodynamic theorists that neurotic conflict had its unconscious determinants, Bandura (1969) preferred to conceptualize neurotic symptoms as products of past learning that are continually maintained by ongoing environmental rewards.

In essence, social learning theory is about the effects of the environment on a person's behavior, and the effects of behavior on the environment. It also attempts to bridge the gap between the inner mental processes of psychodynamic theories and the overt behavior of learning theories.

Meichenbaum (1974) cited Miller and Dollard (1941) as beginning the "conceptualization of cognition" (p. 109), and bringing cognitive process back into serious consideration as a tool for behavior change. Social learning theorists renewed the importance of cognitive mediators as primary determinants of behavior. They influenced CBT methology as well: modeling, for example, is a cognitive therapy tool borrowed directly from social learning theory.

☐ The CBT Model Today

The term, cognitive-behavioral therapy (CBT), is an umbrella idiom for an array of therapeutic interventions. Mahoney and Arnkoff (1978) identified three major forms of CBT: 1) cognitive restructuring therapies, 2) coping skills therapies, and 3) problem-solving therapies.

Cognitive restructuring psychotherapy was first developed by Ellis (1962). Included in this category is Meichenbaum's (1974) "self-instruction training" that combined components of Ellis' (1970) "rational-emotive therapy" and Luria's (1961) description of "inner speech." Also included is Beck's (1976) "cognitive therapy," where the goal is the development of rational, adaptive thought patterns. All three of these therapies consider what clients say to themselves as being defective. Therefore, cognitive therapy changes inner speech which, in turn, changes overt behavior.

Coping skills therapies are Meichenbaum's (1975) "stress inoculation," Kazdin's (1974) "covert modeling," and Goldfried's (1971) modification of "systematic desensitization." These therapies teach individuals an array of coping skills to enhance their adaptation to stressful situations. Consequently, clients experience a greater sense of control over their lives.

Problem-solving therapies encompass many diverse procedures (e.g., Mahoney, 1977; Spivack & Shure, 1974). Problem behavior was defined by Zurilla and Goldfried as "ineffective behavior and its consequences, in which the individual is unable to resolve certain situational problems." (1971, p. 107) The philosophical core is pragmatism: finding the most efficient avenue to help a person in conflict.

The effectiveness of CBT has been studied extensively and thoroughly. Although it is impossible to do a comprehensive survey of recent efficacy research, here is a summary of findings.[1]

For adults, CBT has been effective in treating depression, anxiety, insomnia, phobic reactions, post-traumatic stress disorder, personality disorders, schizophrenia, and obsessive-compulsive disorder. There is evidence to support the use of CBT with sex offenders and adults with other aggressive tendencies. CBT has also crossed over into medicine, where some techniques have reduced the effects of chronic pain and other chronic medical conditions.

For children, CBT has helped those who are depressed, anxious, phobic, obsessive-compulsive, and angry. Youngsters who suffer from attention deficit disorders, learning disorders, behavior disorders, and eating disorders have also benefited from CBT.

CBT has also been successfully integrated into couples therapy, family therapy, group therapy, music therapy (Ulfarsdottir & Erwin, 1999), play therapy (Knell, 1998), bibliotherapy (Ackerson, Scogin, McKendree-Smith, & Lyman, 1998), and story-telling (Friedberg, 1994). Because this model is focused on problem-solving and the development of coping skills, it is often the basis of short-term and solution-focused counseling, brief therapy, and crisis counseling.

☐ Early Cognitive-Behavioral Art Therapy Thinking

Although cognitive approaches to therapy are now several decades old, they have not been widely accepted in the field of art therapy. In 1979 two art therapists began to think

---

[1]Specific references for the research cited in the next three paragraphs that were omitted to save space are available from the author.

and write about the relationship of art therapy to cognitive theories of behavior using the work of George Kelly (1955) as their touchstone.

Kelly (1955) focused on the importance of perception in how people choose to behave, defining perception as an active cognitive process. Each individual develops a set of unique perceptions of his or her world through active interaction with the environment. Kelly labeled an individual's conglomeration of perceptions, a "personal construct system." A personal construct is an individual's hypothesis about how one small aspect of the world works. The personal construct system reflects how people organize the entirety of their perceptions and hypotheses. Personal constructs are inherently bipolar. For example, if one construct is, I find most people to be basically good; the opposite is implied: I find some people to be basically bad. Helping the client to identify and understand their personal construct system was the first goal of Kelly's therapy.

In 1979 Carnes noted that, since imagery, visual thinking, and creativity were aspects of cognition, "personal constructs" could be nonverbal as well as verbal. Thus, making art provides an opportunity to express nonverbal ideas which may be the core of an individual's construct system (p. 71). Carnes also suggested that creating art could help to solve problems, if the personal construct system could be enriched. With a wider personal construct system, the range of solutions would be increased.

Rhyne (1979) also used Kelly's work as one of several theoretical bases for her doctoral research, seeing drawings as personal constructs. By having her subjects draw a set of personal construct "mind states," she could help them come to a broader understanding of themselves and their individual belief systems. Rhyne found that when subjects understood the bipolar nature of their drawn constructs, their meaning was enriched and elaborated. She also gave attention to the link between thoughts and feelings, for within the personal construct model, cognitive and emotional components of experiences are inextricably connected (Rhyne, 1979, p. 251).

Art therapists generally focus on emotional experiences. The misconception that CBT focuses only on the thinking process may be one of the reasons that art therapists have not embraced it more fully. According to both Carnes (1979) and Rhyne (1979), when cognitive processes are used in therapy the emotional components of experiences are not only included, but are an integral part of understanding a person's cognitive process system.

☐ Art Therapy and CBT Today

Although one art therapist stated that "cognitive behavioral approaches appear almost entirely missing from the creative therapies literature" (Reynolds, 1999, p. 165), I found a number of references on the use of CBT in art therapy. Nevertheless, compared to other disciplines, the art therapy literature has a very small percentage of CBT references.

Art Therapy and CBT with Adults

Table 14.1 summarizes the literature describing the integration of art therapy and CBT with adult clients. Bowen and Rosal (1989) found that art therapy with a CBT foundation decreased maladaptive, often bizarre behaviors, and increased the locus of control of a mentally handicapped adult. The client was exposed to the use of positive self-imagery as a means of increasing self-control and self-esteem.

TABLE 14.1. Cognitive-behavioral art therapy techniques with adults

Author(s) & Date	Cognitive-Behavioral Goal(s)	Cognitive-Behavioral Technique(s)	Art Therapy Adaptation
Bowen & Rosal (1989)	To ↑ internal locus of contrtol	Guided imagery of sensory experiences	Crayon drawings & collages of imagery
Rosal, Ackerman-Haswell, & Johnson (1994)	To Identify & label triggers	In vivo techniques & uncovering cognitive distortions	Creating social milieus such as villages & carnivals
Gentile (1997)	To ↑ Internal locus of control	↑ self-control	Using art to externalize internal feelings
Matto (1997)	To ↓ Anxiety in dealing with emotions	In vivo and systematic desensitization	Drawing feeling states from least to most anxiety provoking
Reynolds (1999)	To ↓ Avoidance	Systematic desensitization & flooding	Re-creating photo with high emotional value into tapestry

↑ = Increase; ↓ = Decrease.

A combination of art therapy and CBT was also useful in working with mentally handicapped male sex offenders (Rosal, Ackerman-Haswell, & Johnson, 1994). The men, seen in a group, were able to create social environments with art materials. As the environments were created, the interactional patterns that led to offending behavior were exhibited, noted, discussed, and remediated. When maladaptive social behaviors surfaced, the men were asked to identify precursors to the problematical interactions. Alternate modes of behavior were discussed, and practice of new skills was attempted. Often alternative behaviors were as simple as asking to use another's art supplies, rather than slipping them into pockets or taking them while someone's back was turned.

Women with eating disorders have also benefited from combined CBT/art therapy programs. Gentile (1997) assisted her eating disordered clients by addressing the locus of control issue. Through making art, these individuals were able to gain an internal sense of control, which meant that they did not have to control eating to experience a sense of personal power. The basis of Gentile's work was that transforming verbal information into visual form offered an alternative means of meeting needs. She found that gaining control over one's needs led to an increase in internal locus of control.

Matto (1997) also used art with eating disordered clients in order to integrate meaning into their experiences. Because these women have difficulty with intense emotions, she employed a type of systematic desensitization. She had clients work with the least threatening feelings first, as a means of gaining the strength to create art about more troublesome feelings, and then learn to cope with them. Matto also found that art therapy helped with other CBT goals, such as: challenging irrational beliefs, acquiring mastery and control, and gaining positive inner reinforcement.

Reynolds (1999) found that art making in conjunction with CBT facilitated the grieving process in an adult client. A CBT approach to grief work includes the development of coping strategies and avenues for challenging avoidance, and often includes homework. In her work with a bereaved woman, Reynolds gave the client a homework assignment: to design and create a tapestry in reaction to a photograph that was impossible to view without overt sadness. Like Matto (1997), Reynolds also integrated the use of both "systematic desensitization" and "emotional flooding" into art therapy.

Art Therapy and CBT with Children

It is not surprising that most of the literature on art therapy and CBT is about work with children and adolescents, since behavior management is often needed with troubled youngsters. Sobol (1985) was one of the first to note that some behavioral interventions may be necessary in child art therapy, especially if antisocial or problematic behaviors are exhibited.

Table 14.2 summarizes the literature on art therapy and CBT with children and teens exhibiting a wide range of learning, behavioral, and emotional problems. Based on the writings of these authors, several types of CBT techniques have been adapted to art therapy: cognitive mapping; problem-solving; modeling; relaxation techniques; systematic desensitization; implosion; personal constructs; mental messages and internal speech; mental imagery; externalizing internal processes; exploring and assessing feeling states; and using reinforcements and prompts.

Packard (1977) found that art facilitates the acquisition of new ideas and learning. For children with learning difficulties, new information is often lost or tangled in disorganized mental "pathways." "Cognitive maps" are retrieved and can be reproduced visually in the art room. In Packard's approach, visual images can be "repaved" and essentially cleaned-up. Newly reconfigured mental "layouts" lead to an increased ability to make connections between blocks of information and additional learning. She likened the act of creating art to promoting "mental fitness."

The portrayal of tough personal and social situations through drawings is a technique used by several art therapists to increase problem-solving (Packard, 1977; Rosal, 1985, 1992, 1993, 1996). Having children depict complex life moments can be followed by generating alternatative solutions in pictures. This technique can increase behavioral choice. Similarly, Roth (1987) used reality shaping to model new behaviors and mind sets. With the use of prompts, she encouraged the growth and creation of formed schemas. Roth found that strong schemas led to improved behavior and more adaptive behavioral options.

DeFrancisco (1983), Gerber (1994), and Rosal (1985, 1992, 1993, 1996) advocate the use of four related techniques: relaxation, systematic desensitization, and implosion and stress innoculation. At the heart of these techniques is the induction of relaxed states. Relaxation can be induced through traditional means, such as the use of soothing music, muscle relaxation techniques, or both. Various types of art experiences can induce relaxed states, such as smoothing soft clay or combining the use of broad watercolor strokes with breathing exercises (Lusebrink, 1990).

Reaching a relaxed state, in itself, can be therapeutic. However, once a child is relaxed, other techniques can be used to accelerate behavioral change. Mental imagery can be tapped. Slowly introducing painful images can reduce fearful and anxious responses,

TABLE 14.2. Cognitive-behavioral art therapy with children and teens

Cognitive-Behavioral Technique	Cognitive-Behavioral Goal(s)	Art Therapy Adaptation	Author(s) & Date
Cognitive mapping	To ↓ faulty thinking patterns	Draw situations and events	Packard (1977)
Problem-solving	To ↑ solution generation & behavior choices	Draw solutions to a problem	Packard (1977); Rosal (1985, 1992, 1993, 1996)
Modeling	To learn new behaviors	Reality shaping	Roth (1987)
Relaxation techniques	To ↓ stress & acting out; to ↑ mental imagery	Use of soothing media to enhance relaxation	Rosal (1985, 1992, 1993, 1996)
Systematic desensitization	To ↓ stress & phobias	Use images for slow exposure to feared object/ situation	DeFrancisco (1983); Gerber (1994)
Implosion & stress innoculation	To ↑ ability to cope with stress	Use images to flood/induce emotional responses	DeFrancisco (1983); Rosal (1985, 1992)
Personal constructs	To assess & treat cognitive aspects of a child's life	Draw constructs from child's life to compare/ contrast	Rosal (1985, 1993, 1996)
Mental messages	To ↓ negative inner speech & ↑ self-control	Write/draw messages & change	DeFrancisco (1983); Rosal (1985, 1992, 1993, 1996)
Mental imagery	To link inner world with external behavior; for rehearsal	Induce relaxation & mental imagery; draw and change images	Rosal (1985, 1992, 1993, 1996)
Externalizing internal processes	Uncover mental processes leading to offense; restructure dysfunctional thought patterns	Draw cycle of offense; Before, During & After drawings; draw inside/outside self; masks	Gerber (1994); Gentry & Rosal (1998); Roth (1987); Stanley & Miller (1993)
Assessing feeling states	To ↑ control over negative feelings; to ↑ empathy	Draw feelings states from least to most complex; categorize feeling drawings	Gerber (1994)
Reinforcements & prompts	To ↑ positive, prosocial behavior	Reality shaping; structured painting	Roth (1987); Mellberg (1998)

↑ Increase; ↓ Decrease.

or a flood of images, called implosion, can be summoned. The end result of implosion is an improved ability to handle stressful situations.

Carnes (1979) and Rhyne (1979) used personal constructs with adults. Rosal found that personal constructs are just as effective with children. Children are fascinated with their lives, and having children recreate their vision of the world can be eye-opening, and can be used in the assessment of a child's life-space. The depictions can be used as a springboard for discussion. Children can rank order their pictures (identifying the best scenario through the worst), or they can compare and contrast drawings.

Children can also uncover inner speech. These mental messages can be illustrated and discussed (DeFrancisco, 1983; Rosal). If an internal message is found to be harmful to the youngster, the child is encouraged to change the visual message. According to cognitive behavioral theory, an adaptation of the external message will ease the adoption of an internal adjustment. This holds for mental images as well as for mental messages.

In addition to linking the external and internal worlds, the use of mental images can facilitate rapid behavior change. A child can imagine what it would be like to try on various behaviors. When mental images are drawn, their power is enhanced and a child's ability to change troublesome images is multiplied.

One CBT technique often used with aggressive children and teens can be enhanced with the introduction of art therapy—the externalization of internal processes (Gentry & Rosal, 1998; Gerber, 1994; Stanley & Miller, 1993). This technique requires the visual creation of stages of behavioral action. For some clients, like sex offenders, it might be drawing various aspects of their cycle of offending behavior. For others, this might be drawing before, during, and after drawings of fights or arguments.

A subtler technique is depicting both inner and outer self-images. All these techniques lead to an uncovering of the inner thoughts and feelings that may be the precursors of aggressive or acting out behaviors. Gerber (1994) used art therapy to help youngsters gain control over thorny feeling-states and improve empathy skills. As with Rhyne (1979), this was done by having the clients create feeling-state drawings. The therapist found that working from least complex feelings to most complex emotions facilitated the child's cognitive understanding of moods and control over scary feelings.

There is widespread acceptance of two CBT techniques in child art therapy: reinforcements and prompts. These two techniques are commonly used in behavior shaping. Roth (1987) and Mellberg (1998) have adapted these concepts into art therapy experiences. In Roth's "reality shaping," the use of prompts helps a child to develop clear visual constructs. A structured watercolor protocol was developed by Mellberg that helped teens with developmental disabilities to gain control over the medium and of their behavior. Positive reinforcement was used, concurrently with a sequence of exercises to improve the internal locus of control of these youngsters.

Summary

Art therapy is particularly suited to CBT, because making art is an inherently cognitive process. When creating a piece of art, the artist must be involved in uncovering mental images and messages, recalling memories, making decisions, and generating solutions. Whether drawing or sculpting, creating art involves instant feedback systems and the ongoing reinforcement of satisfying behaviors. Each brush stroke that appears on the paper can suggest or promote further action (feedback) as well as delight (reinforce) the artist. Creating art means that there is a concrete record of inner processes. This concrete record can be discussed, altered, and redrawn to satisfaction. It can also be used to recall past events and as a reminder of positive emotional experiences, as will be described in the case study below.

The overriding goal of CBT is for the client to gain self-control. For adults, cognitive-behavioral art therapy helps to decrease behavioral problems, increase awareness of triggers leading to socially inappropriate behaviors, and improve locus of control. Achieving such goals can help to assist a wide range of adults to cope in more effective ways, and to have more choices in regard to their lives.

For children, developing behavioral self-control is essential to growth. Rather than always needing an adult or a system to be in charge, children in cognitive-behavioral art therapy can learn to manage aspects of their own behavior. For people of all ages, increased self-control can lead to more personal choice and freedom; and personal power, in turn, can lead to a richer and more meaningful life.

☐ Case Illustration

Karen, a 28-year-old computer programmer, had been recently hospitalized for depression. While in the hospital, Karen was exposed to a few sessions of art therapy. She enjoyed the sessions and requested that she be seen in outpatient art therapy. In addition to prescribing anti-depressant medication and outpatient group psychotherapy, Karen's psychiatrist referred her to me for individual art therapy, in order to help her to cope better with her emotions.

Background Information

During our first session, Karen told me about the history of both her depression and her family. While in the hospital, she had learned that she had actually been depressed for several years without realizing it. After a good friend's attempted suicide had set off her own emotional turmoil, including suicidal thoughts, Karen decided to enter the hospital. Karen reported that she had a very stressful job and often found herself in arguments with co-workers and supervisors. Finally, Karen shared her sadness about not being in a relationship. She worried that her weight might be part of her difficulty in meeting and getting involved with men.

Karen's family of origin was troubled. Her alcoholic father had committed suicide when she was 10 years old. Her mother had been unable to comfort herself or her three daughters about his tragic death. The family was left with few financial resources and had become isolated from relatives, friends, and neighbors, due to the nature of the father's death. Karen shared that she was the one who found her father, who had hung himself in the basement of their home.

When asked what she would like to accomplish in art therapy, Karen was very direct. She stated that she wanted to better identify and understand her feelings. She added that while growing up, she was never asked how she felt. In the hospital, the other patients and the caregivers were always asking her for this information, and she found herself speechless. In art therapy she was also asked about her feelings, but was unable to come up with words or images to describe how she felt.

During the first few sessions, it was clear that Karen suffered from many feelings associated with depression, including guilt, anger, anxiety, shame, hostility, sadness, and grief. It made sense that a CBT approach might be useful in working with Karen, since depressed clients were often assisted through the techniques outlined by Beck and his collaborators (1979). Her wish to "understand" her feelings was particularly insightful, since Karen knew that she could easily "act them out." She often found herself in shouting matches at work or with her sisters, and she frequently cried uncontrollably at home. Yet she was usually unable to identify what she was feeling, nor could she identify the origin of powerful feelings. What she knew was that overwhelming feelings led to unproductive interactions with peers and relatives. The first goal, then, was to meet her request.

Cognitive-Behavioral Art Therapy with Karen

To begin, Karen was asked to complete three drawings: 1) Before: life prior to hospitalization, 2) During: events in the hospital that held meaning for her, and 3) After: what she hoped to achieve through outpatient treatment. For her first drawing, she chose a large piece of paper and, with craypas, drew a linear map of what she thought her life "looked like" so far (Figure 14.1), illustrating the ups and downs of her life. For each downward dip of the line, Karen was able to cite an event that caused her to feel blue. The deepest and final dip on the right side of the paper was the recent depressive episode that had prompted her hospitalization.

The first drawing, her lifeline so far, was then compared with the third, what she hoped to achieve (Figure 14.2). Karen described this drawing as a landscape of rolling grassy hills with some "dips." She stated that she would like to be "steadier," and she insightfully acknowledged that even the healthiest of people sometimes had "dips." Because she wanted warmth in her life, Karen had drawn the hills being warmed by the sun.

Based on Rhyne's (1979) work, Karen was asked to produce a set of personal construct "mind state" drawings. Viewing Rhyne's set of mind states, Karen was asked to produce her own list of those she wanted to explore. She was careful to create bipolar sets of feelings, as suggested by both Kelly (1955) and Rhyne (1979). Karen developed a list of 12

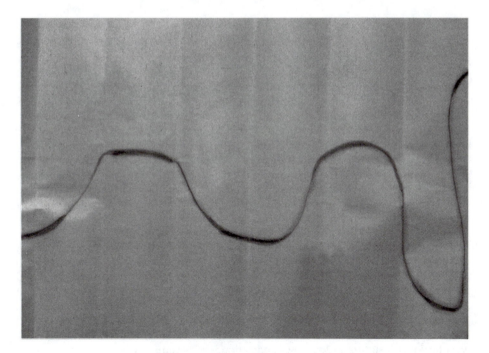

Figure 14.1.

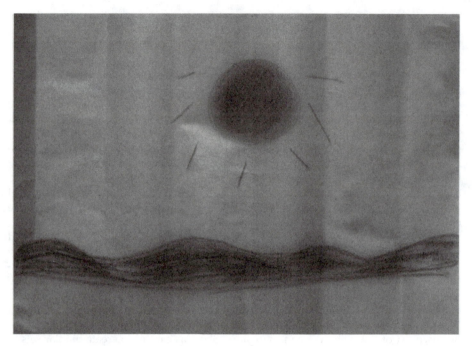

Figure 14.2.

feelings that included some of Rhyne's and some of her own. In weekly sessions over a six week period, Karen drew these mind states. At the end of each session, she discussed the drawings, and what she learned about each mind state as she studied her images.

Once all of her mind state drawings were completed, Karen was asked to place the drawings along her original lifeline drawing (Figure 14.1). After the feeling drawings were placed on the line, she had several insights. First, she realized that it was rare for her to feel peace and serenity (Figure 14.3), and she wondered if she would be able to do so more often in the future. Karen described what serenity might feel like, based on her drawing. Her description included feelings of wholeness, calm, light, and safety. Karen could not find a place on the lifeline drawing for "serene." and so she placed it outside the drawing on the left. The serene drawing was used for homework. She was asked to place this drawing by her bed, and to reflect on the drawing and her descriptions of serenity prior to settling in for the night.

Karen's most surprising realization was that it was the feeling of anxiety (Figure 14.4) that she feared most. Although depression (Figure 14.5) was heavy and dark, it was anxiety that was intense, prickly, painful, and unable to be contained. She also realized that periods of anxiety always preceded and triggered her depressions. Based on this awareness, and with the knowledge that the anti-depressant medication did not assist her with her anxiety, she spoke with her doctor. The doctor was able to prescribe anti-anxiety medication, and taught her when and how to take the drug. Karen reported immediate relief from the flood of negative emotions often experienced at work. Armed with her new insight and her new medication, she became less anxious about being anxious.

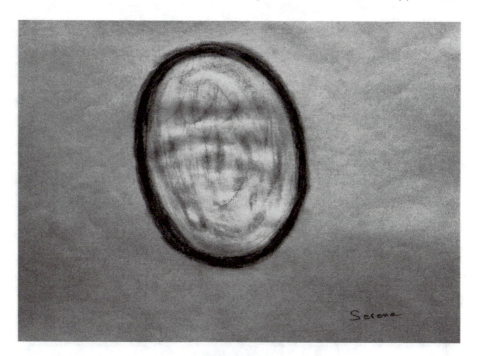

Figure 14.3.

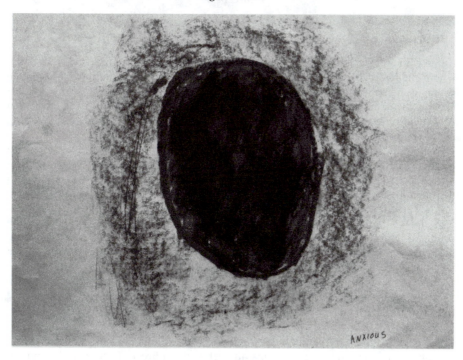

Figure 14.4.

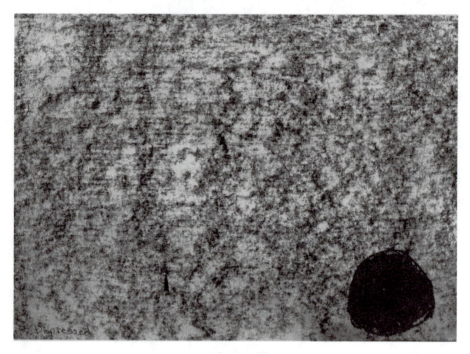

Figure 14.5.

Summary

Karen's Before, During, and After drawings assisted her in comparing and contrasting where she had been emotionally and where she wanted to be eventually. Mind state drawings helped her to focus on the feelings that had been unidentifiable and unmanageable. After about three months of such work on understanding her feelings, Karen continued for the rest of the year in art therapy to work on other concerns, including relationships with family and other significant people.

Although her anxious feelings were not "cured" by her work in cognitive-behavioral art therapy, Karen gained a good deal of control over her anxiety and thus, her depression. She was amazed at how knowing about and checking her anxious states could help to mitigate depressive ones. She began to use the serene drawing as a reminder to soothe herself. Karen also continued to use the personal construct drawings to decipher how she was feeling, if she became stuck when dealing with other matters during the course of treatment. Although she continued to use art throughout her therapy, these particular drawings were kept at hand, and were often called upon by me or Karen to help our discussions of relationships and interpersonal strife.

☐ Conclusion

When engaged in art making, we use a full range of cognitive processes. Tapping into the inherently cognitive essence of making art is at the heart of cognitive-behavioral art therapy. There is evidence that a wide range of visual techniques can enhance CBT.

Imagery is one of the most common tools used by cognitive-behavioral therapists. Since the mental image is effective, the drawn image is a compelling addition to the already effective array of CBT techniques.

Cognitive-behavioral art therapy can be adapted to a wide range of expressive modalities. Adults, teens, and children at various functioning levels can benefit from many different forms of cognitive-behavioral art therapy. CBT is easily modified for use in group and family therapy, including group and family art therapy. CBT techniques are easily translated into art therapy experiences. Some art therapists have done so already, but more work needs to be done.

Cognitive-behavioral art therapy can assist in quick and effective problem-solving, and so is especially useful in brief therapy. Even when additional therapeutic work can enhance the life of an individual like Karen, swiftly getting to the heart of the problem can provide immediate relief. Rapid and solid solutions can help an individual to gain self-control.

Helping a client of any age to develop an internal sense (locus) of control is the primary goal of CBT. Certainly clients engaged in any form of art therapy can quickly develop a sense of control, as they choose art materials, choose how to approach a drawing, and choose how and what to discuss about created pieces. Cognitive-behavioral art therapy accelerates the acquisition of control through combining the inherent internal control building aspects of art therapy with additional techniques such as 1) discovering, promoting, enhancing, and reconfiguring mental images; 2) comparing and contrasting drawings; 3) carefully choosing and portraying problem-specific situations and events; and 4) creating pictorial metaphors of feelings and mind states.

Although there has been a sense among some art therapists that cognitive-behavioral art therapy ignores the emotional component of experiences, this is simply not so. Feelings, as well as thoughts, are cognitive processes. As Rhyne (1979) noted, it is difficult to extricate the feeling component from the thinking component of any human experience. In using the cognitive-behavioral approach to art therapy, both components are explored in order to assist the client. And it is both what we *think* as well as how we *feel* that drives our behavior.

☐ References

Ackerson, J., Scogin, F., McKendree-Smith, N., & Lyman, R. D. (1998). Cognitive bibliotherapy for mild and moderate adolescent depressive symptomology. *Journal of Consulting and Clinical Psychology, 66*(4), 685–690.

Baars, B. J. (1986). *The cognitive revolution in psychology*. New York: Guilford Press.

Bandura, A. (1969). *Principles of behavior modification*. New York: Holt, Rinehart, and Winston.

Beck, A. T. (1976). *Cognitive therapy and the emotional disorders*. New York: International Universities Press.

Beck, A. T., Rush, A. J., Shaw, B. F., & Emery, G. (1979). *Cognitive therapy of depression*. New York: Guilford Press.

Bowen, C. A., & Rosal, M. L. (1989). The use of art therapy to reduce the maladaptive behaviors of a mentally retarded adult. *The Arts in Psychotherapy, 16*, 211–218.

Carnes, J. J. (1979). Toward a cognitive theory of art therapy. *The Arts in Psychotherapy, 6*, 69–75.

De Francisco, J. (1983). Implosive art therapy: A learning-theory based, psychodynamic approach. In L. Gantt & S. Whitman (Eds.), *Proceedings of the Eleventh Annual Conference of the American Art Therapy Association* (pp. 74–79). Baltimore: AATA.

Ellis, A. (1962). *Reason and emotion in psychotherapy*. New York: Lyle Stuart.

Ellis, A. (1970). *The essence of rational psychotherapy: A comprehensive approach to treatment*. New York: Institute for Rational Living.

Friedberg, R. (1994). Storytelling and cognitive therapy with children. *Journal of Cognitive Psychotherapy, 8*(3), 209–217.

Gentile, D. (1997). Art therapy's influence on locus of control with eating disorder patients [Abstract]. *Proceedings of the American Art Therapy Association,* p. 196.

Gentry, H., & Rosal, M. L. (1998). Structured cognitive-behavioral art therapy of adolescents with comorbid depression and conduct problems [Abstract]. *Proceedings of the American Art Therapy Association,* p. 76.

Gerber, J. (1994). The use of art therapy in juvenile sex offender specific treatment. *The Arts in Psychotherapy, 21,* 367–374.

Goldfried, M. R. (1971). Systematic desensitization as training in self-control. *Journal of Consulting and Clinical Psychology, 31,* 228–234.

Kazdin, A. E. (1974). Effects of covert modeling and modeling reinforcement on assertive behavior. *Journal of Abnormal Psychology, 83,* 240–252.

Kelly, G. A. (1955). *The psychology of personal constructs.* New York: W.W. Norton.

Knell, S. M. (1998). Cognitive-behavioral play therapy. *Journal of Clinical Child Psychology, 27*(1), 28–33.

Luria, A. R. (1961). *The role of speech in the regulation of normal and abnormal behavior.* New York: Liveright.

Lusebrink, V. B. (1990). *Imagery and visual expression in therapy.* New York: Plenum.

Mahoney, M. J. (1977). Personal science: A cognitive learning therapy. In A. Ellis & R. Grieger (Eds.), *Handbook of rational psychotherapy* (pp. 689–722). New York: Springer.

Mahoney, M. J., & Arnkoff, E. (1978). Cognitive and self-control therapies. In S. L. Garfield & A. E. Bergin (Eds.), *Handbook of psychotherapy and behavior change* (2nd ed., pp. 689–722). New York: John Wiley.

Matto, H. C. (1997). An integrative approach to the treatment of women with eating disorders. *The Arts in Psychotherapy, 24,* 347–354.

Meichenbaum, D. (1974). *Cognitive behavior modification.* Morristown, NJ: General Learning Press.

Meichenbaum, D. (1975). A self-instruction approach to stress management: A proposal for stress inoculation training. In I. Sarason & C. D. Spielberger (Eds.), *Stress and anxiety* (Vol. 2, pp. 227–263). New York: John Wiley.

Mellberg, C. (1998). Increasing control: Watercolor painting and students with developmental disabilities [Abstract]. *Proceedings of the American Art Therapy Association,* p. 183.

Miller, N. E., & Dollard, J. (1941). *Social learning and imitation.* New Haven, CT: Yale University Press.

Packard, S. (1977). Learning disabilities: Identification and remediation through creative art activity. In R. H. Shoemaker & S. E. Gonick-Barris (Eds.), *Proceedings of the Seventh Annual Conference of the American Art Therapy Association* (pp. 57–61). Baltimore: AATA.

Reynolds, R. (1999). Cognitive behavioral counseling of unresolved grief through the therapeutic adjunct of tapestry-making. *The Arts in Psychotherapy, 26,* 165–171.

Rhyne, J. (1979). *Drawings as personal constructs: A study in visual dynamics.* Unpublished doctoral dissertation, University of California, Santa Cruz.

Rosal, M. L. (1985). *The use of art therapy to modify the locus of control and adaptive behavior of behavior disordered students.* Unpublished doctoral dissertation, University of Queensland, Brisbane, Australia.

Rosal, M. L. (1992). Approaches to art therapy with children. In F. E. Anderson (Ed.), *Art for all the children* (2nd ed., pp. 142–183). Springfield, IL: Charles C. Thomas.

Rosal, M. L. (1993). Comparative group art therapy research to evaluate changes in locus of control in behavior disordered children. *The Arts in Psychotherapy, 20,* 231–241.

Rosal, M. L. (1996). *Approaches to art therapy with children.* Burlingame, CA: Abbeygate.

Rosal, M. L., Ackerman-Haswell, J. F., & Johnson, L. (1994). Humanity behind the offense: Group art therapy with special needs sex offenders [Abstract]. *Proceedings of the American Art Therapy Association,* 127.

Roth, E. A. (1987). A behavioral approach to art therapy. In J. A. Rubin (Ed.), *Approaches to art therapy: Theory and technique* (pp. 213–232). New York: Brunner/Mazel.

Sobol, B. (1985). Art therapy, behavior modification, and conduct disorders. *American Journal of Art Therapy, 24*, 35–43.

Spivack, G., & Shure, M. B. (1974). *Social adjustment of young children: A cognitive approach to solving real-life problems*. San Francisco, CA: Jossey-Bass.

Stanley, P. D., & Miller, M. M. (1993). Short-term art therapy with an adolescent male. *The Arts in Psychotherapy, 20*, 397–402.

Ulfarsdottir, L. O., & Erwin, P. G. (1999). The influence of music on social cognitive skills. *The Arts in Psychotherapy, 26*(2), 81–84.

Zurilla, T. J., & Goldfried, M. R. (1971). Problem-solving and behavior modification. *Journal of Abnormal Psychology, 78*, 107–126.

15

CHAPTER

Susan Aach-Feldman
Carole Kunkle-Miller

Developmental Art Therapy

Our developmental approach to art therapy is based on various perspectives, including analytic ideas about psychosexual (Freud, 1905/1962) and psychosocial (Erikson, 1950) development, especially observations of the separation-individuation process (Mahler, Pine, & Bergman, 1975). We also use studies of cognitive growth (Bruner, 1964), especially Piaget (1951, 1954); and of normal development in art (DiLeo, 1977; Golomb, 1974; Harris, 1963; Koppitz, 1968; Kellogg, 1969; Lowenfeld, 1957; Rubin, 1978). Normal development is our framework for understanding and intervening with clients whose development is not proceeding according to normal expectations (see Table 15.1).

It is critical to think developmentally when working with those at the earliest stages of artistic expression, Piaget's "sensorimotor" and "preoperational" phases, 0–7 in the normally developing child. For those with severe cognitive, physical, and emotional impairments, a detailed understanding of this period is required. We meet their needs by using both traditional media and "pre-art" (i.e., water, shaving cream, beans, rice) materials (Lonker, 1982). We also analyze art behaviors according to levels of functioning, as in the "expressive therapies continuum" (Kagin & Lusebrink, 1978) which describes media interactions for each level in terms of "media dimensions variables" (Kagin, 1969), as well as criteria for assessing and selecting materials.

☐ Assessment

The presymbolic client may have a limited ability to make choices, to express affect, or to use traditional art media appropriately. While one might assume that he would profit from a structured interview, we recommend that the assessment follow a progression from nondirective to structured. Specifically, we suggest an interview that combines two or three of the following: 1) *nondirective work with traditional and pre-art media, 2) structured work with traditional art media,* and 3) *structured work with pre-art media.* With some, the assessment can be conducted in an hour; others may need several sessions. At the end of treatment, the assessment interview can be readministered to evaluate progress.

Parts of this chapter have been previously published by Aach (1981) and Kunkle-Miller & Aach (1981).

TABLE 15.1. Summary of major theories in developmental art therapy

Theorists	Age of Expected Attainment of Skill		
	0–2 Years	**2–4 Years**	**4–7 Years**
Erikson	Trust vs. mistrust consistency of experience separation	Autonomy vs. sharing (2–3) learning to control and let go	Initiative vs. guilt (3–5) develops right and wrong internalizes prohibitions from parents
Piaget	Sensorimotor exploration through body trial-and-error process object permanence	Preoperational (2–7) egocentric learns to use symbolic substitutes learns to classify	
Lowenfeld		Manipulative random scribble controlled manipulation named manipulation early shapes	Preschematic representation of a person cephalopod houses/trees/ animals no particular schema
Hartley, Frank, & Goldenson	Exploration and experimentation Manipulation water play, block play	Product-process phase process of manipulation without intention creation of accidental form product itself important, not the representation	Representation of image with intention beginning of fantasy
Golomb	Delight in action interest in how material moves and feels	Romancing stage use of media as if it had form Reading off stage looks for forms, names parts	
Rubin	Manipulation mouthing materials Forming more conscious control	Naming associating to the form Representing representing qualities of object Containing creation of boundaries	Experimenting exploring different ways of doing
Williams & Wood	Stage—Responding to the environment with pleasure sensory arousing art media as a means of motivation learning to trust	Stage 2—Learning skills that bring success able to use basic art tools and supplies shapes beginning to emerge	

During the *nondirective segment,* the therapist offers a wide selection of materials, including both art and pre-art media (i.e., water, shaving cream, beans, rice). During this phase, the art therapist allows the client to select the media and to determine activity, theme, and content, if at all possible (Rubin, 1978). The amount of time assigned to this phase may vary and will be determined by the initiative and responses of the client.

In the *directive segment,* the therapist presents traditional art media, along with specific instructions. In designing tasks, their purpose is to identify the client's place in the hierarchy of skill development. Activities presented with clay, for example, range from requesting manipulations (pressing, pounding, pinching), to forming shapes, to modeling a person.

Another option is a *structured assessment of the use of pre-art media,* observing the client's media involvement in terms of *orientation, manipulation,* and *organization.* To evaluate *orientation,* we present a variety of qualitatively different (fluid, solid) media and note the response (i.e., aversive, positive). Other tasks examine *manipulative* (i.e., scooping, pouring, banging) and *organizational* skills (i.e., combining, containing) relevant to the material. Throughout the assessment, we gather information about the client's developmental level in the use of materials, response to media properties, use of structured versus nonstructured formats, and capacity to express affect.

Use of Structured and Nonstructured Formats

To evaluate the degree of organization required for optimal creative activity, we compare the client's efforts during "high" and "low project structure" phases of the assessment (Kagin, 1969). We look at differences in several areas—regression versus organization, dependency versus initiative, attention span, and motivation—to determine "project structure" for the initial phase of treatment.

Capacity for Expression of Affect

Levels of affective expression are assessed verbally and nonverbally. Some individuals can talk about their art. Even presymbolic clients can be asked what a scribble "might be," what it "looks like," or of what manipulating the material reminded them. Since mentally impaired adults can produce "named associations" related to age-appropriate issues like sexual fantasies (Kunkle-Miller, 1978), we assume the same potential exists in other developmentally disabled individuals.

Nonverbal behaviors also provide significant affective data, and with some may be the *only* source of information. The client's closeness to or distance from the art therapist, facial expressions, gestures, and the position and muscle tone of the body, are uncensored affective responses which reveal much about anyone, especially those who do not speak.

To identify the preferred modality, we present visual, auditory, tactile, kinesthetic, olfactory, and gustatory experiences, and then note responses in order to develop treatment strategies that will attract the client's attention and sustain interest. For instance, a client who uses an auditory form of self-stimulation (i.e., making inarticulate sounds, talking to himself) may respond positively to auditory stimuli by the art therapist (i.e., pounding clay, tapping markers on paper, or clapping hands). With the disabled, one or more sensory avenues may be impaired, so it is essential to identify which are "open" to therapeutic intervention.

☐ Treatment: The Sensorimotor Phase

This first phase of Piaget, normally 0–2, includes the essentials of motor, cognitive, and emotional growth upon which all later development is based. During this phase, the normally developing infant evolves from a totally undifferentiated state, to one with greater clarity of sensations and perceptions, as well as a refinement of reflexes and movements. By the end of the phase, the child can differentiate between self and other, has a variety of simple schemas, and a basic understanding of cause and effect.

Differentiation of self and other emerges from a close attachment and trusting relationship. Understanding cause and effect relationships also emerges from interactions with the primary caretaker and with objects like toys. Understanding cause and effect and actively investigating the environment signal the end of this phase (Williams & Wood, 1977).

Clients of different ages may demonstrate characteristics of this phase, functioning in part at a developmental age of 0–2. The normal sense of curiosity which leads to investigating the world, as well as the pleasure from that exploration, are often lacking in the developmentally delayed client. Motivation of clients at this stage is a difficult task, one which must take into account functioning level, interests, and chronological issues.

Materials

In the beginning of the sensorimotor phase, the child's primary interest is in his own body, followed by his mother's body; Freud called the body "the first toy." These early experiences enable the child to learn differentiation of various kinesthetic and sensory inputs, as well as a basic definition of self: me versus not me (Winnicott, 1971). Somatic experiences provide a necessary conduit to establishing a basic tolerance, comfort, and familiarity with various sensations and movements for clients of all ages. Movements that are first practiced *without materials* (opening and closing hands, squeezing) can subsequently be used for manipulating materials.

Development of play on a *kinesthetic* level can be a catalyst for the exploration and manipulation of materials. This process may need to begin with pre-art media (Figure 15.1). The primary objective is to "expand sensory, perceptual and motor horizons" (Wilson, 1977, p. 87). Many clients at a sensorimotor level of development demonstrate "resistance to external stimuli," and need simpler steps "to more complex stimuli" (Wilson, 1977, p. 89).

Lonker (1982) believes that such materials decrease resistance by providing *successive approximations* to traditional art media. Pre-art materials include safe (digestible) and manipulable items like "flour, cornstarch, salt, scent extracts, cornmeal, oatmeal, pudding, jello, shaving cream, crazy foam, sand paper, fur, feathers, beans, noodles, spaghetti, sand, water, etc." (1982, p. 14). For those with severe deficits, the use of pre-art materials may need to be restricted. For example, a severely retarded individual may not be able to understand why smearing pudding is permissible during therapy, but not at mealtime.

Interest in traditional art media usually begins near the end of the sensorimotor phase. The interest in sensation and movement noted in earlier efforts with materials is evident in the initial use of crayons and paints. Since some clients may still have a tendency to mouth and ingest media, evaluation of their safety is essential. Materials should be introduced in limited quantities, as some clients may not be able to tolerate

Figure 15.1.

too many novel stimuli at once. The therapist may consider the full range of simple 2 and 3-dimensional art materials in selecting appropriate media.

To Foster Attachment and Differentiation of Self, Other, Object

A client at the sensorimotor phase is similar to a young infant, but due to a variety of factors, resolution of the developmental tasks of infancy may be limited. The capacity for attachment and for the differentiation of a sense of self, other, and object may be impaired. Poor differentiation is evident in poor awareness of people (severely limited responsiveness and initiative, verbally and nonverbally) and of objects (no boundaries in using media).

In order to develop appropriate therapeutic interventions, even with older developmentally delayed clients, emotional development in infancy provides useful guidelines. Mahler, Pine, & Bergman (1975) describe a progression from a time of complete dependence (*normal autism*), to parallel functioning (*normal symbiosis*), to relative independence (*separation-individuation*). We have identified three phases of work with art materials, from *extreme dependency* to *autonomous functioning*, each requiring different interventions.

With a client who demonstrates *extreme dependency and disorientation*, the therapist provides the impetus, and functions as the agent for the play process with materials. The clinician might physically direct and prompt the client through the investigation of a natural material, like beans or leaves. Exploratory movements could include touching, smelling, listening, observing, and perhaps even tasting the material.

With a client who can *respond to interpersonal cues*, the therapist fosters reciprocity (i.e., mirroring, imitation) in the play process—engaging the client to anticipate and repeat behaviors. To establish reciprocal play, use of each sensory modality should be prompted. For example, the therapist might "mirror" the direction (i.e., forward, backward, sideways) of the client's hand movements, or of his rhythm while pounding clay.

With a client who demonstrates *initiative and reciprocity* in play, the therapist alternates directive and reflective roles, functioning minimally as agent and model, while continuing to be facilitating. For example, with a client using a crayon, the therapist could facilitate attention to the mark-making process, reinforce initiative, or promote the selection of colors.

The client at the sensorimotor phase requires intensive and ongoing intervention to facilitate involvement with materials. Although very impaired, the individual can explore and learn about the world, but the art therapist must "join into the play" (Rubin, 1984, p. 237) and "be more than usually active in helping the client learn to use . . . materials" (Wilson, 1977, p. 87).

The therapist needs to modify many elements of media presentation, in order to promote exploration for such a client. To increase the range of movement of an individual with cerebral palsy, the art therapist might present shaving cream or finger paint in a tray. The medium's fluidity increases the potential range of stroking movements and the tray provides containment. In working with these clients, we consider *motivation, prompts, practice steps,* and *reinforcement.* Lonker's (1982) use of *"inherent structure"* is helpful in facilitating investigation at this level.

To Acquire a Positive Sensory Orientation and Simple Motor Schemes

The integration of basic sensory information, and the refinement of simple motor schemes normal for the sensorimotor phase, is inhibited with presymbolic clients. Lonker (1982) suggests that the art therapist operate as a *"guide of the senses,"* "introducing materials which are less obtrusive to his/her touch . . . [and being aware of the client's] sensory limitations in order to develop a trusting relationship" (p. 13). She also recommends the "gradual introduction of each texture or material along with 'talking through,' adding affect to the voice, and gestures" (1982, p. 13). The art therapist thus begins a process of *emotionally desensitizing* the client to initially aversive tactile experiences. The eventual goal is to establish a positive orientation to a variety of qualitatively different media.

To promote independent manipulation and the refinement of a variety of simple motor schemes, the therapist may first need to evaluate various aspects of motor functioning, using toys and natural substances. Motor schemes typically demonstrated at a sensorimotor level include batting, shaking, banging, mouthing, pushing, turning, etc.

To Discover Cause-and-Effect Relationships

As the awareness and coordination of sensation and movement develop, through repeated practice, an interest in cause and effect emerges in art activity, as elsewhere. In persons with disabilities, sensory systems may not provide enough information, or physical impairments may inhibit exploratory movement. The art therapist therefore needs to provide art experiences with sequence and order, where the client can "discover" relationships between cause and effect, like mixing colors of paint (Silver, 1973).

☐ Case Study Sensorimotor Phase: Matthew

Matthew was a totally blind, developmentally delayed 4-year-old, in individual art therapy. He was "tactile defensive" (averse to touching and being touched), and had problems in language (elective mutism), cognition (severe mental retardation), and mobility (semi-independent ambulation). His mental age was 20–35 months (Stanford Binet). His emotional development was at the earliest phase, with poor individuation of self and other, and lack of independence in self-care and exploring the environment. Higher functioning seemed possible, since Matthew's delays reflected not only organic impairments, but also emotional difficulties.

Matthew's behavior during early sessions reflected his emotional problems. There were a variety of self-stimulating behaviors (hand flapping), and no verbal or non-verbal interaction. In response to media, Matthew screeched, cried, and withdrew his hands. Since self-directed activity was minimal, the art therapist used a structured approach.

Temporal boundaries were defined by songs at the outset: "This is Art Time," and at the end, "Goodbye Art Time." Also using song, Matthew and the therapist were physically indicated and named. The goal was to foster identification and differentiation of the event (art) and the individual (therapist). Over nine months, Matthew progressed from screeching and hand flapping, to rocking in rhythm to the songs, to verbalizing segments of the temporal songs (Figure 15.2). For example, the therapist would say, "This is . . ." and Matthew would respond, "art time."

Following the greeting, the therapist initiated playful activities (e.g., hugging, stroking, tickling, knee bouncing, touching, etc.) to stimulate positive affect and to encourage trust. Sometimes music was used too, like singing "Eentsy, Weentsy Spider" while making gentle tickling movements on Matthew's leg, trunk, and arm. The focus was on movement and touch, not materials (Figure 15.3). Though the therapist was the agent, Matthew's initiative was invited by waiting for a response after each play trial.

After about three months, Matthew began to show enjoyment. Soon after, during the "pause period," he began to make movements or sounds that seemed to be a request to repeat the activity. Next, the therapist would wait for Matthew's "request" before repeating a game. The emergence of this "requesting behavior" was seen as a major step toward beginning reciprocal play and comprehending cause-effect relationships.

Efforts to reduce Matthew's tactile defensiveness used pre-art media. Over time, the therapist introduced varied materials, including water (fluid), shaving cream (moldable), and seeds (particle). Through hand-over-hand direction and song, exploratory

Figure 15.2.

Figure 15.3.

movements were encouraged, like batting, stroking, and patting. Over nine months, Matthew began to engage in self-directed exploration of fluid media, like water. He also began to tolerate exploration of other types of media. A decrease in screeching and crying was noted, though resistance continued in efforts to withdraw his hands when the therapist was not directing his efforts.

Matthew needed a structured approach to increase awareness of self and other, to develop understanding of cause-effect relationships, and to promote self-directed sensory/motor exploration. Matthew gradually assumed some of the role as "agent" for the play. As reciprocal play and exploration of materials increased, self-stimulating behaviors decreased.

☐ Treatment: The Preoperational Phase

The client at this phase functions between ages 2–7. It is signaled by a change in the approach to materials, showing discrimination and the organization of sensorimotor responses. There is also progress toward representation and egocentric symbolism, representing the individual's subjective reality. Language is developing, with labeling of thoughts and feelings facilitating the therapy. As these skills develop, the individual is becoming capable and desirous of more autonomous functioning.

Materials

A wider variety can now be introduced, though sand and water continue to provide important opportunities for exploration, and outlets for the expression and release of tension. Also, the fascination with devising routines for organizing and controlling the world generally, and materials specifically, can be successfully initiated on pliable media like sand and water. Activities with these pre-art materials can serve as precursors for organization and composition with traditional art media.

A broad range of media (crayons, paint, clay) is now appropriate, although redirection of inappropriate responses (e.g., mouthing), modeling, or directed practice may be necessary to facilitate stage-appropriate use. Growth is also facilitated by imitation and the emergence of dramatic play, so that art materials can first be investigated through play, before they assume importance for their representational potential.

To Promote Autonomy

Physical maturation provides individuals with the ability and desire to perform increasingly complex tasks with more autonomy. "Muscular maturation sets the stage for experimentation with two simultaneous social modalities: holding on and letting go" (Erikson, 1950, p. 251). Hartley, Frank, and Goldenson (1952) note that children's play reflects a fascination with such sequences as pouring water or sand in and out of cups, a culturally acceptable manner of exploring curiosity about the elimination process. The individual at this stage is attempting to work through separation from mother, with crying and clinging (holding on), negativism, and pushing away (letting go). A preoperational individual who is chronologically older may not be so concerned with toileting, but control and separation issues remain important.

Even severely and profoundly impaired individuals desire some level of independent functioning, so promotion of autonomy is important. Previously an agent for the play process, the art therapist now encourages the client to choose alternatives and reinforces initiative. For a person with disabilities to use materials independently, adaptations may be needed, like attaching a broad piece of foam rubber to the handle of a paintbrush.

A carefully devised project can result in a successful experience and build confidence. To facilitate the finding and selecting of materials with maximum independence, the storage and presentation of supplies must be consonant with sensory and motor skills. When developing projects, we consider the proximity of work surfaces and storage areas, the accessibility of supplies (open or closed containers, high or low shelves), and the quantity of materials.

To Promote the Expression and Differentiation of Feelings

As individuals move through the preoperational phase, they become more cognizant of feeling states, differentiating between affects and their antecedents. Feelings such as anger, sadness, and fear, which were previously generalized as "painful" or "bad," become separated and clarified. Since this is no simple task, the therapist often needs to promote awareness of specific feeling states. This requires developing a sensitivity to affective expressions, from a joyful shriek to an angry punch, so that the individual can name the feeling.

For example, when the client aggressively punches the clay the therapist could comment, "You are really mad at that clay today." Language-impaired clients may require very specific and concrete examples of feeling states. Photographs, especially of the client, showing different kinds of feelings (anger, sadness, happiness, fear, loneliness) may be useful in labeling (e.g, "Point to the picture that shows me how you are feeling today").

The Development of Sensory Discrimination and Percept Formation

Activities with both pre-art and art media can promote sensory discrimination and percept formation. The client can be guided to note and identify characteristics like "full" and "empty," using materials like water or seeds and containers. Using clay or flour and water, characteristics such as "wet" and "dry" can be examined. The client can also be encouraged to perform actions that promote a change in properties.

By describing and labeling the client's efforts, the therapist reinforces identification of these concepts. Providing such feedback in a playful manner enhances attention and motivation. For example, the therapist can improvise songs with lyrics that reflect and accompany the client's efforts. Skills in observation, interpretation, and identification are developed through such an empirical approach to sensory discrimination, as the client plays an active role in the discovery process.

The therapist needs to first identify the motor skills necessary for the use of various media, and then analyze the series of actions required for specific activities. For example, to glue blocks on cardboard, the client must reach for the glue, spread it on a block, turn the block over, and press it down. The therapist can help clients practice by providing verbal cues, such as "touch the glue, spread it on the block." Or she might present such cues in a musical way, in a "Gluing Song" to the tune of the "Hokey Pokey:" "You put your finger in. You take your finger out. You put your finger on the block, and you rub it all about. You turn the block over, and you press it down. And that's how you make it stick!" Planned, consistent arrangements of materials on the work surface also helps, the spatial order guiding the client in the correct performance of the sequence.

To Develop the Capacity for Symbolization

For the presymbolic client, the development of *symbolization* is dependent on *imitation, association,* and *approximation. Imitation* requires the perception of physical or behavioral characteristics and the invention of simple forms of equivalence through enactment (discovery of similarities). These perceptions must be "linked up" or *associated* with the art process in order to transform them into symbolic expressions. *Approximation* of the features of people and objects becomes possible, once there is an association of feelings and ideas with created forms. The presymbolic client has difficulty with abstract thinking processes like imitation and association. Producing symbolic forms and articulating features is often complex, frustrating, and confusing, because of deficits in coordination, ego development, or intellect.

To develop skills in *imitation,* the therapist can promote *simulation* of life experiences in the manipulation and use of materials. Using dramatic play, the therapist may help the client to imitate events (eating), objects (car), or people (mother). Through imitative play using gesture and sound, the client can practice simulating ideas, events, and objects. The client can connect a "form" with an experience or idea, and begin to understand the process of representation and abstraction. *Imitation* thus provides a mechanism for relating form and idea, the first step in symbolization.

The presymbolic client may also need direction and support to *associate* feelings, objects, and events with art media, processes, or products. The therapist can focus on visual, tactile, or kinesthetic aspects. For example, crayon taps may remind the client of raindrops, or the colors brown and red may be associated with peanut butter and jelly. A focus on lines or shapes can also elicit associations, like faces, objects, or animals.

Finally, it is necessary to foster skills in *approximation* in order to promote symbolic art production. Underlying such approximation is the discrimination of characteristics of significant items. To assist emotionally disturbed, mentally retarded clients, Roth (see Chapter 12) provided 3-dimensional models as "conceptual references." She used models to define specific attributes of objects the client showed an interest in representing.

Approximation also depends on knowledge of *techniques.* The presymbolic client is often inexperienced in creating particular shapes and forms. To encourage representing features and properties, teaching of specific techniques may be required. When a blind child wanted to make a puppet, he needed to learn simple techniques for construction using papier-mache. When skills are limited by motor impairments, the therapist should evaluate media and modify project structure. If modeling a figure of plasticine clay is too hard, the therapist could show how to assemble a figure with play dough. The wedge could be sliced into six segments, and distinct body parts identified by the client. Then, using even gross movements, the connections and placement of parts could be attempted.

☐ Case Study Preoperational Phase: Henry

The story of Henry demonstrates interventions appropriate for a preoperational child, while tracing his transition from presymbolic play to symbolic expression. Henry, a developmentally delayed 5-year-old, was admitted as an inpatient to a psychiatric hospital. His presenting problems were: failure to develop speech, delayed self-help skills (encopresis), and a high level of anxiety in strange situations and with adults he didn't know. Although his mental age was 3–11, his emotional issues were typical of a younger

Figure 15.4.

child, like separation anxiety, negativism, and battles for control. Henry demonstrated potential, but his language and emotional disabilities seemed to be inhibiting development.

Henry's behavior during the initial sessions reflected his emotional difficulties. He ran away from the art therapist, avoided eye contact, refused to look at the materials, and lay on the floor, covering his face with his hands. Although the first step in any therapy is establishing trust, with Henry it was even more vital. Respecting his need for distance, the art therapist backed away and began painting at the easel. This allowed the therapist to act as a role model, and to assess Henry's ability to imitate and reciprocate nonverbally. Henry gestured toward the easel, then began to paint. He smeared brown paint, then overlapped additional colors in shapeless forms (Figure 15.4). His motor schemes were those of controlled scribbling. And he reflected some emotional issues related to the encopresis (smearing the brown paint).

Once Henry felt comfortable enough to make eye contact, the art therapist used a "total communications" approach—voice, gestures, sign language, and singing. Sign language communicated without words at his level, facilitating the development of trust. Singing was used as a minimally threatening way of getting his attention and giving direction.

The communications were also aimed at teaching language and the concept of associating or *naming*. The therapist reinforced whatever Henry was doing and making: "You are making circles. What else could you add to the circle?" The intention was to promote both creative behavior and the development of the next level of graphic skill. The ultimate goal was Henry's expression of emotional problems, which would probably be facilitated by the development of symbolic schemas.

Figure 15.5.

Because of Henry's difficulty in establishing relationships, the ability to represent a human face schema seemed critical. To promote this idea, the therapist created a primitive mask, which was then used in "peek-a-boo" games. The focus throughout therapy was on the development of skills that would permit the expression and resolution of emotional conflicts. An emphasis on manipulative and cognitive skills, as well as affective expression, was necessary in order for progress to occur.

After three months of weekly art therapy, Henry began to make paintings with more distinguishable forms and cleaner colors. He made graphic shapes, from a circle to the letter "H" (which he identified with his name), to a house, to a human face (Figure 15.5). During one of his last sessions, Henry painted the outline of a face with a large black mouth, which he then pounded aggressively with markers. For a child who cannot speak, the mouth is a reminder of his frustration. The pounding was probably Henry's way of symbolically expressing his feelings about his disability.

Henry's interactions with the therapist also changed dramatically, from extreme avoidance to reciprocal interaction. The number of "signs" and other communications increased, and Henry's ability to express basic concepts through art improved (Figure 15.6). His graphic skills went from controlled scribbles to preschematic representations (Lowenfeld, 1957).

Henry used art as a language for expressing himself. Developmental art therapy enabled him to make the transition—from exploring without any intent to create a form, to creating basic representational images, which he associated with himself and his environment, to symbolic imagery representing his concerns. By differentiating feelings, developing motor schemes, and learning to create a basic symbol, Henry was able to improve his ways of handling feelings and of interacting with others.

Figure 15.6.

☐ Conclusion

A developmental approach to art therapy, based on understandings of cognitive, emotional, and artistic maturation, has been especially useful with clients at a presymbolic level of expression. The case studies illustrate applications of this approach with two children—one operating at a sensorimotor level and the other in the preoperational phase.

☐ References

Aach, S. (1981). Art and the IEP. In L. Kearns, M. Ditson, & B. Roehner (Eds.), *Readings: Developing arts programs for handicapped students.* Harrisburg, PA: Arts in Special Education Project of Pennsylvania.

Bruner, J. (1964). The course of cognitive growth. *American Psychologist, 19,* 1–15.

DiLeo, J. (1977). *Child development.* New York: Brunner/Mazel.

Erikson, E. (1950). *Childhood and society.* New York: Norton.

Freud, S. (1962). Three essays on the theory of sexuality. In *Standard Edition,* Vol. 7. London: Hogarth. (Original work published 1905)

Golomb, C. (1974). *Young children's sculpture and drawing.* Cambridge, MA: Harvard University Press.

Harris, D. B. (1963). *Children's drawings as measures of intellectual maturity.* New York: Harcourt, Brace & World.

Hartley, R., Frank, L., & Goldenson, R. (1952). *Understanding children's play*. New York: Columbia University Press.

Kagin, S. (1969). *The effects of structure on the painting of retarded youth*. Unpublished master's thesis, University of Tulsa, Oklahoma.

Kagin, S., & Lusebrink, V. (1978). The expressive therapies continuum. *Journal of Art Psychotherapy, 5*, 171–179.

Kellogg, R. (1969). *Analyzing children's art*. Palo Alto, CA: National Press Books.

Koppitz, E. (1968). *Psychological evaluation of children's human figure drawings*. New York: Grune & Stratton.

Kunkle-Miller, C. (1978). Art therapy with mentally retarded adults. *Art Psychotherapy, 5*, 123–133.

Kunkle-Miller, C., & Aach, S. (1981). Pre-symbolic levels of expression. In L. Gantt & S. Whitman (Eds.), *The fine art of therapy*. Alexandria, VA: American Art Therapy Association.

Lonker, S. (1982). *A sensorial approach to art: Pre-art discovery with severely and profoundly impaired children*. Harrisburg, PA: Arts in Special Education Project of Pennsylvania.

Lowenfeld, V. (1957). *Creative and mental growth* (3rd ed.). New York: Macmillan.

Lyons, S. (1981). Art in special education. In L. Kearns, M. Ditson, & B. Roehner (Eds.), *Readings: Developing arts programs for handicapped students*. Harrisburg, PA: Arts in Special Education Project of Pennsylvania.

Mahler, M., Pine, F., & Bergman, A. (1975). *The psychological birth of the human infant*. New York: Basic Books.

Piaget, J. (1951). *Play, dreams and imitation in childhood*. New York: W. W. Norton.

Piaget, J. (1954). *The construction of reality in the child*. New York: Basic Books.

Rubin, J. A. (1978). *Child art therapy: Understanding and helping children grow through art*. New York: Van Nostrand Reinhold.

Rubin, J. A. (1984). *Child art therapy: Understanding and helping children grow through art* (2nd ed.). New York: Van Nostrand Reinhold.

Silver, R. (1973). *A study of cognitive skills development through art experiences: An educational program for language and hearing impaired and aphasic children*. (ERIC Document Reproduction Service No. ED 084 745).

Williams, G., & Wood, M. (1977). *Developmental art therapy*. Baltimore: University Park Press.

Wilson, L. (1977). Theory and practice of art therapy with the mentally retarded. *American Journal of Art Therapy, 16*, 87–97.

Winnicott, D. W. (1971). *Playing and reality*. New York: Basic Books.

CHAPTER Rawley Silver

Assessing and Developing Cognitive Skills through Art

Cognition is the process of knowing, and the study of its development an attempt to explain how knowledge is acquired. My approach explores the role of art in identifying, evaluating, and developing cognitive skills. It is based on the premise that art can be a language of cognition paralleling the spoken word. Cognitive skills can be evident in visual as well as verbal conventions. These skills, traditionally assessed and developed through language, can also be assessed and developed through art activities.

This approach identifies and treats emotional disorders too. Children who cannot keep up with classmates develop feelings of inadequacy. Adults who lose the ability to speak after a stroke feel frustrated and depressed. This approach explores emotions as well as thoughts, and seeks to ease tensions and to build self-confidence. It is particularly appropriate for those who have difficulty articulating thoughts and feelings in words.

☐ Background Literature

Cognition

Jerome Bruner (1966) described cognition as a means of organizing the barrage of stimuli from the outside world. We reduce the barrage by constructing models—imaginary representations. We match a few milliseconds of new experience to a remembered model, then anticipate what will happen next, responding to the model we matched. Thus, we think by representing reality vicariously as well as economically. We represent with the aid of "intellectual prosthetic devices," such as language, and pictorial devices as well: "It is still true that a thousand words scarcely exhaust the richness of a single image" (Bruner, 1966).

Drawings are such pictorial devices. People with inadequate language are deprived of opportunities to represent their experiences, because they lack a major device for constructing models of reality. This alone could account for any cognitive deficiency. If their visual-spatial abilities are intact, however, they may be able to construct visual models of reality, and can then represent their experiences by drawing them.

The Role of Language in Cognition

Language is obviously related to cognition; whether it is essential is the subject of debate. Some evidence suggests that language and thought develop independently, that language follows rather than precedes logical thinking, and that even though language expands and facilitates thought, high-level thinking can and does proceed without it (Arnheim, 1969; Furth, 1966; Piaget, 1970).

Piaget (1970) found that logical thinking exists before language, which appears around the middle of the second year. By the beginning of that year, most children can repeat and generalize their actions. If they have learned to pull a blanket to reach for a toy on top of it, they can pull one to reach anything on top. They can also generalize this action by using a stick to move a distant object, or by pulling a string to reach what is attached.

In normal children, language functions to pin down their perceptions, organize their experiences, and understand and control their environments (Strauss & Kephart, 1955). By labeling perceptions in words, children make them usable again and again. Language also allows vicarious experience. When children cannot obtain a desired result, they can substitute words and obtain it in imagination. By hearing about others' experiences, children can obtain information they would otherwise have to obtain themselves.

Art can serve these functions of language. Like linguistic symbols, art symbols can label perceptions and experiences, and represent particular subjects or classes. The painting of a man can represent the artist's father, authority figures in general, man in the abstract, or all three, just as the word "man" can represent each of these ideas, depending on the context. People with inadequate language are handicapped in representing their thoughts effectively, but if their capacity for symbolization is intact, they may be able to represent their thoughts nonverbally by drawing them.

Left and Right Hemisphere Thinking

The different modes of thinking characteristic of the two hemispheres of the brain are also relevant here. Left-brain thinking (verbal-analytical-sequential) predominates in our educational system, but may handicap those whose preferred mode is visual-spatial-simultaneous (right-brain thinking).

People tend to favor either left or right-brain thinking. Preferences are established early in life, and some prefer visual thinking (Witkin, 1962). To illustrate, imagine that it is now 3:40 P.M. What time will it be in half an hour? One person solves the problem in mathematical and verbal terms; another by visualizing the hands and face of a clock (Arnheim, 1969).

Although our society values more highly the verbal, analytical skills of left-hemisphere thinking, we need and use both. The hemispheres share information across connecting nerve fibers; patterns and incoming data are relayed widely throughout the brain. For people who have difficulty putting thoughts into words or understanding what is said, right-hemisphere thinking could be more than a matter of preference in solving problems and processing information. Such individuals deserve tests and communication channels that can bypass language impediments.

In the 1960's and 1970's, when manual communication was forbidden in schools for the deaf, the day revolved around learning language. Some children (whose handicaps were caused by damage to the brain rather than the ear) had virtually no language at all, but learned nonetheless. One boy could read a map upside down and had remarkable talent in art, but was thought to be retarded. I was unable to interest anyone in testing his intelligence until Dr. E. Paul Torrance (1962) offered to send me his nonverbal test of creative thinking and score the results. The boy scored in the 99th percentile compared with normal children his age (11). But no one in his school was interested, because "language comes first," and he remained in the special class for slow learners until he "graduated" at age 14.

Cognition cannot be separated from creativity. Visual thinking is a crucial and central part of the creative process, according to statements by creative scientists (Lutz, 1978). Michael Faraday visualized the electric and magnetic lines of force; Einstein reported his reliance on mental imagery rather than language; and Kekulé discovered the benzene ring through a vision of a series of atoms linked in a chain and biting its tail like a snake.

Brain wave activity also provides evidence that creative persons use both modes of hemispheric thinking (Martindale, 1975). When presented with creative tasks, people classified as "low creative" showed very little brain wave activity. People classified as "creative" responded with both hemispheres, producing large amounts of alpha waves, balanced nearly equally between the two hemispheres.

Assessing and Developing Cognitive Skills through Art

These considerations led me to an approach to teaching and testing that uses art as the principal medium for expressing and receiving ideas. The reasoning is that this approach is especially valuable to those who rely more on visual-spatial modes of thinking than on verbal-analytical modes; that certain concepts developed through language can also be developed through art activity; and that the understanding of these concepts can be inferred from art forms like drawing, painting, and sculpture.

The concepts under consideration are three thought to be fundamental in mathematics and possibly reading: Space, Sequential Order, and Class Inclusion. Mathematicians have identified three independent structures (not reducible to one another), from which all mathematical structures can be generated (Piaget, 1970, pp. 3, 23). One is based on ideas of space and applies to neighborhoods, borders, frames of reference, and points of view. Another is based on ideas of sequential order applies to relationships. Class inclusion is based on the idea of a group and applies to numbers and classifications. Although these concepts usually develop through language, they can also be interpreted visually. While they seem highly abstract, they are observed in a primitive form in the thinking of normal children as young as six or seven (Piaget, 1970).

Studies of reading disabilities have arrived at similar conclusions. Bannatyne (1971) found that dyslexic children obtain higher scores in certain subtests of the Wechsler Intelligence Scale for Children (WISC) than on other subtests. Regrouping the subtests into three categories—spatial, conceptual, and sequential—he found that these youngsters possessed higher visual-spatial skills, moderate conceptual skills, and lower sequencing skills. As he observed, learning-disabled children often have intellectual abilities of a visual-spatial nature that are seldom recognized, allowed for, or trained, due to the emphasis on linguistic approaches to education.

A Drawing Test of Cognitive and Creative Skills (Silver, 1983/1996)

These considerations led to the construction of a test with three drawing tasks based on the three concepts: *Predictive drawing* assesses the ability to sequence and to deal with hypothetical situations; *Drawing from observation* assesses the ability to represent spatial relationships of height, width, and depth; and *Drawing from imagination* assesses the ability to deal with abstract concepts, creativity, and the projection of feelings.

Scoring is based on studies by Piaget and Inhelder (1967), and others who have traced cognitive development by presenting children with tasks. Although dependent on language skills, their observations about stages of development serve as a paradigm for assessing responses in drawings.

Predictive Drawing.   As Piaget and Inhelder (1967) observed, adults are so used to thinking in terms of horizontals and verticals that the concepts may seem self-evident. The child of four or five, however, when asked to draw trees on the outline of a mountain, may draw them inside the outline. The child of five or six draws trees perpendicular to the incline. Not until the age of eight or nine do children tend to draw them upright.

As for horizontal concepts, a four-year-old may scribble round shapes when asked to draw water in a bottle. Later, lines may be parallel to the base of the bottle, even when it's tilted. An older child may draw an oblique line in a tilted bottle. The lines become less oblique and more horizontal until, at nine, the child draws horizontal lines (Piaget & Inhelder, 1967). In the drawing test, the ability to represent concepts of horizontality and verticality, and to order sequentially, are scored 0 to 5 points.

Drawing from Observation.   In tracing the development of the concept of space, Piaget and Inhelder (1967) observe that young children regard single objects in isolation. In time, they develop a coordinated system, perceiving objects in three directions: left-right, before-behind, and above-below. (One of the characteristics of dyslexia is the confusion of similar letters such as p and q, or d and b, which may be caused by a perceptual disorder.)

The test asks individuals to draw an arrangement of three cylinders differing in size, and a large stone. Responses indicate whether they know that the widest cylinder is the farthest to the left, the tallest to the right, and so on. Responses are scored for the ability to represent horizontal, vertical, and depth relationships; like the others, on a scale of 0 to 5 points.

Drawing from Imagination.   The ability to form concepts, especially of class inclusion, involves making selections, associating them with past experiences, and combining them into a context, like selecting words and combining them into sentences. Selecting and combining are the two fundamental operations underlying verbal behavior, according to linguists (Jakobson, 1964). Receptive language disorders reflect a disturbance in the ability to make selections; and expressive language disorders a disturbance in the ability to combine parts into wholes.

In art, a painter selects and combines colors and shapes; if figurative, selects and combines images as well. Selecting and combining are also fundamental in creative thinking. The creative person makes unusual leaps in selecting, associating, and combining experiences innovatively, whether expression is through language, art, or another medium.

Finally, selecting and combining are related to emotional adjustment. The impairment of concept formation is one of the main ways in which neurological damage impinges on thinking. The effects of mental disorder can often be discovered earlier in concept formation than in other thought processes. Impairment may escape detection in verbal expression, because verbal conventions often survive as "empty shells" even when the ability to form concepts has become disorganized (Rapaport, 1972).

To determine ability in this drawing task, people are asked to select two Stimulus Drawings (from those developed by the author), one from each group, and combine them into a drawing that tells a story. They are encouraged to change the stimulus drawings and to add other images. Drawings are scored on a 5-point scale for the ability to select (content), the ability to combine (form), and the ability to represent (creativity). There are also two optional items: projection and language.

Ability to Select.   There are three recognized levels of this ability. The lowest level is perceptual, the intermediate level is functional, and the highest level is abstract. Hornsby (in Bruner, 1966, pp. 79–85) found that normal children progress from grouping objects on the basis of perceptible attributes such as color or shape, to grouping based on function—what the selected subjects do, or what can be done to them. Adolescents develop true conceptual groupings on the basis of class—invisible abstract attributes.

Children were presented with pictures, asked to select objects that were alike, and then asked to explain why. In the drawing test, similar information is elicited nonverbally, to determine whether an individual selects pictorial elements at the perceptual, functional, or conceptual level.

Ability to Combine.   Piaget and Inhelder (1967) found that the most rudimentary spatial relationship is proximity. Before age seven, children typically regard objects in isolation. They gradually consider objects in relation to neighboring ones and to external frames of reference; drawing a line parallel to the bottom of the paper to represent the ground, and relating objects to one another along this line. Drawings become more coordinated as children take into account distances and proportions (pp. 430–436). In this test, a drawing receives the lowest score (1 point) if subjects seem related on the basis of proximity, 3 points for a baseline, and 5 points for overall coordination, with 2 or 4 for intermediate levels.

Ability to Represent.   Torrance (1980) cautions against separating creativity from intelligence, observing that these are interacting or overlapping variables. In the test, the lowest score is given for drawings that are imitative, intermediate scores for drawings that restructure the stimulus drawings, and the highest score for drawings that are original.

Projection.   The scoring for projection of emotions ranges from negative associations, like life-threatening events, to positive associations, like wish-fulfilling events. Ambivalent or unclear associations receive intermediate scores. This range of scores does not indicate a progression from mental illness to mental health, but provides useful information.

Language.   The scoring for language in titles or explanations of the drawings ranges from concrete to abstract. This score is also omitted from the total score because it is inapplicable to some, such as deaf children who are likely to score low in language regardless of their cognitive skills. Considering language scores separately from cognitive ones also allows one to quantify any changes following programs designed to improve language skills.

To determine whether these test items were related to cognitive maturity, with scores increasing as children grow older, the test was administered to 513 children in nine schools in low-, middle-, and high-income areas in different parts of the United States, as well as to adults. To ascertain validity, scores were correlated with scores on a variety of recognized measures of intelligence and achievement. Reliability was determined through studies of interscorer and test-retest reliability.

The drawing test has served to identify children and adults with cognitive skills that escape detection on language-oriented tests of intelligence or achievement. It has also served as a pre-post intervention measure for assessing progress, as in the case of Joey, reported later.

☐ Developing Cognitive and Creative Skills through Art

For children with scores below age norms, remedial procedures were designed. The art materials and techniques useful in developing cognitive skills include those which readily serve as a channel for representing ideas: drawing from imagination and from observation, painting using a palette and palette knife, and modeling with clay. The objectives are to widen the range of communication, to invite exploratory learning, to provide tasks that are self-rewarding, and to reinforce emotional balance. Emphasis is on demonstration rather than discussion (Silver, 1978).

Developing Concepts of Sequential Order through Painting.   The therapist demonstrates mixing a series of blue tints by placing a dab of blue poster paint on the upper-left-hand corner of a sheet of paper and a dab of white on the upper right. With a palette knife, he or she mixes a series of tints between the dabs by adding more and more white to tints of blue. The therapist then asks the children to find out how many tints they can mix on their own papers, and to use their tints in painting on the paper. Later, red and yellow are added and the children are encouraged to invent colors of their own. Each time one color is added to another, or to tints of white, a sequence has been produced. This kind of learning through doing can be reinforced by cutting up discarded paintings into squares of colors that can be placed in sequence, such as red, red-orange, orange, orange-yellow, and yellow. Children are asked to put the squares in order from red to yellow, from large to small, from light to dark, etc.

Developing Concepts of Space through Drawing from Observation.
To focus attention on spatial relationships, the therapist asks the children to sketch an orange and a green rolled paper cylinder. The arrangement is presented below eye level, in the center of the room. When done, they are asked to change seats with classmates on other sides of the arrangement, and to sketch it again. The therapist may also call attention to spatial relationships, like pointing out that the orange is on the left when seen from one point of view, and on the right from another. Later, children draw and paint other subjects from observation, including one another.

Developing Concepts of Class Inclusion through Stimulus Drawings
(Silver, 1982).   Stimulus drawings are used to stimulate associative thinking and to develop the ability to form concepts. They consist of 50 line drawings of people, animals, places, and things. The basic technique is to present them in groups according to category, to ask individuals to select drawings from different groups, to imagine

something happening between them, and then to show what is happening in drawings of their own. When they are finished, the drawings are discussed. To reinforce selecting and associating on the basis of class or function, the therapist can scramble the stimulus drawings and present tasks, like "Find the ones that belong together" or "This drawing goes with this one. Can you find one that goes with this?"

Developing Concepts of Space, Order, and Class through Modeling with Clay.   The "brick" technique—forming clay into small blocks and pressing them together—is used to build human, animal, and other forms that can be associated with one another. The "slab" technique—placing lumps of clay between parallel sticks and rolling them flat—is used to build boxes or houses. The "coil" technique—rolling clay into "snakes" or balls of different sizes—is used to develop the ability to sequence.

With all these art activities, the therapist keeps daily logs and by dating, numbering, and scoring key drawings, paintings, or sculptures, is able to note changes in the ability to select, combine, and represent ideas; to perceive and represent spatial relationships and sequences; as well as in attitude toward self and others.

Studies Which have Used the Drawing Test and Art Techniques.   These procedures have been used in studies involving normal children (Hayes, 1978), learning-disabled adolescents (Moser, 1980), language and hearing-impaired children (Silver, 1973, 2000a), learning-disabled children (Silver & Lavin, 1977), and normal and handicapped children (Silver et al., 1980). Stimulus drawings have also been used with emotionally disturbed adolescents, schizophrenic adults, adult stroke patients (Sanburg, Silver, & Vilstrup, 1984), and gifted, handicapped children (Silver, 1983).

☐ Joey, a Case Example

Joey, age eight, in the second grade, had been identified as a learning-disabled child with particular difficulty in learning to read. His IQ score was 91, below average as measured by the Canadian Cognitive Abilities Test (CCAT). Only 2 of the 24 children in his class had lower scores.

As measured by the drawing test, however, Joey was far above average in one subtest and far below average in another. In *drawing from imagination,* his score placed him in the 99th percentile, and was the highest in his class. On the other hand, his score in *drawing from observation* was in the 14th percentile, and was the lowest in his class.

These findings raised several questions: Did Joey have cognitive strengths and weaknesses that had escaped detection on the CCAT? Would art activities lead to improvement in cognitive skills, as measured by improvement in scores on the drawing test? If so, would improvement carry over to other school situations? Did Joey's responses to the stimulus drawings provide useful clues to attitudes toward himself and others that might influence his cognitive behavior? If so, would a therapeutic atmosphere lead to improvement?

Joey's remediation teacher was interested in the art techniques. She worked with him individually, once a week for 12 weeks, supervised via correspondence and telephone. While the art program was in progress, the CCAT was again administered. Joey's score increased 8 points, from 91 to 99, whereas the mean score of the 24 children in his class decreased from 113 to 108. When the art program ended, the drawing test was again administered. Joey's score on the *drawing from observation* subtest rose to the 85th percentile, from 4 to 10 points; on the *drawing from imagination* subtest, it declined from 14 to 11 points, placing him in the 83rd percentile.

How can these changes be explained? Was art responsible for Joey's gains and losses? Was it the individual attention of his teacher? There are few answers, unfortunately; Joey's teacher died suddenly, and no one else was available to work with him. When the CCAT was administered the following year, his score had dropped back to 90.

Joey's Drawings from Observation

Joey's pretest drawing is shown in Figure 16.1. Only one of the four objects is represented in the correct position—the tallest cylinder on the right. Joey had confused all the left-right and above-below relationships and failed to show any depth, although two objects were in the foreground. Most eight year olds can perceive and accurately represent left-right (horizontal) and above-below (vertical) relationships, although they often miss front-back (depth) ones, drawing objects in a row. Joey's score, in the 14th percentile, suggests deficits in visual memory or perception. His posttest drawing is Figure 16.2. All four objects are in the correct left-right position. Although Joey's discrimination of vertical and depth relationships is rather crude, all four objects are relatively correct in their height and front-back relationships.

Figure 16.1.

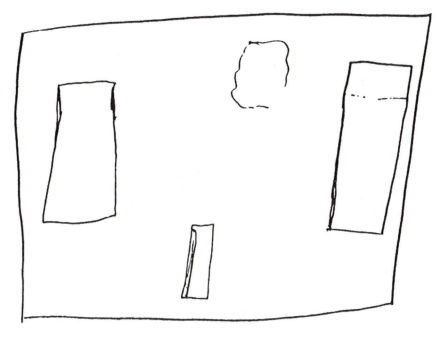

Figure 16.2.

Joey's Drawings from Imagination

Joey's pretest drawing is Figure 16.3. It goes beyond showing what things do, the functional level typical of 8-year-olds. He selected his subjects on the basis of an imaginative idea, implying more than is visible—the conceptual level. His ability to combine subjects pictorially goes beyond the baseline for his age—someone is upstairs. His ability to represent goes beyond imitating or restructuring the stimulus drawings of the test booklet. This drawing is original and expressive of traits that are generally regarded as characteristic of highly creative individuals.

Perhaps the most revealing aspect of this drawing is its projection of emotions. Titled "The Killier" (sic), it seems to represent a doctor operating on a patient who calls out for help, though anesthetized. Upstairs, someone lies in bed snoring, possibly another patient, possibly someone indifferent to what is going on downstairs. Even though Joey's teacher did not ask him to explain, his drawing nevertheless provides useful information about his sense of well-being. Here, the theme has to do with killing and suffering. Although we do not know whether Joey identified himself with the killer, the victim, or both, the world reflected in his drawing is a painful world.

Joey's posttest *drawing from imagination* is Figure 16.4, "The Dog Chasing the Cat." There are several noteworthy differences. First, the world it reflects is no longer painful. Although the cat is being chased, it does not seem to be suffering. Thus, one change was reflected in Joey's projection score, no longer the expression of intense feelings of distress.

Another change is in form: there is a house is in the background, a wall in front of the house, a tree in front of the wall, and a chase in front of the tree—unusual spatial

the Killier

Figure 16.3.

concepts in drawings by eight year olds. There was a gain in score in *ability to combine,* which was offset by lower scores in *ability to select* and *to represent.* Joey seems to have selected the dog and cat on the functional level, simply showing what they do. They also seem static and emotionally flat, compared to his pretest drawing. Was this decrease in expressiveness and creativity the price paid for Joey's gain in spatial skills?

Answers may lie in Joey's drawing from his last art session, the week before the posttest was administered—Figure 16.5, "Seeing an Elephant in the Woods." Using the stimulus drawings, Joey had selected the elephant, the woods, and the mountain climber. The climber in the stimulus drawing is young, but in Joey's drawing he is old, wears dark glasses, and climbs a tree, looking in the wrong direction for the elephant, which is behind the climber.

Joey's drawing contradicts his title: The man could not see the elephant, nor could the elephant be seen from the airplane. The trees would hide it from view, even if Joey had provided the plane with windows. Like his pretest *drawing from imagination*, this

Figure 16.4.

Figure 16.5.

drawing scored in the 99th percentile, suggesting that Joey's expressiveness was intact, but that he was still burdened by feelings of frustration and isolation.

Concluding Observations

Joey had cognitive strengths and weaknesses that escaped detection on the CCAT but were evident on the drawing test. Though his scores on the CCAT were below average, those on the drawing test were far above average—in creativity and in the ability to associate and form concepts, on the drawing from imagination subtest. On the other hand, his scores were below average in the drawing from observation subtest, indicating deficits in spatial thinking. Thus, the drawing test can be useful in assessing cognitive skills which are fundamental in mathematics and reading, and which consequently can affect a child's self-image and self-esteem.

Joey improved in the ability to perceive and to represent spatial relationships, perhaps as a result of the remedial art program. Though gains were evident in his posttest scores, and suggested by his second CCAT scores, there was no evidence of carryover to other school learning. The art program was only 12 weekly sessions—not much time. Perhaps a year-long program with pre- and posttests in reading and math would have clarified the usefulness of the cognitively-based art procedures.

Joey's drawings provide clues to feelings about himself and others. Suffering and frustration are the themes which began with his pretest and recurred in his post-program use of the stimulus drawings. Sadly, the teacher had no training in art therapy, it was not possible for us to meet, and her supervision was restricted to correspondence and long-distance phone calls; therefore, no psychotherapy could be attempted.

What if an art therapist had been able to work with Joey throughout the school year? This is a rhetorical question without an answer, offered as a basis for and encouragement of further research, both with the drawing test and with art techniques based on cognitive development.

☐ References

Arnheim, R. (1969). *Visual thinking*. Berkeley, CA: University of California Press.

Bannatyne, A. (1971). *Language, reading and learning disabilities*. Springfield, IL: Charles C. Thomas.

Bruner, J. S. (1966). *Studies in cognitive growth*. New York: John Wiley.

Furth, H. (1966). Research with the deaf. *Volta Review, 68*, 34–56.

Hayes, K. (1978). The relationships between drawing ability and reading scores. Unpublished Master's thesis, College of New Rochelle, NY.

Jakobson, R. (1964). Linguistic typology of aphasic impairment. In A. de Reuck & M. O'Connor (Eds.), *Disorders of language*. Boston: Little, Brown.

Lutz, K. (1978). *The implications of brain research for learning strategies and educational practice*. (ERIC Document Reproduction Service No. ED 163 068)

Martindale, C. (1975). What makes creative people different. *Psychology Today, 9*, 44–50.

Moser, J. (1980). Drawing and painting and learning disabilities. Unpublished Doctoral dissertation, New York University.

Piaget, J. (1970). *Genetic epistemology*. New York: Columbia University Press.

Piaget, J., & Inhelder, B. (1967). *The child's conception of space*. New York: W. W. Norton.

Rapaport, D. (1972). *Diagnostic psychological testing*. New York: International Universities Press.

Sandburg, L., Silver, R. A., & Vilstrup, K. (1984). The stimulus drawing technique with adult psychiatric patients, stroke patients, and in adolescent art therapy. *Art Therapy, 1*(3), 132–140.

Silver, R. A. (1973). *Cognitive skill development through art activities*. New York State Urban Education Project (Report No. 147232101. ERIC Document Reproduction Service No. ED 084 745).

Silver, R. A. (1976). Using art to evaluate and develop cognitive skills. *American Journal of Art Therapy, 16*(1), 11–19.

Silver, R. A. (1983). Identifying gifted handicapped children through their drawings. *Art Therapy, 1*(1), 40–49.

Silver, R. A. (1993). *Draw a story: Screening for depression.* Sarasota, FL: Albin. (Original work published 1987)

Silver, R. A. (1996). *Silver drawing test of cognition and emotion.* Sarasota, FL: Ablin. (Original work published 1983)

Silver, R. A. (1997). *Stimulus drawings and techniques in therapy, development, and assessment.* Sarasota, FL: Ablin. (Original work published 1982)

Silver, R. A. (2000a). *Developing cognitive and creative skills through art.* [On-line]. Available: iUniverse.com. (Original work published 1978)

Silver, R. A. (2000b). *Studies in art therapy: 1962 to 2000.* Sarasota, FL: Ablin.

Silver, R. A., & Lavin, C. (1977). The role of art in developing and evaluating cognitive skills. *Journal of Learning Disabilities, 10*(7), 27–35.

Silver, R. A., Lavin, C., Boeve, E., Hayes, K., Itzler, J., O'Brien, J., Terner, N., & Wohlberg, P. (1980). *Assessing and developing cognitive skills in handicapped children through art.* (NIE Project No. G79 0081; ERIC Document Reproduction Service No. ED 209 878).

Smith, M. D., Coleman, J. M., Dokecki, P. R., & Davis, E. E. (1977). Intellectual characteristics of school-labeled learning disabled children. *Exceptional Children, 43,* 352–357.

Strauss, A. A., & Kephart, N. C. (1955). *Psychopathology and education of the brain-injured child, Vol 2.* New York: Grune & Stratton.

Torrance, E. P. (1962). *Guiding creative talent.* Englewood Cliffs, NJ: Prentice-Hall.

Torrance, E. P. (1980). *Creative intelligence and an agenda for the 80's.* Viktor Lowenfeld Memorial Lecture at the Convention of the National Art Education Association, Atlanta, GA.

Witkin, H. A. (1962). *Psychological differentiation.* New York: John Wiley.

COMMENTARY

Frances Anderson

Most art therapists who work with clients with disabilities have used aspects of the approaches in this section. My own Adaptive approach (Anderson 1992, 1994) draws on principles from both the Developmental and Behavioral ones; and, as in Silver's Cognitive approach, assessment is an important part of the process. Cognitive-Behavioral Therapy (CBT) is relatively new, so it is less likely that art therapists have utilized it.

Each chapter in this section includes a discussion of the research on which the approach is based. Aach-Feldman and Kunkle-Miller make a convincing case for art therapy with clients who are presymbolic. These are people that one might think unable to benefit from art therapy. Yet, through manipulation of pre-art materials, the authors describe how clients are able to move to a symbolic level of artistic expression. This approach remains one of the few—if not the only one—specifically designed for those with severe developmental delays.

Images and imagery play an important role in all these approaches. Roth supports the notion that, if one can change the art (the external image), this, in turn, can change the client's concepts and behavior. Rosal (1996) elsewhere presented an opposite way of proceeding. With guided imagery and personal construct drawings, she used CBT to change a client's inner images, which, in turn, resulted in changes in overt behavior.

A core component of CBT is accessing the client's mental imagery and the feelings, beliefs and thoughts that imbue these images. Because CBT uses many techniques, no single art therapy example can illustrate them all. Rosal presents a rich tapestry, illustrating the potential this approach has for art therapy—and the potential art therapy has for CBT. Having studied it myself, I believe that CBT utilizing art, imagery, and art making is the among the most important developments in art therapy to date.

The CBT approach and techniques focus on solving problems and developing coping skills, so it is used frequently in solution-centered, crisis, and brief art therapy. Cognitive-Behavioral Art Therapy has been successful for a variety of clients with a wide range of problems. Rosal cites art therapy reports that have used CBT approaches; since many are outcome studies, the evidence supporting it is very strong. In fact, for all these approaches, there are strong case reports of effectiveness.

However, the fact that art therapy is successful in each of these approaches raises a question I have continued to ask throughout my three decades of practice: Given a safe environment and a trusting therapeutic relationship, what are the unique qualities or characteristics that make art therapy so effective? Part of the answer resides in the art product. Part of the answer is found in the client's mental images, and the interactions between these images and how the client makes them concrete in the art.

Part of the answer lies in behavioral principles that are a part of all art therapy. The client is rewarded for his or her efforts in creating artwork and in verbalizing issues surrounding that work. Indeed, it has been argued that engaging in the art making process is itself rewarding. It is this intrinsically reinforcing quality of art that makes art therapy so effective with clients—be they children, adolescents, or adults—with a variety of physical, mental, or emotional disabilities.

Another part of the answer can be found in recent brain research. Goleman (1995), citing a host of studies, concludes that trauma literally imprints the brain. Trauma becomes frozen in our emotional brain—the amygdala (Charney, 1993). It is through mental images, art, fantasy, repetitive play, and repetitive art making that traumatic images can be unfrozen and altered. By making art, a person in a relaxed state can gain control over images, modify them, and move past the traumatic event(s). Then healing can occur (Arrington, April, 2001; Goleman, 1995).

We are getting close to being able to actually document the physiological changes that creating art makes in both the brain and the body (Anderson, 2000; Charney, 1993; Sylwester, 1997, 1998). I believe that in the next decade we will see a whole host of medical studies that document what we have always known: art therapy works. It works with a myriad of clients, with varying problems, and through numerous different approaches, including those described in the chapters in this section.

☐ References

Anderson, F. E. (1992). *Art for all the children: Approaches to art therapy for children with disabilities.* Springfield, IL: Charles C. Thomas.

Anderson, F. E. (1994). *Art-centered education and therapy for children with disabilities.* Springfield, IL: Charles C. Thomas.

Anderson, F. E. (2000). *Art is for all the children: Medical, educational, and therapeutic perspectives.* Keynote address presented at Northern Michigan's third annual conference on art and creativity, Traverse City, MI. April 27.

Arrington, D. B. (2001). *Family art therapy: Home is where the art is.* Springfield, IL: Charles C. Thomas.

Charney, D. (1993). Psychobiologic mechanisms of post traumatic stress disorder. *Archives of General Psychiatry, 50*(2), 294–305.

Goleman, D. (1995). *Emotional intelligence.* New York: Bantam.

Rosal, M. L. (1996). *Approaches to child art therapy.* Burlingame, CA: Abbeygate.

Sylwester, R. (1997). The neurobiology of self-esteem and aggression. *Educational Leadership, 54*(5), 75–79.

Sylwester, R. (1998). Art for the brain's sake. *Educational Leadership, 56*(3), 31–35.

SYSTEMIC APPROACHES

SYSTEMIC APPROACHES

In the first edition of this book, I elected not to include approaches which were most often applied to family or group art therapy. I reasoned that there were a variety of orientations in each, including psychodynamic, humanistic, and psycho-educational, which incorporated interventions ranging from analytic to behavioral. Upon reflection, however, it occurred to me that what I had left out of that book was the thinking broadly known as "systemic"—not a single approach, but rather a way of viewing human beings—as part of a system.

The "system" can be as small as a mother and child, as big as a nuclear family, as large as an extended family, or as vast as the place of any family in its social group or in society at large. The "system" can be as small as a group of two friends, as big as a club, as large as an organization or an institution, or as vast as a village or a country.

Family and group (art) therapy began when workers came to view the patient's problems less as intrapsychic, and more as interpersonal. Both groups and families have developmental histories and dynamics which are central to treatment. In each, the family or the group itself becomes a significant and potent therapeutic modality.

Open and closed groups in art studios have existed since the earliest days of art therapy, and continue to be a way to evoke and to enable the healing power of art. For examples in this volume, see those in the chapters by Kramer, Edwards, Wallace, Rhyne, Garai, Allen, Rogers, Ulman, Wadeson, Henley, and McNiff (cf. also Moon, 2001).

Over time, many different ways of understanding group process and group dynamics have been applied to art therapy groups, with the power of the group itself becoming an increasingly important element. Similarly, family art therapy has developed over the years, with gradually increasing sophistication and a widening range of orientations. In both areas, art therapists have applied others' ideas to their work, often developing their own integrations of different approaches.

I therefore concluded that my reasoning about omitting group and family art therapy from the first edition had been flawed, since I had failed to take into account the special contributions of systemic thinking to work in each—as well as to individual art therapy. So for this second edition, I invited three individuals to write about some ways in which systemic thinking has been applied to art therapy with groups and families.

Barbara Sobol and Katherine Williams not only conduct family and group art therapy; they also teach courses in these areas. Together they have contributed an overview chapter, in which they articulate their understandings of systemic approaches to art therapy with families (Sobol) and groups (Willams). Like the East coast therapists by whom they were trained, their work is grounded in a psychodynamic matrix.

Commentator Shirley Riley, on the other hand, who is from the West coast, represents another kind of systemic orientation, and has embraced postmodern approaches to art therapy. She has spelled out her thinking in greater detail in a recent (1994) book on family art therapy (with Cathy Malchiodi), and a forthcoming book on group art therapy (2001). This new section, then, offers the reader a brief history of both family and group art therapy, and an orientation to traditional as well as emerging paradigms.

☐ References

Moon, C. H. (2001). *Art therapy: Cultivating the artist identity in the art therapist*. Philadelphia: Jessica Kingsley.

Riley, S. (1994). *Integrative approaches to family art psychotherapy* (with C. Malchiodi), Chicago, IL: Magnolia Street Publishers.

Riley, S. (2001). *Art in group therapy*. Philadelphia: Brunner-Routledge.

17
CHAPTER

Barbara Sobol
Katherine Williams

Family and Group Art Therapy

Our lives begin and unfold within the context of families that shape and, in most instances, support our development. Many religions have plumbed the value of group witness and participation for centuries. However, only since World War II have group and family therapy come into prominence as treatment modalities, with many recent adaptations. The focus is increasingly moving beyond the closed system of the self and his or her conflicts to an open, larger system or systems of which the person is a part. "The individual patient is being viewed from a relational perspective, in terms of the early contacts with important others in his or her life and the emotional roles the patient has assumed within the family" (Klein, Bernard, & Singer, 1992, p. 16).

☐ Family Art Therapy

History of Family Therapy

Family therapy has roots in both social work and psychoanalytic psychotherapy. This chapter will focus on the latter. Sigmund Freud, in renouncing his own seduction theory at the beginning of the last century, effectively shifted the focus of the psychoanalytic community away from actual events and relationships in families and toward the study of the child's developing internal mental life. The relevance of actual ongoing family life did not recapture the imagination and scrutiny of most psychotherapists until mid-century. In 1950, child analyst Nathan Ackerman urged the treatment of whole families in child cases (Ackerman & Sobel, 1950). Elsewhere in the 1950's, other prominent analytically trained psychiatrists were engaged in clinical research on the etiology of schizophrenia. Among them were Murray Bowen at the National Institutes of Mental Health (NIMH) in Bethesda, Maryland, Lyman Wynne, Bowen's successor at NIMH, and Don Jackson at Chestnut Lodge Hospital. The study of individual patients expanded to include observation of their families. Family communication—rife with denials and distortions—was studied to determine to what extent it might contribute to, if not sustain or cause, the symptoms of schizophrenia.

In 1959, Don Jackson joined anthropologist Gregory Bateson, psychiatrist John Weakland, and sociologist Jay Haley at the Mental Research Institute (MRI) in Palo Alto,

California, an organization with a grant to study the broader issue of the nature of communication itself. From this early eclectic collaboration, a new theory of family systems began to take shape, driven by Jackson's research interest in schizophrenia, Bateson's fascination with cybernetics (the study of closed information systems and their self-correcting properties), and Haley's fascination with psychiatrist Milton Erickson's techniques to effect change through paradox and hypnosis.

While Bowen and Wynne remained committed to exploring a family's history as a way to shed light on the current emotional system, the MRI group made a radical conceptual and methodological shift, focusing solely on the here-and-now operations of the family system. Leaders in the family therapy movement developed treatment interventions to disrupt, interrupt, amplify, or otherwise disturb the ongoing operations or organization of a family system as first steps toward introducing new and healthier patterns of interaction. Jay Haley (1976) and Cloe Madanes (1981), proponents of *strategic family therapy*, believed that families could get stuck in interactional patterns that maintained problem behaviors, no matter how well-intentioned the desire for change. Strategic therapists made use of dramatic paradoxical directives and other creative behavioral prescriptions to get a family to *do something different* in order to solve a specific—usually behavioral—presenting problem.

Salvador Minuchin (1974) formulated his *structural family therapy* in his work with socially and economically disadvantaged families. Minuchin "believed that problems are maintained by dysfunctional family structures. Therefore, therapy was directed at altering family structures" so that families could develop more competency in solving their own problems (Nichols & Schwartz, 1998, p. 253).

Much of the new therapy was outspokenly anti-psychoanalytic. Little or no value was placed on insight; a high value was placed on short-term treatment, on maintaining the therapist's objective and expert stance, and on behavioral interventions—either straightforward or paradoxical—intended to stimulate change across the whole family system.

Throughout the 60's and 70's, analytically based family treatment and the new systems paradigm developed along mainly separate lines and appeared (or were often treated as) incompatible. However, both schools of thought benefited from an inevitable cross-fertilization and from an influx of new ideas. Early systems theory was rocked and revised by feminist principles (see e.g., Luepnitz, 1988) and by the ideas of social constructivists (see e.g., Anderson, 1990), resulting in a partial return of subjectivity and a higher level of personal engagement and collaboration between therapists and families. Psychoanalytically based family therapy acquired a new richness through the influence of object relations theory, and the willingness of some in the analytic community to acknowledge the value of systems (strategic and structural) ideas (cf. Slipp, 1984).

Core Concepts

From among the evolving concepts and principles of family therapy, a number have endured over time, and to a greater or lesser degree underlie all schools of systemic thought, no matter how diverse. Each of these core concepts, listed below, describes a key aspect of family life. These conceptual categories can be useful to the art therapist in organizing her understanding of a family.

Life Cycle.   According to Carter and McGoldrick (1989), among others, families have a natural developmental *life cycle* with identifiable and predictable phases and crisis points. Events and dynamics of preceding generations powerfully influence how a family handles the critical transition points in its development. A family that is comfortable in one phase of the life cycle (for example, caring for an infant) may not necessarily be comfortable in a subsequent phase (for example, dealing with an adolescent). Therapists from different systems-oriented schools, from Bowenian to strategic, incorporate life cycle concepts, making use of the *genogram* (a three-generation family map) or redefining (*reframing*) a behavioral problem in life cycle terms.

Communication/Behavior.   An axiom in family therapy is that *all behavior*—verbal or nonverbal, active or passive—is *communicative*. Within the family system, communication unfolds in a circular or recursive manner, rather than in a linear or simple cause-and-effect fashion. Families tend to respond to uncomfortable or unacceptable deviations from their habitual circular (and possibly dysfunctional) patterns of behavior by initiating interactions that pull the "deviant" member back into the familiar ways of relating (known as the *homeostasis principle*). A crisis will occur when a family's automatic responses fail to correct the "deviant" behavior.

Structure.   Every family has a discernible structure, that is, the implicit rules that govern the emotional relationships within the family. For example, emotional and physical boundaries within a family are a part of its structure, and in part determine which behaviors or interactions are acceptable and which are not within the family's unwritten rules or norms. Family therapists may invite a family to interact as they would at home in order to observe family structure *in vivo*.

Unconscious Life of the Family.   Every family has a largely unconscious, subjective life of attachments, thoughts, emotions, and representations of self and other, that are experienced internally in each of its members. This unconscious activity profoundly affects the here and now. It may largely determine how particular structures evolve within a family, how emotions are expressed, and how relationships are experienced. The network of internal projections, expectations, and wishes can bind a family together in healthy or unhealthy ways. Therapists who utilize this principle are likely to be exploratory and interpretive in their work with families, with the intent of bringing unconscious aspects of family process into awareness for contemplation or reflection.

☐ Development of Family Art Therapy

Family art therapy may be said to have begun with the work and writings of Hanna Yaxa Kwiatkowska (1978), who was an art therapist at NIMH from 1958 to 1972, and who worked in close collaboration with Lyman Wynne. As part of Wynne's research on schizophrenic adolescents, she developed the *Family Art Evaluation* (FAE), a modification of Elinor Ulman's (1965) diagnostic assessment for individuals. She also created models for adjunctive art therapy and art therapy as a primary treatment for families. Kwiatkowska trained a number of art therapists at NIMH and at the George Washington University, including those who established family art therapy at the Walter Reed Army Medical Center, where an analytic model of family art therapy is still practiced.

Following Kwiatkowska, other art assessments were developed, for whole families (Landgarten, 1987), for couples (Wadeson, 1971), and for families with young children (Rubin & Magnussen, 1974). Others, including Consoli (1994), modified the use of the Kwiatkowska FAE. In 1989, The American Art Therapy Association (AATA) recognized family art therapy with a plenary session at its annual conference. By the mid-90's, AATA had also established a regional symposium on family art therapy to train art therapists across the United States.

Family Art Therapy Today

Family art therapists blend a commitment to the use of graphic expression to promote psychological healing and growth with a commitment to thinking *systemically*. Understanding a client's symptoms as inextricably related to the current ongoing dynamics in his or her most intimate environment, the family art therapist engages some or all of a client's family in artmaking with the therapeutic objective of creating change throughout the family system.

In tracing her own evolution as a family art therapist, Shirley Riley (1994) suggests that art therapy is a fluid modality that may be adapted to support any number of theoretical approaches to family therapy.

Given the proliferation of ideas and techniques in both family therapy and art therapy, the precise "look" of a course of family art therapy may vary widely in both rationale and methods.

For example, "family art therapy" may describe Kwiatkowska's (1978) 18-month treatment in which she used art to explore feelings and relationships and made analytically based interpretations to the family (pp. 137–175). It may also describe Carol Cox's (1992) 6-session treatment in which she used brief, strategic principles to address a specific problem presented by a family. Similarly, a model for short term crisis intervention (Linesch, 1993), a model that follows a social constructivist or narrative therapy framework (Riley & Malchiodi, 1994), a model that uses the principles of paradox (Riley & Malchiodi, 1994; Sobol, 1982), a model of ongoing artwork within the context of play therapy (Gil & Sobol, 1999), and a model combining case management and art therapy with inner-city African-American families (Doby-Copeland, 1999) all fit comfortably under the broad umbrella definition of family art therapy.

Using Kwiatkowska's Family Art Evaluation (FAE) for Assessment and Treatment

Hanna Kwiatkowska's theoretical approach and assessment procedures continue to provide a strong foundation for treating family systems with adolescents as well as families with younger children. The FAE allows the art therapist to gain an understanding of a family along all four core dimensions of family life described earlier in this chapter. As a family moves through a series of tasks in the FAE, a multidimensional "portrait" emerges that elucidates this family's unique relational experience. Additionally, in nearly every FAE series, a receptive art therapist can locate the "emotional center" of the session—a defining moment, image, or set of images that have captured a deep, but usually unarticulated truth about the relationships within the family.

The information yielded by a careful reading of an FAE can help the art therapist chart a clinical course that can aim for either deep insight or behavioral change. Once a clinical path is chosen, the family art therapist may use a non-directive approach or may draw from a wealth of techniques created or adapted for use with families, including a family mural (Rubin), magazine collage (Landgarten; Linesch), family book (Junge), construction projects (Riley; Sobol & Schneider), or work in clay (Kwiatkowska; Keyes) to support the clinical goals. The following case illustrates how images drawn in an FAE may illuminate the relationships within a family, and point toward a direction for the art therapy treatment.

☐ Case Illustration: Darrell

Darrell was referred to my child and adolescent public health clinic twice in one year. As the art therapist, I was expected to balance individual therapy, family therapy, art therapy, and case management in my treatment. At the time of the initial referral, this bright, gifted 16-year-old African-American boy was on the verge of expulsion from high school for disruptive and oppositional behavior and poor academic performance.

Darrell was the only child of his single mother, who had given birth to him when she herself was 16. She was currently in recovery from cocaine addiction and was working as a secretary.

Darrell spent most of his time alone at home during the week. On weekends, he spent a great deal of time at his maternal grandparents' home in another county. His father was only peripherally in his life. Darrell's family on his mother's side had a strong connection to their church community; as a gifted singer, he was often a soloist in the church choir. Darrell also had a history of attention deficit disorder. After one brief, unsuccessful trial of Ritalin in the sixth grade, his mother, committed to AA and NA principles, discouraged further trials of medication.

Only three sessions were held before Darrell broke his most recent behavioral contract at school and was expelled, then swiftly transferred to an alternative public school. The only session in which the full family was present (Darrell, mother, grandmother, and grandfather) had exposed a painful dynamic between the mother and grandmother. As they discussed making plans for Darrell, the grandmother appeared exasperated and critical. Darrell's mother, unable to contain her resentment at her perecption of a lifelong experience of rejection, deflected the session away from problem-solving and directly toward her own pain.

The mental health team at the new school used a structural model of family therapy to empower the mother as the main authority figure for Darrell, and to require the grandmother to play a more minor role.

Although there was a great deal of optimism at the outset, within three months Darrell was permanently expelled from the school and soon permanently "withdrawn" from the county public school system. The family was again referred to my clinic.

In reviewing the new referral for therapy, I read that although the mother had seemed enthusiastic about her newly empowered role, she had not been able to sustain it. She had begun to fall away from the required family sessions, and Darrell increasingly had defied the most basic rules of the program. It seemed that while solutions to problems were being tried, a critical level of information was missing about the emotional dimensions of the family relationships. Because of this, perhaps, all attempts at behavioral problem solving were destined to fail.

I recalled the raw and bitter emotions that had nearly derailed the early family session. In deciding to do the FAE, I hoped that the family would use the art to reveal more about their feelings, while containing them in symbolic form. On the night of the FAE, both Darrell's mother and his grandfather phoned separately to say they would not attend the session. The mother's absence fit my hypothesis that any further exposure of her feelings might be experienced as too painful to tolerate.

The FAE was administered to Darrell and his grandmother by two advanced family art therapy students (Cheryl Doby-Copeland and David Howard) and me. In the *modified FAE* session, family members work at adjacent easels, each making five drawings using chalk pastels and black markers on white drawing paper. The drawings are, in order: a free drawing, a family portrait done in either representational or abstract style, a "warm-up" individual scribble drawing, a jointly developed family scribble drawing, and a final free drawing.

The Family Art Evaluation Session

Throughout the session, there was an easy banter between Darrell and his grandmother, often at a low pitch so that one could hear and experience the light tone but not hear the words. For the first task, the grandmother, an articulate woman, drew simple stick figures with a surprisingly weak hand. Darrell drew vigorously and in a bold style. His sardonic and mocking attitude was striking, and he communicated an emotional distance through his banter and his drawing. His drawing was of a male cheerleader, a boy in a skirt with spiked hair that he titled "Wacky Guy" (Figure 17.1).

The family portraits drawn by Darrell and his grandmother continued the styles and, to some degree, the themes of the first task. Grandmother's family portrait done in a light, shaky hand, again had floating stick figures that barely distinguished one family member from another—except for her daughter, who was shown smoking a cigarette. Darrell's family figures (Figure 17.2) were detailed and highly individualized cartoons; his comments again had a mocking or self-mocking tone. He drew himself in hip-hop clothing—baggy pants, sunglasses, baseball cap. Next to him he drew the smaller figure of his grandmother in a simple, unadorned dress. Spatially, they formed a pair. Separated from them by a few inches were a second pair, Darrell's mother and his grandfather, both in hip-hop clothing. The Darrell figure, all bravado, had no arms.

The joint scribble, requiring family members to work cooperatively at close quarters, often raises the level of anxiety in a family. Instead, as Darrell and his grandmother worked together to develop her scribble, he lost his sardonic edginess. Although he continued to banter, he grew visibly invested in the drawing. He teased, then guided his grandmother into developing the scribble into a full page profile of a horse's head (Figure 17.3), bent down to nibble grass, but looking out at the viewer with a strong, frontal eye and a half-smile. For the title, he wrote "Grazing" at his grandmother's request, then signed both his "baby name" for her and hers for him: "Nonny and Pookie."

The change—the drop in the sarcasm and the concomitant rise in investment—continued into the last drawing. This drawing task often acts as a "recovery drawing," affording family members time back at their own easels after the anxiety of working together. Grandmother attempted the difficult task of depicting an airplane, revealing yet more of a possible cognitive or age-related problem (Figure 17.4). Darrell positioned himself so that he could watch her work, then drew a realistic, accurate, and detailed portrait of her at her easel (Figure 17.5).

Drawing Inferences from the Artworks

For the art therapist to be able to see the relationships among all the pictures and to track how these relationships evolve during the session, it is useful to put the entire set of drawings up on a wall, in a grid formation, where they can be viewed as a whole. Usually, a few images will stand out and evoke a strong subjective response. Working toward a hypothesis about the family relationships requires both the subjective response and a careful objective observation of both the drawings and the interactions. The therapist's objective descriptions uncover formal or thematic connections in the

Figure 17.1.

works; her subjective observations may help her discover the emotional center of the session.

The drawings suggested issues pertinent to each of the four core concepts about family life, as described below. Using my own subjective responses to the art as a guide, I paid particular attention to the family and the horse drawings, which held great evocative power for me.

Figure 17.2.

Life Cycle. Darrell's image of his mother (family drawing) depicts her as an adolescent similar in age and attitude to his image of himself. In the life cycle of this family, it seems that the mother's adolescence and transition into adulthood are unfinished business. Repeating some of his mother's history, Darrell himself— if he is not allowed to finish high school—may be launched prematurely into adult life. The family may need to slow down this transition for him; they may need to revisit the mother's premature launching and renegotiate the mother's entry into adulthood.

Communication/Behavior. Darrell kept up a defensive, distancing posture for the first three tasks, not only with his bantering humor, but also with his images of "wacky" posturing caricatures, several of whom wore sunglasses that kept the viewer at an emotional distance. During the joint scribble, this posture seemed to dissolve. His use of baby names suggested that being physically close to his grandmother may have helped him to drop some of his posturing. This closeness seemed to allow the emergence of the horse, with its direct and open gaze, and Darrell's subsequent guileless watching of his grandmother during the last procedure. While he never stopped joking, during the last drawing his banter had a poignant quality—in a joke about the passage of time.

Structure. The changing images from the family drawing to the horse also contain a suggestion about the structure of the family. Darrell drew mother, grandfather, and himself as adolescents, with the grandmother figure quite close to him, in the background. This placement, followed by an even closer and literal alliance with grandmother in

Figure 17.3.

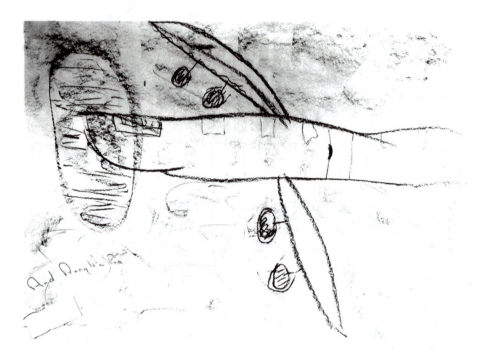

Figure 17.4.

the horse picture, suggests that Darrell can move close to grandmother—to bask in her watchful care—as he demotes his mother to adolescent status, then eliminates her presence altogether. Yet their similar dress and body posture also suggests Darrell's identification with mother. The lack of clarity about mother's position in the family may be contributing to Darrell's confusion and acting out.

Unconscious Life of the Family.   The horse image and the obvious comfort in the process of creating it suggest a powerful attachment between Darrell and grand-mother, and a sense that grandmother provides a holding environment for her grand-son. Mother's absence from the session suggests that grandmother (family) does not provide a "good enough" holding environment for her. The depictions and somewhat derogatory verbal characterizations of mother in the grandmother's drawing also raise questions about possible projective identification. If Darrell's mother experiences her-self within the family as a bad daughter and an outcast, one wonders if this self-image is a projection she has received and absorbed from her mother. Darrell's own images (possibly self-images)—from open and guileless, to wacky, confusing, cool, and even bizarre (his warm-up scribble) suggest that he is struggling and uncertain as to whether he is the "good child" or the "bad adolescent" Are there different projections coming from mother and grandmother?

The Follow-Up Session

Before the FAE session, I had sensed but could not identify unexplored emotional is-sues in this family that were getting in the way of finding good behavioral solutions to

Figure 17.5.

Darrell's expulsions. After the drawing session, it seemed clear that before a good behavioral plan or any attempt to restructure the family roles could be made, the emotional
life of the family needed to be addressed.

The shift in the mood of the session with the appearance of the horse, suggested
that therapy should explore the feelings and thoughts the horse image evoked for both
Darrell and his grandmother. When asked to talk about the horse, Darrell leaned forward
in his chair, abandoning the laid-back posture he had assumed until then. Darrell said
that the horse "is strong, a free spirit, and peaceful, out in nature . . . when I am with my
grandmother, I'm usually happy and peaceful. The eyes and the smile . . . are . . . aspects
of her because she is always watching over me. When I do something good, she smiles
at me. My grandmother is like my guardian angel." Referring to his watching her in
the last picture, he said "she's the main one I focus on for her wisdom. I always keep
her somewhere where I can see her, somewhere in my mind." After this moment of this
reverie, Darrell fell back into his "cool" and guarded stance. Looking at the portrait he
had done of his mother, he slumped in the chair, shrugged, and said, "That's just the way
she is; I can't change her, so I don't worry about it. I just let her go and get on with my life."

From FAE to Treatment Planning

Psychologist Ellen Wachtel (1994) suggests that in an integrated approach to family therapy, a psychodynamic formulation, rather than serving to pathologize a child or family, "enhances the ability to make good sound behavior and systems interventions" (p. 153). In this case, images from the FAE allowed the art therapist to understand the family from both an analytic and a systems point of view, providing a great deal of flexibility for treatment planning.

The Family Art Evaluation session provided an environment that was emotionally safe enough for Darrell to relax his guarded stance and let his imagination produce the smiling horse of the joint scribble. Later, in the follow-up session, the act of looking at the image of the horse seemed to evoke in him the reverie of drawing that picture. He was able to allow himself to express a vulnerable dependency, as well as a striving for manhood. Amazingly, this cool teenager found the words to describe the extent to which he had folded an internal image of his grandmother into his image of himself.

But it also seemed that this peacefulness was gained at the expense of his mother, who may have been emotionally unable to join the session, or had been somehow barred from joining. Both grandmother and Darrell seemed to minimize or avoid a sense of loss. Darrell's laconic rejection of his mother as someone to "let go of," while in some ways mature, seemed a poignant echo of his grandmother's rejection of her daughter. Darrell's ability to bask in the glow of his grandmother's care left an area of family pain never addressed.

Using this understanding as a jumping off place for the family art therapy, I was able to formulate two basic goals and a direction for treatment. The first goal was to create a safe therapeutic space—a holding environment—that could include Darrell's mother. An invitation to the mother to find her own graphic language in art could be extended to her at first within the safety of her own individual sessions, then later in the presence of the other family members.

The second goal was a structural and behavioral one—to ensure that Darrell, who was "chomping at the bit," would be competently managed and guided through this stormy part of his adolescence. It would be foolhardy for the art therapist to ignore the behavioral crisis in favor of an exploration of dynamics; it would be equally unwise to ignore the network of emotions underlying and supporting the dysfunctional behavior. The subsequent family art therapy, therefore, used both frames of reference, shifting gears as both need and opportunity arose. For examples of other cases treated with art therapy within a systems framework, see Riley's work with an adolescent schizophrenic girl (Riley & Malchiodi, 1994, pp. 67–86), and my work with a violent child in a divorcing family (Sobol, 1982).

☐ Group Art Therapy

Some Approaches to Group Therapy

Group therapy does not, at least initially, consist of intimates, but each group member brings within him the introjects developed throughout his life as a family member. Being in a group elicits these patterns of thinking and behavior, and highlights each member's customary ways of seeking comfort and viewing the world. As such, the group experience provides a fertile ground for the growth of self-understanding, as well as rich diagnostic opportunities for the clinician. In group therapy, as in family therapy, process and relationships are at the heart of treatment.

Theoretical antecedents can be seen in the work of LeBon (1895) who wrote about the "group mind," in which individual members become seduced by the group to do things they would not do alone, jettisoning personal responsibility and displaying primitive behavior. McDougall (1920) agreed, but thought that the group could also be harnessed to effect a beneficial change in behavior (Klein, Bernard, & Singer, 1992). Freud, basing his ideas about groups on these authors, focused on the role of the leader, believing that group members' involvement with the leader would bind them together, although their ambivalence could drive them apart. Freud's emphasis on "the process of empathy permits a redifferentiation of each individual to occur by means of imitation and then temporary emotional identification with others. Individuals in groups thereby can reverse the dedifferentiation resulting from initial membership and, in the process, learn more about their own emotional life and that of others" (*Ibid.*, p. 7).

Freud, however, did not use group treatment, and it was the sheer numbers of traumatized servicemen returning to England and the United States during the Second World War that brought about a focus on group as a useful modality. Bion (1959) who, with Ezriel and others, moved to the Tavistock Clinic after his initial work with soldiers, initiated the beginning of the social systems approach to group treatment.

Bion (1959) widened the application of psychoanalytic theory beyond the analyst and his patient. He saw the individual as inextricably part of a group, "even if it is a group to which he insists that he does not belong" (Skolnick, 1992, p. 325). Despite the inevitability of and sometime longing for group participation, the person is nonetheless afraid of groups because of the threat to his individuality. Bion felt that the task of relating to the group of which he is a part is "as formidable to the adult as the relationship with the breast is to the infant, and the demands of this task are revealed in his regression" (1959, pp. 141–142).

One of Bion's (1959) major contributions to group theory and practice is the way he characterized this regression. Believing that the stress of being in groups pushed their members to veer away from the task for which the group had ostensibly been called together and to be beset with irrational beliefs; Bion characterized these beliefs as falling into three *basic assumptions:* fight/flight, dependency, and basic assumption pairing. These beliefs can be experienced by one person, by some people, or by all the members at any given time; and these assumptions may hold sway for a series of groups, or any or all may appear within a single group meeting.

When a member assumes a prominent role and acts as if any of these assumptions were true, that member may be given great power through the accumulated force of the split-off parts of other members being projected onto the leader. It is the leader's job to "illuminate the covert and unconscious shared group processes that [are] interfering with real work on psychological and developmental problems" (Skolnick, 1992, p. 325). Bion also felt that, because of the projections of group members, any member's words might speak in some way for the group as a whole.

Bion's work became combined with the theories of social scientists such as Lewin (1950) and Rice (1969), who brought systems theory to bear on group attributes and activities. The systems approach focuses on the group as part of a larger system, having a boundary that differentiates it from the larger system, "across which transactions occur which require management" (Skolnick, 1992, p. 326). It is important for the group leader to be aware of the input, the conversion, and the output, to use the jargon of this theory. What crosses the boundary to enter the group is transformed in some way before leaving the boundary of the group. The value of this perspective is to heighten the leader's awareness of the place of the group in the larger system, as well as the leader's responsibility to manage the boundaries and to notice the effect that activity at the boundary has on the group. Skolnick, who uses this method, writes: "changing the way members behave in relation to each other, the group, and the environment is as critical to therapeutic change as insight into the historical causes of their difficulties" (p. 328). The combination of Bion's basic assumptions and systems theory led to the social systems focus on roles, tasks, and boundaries in the here-and-now life of the group.

In the United States, the social systems perspective has been mostly utilized in a conference format to teach professionals about the use of power and authority in groups. Even though it is not as widely used in treatment here as in England, Skolnick (1992) maintains that it "provides the therapist with a conceptual flexibility not as yet found in any other framework. As a meta-theory it can enable therapists to bridge and utilize the richness of disparate theories, . . . different time frames, and varying levels of focus. The utilization of this perspective gives the therapist an array of ways to formulate a given moment in the group and also an array of choices about how to intervene" (pp. 344–345). The social systems approach, even though it grew out of classical psychodynamic theories, can be seen as a helpful template through which to view other approaches to group therapy.

Another meta-theory that focuses on group treatment is that of Yalom (1983, 1995), whose theoretical underpinnings are Sullivanian and existential. However, in general, he describes the therapeutic processes that inhere in groups in a way that can be applied to various theoretical approaches. Yalom (1995) lists 11 therapeutic factors that he feels describe the "basic mechanisms of change"in all group therapies. These are: instillation of hope, universality, imparting of information, altruism, the corrective recapitulation of the primary family group, the development of socializing techniques, imitative behavior, catharsis, existential factors, cohesiveness, and interpersonal learning (p. 1). Yalom maintains that therapists with different theoretical perspectives will emphasize differing groups of these factors, and that different patient populations and the resulting goals will also highlight some factors over others.

Rather than being a *leader-focused approach*, like the systems theory approach, this is a *group-centered approach*, in which the leader's goal over time is to recede from centrality, making interventions that encourage group members to do the work of the group. In his book on inpatient groups, Yalom (1983) acknowledges that the leader who works in a short term setting with severely disturbed patients must be much more active than the leader of an ongoing group of healthier individuals.

However, in both cases, the leader's task is not to interpret, but to illuminate the process that is unfolding in the here-and-now. The activation of process involves focusing on the interactions occurring in the group at any given moment, stopping the process and asking the group to observe what has happened, and helping group members to understand and integrate this knowledge, as well as a burgeoning curiosity about their and their fellow members' process. Issues of timing (within the particular session as well as within the life of the group), level of stability of group members, and goal and setting of the group will determine how this unfolds. For inpatient groups, the life of any group may well be a single group meeting, so the goals will be to help patients become engaged in therapy so that they may seek it later, help them to spot patterns of relating to others that could be areas to focus on in subsequent therapy, and help patients to reduce the anxiety caused by being in the hospital.

☐ Group Art Therapy

The foregoing are some models of group therapy that do not involve artmaking. What about group art therapy? Even before managed care, art therapy was largely practiced in groups. Many art therapy articles—including some chapters in this book—report on work with individuals against the background of the groups in which they were treated, without noting the impact of the group in which the art was made.

Surveying the literature, one finds basically three types of art therapy groups: the *studio based* group, the *theme or task focused* group, and the *processs oriented group*. In the studio based group, people come together to make art and are influenced in some way by the presence of others, but the focus is on each individual's process and product and on the interaction between the artist and the art therapist. The first art therapy groups in hospitals, like those led by Hill (1945) and Kramer (1958), were of this sort, while Allen (1992) currently espouses this approach in a community setting.

In this country, the theme or task-based group seems to predominate, with most of the literature describing work with a particular population, the needs of which dictate the theme. Examples include: making "a safe place" in Jacobson's work with Dissociative Identity Disorder (DID) patients (in Kluft, 1993), constructing a torn paper collage about loss with mothers following perinatal death (Speert, 1992), or creating a "symbolic graphic life-line" in groups of patients in a partial hospitalization program (Martin, 1997).

Most of the literature on process oriented groups comes from England, where Waller (1993) writes about group interactive art therapy and Skaife and Huet (1998) speak of group analytic art therapy; although Wadeson's 1980 book also describes some process oriented groups. In this approach, the focus is on group members' interaction with one another and the leader, through words as well as image making.

Within these three general areas, there are so many permutations represented in the art therapy literature that it is not possible to detail them here. It can be seen, however, that there is an increasing progression of interest in systems and process issues as one moves from the studio group, through the themes group, to group interactive art therapy. The groups also become less leader-focused and more group-focused as one moves from studio to interactive approaches. It is important to say that this is not at all a hierarchy, but is simply one way of categorizing what happens in art therapy groups, in order to highlight the fact that each choice the therapist makes entails a sacrifice. Looking clearly at these choices helps the therapist "be awake," as the Buddhist philosophers say, rather than blindly following accustomed practice.

Most of the literature mentions that the art therapist needs to consider such issues as whether the group is to be long or short term, with which diagnostic population, for how long, in what space, for what goal, and using which materials. These and many other variables affect decisions that are part of a complex process that "requires the capacity to hold in mind many disparate elements simultaneously and to recognize the effect that an action in response to one element will have on the other elements" (Deco, in Skaife & Huet, p. 1998, 105). Viewing these and other elements involved in group through the systems and process lenses may help us to see them with heightened awareness.

For instance, there are many reasons why an art therapist might provide a theme to structure the group. She may do this because the patients are not at this time in their lives capable of generating a productive idea and are, because of their illness or their lack of exposure to therapy, dependent on her to provide structure and education. She may want to create an atmosphere that promotes some of Yalom's therapeutic factors, such as universality, interpersonal learning, and group cohesiveness. If so, she probably has, as many therapists do, what Bion would call a *valence for dependency;* and this may be a happy marriage of her orientation and the needs of the group.

However, the therapist could also be acting out of *basic assumption dependency,* in which she and the group are colluding in believing that only the leader is able to provide the theme. Here both the art therapist and the group are acting as if change for group members will come through complying with a directive, rather than from grappling with the uncertainty of relating to each other. This latter task may be as uncomfortable for the art therapist as for the group members, and may be the more salient reason why the therapist offered the group a theme. Recognition of the therapist's heretofore unconscious fears may allow her to bring them into consciousness where they will have less power over her.

Perhaps the group is in an understaffed, busy hospital where patients arrive late to groups, are pulled out of groups for other treatments, or leave early for additional appointments. The therapist decides that the only way to keep any continuity is to work around a common theme, so that new group members may more easily join or others may leave without disrupting the general focus. On the other hand, perhaps the therapist has absorbed the larger group culture and her unconsciously assigned place in that culture, and has relinquished her role as boundary keeper for the group. Though often a nearly insurmountable task, the therapist who is aware of the roles she plays within the larger system may be able to darken the boundaries where the group meets the system, and thus allow for more flexibility within the group.

McNeilly (1983) feels that theme-centered art therapy evokes powerful feelings before the patient is ready to deal with them constructively. The art therapist who uses a theme may feel pressured by the system in which the group operates to come up with significant or interesting diagnostic material more quickly than other therapists, in order to prove the efficacy of art therapy or to promote her authority within the system. It may be this that causes her to act in a manner less helpful to her patients than were she to have looked carefully at her own process.

But what if the art therapist has thoughtfully regarded her place in the larger system, and, after scrutiny, has realized that she has been using careful planning and a directive, leader-centered approach more to defend against her fears and insecurities than to respond to her patients' needs? What if she decides she wants to promote Yalom's therapeutic factors using art in the context of a group interactive approach, in which the leader's role is less central, and the group members learn about themselves through trying to relate to others in the group?

While there are art therapists who write convincingly of incorporating many of Yalom's (1995) approaches in groups that of necessity must remain quite structured (e.g., Sprayregen, 1989), fully opening up the group to allow for its interactive po-tential raises many questions. Including image making in a group is not just adding another item to the list of therapeutic factors. The art process affects and mediates all that happens within the group, posing challenges that verbal groups do not have to confront.

For instance, Skaife and Huet (1998), writing about group analytic art therapy, ask "What are the implications of the therapist taking [an apparently] passive role in a group which has an activity in it, which needs structuring at least in so far as when, and for how long, it takes place?" (p. 24). They echo Yalom who asserts that without the leader providing initial structure, the group may disintegrate, so they do offer enough to help the group get started. However, they leave the time allotted for art making and the content of the art making up to the group, believing that "the group makes use of the tensions around the change in activity to play out issues of power and authority" (Skaife & Huet, 1998, p. 25).

While the elucidation of group members' roles and their relationship to early familial patterns can be beneficial, it also can take away from the art making process. If discussion goes on for too long, there will not be time to make the art. In fact, any discussion takes up time that could be used to engage in the art process; the art products that emerge from customary-length group interactive art therapy sessions are rarely fully realized. The art therapist therefore must choose whether to place some structure on at least the use of time like McNeilly (1990), or to allow the group to come to terms with setting or not setting those limits itself like Skaife and Huet (1998) and, at times, Waller (1993). One remarkable occurrence in many interactive groups is the frequency with which images spontaneously emerge as symbols for the group process. Of course, if the group process is contentious, the universal symbols will reflect this; so our hypothetical art therapist must be able to contain the tension and conflict, and function in the midst of it when utilizing this approach.

Talking about the artwork offers another challenge to the interactive group therapist. She must be aware of all the assumptions about this task. What is paramount? Do she and the members believe that everyone should get a chance to speak about their picture? If so, this diminishes the depth to which the discussion can go, and inhibits spontaneous group interaction around issues raised by a group member's image. If not, there is a sense of frustration that an image has been made but not discussed.

If the art therapist wants to provide equality, is she offering a container that is sufficiently stable and comfortable so that group members feel safe enough to speak, or is she colluding with the members in fleeing from the group task of relating to each other through the art by promoting a discussion style that mitigates against real connection? In group interactive art therapy, the art therapist would almost always make the choice to comment on the process rather than to structure the process, but every time she comments, she is encouraging the group to move to a verbal mode, which involves moving away from the art process.

Moreover, whenever an artist discusses a picture, it is a there-and-then process, since the artist is describing what he drew and thought in the immediate past. This can be beneficial in affording some distance from which to discuss difficult material. But it can also remove the immediacy of group interaction, and the group can revert to a dry show-and-tell format unless the art therapist guides members to attend to the experience of speaking of this material at this moment in this group. These are only a few of the ways art therapists of all persuasions might use the systems or process orientations to scrutinize the design and experience of their groups.

While it is clear that *art therapy in groups* and *group art therapy* are two different but related experiences, there are areas of commonality. Group members gather together and to varying degrees are able, however briefly, to enter into a dialogue with the self from which emerges an image that in some way represents that self—even when the representation is expressive of the manner in which the self is hidden. The art making is an experience of "being alone in the presence of another" (Winnicott, 1958), a very different experience from being merely alone, and one which many psychiatric patients missed early in life. Even in a studio group there are times it is possible to see the resonance (McNeilly, 1990) of images—a convergence of symbols which show that there is some relationship among the group members, even though no common theme or materials have been dictated. Art therapists in more structured groups attempt to create conditions in which this is likely to occur by offering a common theme or task, and art therapists in interactive groups use the similarity of images to explore group process.

Art making within a group offers group members an opportunity to experience both pride and shame (Wadeson, 1980) within a context in which it is possible to live through the shame and live into the pride in the presence of attentive witnesses. The anxiety attendant upon being in a group pushes group members to show themselves writ large, with their habitual patterns of thinking and behaving highlighted further by their interactions with the art materials and the images that ensue from this process. Paradoxically, the group also offers comfort as group members project intrapsychic material into the artwork, where (in some patients) it is symbolized, "acknowledged, and explored," and related to the self and other members of the group. The material can then be acknowledged and accepted as part of the self, bringing about change (Greenwood & Layton, 1987, in Waller, 1993, p. 17).

There are also instances in which group members can appear to be minimally involved in the art process or are merely contained within the group in the presence of the images. Allen (1983) writes of establishing an observer role for patients who are new to the group or who are at the time unable to participate. It appears that she sees this as an initial phase of group participation. However, one patient on an inpatient unit where I worked came regularly to group but never drew. He was severely depressed, unshaven and in his bathrobe, although he always arrived on time and usually helped me wheel supplies back to the closet on his closed ward. Eventually, he was discharged, without ever having participated verbally or artistically.

About eight months later, a well-groomed young man greeted me in the hall. When I clearly did not recognize him, he identified himself as the sad man in my art therapy group. Remarkably, he thanked me for the group, mentioned how much he had gotten out of it, and described in detail the other patients' pictures that had meant the most to him. It appeared that in his depressed state, the images were able to speak to him and linger in his mind, although he did not have the resources to interact with the group members at that time. Perhaps the group also provided "a setting to which an attachment [could] develop which allow[ed] for the introjection of a coherent structure" (Deco, in Skaife & Huet, 1998, p. 107).

For the conditions to exist in which all of the foregoing processes can take place, the art therapist must subject every aspect of the design of the group, her behavior in group, and her understanding of what occurs within the group, to the same intense scrutiny with which she would critique a piece of artwork. The systems and process perspectives are helpful tools in this endeavor and can be applied, with varying intensity, to understanding groups of any theoretical orientation.

☐ Conclusion

Therapy groups are assembled out of the personal distress of the separate lives of individuals. Families assemble for therapy to alleviate the distress within the system. In each case, the whole is greater than the sum of its parts. While each member draws from a deeply personal motivation or experience, the key to the work is the relationships in the room.

In both family and group art therapy, the art process manifests these relationships. The presence of artmaking may at times help participants to avoid relating, but it can also titrate relationships, allowing some families or group members to tolerate being together in uncustomary ways. At best, creating images and viewing the images of others can provide a deep sense of connection and a rich understanding of the dynamics that propel or inhibit relationships. Making art together develops a graphic language that enables people to speak to each other in ways that are simply unattainable by words alone.

☐ References

Ackerman, N. W., & Sobel, R. (1950). Family diagnosis: An approach to the preschool child. *American Journal of Orthopsychiatry, 20,* 744–753.

Allen, P. (1983). Group art therapy in short-term hospital settings. *American Journal of Art Therapy, 22,* 93–95.

Allen, P. (1992). Artist-in-residence: An alternative to "clinification" for art therapists. *Art Therapy, 9*(1), 22–29.

Anderson, W. T. (1990). *Reality isn't what it used to be.* New York: Harper/Row.

Bion, W. (1959). *Experiences in groups.* New York: Basic Books.

Carter, E., & McGoldrick, M. (Eds). (1989). *The changing family life cycle: A framework for family therapy* (2nd ed.). Boston: Allyn and Bacon.

Consoli, J. (Speaker). (1994). *A three-step family systems approach for assessment, confrontation, and treatment planning* (Audiotape #24). Annual AATA.

Cox, C. T. (1992). *Take back the night: Healing trauma through short-term family art therapy* [Videotape]. Bowling Green, OH: WBGU Television Learning Services at Bowling Green State University.

Deco, S. (1998). Return to the open studio group: Art therapy groups in acute psychiatry. In S. Skaife & V. Huet (Eds). *Art psychotherapy groups* (pp. 88–108). New York: Routledge.

Doby-Copeland, C. (Speaker). (1999). *African-American families in art therapy: A strengths-based approach* (Audiotape #105). Annual AATA.

Gil, E., & Sobol, B. (1999). Engaging families in therapeutic play. In C. E. Baily (Ed.), *Children in therapy: Using the family as a resource.* (pp. 341–382). New York: W. W. Norton.

Haley, J. (1976). *Problem-solving therapy.* San Francisco: Jossey-Bass.

Hill, A. (1945). *Art versus illness.* London: George Allen & Unwin.

Jacobson, M. (1992). Group art therapy with multiple personality disorder patients: A viable alternative to isolation. In E. Kluft (Ed.), *Expressive and functional therapies in the treatment of multiple personality disorder* (pp. 101–123). Springfield, IL: Charles C. Thomas.

Junge, M. (1985). The book about Daddy dying: A preventive art therapy technique to help families deal with the death of a family member. *Art Therapy, 4,* 10.

Keyes, M. F. (1974). The family clay sculpture. *The Arts in Psychotherapy.* pp. 25–28.

Klein, R., Bernard, H., & Singer, D. (1992). *Handbook of contemporary group psychotherapy.* New York: International Universities Press.

Kramer, E. (1958). *Art therapy in a children's community.* Springfield, IL: Charles C. Thomas.

Kwiatkowska, H. Y. (1978). *Family therapy and evaluation through art.* Springfield, IL: Charles C. Thomas.

Landgarten, H. B. (1987). *Family art psychotherapy: A clinical guide and casebook.* New York: Brunner/Mazel.

Landgarten, H. B. (1993). *Magazine photo collage: An assessment and treatment technique.* New York: Brunner/Mazel.

Linesch, D. (Ed.). (1993). *Art therapy with families in crisis.* New York: Brunner/Mazel.

Luepnitz, D. (1988). *The family interpreted: Feminist theory in clinical practice.* New York: Basic Books.

Madanes, C. (1981). *Strategic family therapy.* San Francisco: Jossey-Bass.

Martin, E. (1997). The symbolic graphic life-line: Integrating the past and present through graphic imagery. *Art therapy, 14*(4), 261–267.

McNeilly, G. (1983). Directive and non-directive approaches to art therapy. *The Arts in Psychotherapy, 10,* 211–219.

McNeilly, G. (1990). Group analysis and art therapy: A personal perspective. *Group Analysis, 23,* 215–224.

Minuchin, S. (1974). *Families and family therapy.* Cambridge, MA: Harvard University Press.

Nichols, M. P., & Schwartz, R. C. (1998). *Family therapy: Concepts and methods*, 4th ed. Boston: Allyn & Bacon.

Rice, A. K. (1969). Individual, group and intergroup processes. *Human Relations, 22*, 565–584.

Riley, S., & Malchiodi, C. (1994). *Integrative approaches to family art therapy.* Chicago: Magnolia Street.

Rubin, J. A. (1978). *Child art therapy.* New York: Wiley.

Rubin, J. A., & Magnussen, M. (1974). A family art evaluation. *Family Process, 13*(2), 185–220.

Skaife, S., & Huet, V. (Eds.). (1998). *Art psychotherapy groups.* New York: Routledge.

Skolnick, S. (1992). The role of the therapist from a social systems perspective. In R. Klein, H. Bernard, & D. Singer (Eds.), *Handbook of contemporary group psychotherapy* (pp. 321–369). New York: International Universities Press.

Slipp. S. (1984). *Object relations: A dynamic bridge between individual and family treatment.* Northvale, NJ: Jason Aronson.

Sobol, B. (1982). Art therapy and strategic family therapy. *American Journal of Art Therapy, 21*(2), 43–52.

Sobol, B., & Schneider, K. (1996). Art as an adjunctive therapy in the treatment of children who dissociate. In J. Silberg (Ed.), *The dissociative child* (pp. 191–218). Lutherville, MD: The Sidran Foundation Press.

Speert, E. (1992). The use of art therapy following perinatal death. *Art Therapy, 9*(3) 121–128.

Sprayregan, B. (1989). Brief inpatient groups: A conceptual design for art therapists. *American Journal of Art Therapy, 28*, 13–17.

Ulman, E. (1975). A new use of art in psychiatric diagnosis. In E. Ulman & P. Dachinger (Eds.), *Art therapy* (pp. 361–386). New York: Schocken.

Wachtel, E. F. (1994). *Treating troubled children and their families.* New York: Guilford.

Wadeson, H. (1980). *Art psychotherapy.* New York: Wiley.

Waller, D. (1993). *Group interactive psychotherapy.* New York: Routledge.

Winnicott, D. W. (1958). *Through paediatrics to psychoanalysis.* New York: Basic Books.

Yalom, I. (1983). *Inpatient group psychotherapy.* New York: Basic Books.

Yalom, I. (1995). *The theory and practice of group psychotherapy* (4th ed.). New York: Basic Books.

COMMENTARY

Shirley Riley

I have been invited to discuss the growth of systemic and postmodern thinking in relation to the practice of art therapy. As described in the preceding chapter, art therapy grew up during a heady time of innovation in both group and family therapy. The pioneers in these areas changed our thinking about clients, by recognizing that every individual is embedded in multiple systems; and by proposing treatments carefully designed to facilitate systemic changes.

The family system that did or did not nurture the individual, the position that family had in the socio/economic/cultural systems, and its place in the larger system of politics and nationality—all were vitally important. It became apparent that the nuclear family and its generational belief system—whether two-party or single parent, kind or cruel, rich or poor—assigned roles and beliefs to each member. Although this is not news in the year 2001, these ideas were a radical departure from the prevailing psychiatric views of the time. Systemic thinkers had created a new reality for the practitioners of psychotherapy.

In concert with the spread of these beliefs, the use of art in family therapy was making its mark. For therapists enthusiastic about seeing the individual in a larger context, the art made by families, or by individuals reporting on their families, gave credence to the systemic perspective.

For example, as I worked with families, their group drawings were a veritable testimony to this approach. Johnny drew all over Mom's attempt to structure a theme; Dad made flowers and trees for his daughter and never came close to his wife's contributions; and Sally made "helpful" additions to everyone's images. When the family took a look at these murals, they became aware of their interactions. They could "see" that they were in a system of relationships.

The therapy proceeded from there. I do not mean to minimize the knowledge gained from their art. However, the greatest benefit for me as therapist, was that I could extricate the identified patient from the position of having caused the problem. The "problem" became a twist in the family system that needed to be set right. With this as the context, everyone could now work to solve it as a team.

There was no longer a need to peek under every personal bush and find a "borderline" hiding in the tulips. The labels had been hard to use, since the external social or family system was often more pathological than the clients. What exactly is the *DSM-IV* diagnosis for a crime-ridden neighborhood where survival is the primary goal? And how could therapists bill the insurance companies when a large family of six or seven were all involved in activities that kept the targeted behaviors in place? This remains a challenge, and a serious threat to using systemic approaches.

The solution has often been to treat family members as individuals, which may defeat solving the problem. If the family has constructed the difficulty, how can they deconstruct it without working together? The language of art helps so much, because it can be observed by all members. Messages that are too delicate or powerful to speak directly can be conveyed in visual form. Competent family art therapists began to use the theories of Minuchin (1974), Haley (1963), Bowen (1978), or the Palo Alto group (Fisch et al., 1982; Weakland et al., 1995), to name a few, to achieve a reduction or elimination of the unwelcome behavior in a reasonable amount of time. Family art therapists found that they were comfortable and successful when they adapted a systemic approach to their work.

Families, or individuals seen in a family (systemic) context, were happy to have therapy do the job, so that they could get on with their lives. The surprises continued. The effects of brief therapy lasted a long time. The recidivism rates were no higher with short term therapy than with long term treatment. The reason seems clear to me. When a group of people change in connection with each other, the behaviors that reinforced the toxic problem are gradually dissolved. Teamwork provides the support to continue the new interactions; and since the problem belongs to everyone, it is a smaller load for each person to deal with.

However, not all art therapists are as enchanted as I am with these ideas. It is very tempting to see a client alone. The art projects can develop into wonderful creative statements, and the intimate process is gratifying. On the other hand, families are full of children of all ages who avidly draw imagery that is helpful, but not always clear or artistic; the adults often suffer angst about making art until their expectations are more relaxed; and the art therapist has to be content with using the art primarily as systemic information that is interpreted by the family. The systemic art therapist needs to look at the whole, rather than at the parts.

Change did not stop here. In line with more recent developments, some clever clinicians learned what art therapists have known all along. We did not realize we were "narrative" therapists, until Michael White and David Epston (1990) wrote some interesting papers demonstrating their technique of externalizing the problem that had conquered one member of the family. They rallied the family around the externalized problem, and then worked as a team to banish the unwanted behavior from the family.

Yet art therapists have always externalized problems! How many hundreds of times have clients been asked to picture their concerns? Once the client and art therapist can gaze at the problem together, there is a better understanding of how it "looks." Many modifications are possible with an image of a "problem," like reducing its size. The drawing can be cut up and distributed to family members, and each person can then deal with a reduced portion. Smaller pieces become less threatening. I am sure the reader can imagine how these interventions become tangible metaphors that do not require explanation.

It seems that we were already postmodern in our thinking, simply by bringing the clients' reality into the session using art, and thus making the issues known to everyone present. If we are thinking in a postmodern fashion, we are also not imposing our reality on clients' images. We are not "assessing" the product. We are not giving it a label, such as "passive aggressive" or "resistant." Contemporary "solution focused" and "narrative" therapists are not so interested in pathology; rather, they are interested in strengths.

Although art therapy has always used externalized images and invited changes based on the knowledge emerging from these images, few of us have felt comfortable giving up the position of "knowing." In 1988 Anderson and Goolishian proposed a therapeutic stance of "not knowing." This was named the "social constructionist" view. They believed that too often the therapist's belief system is imposed on the clients, albeit unconsciously. To be "postmodern" as I see it is to give up programmed knowledge. It is essential to become the student of the client, and to learn from each client the meaning of the situation they bring. By "co-constructing" therapy with the client, the therapist becomes a collaborator in the therapeutic conversation. This position required a relinquishing of power and was a creative leap in therapeutic relationships.

The narrative, the story told and believed, became the key to change. The story was accepted as the "truth," not second-guessed as a "defense" or some other psychological term for not telling the truth. In fact there was no "truth," only the narrative, and the possibility of finding alternative stories buried in the dominant tale. The therapist became a detective, searching for more satisfactory meanings in the script.

A social constructionist/narrative philosophy is my preferred way of thinking about and conducting art therapy. However, although this is an exciting philosophy, a vital component of storytelling was still missing. The stories needed to be illustrated! Illustrations made the story more "real" for the participants in the therapy. It became more of a "here-and-now" experience. The pictures broadened and deepened the collaborative exploration for new solutions, within the reality of the storyteller.

Art therapy is also a tool to tap into mind/brain functions that aid both creativity and cognition (Demasio, 1994). Even a layman's knowledge of neuropsychological functions of the brain confirms that bringing imagery into the session is helpful. The interplay—between the verbal explanations and the visual renditions—greatly enriches the opportunities for the client.

It is not only the image itself, but the making of the image that is important. Introducing sensory and kinesthetic experience can add to the success of the therapy. This reality is vividly demonstrated with elderly clients in the early stages of dementia. By including movement, art, and touch in the therapy, the clients become less forgetful, less unfocused, more able to make connections, and more cognitively competent. Their needs in a declining state dramatize what we all require to evoke our best cognitive performance. Stimulating feelings and emotions facilitates intellectual functioning, enhancing decision-making potential.

For those of us who have been mental health workers for a long time, there is a growing awareness that it is very hard to separate any one school of therapy from others. I believe that therapies grow from and with others, and that there are more changes currently in the position of the therapist vis à vis the client than in any other aspect.

Where once we were the "experts," seeing information in knotholes, and pathology in baselines, now we are collaborators. If we are concerned about a knothole, we explain the reason why others have considered this diagnostic, and ask the clients what they think. What they think is what we believe. The discipline is not to impose judgment on the clients. I believe that few art therapists judge their clients, but many judge their artwork. For me, art and artmaker are fused; therefore, I cannot be wise about one and not the other.

Faith in the client is central to postmodern beliefs. Casting out the search for pathology, and looking to the external pressures of society and culture—rather than within the individual psyche—is another keystone. A broad world view is also the core of systemic thinking. None of these beliefs can be pretended in the therapeutic relationship. The contemporary therapist allows a form of transparency that lets the client into his or her philosophy—of life and of therapy. The two ways of being in the world should not be divided.

Postmodern belief systems are a release for the therapist. Not to be wiser than our clients is more respectful and less stressful. We can look forward to collaborating with individuals, families, or people in group therapy—where that "system" becomes itself a significant treatment tool. We can enjoy the art, as it reflects the process of the therapy, and reveals material that invites an alternative understanding of life events. I confess that I am passionate about having a philosophy that includes as many levels of creativity as I am capable of. My realities at this point in my professional and personal life are in some harmony; I respect and am curious about yours.

☐ References

Anderson, H., & Goolishian, H. (1988). Human systems as linguistic systems: Preliminary and evolving ideas about the implications for clinical theory. *Family Process, 27,* 371–394.

Bowen, M. (1978). *Family therapy in clinical practice.* New York: Jason Aronson.

Demasio, A. R. (1994). *Descartes.* New York: Avon Books.

Fisch, R., Weakland, J., & Segal, L. (1982). *Tactics of change, Doing therapy briefly.* San Francisco: Jossey-Bass.

Haley, J. (1963). *Strategies of psychotherapy.* New York: Grune & Stratton.

Minuchin, S. (1974). *Families and family therapy.* Cambridge, MA: Harvard University Press.

Weakland, J. H. & Roy, W. A. (Eds.). (1995). *Propagations: Thirty years of influence from the Mental Research Institute.* New York: Haworth.

White, M., & Epston, D. (1990). *Narrative means to therapeutic ends.* New York: W. W. Norton.

INTEGRATIVE APPROACHES

INTEGRATIVE
APPROACHES

While divergent viewpoints can be 'integrated' as a conceptual act and even rationalized with an eclectic philosophy, the rationale must not be so broad as to espouse laissez-faire. Integration of divergence need not mean that "anything goes." (Bernard Levy)

It is all well and good to read about different theoretical approaches to art therapy, and to be stimulated by different styles of thinking and of working. But what is the practitioner to do with all this information? Is it best to select one primary orientation? Is it wiser to use whichever one seems right at any particular moment? Or is there a way to integrate more than one approach into a workable synthesis?

Elinor Ulman's chapter reminds us of the dilemma faced by early art therapists, who felt a need to choose between *art as therapy* as espoused by Edith Kramer, and *art psychotherapy* as developed by Margaret Naumburg. Given these two approaches, both grounded in Freudian theory—one with the emphasis on art and one with the emphasis on therapy—which direction should the clinician take? Unlike those who saw them as incompatible, Ulman insisted that they were not, and integrated them into her own theory of art therapy.

Harriet Wadeson, who entered the field a little later, describes her dilemma, as she gradually learned about the many different ways of viewing human beings and psychotherapy. In her chapter on an *eclectic* approach to art therapy, she gives a clear account of how she came to know and to value diverse theories, and how she solves the problem of *which* one to use *when* in her clinical work.

Many art therapists, perhaps a majority, approach their work in the fashion described by Wadeson, shifting gears as the situation seems to require. In fact, it seems to me that most art therapists are primarily *pragmatic,* selecting the approach that best fits the therapeutic moment. Robert Ault, whose Commentary ends this section, once described four different approaches, each to be utilized *depending on the needs of the patient(s).* The ones he identified roughly parallel the first three sections of this book: *Analytic* (Psychodynamic), *Gestalt* (Humanistic), *Functional,* and *Psycho-Educational* (Psycho-Educational).

For this second edition, two chapters have been added to this section. Like the two from the first edition that focus on theory selection as the primary issue, I believe that all of them represent the kind of genuine *integration* of which Bernard Levy was speaking in the quotation above.

Although several of the chapter's authors in the first edition mentioned using other creative modalities at times (Edwards, Wallace, Garai, Rhyne, Aach-Feldman &

Kunkle-Miller, and Wadeson), and others have reported such work elsewhere (Lachman-Chapin, Robbins, and myself), a multimodal approach was not the keystone of their thinking. Since intermodal work has become increasingly popular among art therapists in recent years, I have added chapters on using all of the arts in an "expressive therapy" approach. The one by Natalie Rogers would fit equally well here, but was finally placed in the Humanistic section because of her clear explanation of a "person-centered" approach (to "expressive therapies").

Two other new chapters integrate expression in all of the arts. As is true for Rogers, the visual arts are central—the "trunk" of their expressive arts' "trees," to use Shaun McNiff's metaphor. In addition, each integrates one or more frames of reference about human beings with their use of the arts. For Rogers, it is the person-centered approach of her father Carl (originally "client-centered"). For McNiff, it is the integrative function of the imagination in mental and physical health. Finally, David Henley's arts-based therapeutic education operates from a base of psychodynamic understandings, while using cognitive and behavioral interventions.

The chapters in this section are not the only ones which integrate understandings from more than one perspective. Jung, for example, is mentioned by Allen, McNiff, Rogers, and Garai. The developmental art therapy chapter, like Henley, explicitly utilizes psychodynamic, cognitive, and behavioral theories in its therapeutic mix.

The authors of all of the chapters in this section describe work done, at least in part, in a group setting. Some note the power of the group itself as a modality which can facilitate a genuinely transformative creative process. This point was also made by Pat Allen and by Natalie Rogers in their chapters in Part II. So, from another point of view, it may be said that each art therapist's preferred theory of group dynamics is being integrated into the work described here. Similarly, the writers in Part IV (Systemic) have integrated psychodynamic, narrative, and other approaches with their understanding of families and groups as systems.

As Bernard Levy said, it is critical that using more than one orientation to inform one's conduct of art therapy not be understood as "anything goes," but rather as a carefully considered integration of mutually supportive frames of reference. These issues, as well as the variables in theory selection, will be considered further in the Conclusion, which ends this book.

18

CHAPTER   Elinor Ulman

Variations on a Freudian Theme: Three Art Therapy Theorists

Any particular scientific outlook represents only one possible way of organizing the raw material under consideration [but] . . . one often gets the impression that one theoretical outlook is the correct one . . . one seldom hears acknowledgment that the organizational symbols behind one's outlook are, to some extent, subjectively chosen. We select our conceptual framework not only on the basis of intellectual judgment but also because it is congenial to our way of thinking and because the type of clinical work that follows from it suits our personality. Being aware of this subjectivity . . . introduces a welcome tentativeness.
(Susan Deri)

Inspired by the above quotation, I explore the connection between the theoretical ideas and the personal value systems of three writers on art therapy: Margaret Naumburg, Edith Kramer, and myself. By doing so I hope to promote among art therapists that "tentativeness" that Deri saw as welcome for the analysts she was addressing. All three of us claim intellectual descent from Freud, but differences among us have shaped the development of art therapy in several different directions.

I begin by noting briefly the salient features of Freudian theory that some find congenial and that arouse the misgivings of others. Then I recapitulate some early definitions of art therapy by these three authors. Next, I speculate about personal factors that may have entered into their choice of beliefs. Last, I present case material to illustrate my preferred methods, and to dramatize the complexity of the issues that must be faced when circumstances dictate the choice of any approach to art therapy.

☐ Some Features of Freudian Thinking

What are the key features of the theory that tend to determine people's choice of Freud as a guide to understanding themselves and other people and to shaping therapeutic

This chapter has also been published as an article in *The American Journal of Art Therapy*, 1986, 24(4).

interventions? Fundamental, I believe, is the concept that *conflict is inherent in the nature of man.* The human need for reconciliation of opposing internal forces has been recognized under many non-Freudian guises. Traditional symbols such as *original sin* give way to Freud's new metaphor—the epic struggle of *ego and id.*

Many people shrink from what they perceive as the harshness of the view that conflict is inborn, preferring to believe against all odds that everyone is born good, but in generation after generation that goodness is somehow distorted by wicked parents or society. (But who made society?) To some of us, however, it seems that recognizing how hard it is to grow up into a good human being makes for a feeling of compassion toward ourselves and others. It is much less discouraging to view one's struggles as one's share of man's fate, than as signs of one's inborn inferiority or victimization on the part of evil parents or society (the collective parents).

Another aspect of Freudian thinking that attracts some as much as it repels others is the concept of *sublimation.* The theory of sublimation postulates that humanity's great achievements—in art, science, and heroic self-sacrifice, as well as more everyday civilized social behavior—are fueled by sexual and aggressive energies. Is the thought that out of the dungheap springs the rose cause for disgust or for amazed admiration? For those who find Freud's thinking congenial, the idea of sublimation does not denigrate the rose on the basis of its humble origin; rather, it recognizes in the rose a testament to a miraculous transformation.

Inner conflict and sublimation are only two facets of Freudian thinking that are understandably rejected by many people. Both can be looked upon as corollaries of Freud's basic discovery: the key role of the *unconscious* in human life. This concept, too, is rejected by many. The thought that one is truly *unaware* of a very important—even powerful—part of oneself is frightening, and therefore not easy to accept. Acceptance entails, among other things, a high tolerance of ambiguity. Insofar as the art therapists we are considering ascribe to Freud's views, we can assume considerable common ground among them, whatever their differences.

☐ Three Theories of Art Therapy

Naumburg

Although both Naumburg and Kramer relied on psychoanalytic insights, the divergence between them (in both practice and theory) tended to widen over time. A knowledgeable friend once remarked that Naumburg took the psychoanalytic patient off the couch and stood him in front of an easel. The consequences of her doing so were far-reaching. In Naumburg's own words, art therapy as she practiced it based

> its methods on releasing [the unconscious by means of] spontaneous expression; it has its roots in the transference relation between patient and therapist, and on the encouragement of free association. It is therefore closely allied to psychoanalytic therapy . . . (Naumburg, 1958a, p. 516).
> . . . Treatment depends . . . on a continuous effort to obtain [the patient's] own interpretation of [his or] her symbolic designs. . . . The images produced are a form of communication between patient and therapist; [they] constitute symbolic speech (Naumburg, 1958b, p. 561).

Here I want to state parenthetically my opinion that Naumburg's professed application of psychoanalytic techniques in art therapy is not to be taken entirely at face value. In particular, she speaks somewhat loosely of *free association;* what she reports sounds more like *conscious interpretation* by her patients of their art products. They are not asked to make the difficult attempt to abandon censorship of speech that is demanded of the analysand. Likewise, what she terms *transference* often sounds more like a *therapeutic alliance* between herself and a patient.

Naumburg (1958a) cited the advantages of introducing painting and clay modeling into psychoanalytically oriented psychotherapy as follows:

> First, it permits the direct expression of dreams, fantasies, and other inner experiences that occur as pictures rather than words. Second, pictured projections of unconscious material escape censorship more easily than do verbal expressions, so that the therapeutic process is speeded up. Third, the productions are durable and unchanging; their content cannot be erased by forgetting, and their authorship is hard to deny (p. 512). Fourth, the resolution of transference is made easier: The autonomy of the patient is encouraged by his growing ability to contribute to the interpretation of his own creations. (p. 514)

Thus, art is seen as an added ingredient that makes possible an improved and stream-lined psychoanalytic procedure. Naumburg viewed art therapy as a *primary* as well as an *adjunctive* form of treatment. The client's experience of the creative process is not even mentioned at this point as a benefit of the kind of art therapy Naumburg had come to advocate. But it was not always so. A decade earlier she had written:

> A vital implication [of] studies . . . made on children's art expression as an aid to diagnosis and therapy is that imaginative, creative expression is, in itself, a source of growth and sustenance as well as a language of communication in the life of every individual. (1947/1973, p. 89)

Kramer

Kramer's basic ideas have more in common with those of the earlier, rather than the later, Naumburg. Throughout her writings Kramer finds in art itself the explanation of the art therapist's special contribution to psychotherapy. She went beyond Freud himself in her use of "the insights of Freudian ego psychology to elucidate the problem of quality in art" (Kramer & Ulman, 1977, p. 22), but her understanding of the healing quality inherent in the creative process is firmly based in Freudian personality theory. In an early formulation (Kramer, 1958) she described art as "a means of widening the range of human experiences by creating equivalents for such experiences" (p. 8). Using these equivalents the artist can choose, vary, and repeat what experiences he will. He can reexperience, resolve, and integrate conflict. Throughout history "the arts have helped man to reconcile the eternal conflict between the individual's instinctual urges and the demands of society" (1958, p. 6). But the conflicting demands of superego and id cannot be permanently reconciled. The art therapist makes creative experiences available to disturbed persons in the service of the total personality. He must use "methods compatible with the inner laws of artistic creation" (p. 6).

Three of Naumburg's four books on art therapy had already appeared when Kramer published her first book in 1958. Later, practices stemming from Naumburg's "dynam-ically oriented art therapy" (the title of her last book, 1966) came to be known as *art psychotherapy,* and Kramer herself coined the phrase *"art as therapy"* to define her work (1971). When I began to work on my own definition of art therapy in 1961, these terms were not yet current, but I will use them retroactively in discussing later developments.

Ulman

It is almost a half century since my first attempt to define art therapy so as to encompass *both* art psychotherapy and art as therapy. In 1961, I stated my belief that "the realm of art therapy should be so charted as to accommodate endeavors where neither the term art nor the term therapy is stretched so far as to have no real meaning" (p. 19). I designated

> therapeutic procedures as those designed to assist favorable changes in personality or in living that will outlast the session itself.... Therefore, specialized learning that leaves the core of the personality untouched is not part of therapy.... The art therapist often must tolerate defensive or escapist uses of art materials but this is never his goal. (1961, p. 19)

I then offered a very condensed definition of *art:*

> Its motive power comes from within the personality; it is a way of bringing order out of chaos ... chaotic feelings and impulses within, the bewildering mass of impressions from without. It is a means to discover both the self and the world, and to establish a relation between the two. In the complete creative process, inner and outer realities are fused into a new entity. ...
>
> The proportions of art and of therapy in art therapy may vary within a wide range. The completion of the artistic process may at times be sacrificed to more immediate goals. Stereotyped, compulsive work used to ward off dangerous emotions must sometimes be permitted. Communication and insight may take priority over development of art expression. On the other hand, where no fruitful consolidation of insight can be foreseen, the exposure of conflicts may be deliberately avoided in favor of artistic achievement. (1961, p. 20)

☐ Discussion

In the 1950's it was relatively easy for both Naumburg and Kramer to assert that their own views and procedures represented all that art therapy was or ought to be. But as early as 1961, when I first put forward what was intended as a comprehensive definition of art therapy, it seemed clear that no discussion of psychoanalytically based art therapy could afford to ignore the divergent ideas of both these thinkers.

Although both leaned heavily on Freudian personality theory as the basis for understanding people's psychological needs, they saw its implications for the *practice of art therapy* quite differently. Kramer subscribed more fully to Freudian *principles,* but it was Naumburg who emulated the psychoanalyst's *techniques.* Kramer developed her own methods of eliciting the most effective possible art, in the name of therapeutic gains for her young clients.

☐ Subjective Factors in the Development of Theory

What personal attitudes are likely to have played a part, not only in their general choice of Freudian views, but also in their development of art therapy theory on the basis of those views?

Contrasts Between Naumburg and Kramer

Naumburg, born in 1890, grew up in New York, where her immigrant father had become a successful businessman. Her parents were of their time, and it was left to Margaret's generation to rebel against the rigid conventionality of their late 19th century beginnings. Perhaps this accounts for the embattled quality of her writings. In both her early career as an educator and her later career as a therapist, she tilted against the establishment, whether academic or psychiatric (Frank, in Detre et al., 1983, p. 114).

Naumburg's education and experience seem to have inclined her toward eclecticism. She was a critical thinker who made her own synthesis of ideas from various sources, not an idea-hopper flitting from one theoretical notion to another. Perhaps it was just chance that Naumburg's first experience with personal analysis was with a Jungian; Jungian ideas were certainly important in her early thinking about art therapy (Naumburg, 1950, pp. 15–34). She later undertook treatment with a Freudian psychoanalyst, and it was largely from Freudian sources that she subsequently derived her techniques: associative work, attention to transference, and the liberation of repressed material. In fact, she acknowledged primary indebtedness to Freud, Jung, and Harry Stack Sullivan (Frank, in Detre et al., 1983, p. 114; Naumburg, 1953, p. 3).

Kramer was born about a quarter of a century after Naumburg. Her early years were spent in pre-Anschluss Vienna. Many members of her family and their friends were in the arts. Her parents were unconventional people who had rebelled against their own families' middle-class values. Some of their associates were the younger members of Freud's early circle, so she was familiar with psychoanalysts and their ideas, and her own analysis was along orthodox lines. While she is open to theoretical developments springing from ego psychology, Kramer has never subscribed to any school of thought that repudiated Freud's teaching.

An important key to the ideas of Kramer and Naumburg lies in the place held by *art* in the life of each. Kramer is first and foremost an artist; painting has been the abiding passion of her entire life. Small wonder, then, that artistic sublimation, which has been such an important reward of her lifework, should be the cornerstone of her beliefs about how art therapy works. Her primary commitment to art also made her happy with being an *adjunctive* therapist, for unlike a primary therapist, this left her free to devote four out of every twelve months exclusively to painting. (Some adherents of Kramer's general thinking do not agree with her view that art as therapy cannot stand alone as a primary form of treatment.)

Naumburg knew a great deal about art and art history, and her responses to the art of her own time were knowledgeable and sensitive (Frank, in Detre et al., 1983). Also, she undoubtedly learned much from observing the work of her sister, Florence Cane, at the Walden School (Cane, 1951/1983). Thus, she was able to introduce the teaching of art into her work as a therapist when appropriate (Naumburg, 1966, p. 131). She also recognized that art therapy often enhanced the quality of a patient's art, because it released the same unconscious forces operative in all art (Naumburg, 1953, p. 7). Most of the illustrations she chose for her publications are expressive artworks—far from the impoverished stick figures that sometimes suffice (or are encouraged) in art psychotherapy.

Despite Naumburg's understanding of art, her primary identity was not that of an artist. She has been described as *"an educator who became a psychologist and an art therapist"* (Kniazzeh, in Detre et al., 1983, p. 115). Naumburg came to view art therapy as an independent mode of treatment that offered numerous advantages over the "talking cure," where treatment depended entirely on verbal exchange. In her later years she yearned for recognition as a psychotherapist, especially in psychoanalytic circles. The role of *primary* therapist, with its implied responsibility 365 days a year, suited her to a tee, for *art therapy* was central to her life.

Ulman's Background

My own personal history and inclinations were likewise influential in the development of my beliefs about art therapy. I am about five years older than Edith Kramer, and we entered the art therapy field at about the same time. I grew up in Baltimore. My parents were middle-class liberals, and most of their associates were teachers and professional people. I was the first member of the immediate family to become an artist; painting was my first profession and my main occupation for about eight years. In 1966, explaining my emphasis on particular aspects of art therapy, I wrote, "When I started working in a psychiatric clinic in the early 1950's, I envisioned myself as a potential art *teacher,* not as an art *therapist*" (p. 9).

I add today that my landing in a psychiatric setting at all was fortuitous. I was an artist but, having become blocked in my painting, was earning my living in other ways. Homesick for the world of art and artists, I looked for a career with a legitimate relation to art, even if unable to resume being a painter myself. I went on (in 1966) to say the following:

> Guided by the new approaches to art education enunciated by such writers as Florence Cane (1951/1983) and H. Schaeffer-Simmern (1948), I wanted to be the kind of art teacher I wished I had had. Naumburg stood alone at that time as a spokesman of psychoanalytically oriented art therapy. I did not feel qualified to follow in her footsteps, but was pleased and excited when some of the clinic patients led me a little way along that road. A much larger number of my patients, however, did not try to translate the symbolic content of their pictures into words, yet it seemed to me that they too were getting something valuable from their work in art that nothing else could supply. . . . It was eight years later that Edith Kramer's book *Art Therapy in a Children's Community* [1958] was published. . . . Kramer analyzed from the vantage point of Freudian theory the place of the arts in the emotional economy both of the individual and of society. The subtle relationships between psychoanalytic and artistic insights began to come clear to me, and I was provided with theoretical backing for my unarticulated feeling that my functioning as an artist-teacher and an art therapist were not so far apart. (p. 9)

At this point I need to mention other personal factors that helped determine my thinking. First, I had entered analysis shortly before my first foray into art therapy. The three analysts I eventually saw, though to varying degrees unorthodox, gave their primary allegiance to Freud. Certainly, my hours on the couch were not devoted to the discussion of rival psychological theories or philosophies of life, but it seems likely that my analysts' attitudes exerted influence in my eventual adoption of a generally Freudian outlook.

Second, though I drifted into art therapy specifically because I was a frustrated painter, I am as much a word person as a visual person. My talent and taste for literary expression are at least equal to my talent and taste for the visual arts. I found the world of verbal psychotherapy fascinating and wanted to develop an understanding of art therapy that embraced Naumburg's ideas as well as Kramer's.

Having welcomed Kramer's exposition of the psychological and social functions of art, I made my own formulations concerning the place of the arts in human development.

In the terminology of Susanne Langer, the business of the arts is to give form to feeling, and this is the basic method whereby man creates his world. Every child needs to be an artist insofar as he must find a means to conceive himself and the world around him and to establish a relation between the two. ... But the task does not end with childhood, and the arts serve throughout life as the meeting ground of the inner and outer worlds. (Ulman, 1971, p. 93)

Later (1977), I elaborated further on the same theme:

Cultural history and the developmental history of each human being alike bear witness to a universal inclination toward the arts as a means of reconciling two conflicting demands: the need for emotional release and the need to discover order and impose organization. ... The artistic process calls on the widest range of human capacities. Like maturation in general it demands the integration of many inescapably conflicting elements, among them impulse and control, aggression and love, feeling and thinking, fantasy and reality, the unconscious and the conscious. ... The function of the arts has been explored in terms of numerous theories. ... The common thread uniting these many views is recognition of the inherently integrative character of the arts, that is their power to unite opposing forces within the personality and to help reconcile the needs of the individual with the demands of the outside world. ... True mastery of life's tasks depends upon a disciplined freedom, whose model may be found in the artistic process. (Ulman, 1977, p. 14)

Since I came to art therapy from my own experience with *art*, it is no surprise that my enthusiasm for *art as therapy* happens—for this very personal reason—to be greater than my enthusiasm for *art psychotherapy*. However, I recognize the validity of both applications of psychoanalytic theory to art therapy practice. Art psychotherapy and art as therapy can exist side by side in the same room at the same time, or in the work of the same therapist at different times. In my own life as a clinician I moved between the two, using art as therapy where I could and shifting to art psychotherapy where the situation seemed to call for it.

☐ Art as Therapy with Adults

The following two case vignettes are intended to make clear what I mean by art as therapy, and why I have found so much satisfaction in it.

Mary

Mary readily became interested in using art materials. She had no extraordinary aptitude for art, very little formal education, and showed no signs of unusual intelligence or verbal skill. She had lived on a farm her first few years, then had grown up in an orphanage. She was in her late 20's when I met her in the psychiatric ward of a general hospital. She had been diagnosed as a paranoid schizophrenic, but soon after admission, her more florid symptoms abated. Figure 18.1, however, suggests the severity of her illness. In it we sense the horrifying self-denigration and the violent extremes of her sexual ambivalence.

Other early drawings reflect the childhood stereotypes Mary brought to the renewed experience of using art materials. Like Figure 18.1, they had an extreme rigidity, a quality she came to recognize and deplore in her art. Gradually, her work became

---

Some of this case material was published in a slightly different form in Ulman, 1966, and Ulman, 1971.

Figure 18.1.

Figure 18.2.

less symptomatic, and took on the decorative charm of folk art. At first proud of these productions, she later disparaged them as "too proportionate," her term for the stiffness and "hardness" she had come to dislike as much in her work as in her personality.

Figure 18.2 was painted when Mary had been in the group for about three weeks. We were equally excited about it. I took pleasure in her new-found grace, as she stepped back to decide where her picture needed another flower. She joyfully declared, "It's the first thing I've ever done in my life that isn't *neat!*" She went on to talk of her restuarant job and how she and the other waitresses drove each other frantic, because she went into a tailspin if the salts and peppers she'd arranged a certain way were moved around.

Mary developed pride in the originality of the many pictures she made without any models or assistance from me. At first, she begged me to do her work for her, and got very angry at my unwillingness. Then, almost in the same breath, she would accuse me of not letting her do anything her own way. Now she was sorry that her brutal ex-husband wasn't around to see her artwork. "He never thought I could do *anything,* . . . He took my mind away from me. But it started in the orphanage. In the orphanage everything was thought for us, even time. I have no meaning of time."

Through art, Mary caught a glimpse of her own worth and capability. The flower picture taught her, too, that she could relinquish her obsessive-compulsive defenses without precipitating disaster. Instead, the free play of feeling, controlled and channeled into her art, allowed her to function more effectively than she ever had before.

Mary's pictures suggest another sacrifice we sometimes make when we opt for art as therapy. The closer the work comes to art, the less its diagnostic value is likely to be. "Bad art always invites speculation about the artist and good art never does" (Kramer & Ulman, 1977, p. 21). Mary's early work, as shown in Figure 18.1, is a raw, easy-to-decipher presentation of symptoms. Figure 18.2, on the other hand, tells no more about her than that, at a given moment, she was able to function fully in artistic terms.

What is true in the small world of art therapy is also true in the larger world of art.

> Daydream art, self-serving autobiographical apologias, and unintended revelations of pathology inevitably invite speculation about their authors' problems and motivations. Great art, on the other hand, invites us to think not about its author and his experiences, but about our own experiences and ourselves. ... Every great work of art has a life of its own quite separate from the biography of its maker. (Kramer & Ulman, 1977, p. 21)

Mary's story gives justification to the frequent claim that art can serve the expressive needs of inarticulate people. Janet, on the other hand, was adept in the use of words but used them mainly in the service of defense. Her experience exemplifies the usefulness of art in cutting through the emotional smokescreen some highly verbal people are able to erect.

Janet

Janet's story, like Mary's, exemplifies the aspect of art therapy that depends less on interpretation than on the experience of a special kind of functioning. The artistic process itself is a momentary sample of effective living, providing an invaluable glimpse into modes of thought and action that have wide application outside the artistic realm. Furthermore, a client may derive potentially useful insights from art experiences neither designed for, nor subjected to, analysis of their symbolic implications.

Janet's work illustrates this kind of therapeutic art experience. She was a pretty, intelligent, young alcoholic woman. Before joining the art therapy group at the clinic where I worked, she had made many attempts to learn about perspective and to discover rules that would help her achieve "correct" graphic representation. She was justifiably dissatisfied with the tight, flat landscape she made on her first visit. She was trying, she said, not to get lost in details, not to be overprecise; as a result, her picture turned out to be at the same time both vague and overworked.

My first intervention was to introduce Janet to rhythmical exercise and scribbling, as a way of searching for more inwardly derived, less conventional imagery (cf. Cane, 1983, pp. 56–80). Figure 18.3 was developed from a scribble, about a month after Janet started attending the art therapy group. The strength, movement, and depth she was now able to achieve constituted an artistic accomplishment. Janet herself translated this into psychological terms, saying, "For the first time I really know what my therapist means when he says I must learn to trust my intuitions." In these words she acknowledged a new experience of inner freedom and a new awareness of modes of action more effective than her habitual overintellectual attempts at planning and controlling her life.

Janet mentioned that the scribble had suggested to her a dress form, and that she had placed it in her own preferred position, inside a window looking out. She thus spontaneously called attention to symbolic details that identified the figure as a self-image, but the picture's most significant symbolic association was never talked about.

One of Janet's legs had been amputated when she was still a child; her disability dated back to a congenital malformation, and was at the root of many severe problems. Janet and the clinical staff were well aware of these ramifications. Their symbolic expression in the dress form, full of life yet immobilized, impaled on its single peg leg, offered Janet little new insight on a conscious level. It seems likely, however, that Janet's enthusiasm about this esthetically transformed self-representation helped her at an unconscious level to better accept her mutilated state.

Figure 18.3.

In another connection Janet remarked, "I'm all id and superego," and indeed the observation was apt—the id drunken, violent, promiscuous; the superego wearing an Alcoholics Anonymous halo and a mask of sweet devotion to helping others. In her experience with art, Janet found at last and recognized some moments of successful ego functioning.

Figure 18.4 was painted more than a year after the dress form. Its chill and loneliness say something about Janet, but also evoke a similar mood in many others. At a modest level, Janet here achieved the quality of art.

Like many adults, Janet readily translated into words the insights derived from her art experience. Insight often accompanies the changes brought about in adults by art as therapy, even though the therapist has not set insight as a goal. We note that in Janet's case it was the formal qualities of her pictures that spoke back to her, confirming what she had experienced while making them. Subject matter was fairly unimportant.

This kind of spontaneous verbalization of new insights happens frequently with adults who use art as therapy, but is far less likely to occur with children. The line between art as therapy and art psychotherapy is more likely to become blurred with adults than with children.

☐ The Consequences of Therapeutic Choice

Sometimes circumstances other than the needs of a given client dictate the choice between art psychotherapy and art as therapy, and every choice entails a sacrifice of whatever lies along and at the end of the road not taken. Sometimes an art therapist is free to choose within a wide range—a range whose limits are set only by her own capabilities. At other times choices are limited by other factors, like availability of personnel, money to pay for their time, institutional policies, etc.

Greta

To dramatize the consequences of choice between art as therapy and art psychotherapy, let us consider two pictures by Greta, a good-looking, sun-tanned, blonde woman in her early 30's. She came to the day hospital where I was working a few hours a week, and was told, in my absence, about an opening in the art group. Greta enthusiastically agreed to the 4-week commitment to attendance, the rule that the staff and I had set.

Unfortunately, the staff member who introduced Greta to the various therapeutic activities available did not know enough about either art or art therapy to explain how different this particular group was from a regular art class. In keeping with the nature of the entire program—it consisted of group activities followed by group discussion—and because I was available for very few hours each week, we had arrived at a structure that would make the most of the limited possibilities. At each session, the group agreed on a theme suggested either by me or by one of them. Art work was limited to 45 minutes, after which the pictures were put up and subjected to group discussion. Thus, in setting the stage for art psychotherapy, we had made it very unlikely that art—and hence art as therapy—could flourish.

On Greta's first visit, the group agreed on an idea from one of them. Draw the *animal* you would like to be if you were born back on this earth as an animal. Greta was furious at the regimentation, the strict time limit, and the pressure to discuss the pictures and listen to others' comments. Figure 18.5 is the eloquent expression of her rage. She called it a "Bird of Paradise" and claimed to see nothing in it but the beauty to which she

Figure 18.4.

Figure 18.5.

aspired. A member called it "the terrible tyrant of the classroom." He and I sensed that Greta's tightly controlled ferocity was largely directed at me.

The art psychotherapy character of the group had accidentally revealed the potential value that art as therapy might have had for Greta. Half regretting that I could not transform the setting into one more congenial to her, I nevertheless looked forward with great interest to further experiences of her power for vivid graphic expression and wondered whether the group would permit her to maintain the massive denial with which she had greeted her first revelation of feeling.

I was never to find out. Greta managed to evade the next three sessions of the art group. Corralled by a staff member into meeting her obligation, she showed up for the last session before the Christmas break. Knowing how hard the holidays are for people suffering from mental breakdown, I assigned a topic: Try to put into a picture your feelings about the upcoming holiday. Greta was subdued and withdrawn, obviously depressed, quite different from the rather arrogant bird of paradise of our first encounter. She worked slowly; in itself her weak drawing with its many Christmas greetings (Figure 18.6) expressed little.

Figure 18.6.

By this time a change had taken place in the day hospital schedule, and the drawing time of the art group of eight was immediately followed by a meeting of the entire community—about 30 clients and all staff members who were available to attend. We decided to carry the artworks to the meeting and pin them on the wall, where they might attract the attention of others and become the focus of the larger group's discussion.

The leader was usually a young psychiatrist who was a great confronter. He zeroed in on Greta's six-pointed star, asking why she chose a Jewish symbol to hang from her Christian tree. For a few minutes Greta tried to maintain that the Star of David was simply easier to draw because it could be made from two triangles. Dr. Miller pooh-poohed this excuse; he and Greta both knew she could easily draw a five-pointed star.

Suddenly, the floodgates opened. Greta started by telling the community about her father. He had been a fairly high official in Hitler's Germany; Greta knew him only as the warmer and more loving of her parents. Now, as an adult American with many Jewish friends, she could not come to terms with the knowledge that this beloved man had been responsible for the death and torture of many innocent Jewish victims.

Then she turned to the special meanings that Christmas had for her. It was on Christmas that her sister had been almost killed in a skiing accident, and her mother had coldly withdrawn, leaving all the responsibility on Greta's young shoulders. And what about the loving father? He had been jailed after the war and was awaiting trial for his crimes when, just a year before her sister's accident, he was found hanging in his cell on Christmas Eve.

Dr. Miller was famous for not permitting community members to leave the meeting no matter how urgently they pleaded. Having finished her story, Greta asked if she could leave. Dr. Miller, rendered speechless like the rest of us, merely nodded. The whole group was stunned. As we stared at Greta's weak, empty little Christmas cryptogram, I'm sure I wasn't the only one to think of the red heart hanging from the tree as linked with Greta's father hanging in his cell.

This cathartic outpouring was entirely new in the day hospital staff's experience with Greta. It seemed to have resulted from the Christmas theme assigned in art therapy in keeping with the methods of art psychotherapy.

Greta's time in the hospital's 30-day treatment program was almost over, and I did not see her again. From the two experiences we had, there is no way to guess which art therapy approach would have yielded more benefit to Greta. Only one thing is sure: under the circumstances at the day hospital, she couldn't have both. We had made our plans with the hope of offering the best we could to the greatest number of clients; inevitably, this was not always the best possible treatment for every client all the time.

☐ Conclusion

I hope this glance at the work of three theorists will encourage a rising generation of art therapists to become acquainted with the broad range of practices and to maintain the flexibility that will enable them to choose the best available method in their work with each individual client. In 1961 I wrote that: "when we talk about cause and effect, art therapists are in the same boat as the rest of psychiatry—mostly at sea. If favorable changes occur we don't know exactly how much an esthetically valid painting or how much a dramatic new spoken insight had to do with it" (p. 19).

Freudian-based art therapy, as it has descended and evolved from the theoretical and practical differences among Naumburg, Kramer, and Ulman, presents great possibilities for favorable change. Yet we must also face up to the limitations of therapeutic work, whatever its theoretical basis. It has been remarked that the net achievement of psychological treatment in general has been to cure the healthy and maintain the sick.

Accepting this as a realistic expectation of our endeavors is perhaps less cynical than it seems at first blush. The sick may be maintained in the desperation of an old-fashioned back ward or in the dignity of a day hospital whose program may offer art therapy, among other beneficial opportunities. It is a mistake to underestimate the vast amelioration that may take place short of cure.

☐ References

Cane, F. (1983). *The artist in each of us* (Rev. ed.). Craftsbury Common, VT: Art Therapy Publications. (Original work published, 1951)

Deri, S. K. (1984). *Symbolization and creativity.* New York: International Universities Press.

Detre, K. C., Frank, T., Kniazzeh, C. R., Robinson, M. C., Rubin, J. A., & Ulman, E. (1983). Roots of art therapy: Margaret Naumburg (1890–1983) and Florence Cane (1882–1952), a family portrait. *American Journal of Art Therapy, 22,* 111–123.

Kramer, E. (1958). *Art therapy in a children's community.* Springfield, IL: Charles C. Thomas.

Kramer, E. (1971). *Art as therapy with children.* New York: Schocken Books.

Kramer, E., & Ulman, E. (1977). Postscript to Halsey's 'Freud on the nature of art.' *American Journal of Art Therapy, 17,* 21–22.

Naumburg, M. (1950). *Schizophrenic art: Its meaning in psychotherapy.* New York: Grune & Stratton.

Naumburg, M. (1953). *Psychoneurotic art: Its function in psychotherapy.* New York: Grune & Stratton.

Naumburg, M. (1958a). Art therapy: Its scope and function. In E. F. Hammer (Ed.), *The clinical application of projective drawings* (pp. 511–517). Springfield, IL: Charles C. Thomas.

Naumburg, M. (1958b). Case illustration: Art therapy with a seventeen year old girl. In E. F. Hammer (Ed.), *The clinical application of projective drawings* (pp. 518–561). Springfield, IL: Charles C. Thomas.

Naumburg, M. (1966). *Dynamically oriented art therapy: Its principles and practice.* New York: Grune & Stratton.

Naumburg, M. (1973). *An introduction to art therapy: Studies of the "free" art expression of behavior problem children and adolescents as a means of diagnosis and therapy.* New York: Teachers College Press. (Original work published 1947)

Schaeffer-Simmern, H. (1948). *The unfolding of artistic activity.* Berkeley and Los Angeles, CA: University of California Press.

Ulman, E. (1961). Art therapy: Problems of definition. *Bulletin of Art Therapy, 1*(2), 10–20.

Ulman, E. (1966). Therapy is not enough. The contribution of art to general hospital psychiatry. *Bulletin of Art Therapy, 6,* 3–21.

Ulman, E. (1971). The power of art in therapy. In I. Jakab (Ed.), *Conscious and unconscious expressive art—Psychiatry and art,* Vol. 3 (pp. 93–102). Basel, Switzerland: S. Karger.

Ulman, E. (1977). Art education for the emotionally disturbed. *American Journal of Art Therapy, 17,* 13–16.

Harriet Wadeson

An Eclectic Approach to Art Therapy

In responding to the editor's invitation to contribute to this book, my secretary typed that I would be happy to write a chapter on "The Electric Approach to Art Therapy." I didn't correct the letter, but added in the margin that this is indeed highly charged work. And so it is. The power of an eclectic approach is the personal nature of its development. Nothing is taken for granted. It is not simply because I believe that many theories have something to offer, nor that any one theory may be too limiting—although I find both to be true—that I choose to be eclectic and encourage my students to be so as well. My rationale is far more fundamental, intrinsic to my convictions of what therapy is and what it is about.

The instrument of the therapy is the self of the therapist in concert with the self of the patient. Our basic tools are not paint or brushes any more than they are words. Whatever happens in art therapy occurs within the container of the transference relationship (psychoanalytic theory: Moore & Fine, 1968). Margaret Naumburg (1966) was particularly emphatic in making this point. I also believe that the therapeutic endeavor is a creative enterprise. Since the selfhood of each therapist is unique, each clinician's creative work in this realm will bear the imprimatur of that self, with all its life experience influencing each moment of the therapeutic relationship. Just as my painting will be different from yours (even though we may have attended the same art school), so we will practice therapy differently, each according to our own style, even though we may share similar views of psychodynamics and treatment objectives.

Each existing theory orients us somewhat differently. No doubt these theories were developed in consonance with the unique needs and life experiences of their authors. It follows, therefore, that if we are to make the most of our unique potentialities, it is up to us to select and synthesize from among the many theories and treatment models available to us in accordance with our needs and world views.

It is important to note that this is an active and ongoing process. Being eclectic does not mean slipping into a ready-made garment and going to work. The process requires far more creativity. We may select a hat from one store, a sweater from another. We hope the shoes won't clash with the rest of the ensemble. We might outgrow them or discard a style that pinches for one that is more comfortable. It is in this way that we create ourselves as art therapists. Nevertheless, it is not necessary for us to weave our own garments. We can select ready-made slacks and shorten them only if they are too long. To switch metaphors, we don't have to reinvent the wheel.

When we look at the theories that we wear, however, we must recognize them for what they are. They are not skin or blood or bones. They are made up to serve a purpose. For example, there is no such thing as an id. (Have you ever seen one?) There is only a concept. If that concept helps us to organize our understanding, then it is useful. On the other hand, if we are referring to "repressed" aspects of the "self" that are more encompassing than "basic drives," we may find the Jungian "shadow" a way to express our understanding.

An eclectic approach is a more difficult road. It requires choices. There isn't a unified system into which the complex data for understanding and changing human dynamics can fit. Nevertheless, for me it is the only way. It is consonant with my belief that therapy is growth, and that growth is a mystery. The art therapist participates with the client in the client's growth. And the art therapist must grow as well. An aspect of that growth is the continuing search for understanding, the ongoing refinement of one's thinking. This is an active process of attending to all possible influences, including new ideas and theories.

And the mystery? Ultimately the process of growth is a mystery to us. It is a continuation of the process of creation. As an art therapist I am in a position of awe in relation to that process. As a searcher and a seeker in the understanding of human creation and growth, I must be open to new possibilities.

☐ My Eclectic Layer Cake

In a brief chapter such as this, it is not possible to present a full description of the eclectic synthesis that informs my view of art therapy at this time. The best way to summarize it appears to be an historical review of the layers of my own theoretical development.

As I have stated elsewhere (Wadeson, 1980), I began with Father Freud during teenage baby-sitting stints at the home of my-uncle-the-psychiatrist. I had never dreamed dreams could be so illuminating (Freud, 1900/1950). When I began working at the National Institutes of Mental Health (NIMH), the neo-Freudians who reigned supreme were being joined by the systems folks who were studying family dynamics, which they later published (Bowen, 1961). I read Jung (1959) but found him too spiritual. Later, I was ready for him. I was working with adolescents at NIMH then, and leaned on Erikson's (1950) developmental model.

During the mid-60's I began venturing forth from NIMH and the medical model into more humanistic realms. I read existential philosophy (Heidegger, 1962, 1964; Jaspers, 1952, 1963; Kierkegaard, 1957), and began to replace the idea of psychic determinism with the notion of individual responsibility for creating one's life. I began to see perception as an active, selective process. This view was more hopeful, and therapy took on new dimensions and possibilities for me. I suppose I was always a closet phenomenologist, but in conjunction with existentialism it took on new validation (Boss, 1958). When I changed projects at NIMH and moved from affective disorders to acute schizophrenia, my immediate interest was to try to understand what it was like to be schizophrenic. There are plenty of observations by others of acute schizophrenics, but I wondered what it was like for *them*. So I directed my research to the phenomenology of schizophrenia (Wadeson & Carpenter, 1976). Art therapy was a natural channel for the expression and reification of the inner experience.

Consonant with an existential view was a shift from viewing the patient as object. It became increasingly apparent that the patient was not a constant with a fixed symptomatology. There were patients who behaved very differently in their art therapy sessions with me than they did with their psychiatrist or in the dayroom. Since most of the patients with whom I worked were diagnosed psychotic and were free of medication for research purposes, the shifts in their behavior were often quite dramatic. I began to see how much influence the therapist has. It became clear to me that I could not understand my sessions with patients without exploring my half of the equation. I began to scrutinize the therapeutic relationship.

From a practical standpoint, I found Fritz Perls' (1969) Gestalt therapy helpful. Attending to the messages my body was sending me, I became more self-aware in this endeavor. This was particularly useful during art therapy sessions. For example, I began to notice that at times my eyes would go out of focus. I came to recognize that this signaled boredom or apathy on my part, and was almost always related to the patient's enacting some distancing maneuvers. Now, the moment my eyes go out of focus, I interrupt the patient and inquire about what's going on.

I find Gestalt therapy's concept of "disowned parts" an interesting companion piece to the concepts of "projection" in Freudian theory and of the "shadow" in Jungian psychology. Taken together, these three constructs round out a significant area of psychopathology or malfunctioning. The three ideas do not contradict one another, but rather are complementary, each adding a dimension to our understanding of what happens to those aspects of ourselves we find difficult to accept.

Of the major triumvirate of psychoanalysis, humanistic psychology, and behaviorism, I find the latter the weak sister. Yet I borrow from that approach too. I believe that there is never a session in which I do not use positive reinforcement. Particularly around sexual issues with couples, I am likely to use behavioral approaches for restructuring the interaction.

More recently I've focused on group dynamics. I find art expression especially valuable in both reflecting and advancing group process. The art activity makes everyone a group participant. Yalom's (1975, 1983) articulation of group therapy theory and practice has been especially clarifying for me. Promoting experiences of universality through the commonality that can be readily viewed in the content of the art productions, and the exploration of the here-and-now through art expression, make the marriage of group therapy and art therapy a dynamic union.

Finally, there are two significant influences that form the matrix of human experience and are sometimes overlooked in theories of psychotherapy. One is the physiological. Much of the research at NIMH with which I was affiliated resulted in significant correlations between biochemical variables and psychopathology. Given this information, coupled with epidemiological studies pointing to genetic links for certain clinical syndromes, the possibility of hereditary predispositions in mental illness is a very strong one.

The second influence is societal. It is so pervasive that it is difficult to define briefly. Hopefully, two examples will suffice. It seems to me that most emotional problems stem from feelings of inadequacy or unworthiness. In our society children are usually raised in an isolated nuclear family, are often pushed to achieve, and are seldom cherished just for being who they are. Child rearing is different in many other cultures where an extended family, as well as parents, dote on the growing child. In our culture, therefore, child-rearing patterns along with economic pressures and rapidly changing social values may contribute to emotional disturbance.

Whereas the first example deals with etiology, the second deals with disposition. No matter what the treatment, the proof of the therapeutic pudding must come later, in the world in which the patient lives. In some instances, a child may have to return to hostile parents or an adult to the unemployment line. So it does seem obvious to me that both physiological and societal factors must be recognized in our understanding of the people we treat and the treatment we undertake with them.

In sum, I have only alluded to the sources for the content of my eclecticism. Hopefully, the following examples will provide a view of how they come into play in the clinical situation. Please bear in mind, as you view them, that an eclectic approach is not a fragmented one. The pieces that come together from diverse sources must integrate as a whole, if the art therapist is to have a basis for understanding the therapeutic process and directing it in a meaningful way.

☐ An Art Therapy Example

Susan, a bright, capable teacher, was a member of a private practice art therapy group of eight women. In the third month of treatment, the group was discussing their feelings toward me, spearheaded by Susan, who at 34 was amazed by how childlike she felt in relation to me. Others were also animated in expressing their feelings, so I suggested that they all draw pictures of their relationship with me. Figure 19.1 is Susan's.

Figure 19.1.

She spoke of feeling very young, wanting my protection, affection, and approval, and represented herself as a child close to me with my arm around her. The figure on the right came as a surprise and represents her defiance and anger at being a dependent child. I am no longer with her, and she is larger. I asked her if she was willing to act out her picture and she agreed. First, she assumed the position of the child and I put my arm around her. Then I sat down and she assumed the position of her larger self. She commented that she felt nervous and sort of frightened in the first position; and that the second position felt much better.

Fundamental to understanding the theoretical frameworks that I used in conceptualizing and dealing with this event in Susan's therapy is a recognition of the facilitating function of art expression. Although Susan had recognized uncomfortable feelings in relation to me prior to her drawing, it was the pictorial image formation process that brought into awareness an unexpected side of her feelings. Therefore, it is important to bear in mind, as a foundation to the approaches to be discussed, the power of art expression as a ladle for dipping into the unconscious soup. With that as a basis, I will discuss the theoretical frameworks from which I approached this episode in Susan's therapy:

1. *Freudian Psychoanalytic*: The subject is transference. In her reaction to me, Susan recognized the parallels to childhood relationship to authority and the adaptations that evolved. The therapeutic situation plunged her into feelings of dependency that she had not experienced in some time.
2. *Gestalt Therapy*: The technique I used in asking Susan to "enact" her picture is drawn from Perls' (1969) dreamwork. His view is that the objects in a dream are all self-representations, and clients can best process their dreams by "becoming" the objects in them and thus reown "disowned" parts. I believe art expressions may be viewed and worked with in the same way. In Susan's case, the enactment deepened the "owning" of her feeling states, forming a synergy between the imagistic and the kinesthetic.
3. *Jungian Analytical Psychology*: Both the dependent child and the angry defiant adult bear elements of the concept of the "shadow" (Jung, 1964). Both these aspects of "self" were unacceptable to Susan and were usually repressed, causing her difficulty by being unacknowledged. By bringing these shadow elements into the light, Susan was able to work with them, rather than to be unconsciously subverted by these denied aspects of self.
4. *Developmental*: In Susan's picture and its processing, we see her move from dependent child to defiant adolescent. By working with her shadow she was able to grow into an adult in relation to me, no longer dependent on my approval or angry. She was also able to see me more realistically.
5. *Existential*: Susan recognized her responsibility for her feelings. She was quick to see that they emanated from her perception of me, rather than from anything I was doing. Recognizing herself as the creator of many life experiences, she also recognized her power to change them.
6. *Group Therapy Theory*: In Yalom's view (1975, 1983), group therapy should be based on a theory which postulates that humans learn and develop in the context of interpersonal relationships (Sullivan, 1953). It follows, therefore, that individuals can best learn about themselves by examining their relationships with others. There is no better place than group therapy for obtaining this sort of feedback in the here-and-now. Often history-taking is not necessary, as the group becomes a microcosm in which

members display their relationship patterns in the ongoing group interactions. The group often provides an awareness of the universality of experience; members feel less negatively unique, less isolated, less alone.

Such was the case for Susan in this instance. The pictures made by other group members at this session also displayed dependency and/or anger toward me. The social microcosm aspects of Susan's behavior were represented in her risk taking. It was she who opened the sensitive subject of feelings about the therapist early in the group's life. This was the first time anyone had enacted a picture. Not everyone was willing to be as open or risk as much during this session as Susan did. She demonstrated some of her very significant interpersonal strengths.

☐ Locked into Theory

In the next example, my intention is not to erect a straw man to knock down, but to present a somewhat extreme example of the problem of being theory-bound. Please bear in mind that the purpose here is not to disparage the use of a well-integrated theory, but rather to point out the problem of narrow adherence.

I was giving an art therapy presentation to a staff unfamiliar with art therapy. The senior psychiatrist was particularly impressed by Figure 19.2, a depiction of a delusion drawn by Vickie, a young woman diagnosed as acute schizophrenic. Prior to entering the hospital, she had the repeated experience of a "big black man, a killer" stalking her in a back alley.

By drawing a picture of him, she was able to explore her delusion more fully and make more sense out of her confusion over what was real and what was not. And the drawing communicated an experience that had previously remained private for this withdrawn young woman. Its expression in imagery and our subsequent discussion of the picture and the experience markedly undercut the isolation of this patient who, prior to hospitalization, had remained shut in at home alone for several months.

But the senior psychiatrist had other ideas about the picture. He saw it as a penis within the vaginal canal. It seemed to me that his classical analytical training influenced him to seek out only sexual symbolism. Is this really the picture's deeper meaning? How do we know? I believe these questions confront us with larger issues of how we approach our work: how we understand the imagery presented to us, the understanding we gain of our clients, and what outcomes these understandings shape in the way we develop treatment goals and the way we relate to our clients. The psychiatrist who interpreted Figure 19.2 as an image of sexual intercourse probably would have had a different sense of the patient's dynamics than I did. Perhaps he would have conducted the treatment differently and would have related to her with a wish to uncover repressed sexual conflicts.

I believe it is important to meet clients where they are (fundamental to social work theory and others), and to build an empathic bridge (Kohut, 1959) between the patient and myself. In Vickie's case this bridge served to reach the island of isolation she had created. Bridging this sort of isolation is particularly important for psychotic patients whose delusional, idiosyncratic ideation separates them from the basis of a consensual reality to which others ascribe. Furthermore, the empathy of the art therapist often provides the "corrective emotional experience" (Alexander & French, 1946) that is one basis for a humanistic approach to therapy.

Figure 19.2.

But suppose the psychiatrist's interpretation is correct? An important foundation of my commitment to an eclectic approach is that I have found no single theory that can fully explain unconscious processes. There are no indisputable answers. We can no more claim that his interpretation is erroneous than we can say that it is correct. So how do we find out?

As a phenomenologist, I would rely on the patient's experience, first through imagery, then through fantasy. I would utilize free association (Freudian), active imagination (Jungian), perhaps enactment (Gestalt and psychodrama), and so forth. I would use tools from many therapeutic approaches, capitalizing on those to which the client responded most readily. Ultimately I would probably recognize that some areas would still remain shrouded in mystery, but my experience as an art therapist has taught me that there is so much that the art expression provides, that it is not necessary to make speculative leaps into insubstantial interpretations.

This conclusion leads me into another concern about being locked into theory. The internal consistency of a theory enables the clinician to arrive at a relatively neat and comprehensible formulation of a client's psychodynamics. Of course, the problem is that sometimes the client is made to fit the theory rather than vice versa. Having a dynamic formulation may relieve the therapist's anxiety, and can serve as a platform on which to erect therapeutic work. It is more difficult to remain open to many possibilities, and to recognize that the data are never all in.

This sort of openness to possibilities, this working with hunches rather than more solid formulations, may be easier for art therapists than other clinicians. As artists, we may be characterized by some of the attributes Frank Barron (1968) found in creative people, particularly a tolerance for ambiguity and a preference for complexity.

Therefore, with a recognition of the essential complexity in every human existence, and a tolerance for the ambiguity in a situation in which we are presented with an abundance of data (images, statements, behavior), my hope is that my anxiety will not push me to premature closure in an attempt to fathom my client's problems. I believe an eclectic approach encourages me to cast my net widely for the many sources of knowledge that may inform my understanding, and to take the time to weave a synthesis of ideas. Hopefully, an eclectic approach also prevents me from coming to premature formulations based on what I may have found to be a tried and true theory.

☐ Toward Future Art Therapy Theory

Art therapists have utilized various theories of human development, psychopathology, and psychotherapy to inform their work. We adapt our work to these theories or we adapt these theories to art therapy. Many recognize a need for a theory of art therapy that would integrate human psychology, creative art expression, and the meaning of visual imagery.

A brief glimpse of artwork by a psychiatric patient may indicate some of the directions for future theory. Figures 19.3 and 19.4 were drawn by Craig, a young paranoid schizophrenic hospitalized at the National Institute of Health's Clinical Center, where I saw him. He had been dragged into the hospital by seven policemen, and was considered dangerous by the staff. His shaggy appearance and suspicious, menacing glances added to the effect. Artwork was an important outlet for him. Although his pictures expressed "secrets" he feared revealing, his love of drawing and the communication it afforded lessened the isolation his idiosyncratic ideation created.

The two pictures reproduced here were made prior to Craig's hospitalization. He stated that Figure 19.3, delicate traceries on notebook paper in pencil and blue ink, was drawn "in a shit house" when he was working at a factory. Figure 19.4 was also drawn on notebook paper with pencil and blue ink. He described it more fully, saying that it was himself. The underneath part is "strong and grasping," the sphere is "selfless" and represents his "mind." He explained that the roots are holding the sphere and that the

Figure 19.3.

underneath shows "control" of the body over the mind. "In order for the mind to exist, the body controls or comforts it," he said.[1]

An art therapy theory would be able to account for many aspects of Craig's art-making activity. First, there would be an understanding of why and how a very psychotic patient

---

[1]For additional examples of Craig's artwork, see Wadeson, *Art Psychotherapy*, 1980, pp. 140, 153–157, 159–161.

Changes

Figure 19.4.

did not decompensate further as so many others did upon hospitalization. It was clear that making art, in and of itself, was a stabilizing process for Craig.

Second, Craig's frightening physical aspect, his fear that people would take his "secrets" from him, and his elaborate delusional system alienated him from others. But his art created a bridge for him. Staff and patients were intrigued by his pictures, showing their interest, and often admiration. But even more significant was the opportunity art therapy sessions provided. It was there that he began to build trust, through my interest in the meaning of his imagery. In his pictures he portrayed an elaborate inner world of strange beings and unearthly landscapes. The isolation experienced by delusional patients cannot be overemphasized. An art therapy theory would note art's potentiality for bridging.

Most obvious, of course, an art therapy theory would facilitate the understanding of imagistic expression. There would be recognition of the delicacy and loving care that this fearsome, often wild-looking young man devoted to Figure 19.3. Evident also in this picture is some of the control of which he spoke in reference to Figure 19.4. This latter drawing is an interesting contrast to the former. The upper tree is quite truncated in comparison to the more conventional tree of Figure 19.3 and the unusual underpart of the second tree in Figure 19.4. This underground aspect is original, creative, bizarre. The artistry in art therapy is the ability both to encourage art expression and to help the patient relate to it. In this case, although Craig had been fearful of disclosing his private meanings, sufficient trust had developed between us for him to associate to his picture quite freely.

But even with his somewhat unclear explanation, how do we understand such an image? Hopefully, an art therapy theory might provide direction. For the present, we note the power and importance of what is underground, what is hidden from view. Craig has related this portion of the picture to control. He has spoken of mind and body, but the locus of control is unclear from what he says. The roots appear to grasp and to be quite separate from the portion of the tree above ground. We gain a sense of Craig's struggle for control, both from the content of this picture and from the style of all his pictures. We see the separation, both graphically and thematically, between the upper and the lower.

We see a young man with a highly original creative energy who has had difficulty getting along in the world, who has managed to frighten almost everyone—family, employers, hospital staff—almost everyone except his art therapist. Even a famous psychiatrist renowned for his writings on schizophrenia, who served as consultant to our ward, was afraid Craig wanted to kill him and would not see him alone. I found Craig gentle, sensitive, a very caring human being. What might an art therapy theory tell us about this discrepancy?

Finally, there is the question of creativity. How does it move us? What is the healing nature of art making? Certainly it operated for Craig. And what is the nature of a therapeutic relationship that has creativity at its center? Perhaps this phenomenon allowed me to know an aspect of Craig that others didn't see.

☐ The Selectric Electric

I have strayed from "An Eclectic Approach" only to return to it. My hope is that as we develop our profession, and gradually build what will come to be art therapy theory, we will learn from and integrate whatever wisdom we may. There are many paradigms, more than one lens through which to view our complex world. They enable us to see a number of different relationships within the "reality" we attempt to understand.

I hope this chapter has made clear that I believe theory to be an essential foundation to our work. An eclectic approach respects the contributions of many theorists, and enables the clinician to draw on many sources of knowledge. It places a great deal of responsibility on the therapist to form a functional synthesis, integrating theories with one another and applying them to practice in the most efficacious way.

For those who feel a need for art therapy to have its own theoretical base, I believe this book begins a process for developing and drawing together various strands that can be woven into an art therapy theory. We look to the articulation of knowledge of human growth and behavior, to metapsychological viewpoints, to formulations of psychopathology, to treatment rationales. We have a rich heritage for a foundation. To that we must add an understanding of what is unique to art in therapy: expression in images, working with art materials, the client-therapist relationship around art making, and the place of creativity in art therapy. It is an exciting challenge.

For starters, I would like to return to the thoughts of my typist. I highly recommend her Selectric-Electric approach to art therapy.

☐ References

Alexander, F., & French, T. (1946). *Psychoanalytic theory: Principles and application*. New York: Ronald Press.

Boss, M. (1958). *The analysis of dreams*. New York: Philosophical Library.

Bowen, M. (1961). The family as the unit of study and treatment. *American Journal of Orthopsychiatry, 31*, 400–460.

Erikson, F. (1950). *Childhood and society*. New York: W. W. Norton.

Freud, S. (1950). *The interpretation of dreams*. New York: Modern Library. (Original Work Published 1900)

Heidegger, M. (1962). *Being and time*. London: SCM Press.

Heidegger, M. (1964). *Existence and being*: Chicago: H. Regnery.

Jaspers, K. (1952). *Reason and anti-reason in our time*. New Haven, CT: Yale University Press.

Jaspers, K. (1963). *General psychopathology*. Chicago: University of Chicago Press.

Jung, C. (1959). *Basic writings*. New York: Modern Library.

Jung, C. (1964). *Man and his symbols*. Garden City, NY: Doubleday.

Kierkegaard, S. (1957). *The concept of dread*. Princeton, NJ: Princeton University Press.

Kohut, H. (1959). Introspection, empathy and psychoanalysis. *Journal of the American Psychoanalytic Association, 7*, 459–483.

Moore, B., & Fine, B. (1968). *A glossary of psychoanalytic terms and concepts*. New York: The American Psychoanalytic Association.

Naumburg, M. (1966). *Dynamically oriented art therapy: Its principles and practice*. New York: Grune & Stratton.

Perls, F. (1969). *Gestalt therapy verbatim*. Moab, UT: Real People Press.

Sullivan, H. S. (1953). *The interpersonal theory of psychiatry*. New York: W. W. Norton.

Wadeson, H. (1980). *Art psychotherapy*. New York: John Wiley.

Wadeson, H., & Carpenter, W. (1976). Subjective experience of acute schizophrenia. *Schizophrenia Bulletin, 2*, 302–316.

Yalom, I. (1975). *The theory and practice of group psychotherapy*. New York: Basic Books.

Yalom, I. (1983). *Inpatient group psychotherapy*. New York: Basic Books.

CHAPTER

20

Shaun McNiff

Pandora's Gifts: The Use of Imagination and All of the Arts in Therapy

☐ The Integrating Realm of Imagination

The idea of using all of the arts in therapy provokes fear in some and excitement in others. Perhaps this discrepancy is connected to the way in which the reputation of the mythic figure Pandora, the "all-giver," changed from being the source of bounteous gifts to the cause of pandemonium (Gaskell, 1960; Walker, 1983). Pandora's "many things" came to be perceived as "too much." The word pandemonium (pan, demonium), meaning the universal release of daimons/spirits, became associated with a state of being overwhelmed.

The linear mind does not respond favorably to the stream of images and sensations flowing from Pandora's original vessel, a honey vase from which blessings were poured. The vase became a box "only in the late medieval period" (Walker, 1983, p. 767) due to a misunderstanding of the original image. When Pandora, the first woman, "out of curiosity for new experience" (Gaskell, 1960, p. 558) opened the vessel she was forbidden to touch, all of the evils of the world were released. By the time she was able to shut the lid, only Hope stayed within the enclosure. Pandora became a symbol of chaos, and her many blessings were lost.

Within general culture the Pandora image has developed into a reminder of what "we do not want to do"—don't open the lid and let everything out; keep it all under control, and so forth. However, those who are stimulated by a creative interplay of diverse elements are more apt to welcome the endless possibilities suggested by the original image of Pandora. Negative assumptions about the Pandora aspect of consciousness can be altered by an understanding of how the creative imagination is an integrating intelligence, which actually requires a fluid mix of ingredients. The ills of Pandora's many things become necessary elements of a creative integration, that does its best work with a rich variety of ingredients.

318

In the mid 1600's, the empirically minded philosopher Thomas Hobbes viewed imagination as a connecting power that functions organically, in contrast to mechanistic chains of thought. The formative power of imagination integrated all faculties and ways of knowing—the arts, science, reason, perception, memory, and emotion. From the radical empiricism of Hobbes to the more transcendent Romantics, imagination was viewed as a mediating intelligence. In 1744 Mark Akenside described the imagination as a "middle place" between perception and reason, and Samuel Taylor Coleridge (1817/1907) emphasized imagination's role as an "intermediate faculty."

The identification of imagination as a middle realm suggests a state of consciousness where the different elements in a situation can meet, influence one another, and create new patterns of interaction. The release of Pandora's many things will find its way to order and creative transformation, within an environment that understands and protects the natural movements of the integrating imagination.

In 1804 Jean Paul Richter described the imagination as the "faculty of faculties" which he likened to the process of pollination: "In genius all faculties are in bloom at once, and imagination is not the flower, but the flower-goddess, who arranges the flower calyxes with their mingling pollens for new hybrids" (1804/1973, p. 35). Imagination, as Richter suggested, is the "conductor" of creative action, a force that operates by making fresh links between previously separate entities, always open and receptive to new possibilities while forever seeking out opportunities. It would be sheer folly for the creative imagination to arbitrarily declare any aspect of inquiry off limits. As a "conductor" of the complex of forces and thoughts moving within a person, the imagination functions as an inner leader.

During the twentieth century the intelligence of the imagination has been over looked by education and psychology, in spite of the testimony of great thinkers like Albert Einstein, who declared that "imagination is more important than knowledge." Our multi-dimensional lives give a new relevance to the idea of imagination as the power capable of gathering and fusing infinitely variable materials and ideas.

☐ Using All of the Arts in Therapy

Paolo Knill, who has created a method called "intermodal expressive therapy," repeatedly refers to the use of all of the arts in therapy as a "discipline" that can be compared to a more singular focus on painting, piano, poetry, or theater. He emphasizes how we need to pay more attention to "the basic human need or drive to crystallize psychic material; that is, to move towards optimal clarity and precision of feeling and thought" (Knill, Barba, & Fuchs, 1995, p. 30). Stephen Levine's (1992) approach to using all of the arts in therapy trusts that in the sometimes difficult and disintegrating movements of creative imagination "lies the cure" to our psychic ills. In *Foundations of Expressive Arts Therapy* (1999) Stephen and Ellen Levine note that, even though the "multidimensional approach" to all of the arts has been "accused of eclecticism in the sense of an incoherent collection of approaches" (1999, p.11), the process of creative imagination unifies the multiplicity of experiences that often cause our emotional fragmentation.

The idea of using all of the arts in therapy consistently raises concerns that those who work in this way will be dilettantes—"jacks of all trades and masters of none." I don't deny these worries about quality. But aren't our goals in both creation and therapy focused on the integration of the varied elements of our lives? Are we better served by keeping Pandora's discoveries securely locked inside a box, or by learning how to move with them in creative and ever-changing ways? Is the most complete exercise of intelligence and creation possible without accessing all of our resources?

One way of responding to the dilettante challenge is by training therapists who are skilled in the process of integrating the arts.[1] In 1974 I founded the first graduate program with the goal of achieving this outcome. Paolo Knill's intermodal expressive therapy and other ways of integrating the arts grew from our community. We studied traditions in the West and within all of the world's indigenous cultures where different expressive media are used to further healing (McNiff, 1979). However, the potential of integrated arts training will be limited if the only goal is the creation of yet another mental health specialization and "brand name." The more intriguing task is the exploration of how all therapists—and artists—can open their work to a more complete process of expression.

In this chapter I hope to demonstrate how work in art, as in all creative modalities, requires multi-sensory activity. In *The Arts in Psychotherapy* (1981) I also suggested that the natural "integration of the senses in artistic expression" restores a "forgotten balance" that is the basis of healing (p. ix). So rather than getting caught in arguments about dilettantism, eclecticism, and professional association guidelines for a discipline, I will try to show how the practice of art therapy is enhanced by—indeed, requires—a more comprehensive understanding of expression through all of the senses.

Can we learn to approach multiplicity—whether in Pandora's box or in the therapy room—as an opportunity rather than as a plague? In environments that support the expression of creative imagination with both children and adults, there is typically a mix of different modalities. We find repeatedly that the ecology of different sensory expressions not only increases the creative vitality of the whole environment, but also furthers imaginative expression within a particular medium. I have always chosen to use different arts in my studio practice, because the breadth of resources and materials enriches the creative process and is more satisfying for participants.

I have increasingly observed that the healing effects of the art therapy experience are connected to a successful activation of creative "energy." Consequently, a primary objective of my practice has been the creation of a space that generates expressive energies which then act upon the people within it. In keeping with Reiki energy practitioners, I have found that within a free and safe environment, the creative medicines of the artistic process find their way to conditions in need of transformation (McNiff, 1998).

In constructing this environment I am concerned with the overall feel of the studio. I strive to create an atmosphere which fosters access to that intermediate realm of imagination which acts upon us through its transformative forces. I often drum and play other percussion instruments as participants paint or work with visual art media. There is a high level of emotional release and relaxation connected to the drumming that helps people to move more spontaneously. Participants describe how the drum enables them to work in a bodily way, how it stimulates a flow of imagery, and how it helps them connect to the forces of creation.

For example, I have discovered that drumming helps people to make bolder and more expressive gestures. When we encourage spontaneous expression on large surfaces with

---

[1] If we think in terms of more universal access to all of the arts in therapy, then we are subject to the valid criticism that therapists are using the media of other professional groups without proper training. However, there are many Registered and Board Certified art therapists who do not have highly developed skills with all of the media they use with clients. Are they to be restricted to offering only materials in which they are proficient?

wide brushes or oil sticks, for example, the drum furthers the use of the whole body. Percussive music has a similar effect on artistic expression on small surfaces and with precise tools. In big and small paintings, rhythm supports movement.

Repeatedly, I have seen how a person who at first timidly moves with a paint brush, becomes an "expressionist" with the help of the drum. Others who fear expression, can let go of restrictive thoughts. Faint or tight lines and other signs of inhibition are often caused by feeling that we have nothing of value within ourselves to express. People are also blocked by feelings of technical ineptitude. Moving with the drum beat, we realize that expression can be more than what we initiate alone. Paintings can be created in response to, and in synchrony with, the expressions of others.

The drum helps to sustain expression within the painting, just as the rhythmic element provides continuity for a musical composition. The person who lacks self-confidence or a clear sense of where to go with a painting, simply makes strokes, taps, and marks in synch with the drum beat. Images take shape through the natural flow of incremental gestures. Rhythm enables us to appreciate how the painting process, like music and dance, involves a sequence of expressive gestures that occur within the context of space, time, and kinesis.

The painting itself can be viewed from the perspective of rhythm. Visual patterns, repetitions, ascending and descending lines, and other features are related to elements of the music. When multiple art forms are used, we may be even more apt to experience ourselves making gestures within a supportive environment of expression. I believe this use of different artistic media creates an environmental energy, or imaginative realm, that truly acts upon the individual. It counteracts the common problem of a person feeling pressure and inhibition because of a belief that expression comes completely from within themselves. When we feel empty and blocked, the environment itself can be a source of stimulation.

My work with all of the arts in therapy began in response to the way in which patients in the psychiatric hospital to whom I was offering art, spontaneously expressed themselves with poetry, drama, voice, and movement as well. Was I to say that these communications were off limits? Was I to close Pandora's box or was I to allow the different expressions to emerge, trusting that they would find their way to creative integration? Did I have to be an expert in these different media in order to welcome what was expressed naturally in the studio environment? Could I open myself and the art studio to a natural multimodal flow of expression? The different art forms introduced a broader spectrum of expression, and they were clearly manifesting needs for communication that could not be met exclusively by the visual arts.

Stories, poems, creative writings, and imaginal dialogue have always played an important role in my work as ways of engaging visual art imagery (McNiff, 1993). But from my first art therapy experiences, I discovered how limiting verbal explanations can be. I explored ways of responding to art with art, and in keeping with Jung's practice of "active imagination," I found that we can amplify and focus our engagement with an image by imagining it further (McNiff, 1998). Explanation certainly has its place in art therapy, but I have also experienced how it can arrest the ongoing flow of the creative process. The exclusive use of verbal language as a mode of relating to images tends to keep us within the realm of what I call "explanationism." Even my experimentation with imaginal dialogue was restricted by the linear structure of narrative (McNiff, 1993).

In recent years in my studios I have explored how we can use movement, vocal expression, and performance to more completely access the creative energies manifested by images. While other colleagues who engage all of the arts in therapy give relatively equal focus to all media (Knill, Barba, & Fuchs, 1995; Levine 1992; Levine & Levine, 1999), I have always used the visual arts as what I call the "trunk of my tree." I introduce the other arts in order to more completely perceive and express the energetic qualities of images. Sound and bodily movement, for example, help us to resonate more closely with the vibrational qualities of images approached as energetic fields of interacting colors, movements, and forms. There is as much physics to a painting as there is psychology, and the energetic medicines have healing powers that are not released through verbal explanation.

Pandora's many ingredients can be released in such a studio atmosphere, and in keeping with the dynamics of the creative process, they are allowed to find their way to areas of need. The healing process of creativity corresponds to the ecological forces of nature. Outcomes cannot always be planned in advance, and I am usually surprised by what a person does and how a problem is resolved.

Talking about paintings will always be an essential feature of art therapy. But I have found that it can sometimes be more helpful to respond to a painting of swirling lines with movements that correspond and mirror, amplify, diminish, or redirect the expression of the visual art work. Vocal improvisations add yet another dimension to our experience of a painting. These multi-media engagements expand the sensory interplay. We can respond to any visual configuration, scene, or combination of colors through sound and movement. The simplest and most elemental figurative and nonfigurative compositions often elicit the most direct and spontaneous artistic responses in other media. Body movement and vocal improvisation deepen our relationships to paintings, and actually augment our understanding of them. This expansion of the process of communication reminds us that pictures can evoke more than verbal explanations.

My role is one of keeping the space safe and creative. This process is similar to Winnicott's attempts to create a "holding environment" that supports the person in finding understanding. Winnicott was dismayed when he realized "how much deep change" was "prevented or delayed" by his interventions. He concluded that the analyst' s role is the creation of environments that act upon people: "If only we can wait, the patient arrives at understanding creatively and with immense joy, and now I enjoy this more than I used to enjoy the sense of having been clever" (Davis & Wallbridge, 1981, p. 25).

This method of using all of the arts in therapy establishes an environment of creative energy that influences people, in contrast to an emphasis on linear treatment plans for individuals. The creative atmosphere is an agent of therapeutic transformation. However, such "process medicines" complement, but certainly do not replace, the conventional treatment plan. Within the overall environment of the studio, I adjust and plan according to the unique needs of individuals. One person might need to warm up with body movement in order to paint with more fluidity, whereas another might need to sit down and meditate in order to benefit from stillness and quiet focus.

From the beginning of my art therapy practice I have focused on the healing effects of groups of people working together in studios (McNiff, 1973). Maxwell Jones' practice of the therapeutic community (1953, 1982) and Rudolf Arnheim's interpretation of Gestalt psychology (1954, 1972) helped me to understand that the structures of environments generated therapeutic forces. Where others might direct their primary attention toward specific techniques for integrating the arts, I am more interested in the larger "ecology of imagination" (Cobb, 1977), and in a therapeutic community of creative expression.

Even if an art therapist chooses to work only with visual media, there is a need for a deeper appreciation of the interplay among different sensory modalities within the creative process. In the following section I will focus on how an understanding of the kinetic basis of painting furthers expression within visual art therapy. Hopefully this illustration will show how the different arts inform and enhance one another, and how even the most focused practice in a particular medium is advanced through an understanding of how all of the faculties work together within the process of creative expression.

☐ The Primacy of Movement

I will typically introduce painting and drawing activities by encouraging people to move in a relaxed way, without thinking about what they are going to do next. I urge them to move freely while they paint, without an initial regard for results. As they become immersed in the painting activity, they also see that the movement will "start to direct itself." It helps to demystify painting and drawing when we approach them as movement. When we paint, we are dancing. When we dance, we sculpt fleeting forms and create fleeting images. Neither kinesis nor touch can be separated from the process of creating a picture. In my experience, the expressiveness of a painting is furthered by improving a person's ability to move with greater spontaneity and grace.

I try to keep people focused on elemental gestures. I encourage repetition and simplicity, knowing that structure and other forms of communication will emerge from basic motions if we can stay with them and let go of the need to plan everything in advance (McNiff, 1998). We avoid inhibiting ideas about what a painting or poem "should be" by approaching it as movement.

We have all heard the child or adult patient say, "I can't think of anything to draw." The same poverty of ideas tends to apply to the other arts when they are approached through mental or even visual planning. Movement offers a guaranteed starting point. Rather than focusing on the quality of the visual image, I recommend concentrating on the character of the movement and the creative energy it generates. When the person says "I can't think of anything to make," I reply, "That's fine. You don't have to think of things in advance. Just move with the materials. Close your eyes if it helps, and feel the movement and the way the art materials make contact with the surface. Imagine the painting as a dance. Focus on the quality of the movement. Don't be concerned right now with the visual appearance of the picture."

As I drum and use other percussive instruments to create rhythms, people begin to let go and move more spontaneously in their paintings. Not only does the accompanying music further the painting, but I find that people will often move with their brushes and oil sticks in synchrony with the rhythms. In some cases the paint is applied percussively and rhythmically through striking motions, slaps, taps, rubs, and other gestures evoked by the music. There are also clear variations in the visual marks and patterns which emerge, in keeping with changes in the music. Painting, movement, and tactile sensibilities are naturally integrated in the making of a picture. The music and sound tend to energize the painting process, and I have never observed them controlling or in any way interfering with the artist's freedom of expression.

By approaching painting as a multi-sensory activity we benefit from a more complete circulation and ecology of expressive energy. It is helpful to view every gesture as part of an ongoing flow of movement. Every stroke simply emerges from the one that went before it, and then becomes the source of yet another gesture.

People need to learn how to move from within themselves, from the particular place where they are at the moment. Many find it difficult to act creatively because they attempt to be in a place other than where they are at the moment. They lose balance and the ability to move with the forces of the environment that will ultimately support expression. They expect something other than what they are doing at that particular time, or they think that what they are doing is inadequate. They become blocked and caught up by negative and confusing thoughts.

The movements of any person on the surface of a painting can become truly fascinating, when they are made with total concentration and abandon. If people need guidance after making their first gestures, I encourage them to simply build upon what they are already doing. When we begin to move in a more relaxed way, the movements not only emerge from one another, but even seem to perfect themselves. The improved quality comes from within the movement itself.

Simple experiences with movement help us to see how we frequently overdo it in other parts of our lives. I might say to a person in need of direction, "Try to keep moving, don't stop, and trust that a new movement will always come out of the one that went before it. Put everything you have into the movement. Even if you make a slow and delicate gesture with your arm, fill it with all your energy and with total concentration. Identify completely with it. Be aware of your breath and view stillness as a pause between movements. Let another gesture come forward and yet another one from it. If you can keep moving in a relaxed way, without thinking about what you are going to do next, you will discover that the movement will start to direct itself."

If we are able to let go of the need to mentally direct expression, we will discover that the movement "happens" to us. When we reach the state of being moved by a force which is more than our conscious mind acting alone, we have entered the realm of *imagination*. It is our body which is moving, yet it is propelled by forces outside of ourselves as well as within ourselves. As Ahab said in *Moby Dick*, "Is Ahab, Ahab? Is it I, God, or who, that lifts this arm?"

Nothing will happen, however, unless there is sustained movement from one moment to another. The direction is not always clear, and the outcome rarely known at the start of an imaginative act. What matters most is the commitment to beginning, and the acceptance of what will emerge. By focusing on the movement basis of painting, the mind follows the lead of elemental gestures.

☐ Letting Go while Staying Focused

Those who have encountered the powers and gifts of the creative imagination know firsthand that it is usually the overly controlling mind, excessive effort, and narrow expectations which restrict access to the middle realm of imagining—which requires a paradoxical *discipline* of letting go while staying focused, and allowing the creation to emerge.

Children's play can teach us so much about the creative process. As Hans-Georg Gadamer (1994) insists, the fulfillment of play requires the player to become lost in play (p. 102). The fear of losing control is the primary reason why many people are reluctant to open themselves to unplanned expression. This fear may be magnified when making art is accompanied by other forms of expression.

Free movement can evoke a sense of primal isolation or coming apart at the seams, and spontaneous drama may trigger the paralysis of stage fright or the dread of being exposed. These fears can be motivating forces for expression, if the space is safe, and if participants are convinced that their expression will be welcomed and respected. Lifelong fears of being rejected and judged can be reversed, if every gesture is witnessed with a sense of appreciation and even sanctity. This is the most distinguishing characteristic of the art therapy studio.

Rather than letting ourselves go within the creative process like a child at play, we initially guard ourselves against "pandemonium." Our defenses are constructed on the basis of real life experiences of being overwhelmed and confused. Opening to the gifts of Pandora is not without challenges. Creative exploration can be difficult, and it is sometimes painful and disruptive.

Nevertheless, the experience of making art consistently suggests that what disturbs us the most may also have the most to offer. In medicine, the toxin can become the anti-toxin. Similarly, engaging and knowing the power and the pain of rage, fear, and ecstasy, allows us to harness their energy in our lives. Over and over again, I have found that the images and expressions we create never come to harm us. Indeed, even when full of pain, they instruct and strengthen us. The goal of this approach to art therapy is the creation of a space where we can open ourselves to the complete spectrum of human expression, trusting in the intelligence of the creative imagination.

Creative vitality can be viewed as a condition in which all of our resources are simultaneously engaged. The process of transformative integration is the basic dynamic of health, as well as creation. This approach to art therapy, then, relies on the making of a space where these creative powers can be activated, and where we in turn can be healed by them.

☐ References

Akenside, M. (1744). *The pleasures of imagination*.

Arnheim, R. (1954). *Art and visual perception: A psychology of the creative eye*. Berkeley and Los Angeles: University of California Press.

Arnheim, R. (1972). *Toward a psychology of art*. Berkeley and Los Angeles: University of California Press.

Cobb, E. (1977). *The ecology of imagination in childhood*. New York: Columbia University Press.

Coleridge, S. (1907). *Biographia literaria*. In J. Shawcross (Ed.). London: Oxford University Press. (Original work published 1817)

Davis, M., & Wallbridge, D. (1981). *Boundary and space: An introduction to the work of D. W. Winnicott*. New York: Brunner/Mazel.

Gadamer, H. G. (1994). *Truth and method*. New York: Continuum.

Gaskell, G. A. (1960). *Dictionary of all scriptures and myths*. New York: The Julian Press.

Jones, M. (1953). *The therapeutic community: A new treatment method in psychiatry*. New York: Basic Books.

Jones, M. (1982). *The process of change*. Boston: Routledge.

Knill, P., Barba, H., & Fuchs, M. (1995). *Minstrels of soul*. Toronto: Palmerston Press.

Levine, S. (1992). *Poesis: The language of psychology and the speech of the soul*. Toronto: Palmerston Press.

Levine, S., & Levine, E. (1999). *Foundations of expressive arts therapy: Theoretical and clinical perspectives*. London: Jessica Kingsley.

McNiff, S. (1973). A new perspective on group art therapy. *Art Psychotherapy*, (pp. 243–255).

McNiff, S. (1979). From shamanism to art therapy. *Art Psychotherapy, 6*, 3.

McNiff, S. (1981). *The arts and psychotherapy*. Springfield, IL: Charles C. Thomas.

McNiff, S. (1993). Letting pictures tell their stories. In C. Simpkinson & A. Simpkinson (Eds.), *Sacred stories: healing in the imaginative realm* (pp. 169–179). San Franciso: Harper Collins.

McNiff, S. (1994). *Art as medicine: Creating a therapy of the imagination*. Boston: Shambhala.

McNiff, S. (1998). *Trust the process: An artistic guide to letting go*. Boston: Shambhala.

Richter, J. P. (1973). *School for aesthetics*. (M. R. Hale, Translator). Detroit: Wayne State University Press. (Original work published 1804)

Walker, B. (1983). *The woman's encyclopedia of myths and secrets*. San Francisco: Harper and Row.

David Henley

Lessons in the Images:
Art Therapy in Creative Education

Learning prospers when we reinstate the vague and inarticulate to its proper place in our mental life. (William James)

One morning, in a school for disturbed teenagers, 16-year-old Mel was reading *The New York Times* as part of current events, and latched onto an article on the bombing of Dresden in World War II. Although the city had no military value, the allies fire bombed this medieval architectural treasure purely to terrorize and break the will of the German people. The firestorm annihilated thousands of civilians, and is one of the few war atrocities perpetrated by American and British forces. The article covered a recent candlelight peace march, commemorating the 50th anniversary of the terror-bombing.

Disturbed by the story, Mel said that "history is always written by victors who retain power," and that he himself is often wrongfully attacked by adults who are "always right, only because they're in charge." He described his "own war" against those who wield power, who "never have to worry about the consequences of being wrong"—like the allies, and like his teachers.

These adolescent issues of power and authority were expanded upon when, as part of the current events activity, I suggested making some images about the article. Mel created a colored pencil drawing (Figure 21.1) of a flaming candle, featuring a cloud of smoke and dripping red wax. Though reluctant to talk about it, Mel did point out the split in the image: the mushrooming cloud representing the ever-present threat of world war, and the candle symbolizing a gesture towards world peace.

As he spoke, he continued to doodle in his characteristic style, adding some cannabis references, along with a snow-boarder blowing a smoke ring of the "peace weed" toward the boiling clouds. These drug references were received with the same seriousness as the candle image, since they were an integral part of the metaphor. While discussing the topic, we were able to explore Mel's sometimes explosive hostility to authority, and its relationship to his engulfing, infantilizing mother and absentee father.

As this vignette illustrates, almost any meaningful learning experience can become a vehicle for therapeutic growth. The mission of education is usually the acquisition of academic skills, but it is expanding to include increased therapeutic support; as

Figure 21.1.

violence, substance abuse, and other problems reach epidemic proportions in the schools. Believing that academic work can be a springboard to emotional problem solving, I have developed a "therapeutic curriculum" (Henley, 1997, 1998, 1999).

The key to such a curriculum is tailoring educational work to the children's own interests, no matter how negative or inappropriate they may be. In disturbed adolescents, these include negativity, anarchy, drugs, and violence, all of which find impoverished expression in contemporary media. Yet Shakespeare, too, conjured up as much graphic violence, sexual perversity, lawlessness, and psychedelic imagery as any contemporary video or computer game! Like therapy, this curriculum "goes to where the child is" by using any content that engages him in learning. Just as Shakespeare was able to transform graphic descriptions of maternal incest and rape into Hamlet, so too can the disturbed child transform his own negative perceptions and feelings into something poetic and powerful.

☐ A Brief History of Therapeutic Education and Art

In 1799, a young physician named Jean Itard (1802/1962) took on the challenge of taming and educating a "wild child." The boy, probably autistic, was found naked and scarred, roaming the forests of France in a primal state. With highly developed animal senses, void of language or habituation to people, he was approached by Itard with sensitivity and empathy. His methods of educating and civilizing the feral child paved the way for humanitarian therapeutic approaches.

Over a century later, educator John Dewey (1916) stressed the importance of personal involvement in learning: "When excitement about subject matter runs deep, it stirs up a store of attitudes and meanings derived from prior experience. As they are aroused into activity they become conscious thoughts of emotionalized ideas" (1934, p. 65). Dewey also recognized the role of the unconscious in creative education: "New ideas come to consciousness only when work has been done in forming the right doors by which they may gain entrance. Unconscious maturation precedes creativity in every line of human endeavor" (1934, p. 65).

Psychoanalytic ideas were implemented in Margaret Naumburg's progressive school, Walden. Naumburg (1917), who had studied with Dewey at Columbia and later founded the field of art therapy in America, put into practice her ideas about fostering learning through spontaneous creative expression. To help accomplish this mission, she hired her sister, Florence Cane (1951), to teach art in a uniquely empathic fashion.

In the 1930's, art education pioneer Viktor Lowenfeld (1939) began his seminal work with blind children in Europe. Influenced by the child-centered teacher, Franz Cizek, he stressed motivation as the core of creative expression. Lowenfeld stimulated self-expression by bringing feelings, bodily sensations, memories, and ideas into greater sensory proximity (1957). And he fostered a therapeutic alliance, enhancing the children's investment and their willingness to take creative risks (Ulman, 1987). Henry Schaeffer-Simmern (1948) also emphasized sensory involvement: "Even the simplest drawing, so long as it is the result of visual conceiving, always points to the producer's relationship to the subject represented. It is this innermost connection between subject matter and artistic form which assures the organic unfolding of one's inherent creative capacities" (p. 154).

Art therapy in educational settings began in earnest with the work of Edith Kramer, who documented her "art as therapy" approach at the Wiltwyck School (1958). Her pioneering work with these disturbed children centered upon harnessing the drives in the service of the ego, in order to achieve maturational growth and sublimation through the art process—ideas which are central to the therapeutic curriculum.

 #28

written book about focusing on art process vs. product

☐ Case Background and Setting

In order to illustrate the therapeutic curriculum, I return to Mel, and a composite of one day of programming in a public school envisioned as an alternative to behaviorally-based special education programs. It was designed for children 5–21, whose emotional and behavioral issues made it difficult for them to function in regular programs. A bright, creative, and fascinating teen, Mel's intractably negative behaviors had led to a series of failed placements in both public and private schools. His was a complex clinical picture, with symptoms associated with ADHD (Attention Deficit Disorder with Hyperactivity) and immature forms of both borderline and bipolar disorders. Emotionally, Mel functioned at an arrested level of development, with frequent regressions.

His ADHD symptoms included hyperactivity, impulsivity, inattention to tedious or low-reward tasks (most school work), and frequent mood swings. Mel also suffered from a body-ego disturbance, impulsively invading the personal space of his teachers and peers, who complained that he was "always in their face." There were also bouts of self-injurious behavior, particularly when his bottomless need for attention was rebuffed. At times, Mel would become verbally abusive, turn his aggression toward himself or others, or withdraw.

Like many troubled teens, Mel often attempted to self-medicate with recreational drugs. The after-effects of these binges ranged from nasty, groggy moods to hair plucking, skin picking, and cutting. Like others with similar disorders, Mel possessed "islands" of ability, with unusually strong world knowledge (he read and watched the news avidly), and a capacity for insight. His precocious drafting ability was complemented by a ferocious sense of sarcasm. His hard-hitting caricatures and cartoons of teachers and administrators revealed astute powers of observation and criticism. This ability to lampoon others awarded him special status in the social hierarchy of his peers.

In this program, I was a "teacher/therapist," meaning that I was to implement both educational and therapeutic initiatives as part of an interdisciplinary support team. Since this was an alternative progressive school, I was free to write curricula which infused the arts therapies into every facet of the school day. Treatment approaches were also eclectic—behavioral, cognitive, object relations, psychodynamic—implemented when appropriate to the situation, as I shall now illustrate.

☐ The Therapeutic Curriculum Illustrated

The opening moments of the school day were, like any time of transition, marked with high anxiety and low productivity. The students filtered in huddling and chatting, recounting "war stories" about the night's adventures, and exchanging social gossip. To allow for—yet contain—such discharge, a morning ritual of hot drinks, snacks, and taped music videos served to ease the transition. Eventually, the students were called to order, and told the plan of the day.

First Hour: Generating Ideas and Issues

Each academic day began with current events, with the entire class perusing the *New York Times*. Sipping tea and thumbing through the paper, we resembled a large family in the midst of a morning routine. Beyond cementing community ties, this ritual helped to contain distracted, unsettled, or agitated behavior. For those who were bleary-eyed, staring at the paper—even if only at sports scores or TV listings—camouflaged inactivity through appropriate means.

The *Times* also provided content they could relate to, since the news is full of lurid but compelling material involving sex and violence. The stories served as conduits for their own projections and anxieties, through real life factual material. The *Times* also offered a model of how to transform provocative content in an understated and poetic way. The vocabulary sets a standard, particularly since the writing style in the *Times* has become more casual.

In the opening vignette, I described how Mel latched on to the article on the anniversary of the Dresden bombing. His self-selected topic may have acted as a metaphor for his own anxieties—over fears of annihilation and the ultimate authority of those in power. Like his peers, Mel did not always reach such high levels. Emotionally disturbed children typically oscillate between different modes of functioning, depending on inner resources. More often than not, the child's weak ego leads to aborted attempts or chaotic discharge of drive energy, which may preclude the culmination of the process in a product (Kramer, 1971).

Second Hour: Finding Issues in the Classics

The second hour involved bibliotherapy, in which the students read literary classics, works chosen for their relevance to teens, as well as for their academic content. Often issues were projected onto the characters, especially through identification with the aggressor or the victim.

One day the group viewed a video of the play they had been reading— Shakespeare's *Henry V*—a sprawling historical epic of violence, loyalty, and political intrigue, as the young man struggles to mature into a King. There is a moment in the play when King Harry has to confront a childhood friend, Bardolph, a loving but hopelessly alcoholic character, brought to him on charges of looting a French church during the battle of Agincourt. Despite affection for his old friend, Harry had to put his kingly duty before personal loyalty, and Bardolph was sentenced to hang. Mel took his turn to read: "we will have all such offenders cut off. For when lenity and cruelty play for a kingdom, the gentler gamester is the soonest winner."

As the old man was strung up, the King made tearful eye contact, and memories of their lives together flashed before his eyes. A few students, including Mel, were clearly moved by this passage. Most related it to times when they too had to decide whether or not to expose a guilty friend, in order to protect themselves or their peer group.

Invited to write or draw about this issue, Mel produced Figure 21.2, in which King Harry faces his audience with clenched fists, choked with emotion, but resolute in his actions. To his left, the executioner wields his broad sword to show support for the King. Poor Bardolph is shown hanging, left as an example to others to abide by their society's code of ethics. A cross seems to bear down upon the King's back as it slants toward the corpse, as well as another on the King's cloak— symbols referring perhaps to hopes for redemption or salvation, though it is not clear whether it is sought for the victim, the king, or both. Whatever its symbolism, Mel had engaged a metaphor of archetypal proportions, and defended against pressures exerted by the primary process.

Despite the urgency and evocative nature of the theme, Mel maintained an intact narrative and realistic drawing style. Although drawing the death of the King's childhood

Figure 21.2.

friend might have sparked his own self-destructive tendencies or fears of annihilation, these seemed neutralized in his academic yet evocative treatment of the subject. The choice of colored pencils may have also supported the containment of his emotions and conflicts. Since both intellect as well as emotion were simultaneously engaged, this activity probably bolstered his tenuous ego.

The drawing represented higher-order defensive measures indicative of sublimation, wherein drive energy is partially neutralized. The vignette exemplifies one aspect of this approach, as the ego is supported in its bid to relieve strong internal pressures, through a form that remains personally powerful yet socially meaningful. For the piece was not only a document of personal insight; it was also valued by the group. Like all powerful art, it stood as a collective truth for Mel's peers to share.

Third Hour: Focusing Ideas

During the third hour, students were encouraged to develop ideas stimulated by individual readings or group activities. One day, Mel decided to follow up on another article from the *Times* about the reintroduction of wolves to Yellowstone Park after 70 years of extirpation. During the class discussion, Mel had taken the position that nature should take precedence over short-term human economic needs. He declared that "a bounty on the skins of offensive people might provide a lesson in tolerance." I encouraged him to direct his passion to several resources on hand in the classroom, like Lopez's (1978) study of wolf/human behavior.

Perusing this book, Mel became interested in wolf mythology, particularly the story of Romulus and Remus, the Roman wolf children. I directed him next to Candland's (1993) study of reported instances of wolves actually raising human babies along with wolf siblings. Engrossed in these tales of feral children (like the wild boy of Aveyron), Mel lifted an image from the Lopez book. From a medieval manuscript, it shows a she-wolf carrying off a boy (Figure 21.3). Mel joked about whether this odd couple might be accepted by the Yellowstone pack. Turning serious, Mel lamented that adopted cubs were often ostracized or even killed by the pack.

Using the book's illustrations, Mel sketched a series of postures (tail raising, teeth baring, bowing), any of which might signal acceptance or rejection. He then drew parallels to life in the classroom, where the "alpha" or dominant males influenced whether he—who was overweight and unattractive—was considered fair game for teasing or acceptance as a peer. Mel observed how the alpha male was sometimes challenged by other aggressors, creating an atmosphere of uncertainty and tension in the class until the hierarchy was again stabilized—just like in the wolf-pack. Mel then referred to his drawn she-wolf as an "alpha" in her own right, capable of vigilant protection and tender nurturance.

Perhaps he used this topic as a way to work out his own position in the class, always a source of anxiety. Given Mel's abandonment issues and continued neediness for parental attention, his image also speaks clearly of an all-powerful mother. Note the special care with which he modeled the alpha she-wolf, who firmly yet gently holds him in her jaws. For Mel, there was a fine line between maternal engulfment/annihilation and maternal "holding," nurturance, and care. Judging from the figure's grin, the quality of attachment seems to be one of bliss rather than fear.

Although the material had stirred anxiety over social status and maternal care, in researching the subject Mel seemed to gain a measure of mastery. Naumburg wrote (1947, 1966) that the image fixes in time and space unconscious material that would otherwise remain evanescent —hence, insight and maturational growth become a possibility

A Drawing from midieval manuscript shows a werewolf grasping a human victim

Figure 21.3.

during such an art therapy experience. In this case, mastery came in the form of marshaling powers of reason via the cognitive domain (Silver, 1978), to neutralize potentially overwhelming unconscious forces.

Fourth Hour: Overcoming Resistance to Writing

In language arts, writing of any kind can be agonizing for students with emotional or learning difficulties. Faced with assignments like journaling or critical essays, compliance often declines, with the barest effort being expended. Even creative writing requires extra stimulation in order for disturbed students to stay on task. Lowenfeld (1982) taught that students can often overcome resistance when given a novel motivation to fuel their efforts. Phototherapy was such a stimulus, introduced to help the class compose visual ideas, which could then be translated into prose.

The first task was to learn to truly "see," using the camera's lens as a viewfinder. I showed them the work of artists, like painter Georgia O'Keefe and photographer Alfred Steiglitz, who used devices such as cropping, framing, and magnifying images. Small supervised groups were then allowed to explore the school with cameras, in search of suitable material to photograph.

Most of the students handled the freedom well, but even with close monitoring, Mel barged loudly into the general office where he found the principal. He then thrust the camera into the principal's face, and began to shoot. Although he followed the requirements, cropping the portrait in an interesting way, the print (Figure 21.4) accurately captures the principal's distressed feelings about having his personal space invaded.

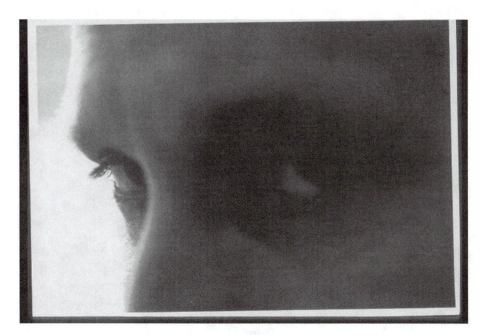

Figure 21.4.

After the contact sheets were developed and enlarged, Mel composed a prose poem about the mask-like portrait. His choice of the principal alluded, once again, to issues of power and authority. But this loaded subject precipitated more incursions of primary process material, as his writing took on a delusional, even paranoid, quality. In the flowing free-verse of his poem, Mel described the principal as "a restroom spy with unnatural hearing and smell, who knew everything one did in there, yes, you could hear him laughing and whispering through the toilet stall," etc.

Upon reading the draft of his wild verse, I offered some suggestions intended to tone down its exaggerated quality. The next version was not only unchanged, but had escalated to include sexual obscenities. Mel was soon out of control, brashly reading his work aloud to the class. I cautioned him that he was now in violation of the "private expression rule" (Henley, 1992, 1995), which stipulated that creations of a graphically obscene or violent nature could exist only in privacy. No form of exhibition would be permitted, since such work might disturb others or be detrimental to the school community. Therefore, I calmly stated, the work in its present state needed to be censored. Disregarding this warning, Mel continued to perform the poem, ad libbing in different voices, to the delight of his peers.

As part of Mel's individualized education plan (IEP), he was subject to a mutually agreed upon behavioral contract, which spelled out the contingency plan for dealing with out-of-control behavior. After several cues to regain control himself went unheard, Mel was asked to relocate to the time-out area. In defiance, he stood inches from my face, mimed blowing smoke at me, and again refused. A "code" was called (as per school policy), and reinforcements arrived to escort him to time-out (a cubicle in the hallway). Mel's passions had been aroused to the point that he lost self-control, bringing into question the stimulation of the activity.

Figure 21.5.

Fifth Hour: Behavioral Consequences

Because Mel was able to relocate without becoming assaultive, his contract permitted him to take his pen and sketchbook into time-out. He drew quietly for most of the hour's "cool-down" period. After convincing me that he could handle returning to the group, he was welcomed back to class. During his period of seclusion, Mel had produced several images alluding to our confrontation (Figure 21.5). He drew himself looming over me, about to flick an ash in my face, as his shirt exclaims "No Life!" His broad stance, threatening gesture, and troubled expression all capture his defiant posturing. Again, Mel was able to show some ego strength: the form of the drawing remains remarkably intact, despite conveying strong emotion. This extraordinary caricature was drawn in one continuous, elegant contour line. His confident drafting, the dramatic perspective, and its complex layers of meaning, all contribute to the work's expressive power.

Typically, Mel presented the drawing to me without comment, yet his demeanor suggested that it was meant to be a conciliatory gesture. In using a drawing to express his contrition, he was able to bypass authority issues and "save face." By using the language of art to communicate the depths of his suffering, Mel was able to accomplish a "supreme act of integration" through a work which fits Kramer's (1971) definition of "formed expression." The drawing possesses an economy of means, a sense of inner consistency and truth, as well as conveying an emotional charge and power with which others can identify. The sum of these successful elements suggests that sublimation had been achieved.

The second picture of the series (Figure 21.6) is more regressed, with the mood of defiance deflating into resignation and self-pity. References to childlike self-soothing surround him: a ring toss, blocks, a walkman, all coexist with an inventive use of

Figure 21.6.

descriptive text. While the content of the work is more raw, this takes nothing away from the image as a form of cathartic release and a further achievement of formed expression.

It was perhaps the resilience of our therapeutic alliance which allowed these contradictory feelings to be fully expressed, as they were "held" without my judgment or placing blame. Indeed, it was I who had overstimulated Mel with the photo project. With all of us taking some responsibility for the meltdown, Mel was welcomed back with a clean slate, and encouraged to take his rightful place in the class.

Discussion

In a 1917 paper entitled "A Direct Method of Education" Naumburg wrote: "Up to the present time, education has missed the real significance of the child's behavior, by treating surface actions as isolated conditions. Having failed to recognize the true sources of behavior, it has been unable to effectively correct and guide the impulses of human growth" (Frank, 1983, p. 113).

In the case vignettes, we see an illustration of Naumburg's tenet. Throughout each of the activities, Mel's issues were recognized as an integral part of his overall learning experience. The themes stimulated both fresh ideas and long-standing conflicts, which sometimes provoked Mel into losing control over his behavior.

Yet this provocative process is also at the center of the therapeutic curriculum—to take creative and therapeutic risks, in order to elicit impassioned participation and ply the depths of causation, as Naumburg had urged. At the same time however, there is an emphasis on self-control, self-monitoring, and social responsibility. The dynamic tension that exists between these two is an integral part of the approach. An expected outcome of the personal relevance component is that disturbing responses are likely to be elicited. And one must use caution when using themes as motivational stimuli that may tap into a child's issues.

A tragic example is the case of Kip Kinkel, who in 1999 murdered his parents and several classmates after years of emotional suffering. Just prior to his killing spree, Kinkel's high-school teacher had taught Shakespeare's "Romeo and Juliet" using an MTV-style film version, in addition to reading the play. Set in contemporary Los Angeles, the rival families are shown as barrio gangs, whose unbridled gunplay and violence captured the students' imaginations—and became an obsession for Kinkel. When police entered the home and found the slain parents, their grim search was set to music. Kip had left the film's soundtrack on continuous play at top volume. The eerie music enveloped the officers, its themes creating a dramatic backdrop to the crime. As an educational intervention, the teacher had chosen a powerful stimulus—one that engaged this student's interest in ways that had unforeseen and tragic consequences.

Acknowledging the potential power of such stimuli, we need to utilize children's capacity for reason as a way to cope with provocative themes. By engaging the intellect, cognitive therapeutic approaches can be used to bolster self-reflection while objectifying potentially disturbing material. Distorted belief systems, irrational worries, and skewed perceptions can all be tempered through intellectual inquiry. Hence, when Mel became worked up over current events, world history, or literature, he was drawing upon his intellect to process and defuse his own issues as well.

When intellectual approaches fail to neutralize the overwhelming emotions of children with weak egos, however, we can expect regression and breakdowns of impulse control. Behavioral approaches may then need to be pressed into service. As with Mel, this might take the form of a mutually agreed upon contract, spelling out contingency plans for dealing with acting out behavior. He understood that we would negotiate and accommodate acting out for only so long, before action would be taken. Because of his problems with limits, their parameters needed to be crystal clear. Only then could Mel anticipate the consequences of his actions and feel secure, even when out of control. With limits set, we could do our work with fewer regressions and a strengthened therapeutic alliance.

A solid alliance with Mel enabled me to set limits when necessary, while not doing fatal damage to our rapport. As he tended to vilify me as the all-bad "mother," it was critical to absorb this negative transference and to convey a sense of forgiveness after each incident. Emphasis was always placed on his returning to class with a blank slate and a fresh start.

Yet, even with this response, Mel's splitting defenses often remained mobilized. Figure 21.7 reflects what a strain it was for him to maintain our alliance, especially when we were in conflict. This image was presented to me the morning after a particularly bitter confrontation. In Mel's dream I loom over him, imperiously gesturing, while he sweats out the nightmare under the covers. I declare that Mel is in a "no cue situation," meaning that his behavior had escalated to the point that no further warnings would be given before he would be removed from the class.

I was represented as the voice of the auxiliary ego and the superego. That Mel carried our behavior contract with him into the realm of primary process, attests to the gravity of these struggles, as they fully engaged his psyche. The program had become internalized for this child, which I believe contributed to its therapeutic efficacy.

Figure 21.7.

☐ Conclusion

The approach described in this chapter is not simply a matter of practicing art therapy in educational settings as a clinical support service (cf. Bush, 1997). In the therapeutic curriculum, work is not separate from the academic experience, but is an ongoing process integrating a range of expressive modalities: art, photography, poetry, and bibliotherapy.

The mission of the therapeutic curriculum is to support a child within the "least restrictive environment" as stipulated by the mainstreaming law. My interpretation of this statute is that the content of academic courses should include elements of emotional problem solving. Only then can the school experience address the whole child on a sustained basis. Given that school lasts for 12 years (up to 16 in special education), long term therapeutic work can be accomplished. This stands in stark contrast to the "revolving door" that characterizes profit-driven HMO's.

The therapeutic curriculum can also be adapted to assist the "normal" school child in coping with life's stresses and transitions, without diluting academic rigor. For children whose problems remain at subthreshold levels and do not require IEP accommodations, a more empathic approach may also enhance their adjustment and motivation. Rather than being a means of damage control after symptoms of maladjustment appear, the therapeutic curriculum can be proactive and preventive. And the work goes on all the time as part of normal school activity.

I have also used the therapeutic curriculum in a summer camp setting with ADHD children, who became adept at utilizing metaphors during ordinary group activities (Henley, 1999). For example, after leading a fishing expedition with a group of bright seven-year olds, I asked them whether they'd ever felt "like a fish out of water." They immediately grasped the connection between their own anxieties and those of the fish— which they had caught and put into the camp's aquarium. They were able to project their feelings onto the fish, and to explore instances where they felt alienated, isolated, or abandoned. They made pictures about being afraid to be left overnight at Grandma's, having to move to a new house, or having new step-siblings when their parents remarried. Expressions of great profundity were generated by an otherwise unremarkable summer camp activity.

Ideally, the therapeutic curriculum intervenes during formative stages of development, wherein we hope to promote healthy coping capacities that will endure into adulthood. For it is our children who will inherit and define the future health of our culture and, indeed, the world.

☐ References

Bush, J. (1997). *A handbook for school-art therapy: Introducing art therapy into a public school system.* Springfield, IL: Charles C. Thomas.

Candland, K. C. (1993). *Feral children and clever animals.* New York & London: Oxford University Press.

Cane, F. (1951). *The artist in each of us.* Craftsbury Common, VT: Art Therapy Publications. (Reprinted in 1983)

Dewey, J. (1916). *Democracy and education.* New York: MacMillan.

Dewey, J. (1934). *Art as experience.* New York: Minton Books.

Frank, T. (1983). Margaret Naumburg, pioneer art therapist: A son's perspective. *American Journal of Art Therapy* 22(4), p. 113.

Henley, D. (1992). *Exceptional children: Exceptional art.* Worcester, MA: Davis.

Henley, D. (1995). Political correctness in the artroom: When limits get pushed. *Art Education*, *48*(2), 57–66.

Henley, D. (1997). Expressive arts therapy as alternative education: Devising a therapeutic curriculum. *Art Therapy*, *14*(1), 15–22.

Henley, D. (1998). Art therapy as an aid to socialization in children with attention deficits. *American Journal of Art Therapy*, *16*(3), 2–12.

Henley, D. (1999). Facilitating socialization within a therapeutic camp setting for children with attention deficits. *American Journal of Art Therapy*, *37*(2), 40–50.

Itard, J. (1962). *The wild boy of Aveyron.* New York: Appleton-Century-Crofts. (Original Work Published 1802)

Kramer, E. (1958). *Art therapy in a children's community.* Springfield, IL: Charles C. Thomas.

Kramer, E. (1971). *Art as therapy with children.* New York: Schocken Press.

Lopez, B. H. (1978). *Of wolves and men.* New York: Scribner.

Lowenfeld, V. (1939). *The nature of creative activity.* London: Routledge.

Lowenfeld, V. (1957). *Creative and mental growth* (3rd ed.). New York: Macmillan.

Lowenfeld, V. (1982). *The Lowenfeld lectures* (J. A. Michael, Editor). University Park, PA: Penn State Press.

Naumburg, M. (1917). *A direct method of education* (Bulletin No. 4). New York: Bureau of Educational Experiments.

Naumburg, M. (1947). Studies of the free art expression of behavior in problem children in diagnosis and therapy. *Nervous & Mental Disease Monograph* No. 71. (Reprinted in 1973 as *Introduction to art therapy*. New York: Teachers College Press)

Naumburg, M. (1966). *Dynamically oriented art therapy.* New York: Grune & Stratton.

Schaeffer-Simmern, H. (1948). *The unfolding of artistic activity.* Berkeley: University of California Press.

Silver, R. (1978). *Developing cognitive and creative skills through art.* Baltimore: University Park Press.

Ulman, E. (1987). Introduction to "Therapeutic aspects of art education" by Viktor Lowenfeld. *American Journal of Art Therapy*, *25*, 111–112.

COMMENTARY

Robert Ault

Following dinner the three couples retired to the living room for coffee and conversation. All of us were mental health professionals, and as we talked the conversation got around to psychoanalysis, and the discovery that we had all been analyzed at Menningers. We began to compare notes, and found that we had each had very different experiences and perceptions of the analytic process, although it had been carefully crafted with the same philosophical foundations and technique. I offered that my analyst had never in four years acknowledged that he had seen one of my paintings. Another said his analyst hardly ever spoke, while another said he couldn't get a word in edgewise. To our astonishment, we discovered that the most glaring variable in this presumably highly structured treatment process was the personality of the analyst.

As I reflected on the similarities and differences among the chapters in this section, I was reminded of that evening. Having known the authors for many years, it seemed to me that the greatest consistency was with the personalities of the therapists. Each described the importance of a "holding environment," which all created very well; yet they varied not only as dictated by patient needs, but also by their individual personalities.

It is not something that is talked about much in theoretical descriptions of clinical work, yet it is there; and Elinor Ulman and Harriet Wadeson allude to it in their chapters. It is something each art therapy educator struggles through with each student, for the real core of the work may depend as much on what you *are* as a human being, as on what you *know* of theory and technique. It always seemed to me that the best service I could provide to a student was to help them find a way of doing art therapy that was consistent with who they were as individuals.

The overall theme of the chapters in this section is the integration of art making into the therapeutic process of art therapy. In each, engagement in a creative endeavor—using one or more art forms—is integral to the healing process. I have always believed that the healing power of the creative process, as it is played out in art therapy, is the engagement of both patient and therapist, in an exploration that demands the courage of risk and pain to which each is willing to commit.

I once worked with a young man who had been hospitalized several times, and had had several unsuccessful attempts at therapy. They sent him to art therapy as a last resort. There, we made art, but some days we drove around in a van, listened to rock music, and fished. He refused to talk about his problems or his abandonment by his father. I wasn't sure what I was doing, and felt guilty charging for such poor "psychotherapy," but I did observe that he seemed to get better.

At his discharge conference, I described what had gone on, as well as my puzzlement about the outcome. The consultant on the case commented: "Do you know how hard it is to find a therapist who can tolerate *not* doing therapy?" He went on to say that at times one needs not only to *talk about* metaphors, but to be willing to *enter into* the metaphor itself. I believe the arts, as well as the other activities, contributed to this patient's success in finding meaning, and in resolving those forces that were tearing up his life.

As I read the chapters in this section, I often found myself thinking "Yes, I know what you mean. Been there, done that!" At other times, I had a hard time imagining how something would possibly work with some of the patients I see. For example, I use music, but more often as a background than as an active element in the process. I am sometimes accused of playing "elevator music for a mortuary." Such music is intended to lessen stimulation, rather then elevating it, for often the patients are already hyper-stimulated, and tend to disintegrate or regress in a heightened environment. It is easier to open them up than it is to integrate an experience for them in a meaningful way. I am thinking of those with schizophrenia or post-traumatic stress disorder; how fragile they are at times, and how they often shy away or withdraw even further into themselves. "Pandora's Box" for them would not be an opening to the treasures of inner life, but to the terror of their worst nightmares.

For creative imagination to work as an integrating "intelligence," as Shaun McNiff proposes, there has to be a degree of reality testing and other ego functions available in order for it to be a positive experience. Many patients speak enthusiastically of the "release"—even "exorcism"—they feel in group arts activities, yet they may also regress. I recently treated a nun who experienced a group using art and music as a turning point in her life, but it was followed by a need to be hospitalized and stabilized. We spent much time integrating this event, which was indeed seen as a "special life experience," but one she was not fully prepared to assimilate. McNiff wisely cautions the reader by describing how important it is for the therapist to create a safe "holding environment."

David Henley also speaks about how all of the arts can be integrated into the education of children with special needs. He describes how he attempts to help youngsters to open up in a highly structured holding environment. The thought and creativity that go into the daily task of fostering both maturation and sublimation are surely very taxing on the therapist, and I was reminded of just how hard the work really is when done right.

While reading this chapter, I also recalled a time I looked up the word "see" in the dictionary. There was a list of 23 different meanings and uses, and our speech is filled with them. I don't believe it is an accident that our language is so rich in referring to visualizing as understanding—such as "Do you *see* what I mean?" or, "Do you *understand*?" It makes a great deal of sense to integrate visualization techniques into academic activities.

Flying back to Kansas one evening, I found myself sitting next to a pilot with many years' experience. I asked him if he ever felt flying to be a routine business with much repetition. He answered, "No. Every time I get at the end of the runway and push the throttles forward, it's a whole new ball game." I have often thought of his remark and my own work as an art therapist for over 40 years. Each new patient is a new course of challenge and exploration. I get to hear the stories and share the deepest of human convictions, conflicts, and spirit. It is an opportunity to create, and to be in the presence of the energy that comes from sharing this. It is the wonderful integration of all I know as an artist and all I have learned as a therapist. When asked by students; "How do you know what to do?" I can answer with ease, "Don't worry, just watch and listen; the patient will help you."

CONCLUSION

Judith Rubin

*As· a psychotherapist I found it particularly heartening that the use of art in therapy seems to have the effect of reducing the differences between Freudians, Jungians, Kleinians, and adherents of other schools. . . . Art not only bridges the gap between the inner and outer worlds but also seems to **span the gulf between different theoretical positions.** (Anthony Storr)*

Most people are attracted to art therapy because they like both art and human beings, and they tend to be curious, as well as compassionate and creative. For some individuals, their curiosity extends beyond understanding the people they see and the art that is made, to the creative process that seems to work so well in healing. This very combination can make theory-building endlessly fascinating.

Since, in many ways, art therapy is still "a technique in search of a theory," it has been fortunate that restless thinkers, like the authors in this book, enjoy the challenge of theorizing. All of them have worked out ways of applying theoretical constructs— by synthesizing what they know about the therapeutic power of art with what they understand about one or more theories of psychotherapy.

The question of which theoretical framework(s) any art therapist ought to adopt is not unique to me or to this book. Although the debate continues, almost all of us agree with Elinor Ulman that "art therapy ought to be applicable to any endeavor that genuinely partakes of both art and therapy" (1961, p. 13). This broad-based definition leaves considerable leeway for a variety of viewpoints, like those presented in this volume.

Equally important, it highlights the two elements whose synthesis is the essence of our work: art + therapy. And it reminds us that, while art alone may be highly therapeutic and therapy alone can be very artistic, art therapy is the product of a marriage between the two. Perhaps the most critical issue for practicing art therapists is just how to make that marriage one in which neither partner loses its identity.

For that reason, the question of how to relate one's identity as an artist to one's identity as a therapist will always be vital. As Bob Ault once asked, "If someone shook you awake at 3:00 in the morning and asked 'Are you an artist or a therapist?' how would you answer?" (1977, p. 53). Arthur Robbins, addressing a recent graduate, sensitively stated: "You do not want to see yourself as a psychotherapist. The smell of paint and sense of excitement about the art room moves in your arteries, and you have a strong identification with your fellow artists. Consequently, you search for constructs that

---

For a more detailed history of the discussion of theory within the American art therapy community between 1970 and 1983, see the Conclusion of the first edition of this book.

resonate with your experience as an artist, as the technical notions of psychotherapy seem alien and have the ring of jargon" (1981, p. 2).

One of the most striking developments in the field during the past decade has been a return to the studio, and the development of a variety of studio-based approaches, like the one described by Pat Allen in her chapter. At least two other new chapters, those by Rogers and McNiff, describe group art activities in a studio setting. And a recent book on *Art Therapy* by Cathy Moon (2001) is subtitled *Cultivating the Artist Identity in the Art Therapist*.

Most art therapists, including many authors in this book, yearn to find meaning in their work and to do it well, without abandoning their creative core. Some use their own art to stimulate patients to be more creative, as in Silver's Stimulus Drawings. Some make art along with their clients, like Lachman-Chapin or Allen. Others focus on the liberation possible through creating free and spontaneous art, like Rogers or McNiff. And yet others stress the potential strengthening of making formed expression, like Kramer or Henley.

For most, regardless of orientation, creativity is synonymous with mental health in that both reflect the capacity to be freely in charge, whether of materials or of the self. In fact, it was a playful psychoanalyst named Donald W. Winnicott who wrote: "It is only in being creative that the individual discovers the self" (1971).

Winnicott's (1971) concept of the "holding environment" is one that is referred to by many contributors to this book, since it describes the kind of space essential for authentic creativity as well as growth. His appeal to non-analytic art therapists is probably based on the fact that he was so creative as a therapist, as in his invention and use of the "Squiggle Game," a graphic way to communicate with patients.

Jung, like Winnicott, is cited by many contributors who are not analytically oriented. His understanding of what I would call the "*creative unconscious*," and his reverence for the image have a powerful appeal for art therapists. Jung, who built, drew, and painted as part of his own self-analysis, was also an artistic theorist. A minister's son, he stressed the mystical and spiritual elements in analytic therapy; whereas Freud, a rationalist, was determined to prove the scientific validity of the radical new depth psychology.

Ironically, both polarities are more important in mental health than ever before. Psychobiological approaches dominate contemporary psychiatry, while neuroscience and cognitive-behavioral therapy currently dominate psychology. At the same time, in a technological world of virtual realities, where human values and connections often seem to have been lost, the hunger for meaning has intensified. Spiritual and transpersonal approaches have grown in popularity among healers in all disciplines, and are evident in the self-help materials hungrily lapped up by the public.

Art therapy, drawing as art has from time immemorial on the human spirit, offers a wonderfully appropriate and appealing avenue for authentic expressions of the human soul. Even the most rational among us knows of the deep inner well from which we draw when we express ourselves. And although we operate from many different perspectives, one that cuts across all of our theoretical differences is that of the human spirit, which is so essential to our creative capacity. I believe that art is indeed the signature of the soul, and that what we create are "*soul prints*."

Yet, as you have seen, each of the art therapists in this book has a slightly different idea of how to go about using art to help human beings to free their souls and to live more fully. In addition to the virtues of the theories themselves, two major variables in theory selection have been identified: the patient and the therapist, both of which play a role in the theoretical equation developed by each of us.

Arthur Robbins felt a need to look beyond analytic theories stressing sublimation, largely because of his experiences with psychotic and borderline patients who were unable to sublimate. Mildred Lachman-Chapin emphasizes the special relevance of self psychology for work with those whose problems began in the earliest months and years of life. In contrast, Janie Rhyne notes that the confrontational and demanding approach of Gestalt art therapy is not for those whose psychological state is too fragile, a point Bob Ault also makes about Shaun McNiff's approach.

There is a parallel in the history of how different theories evolved. "One source of difference between schools of psychotherapy that is often overlooked and which needs to be made explicit is the difference in types of patients on which the founders of the different schools based their initial observations" (Stein, 1961, p. 6). After citing some well-known examples (like Freud seeing hysterics and Sullivan schizophrenics), the author goes on to draw the logical conclusion: "With these differences in basic data and sources of observation, it is not surprising that each school should develop its own special theory and technique (pg. 6)." It therefore makes sense that "one school might well have a good deal more to say about one specific type of patient than another" (p. 7)—or, one might add, about one aspect of a patient rather than another.

Many therapists believe that there is a "need for different theories to deal with different sets of empirical data [and that] ... no single theory is fully sufficient to order even one set of clinical observations" (Gedo & Goldberg, 1973, p. 172). The idea is that different models of the mind fit different patients, as well as the same patient functioning at different developmental levels at different times (cf. Rothstein, 1985). Schaverien's commentary makes this point in another way, articulating the contribution of each psychodynamic approach to her work with a single patient.

Listening Perspectives in Psychotherapy (Hedges, 1983) clarifies the importance of being able to hear a patient's communications in terms appropriate to their etiological source. The author defines *"listening perspectives"* as different *"clinical frames of reference,"* which provide a "backdrop" for hearing patients' verbalizations. A recent book on *"learning to listen from multiple perspectives"* (Frederickson, 1999) also articulates different ways of listening, based on different aspects of psychoanalytic theory.

In addition to understanding what is being *said*, art therapists need to develop an appropriate set of *"looking perspectives,"* so that we can look each time in a way that truly fits the process or product in front of us. Indeed, just as the same behavior can have different meanings depending on the theoretical filter through which it is perceived, the same painting, sculpture, or creative process can have different meanings, depending on the theoretical lens through which it is viewed.

In the two chapters explicitly dealing with the problem of selection among different theories, both authors stress the related importance of the style of the individual therapist, as do commentators Bob Ault and Shirley Riley. Just as theoreticians develop ideas that fit their personalities and ways of working, so anyone's way of being an art therapist must be synchronous with one's authentic self. It is really impossible to "put on" any approach that does not comfortably "fit."

In finding a "goodness of fit," however, we need to be careful that the theory and methodology we espouse does not conceal unrecognized needs or conflicts within ourselves. It is all too easy, especially if one is articulate, to find or create a theoretical rationale for almost any therapeutic stance.

And to the extent that our theory, as well as our practice, is determined by forces of which we are unaware, then it is no more than an externalization of our own intrapsychic issues. Insofar as we have, usually through our own therapy, come to know and to accept these forces, we can hopefully be in charge of them.

We can then try to evaluate them objectively, in light of what we know and understand about the human and artistic needs of those with whom we work. Only after this step of self-analysis, are we ready to think or talk about the mature and creative use of the self in art therapy. The next step toward that goal is to be open-minded—about how one perceives what is happening, how one approaches the patient, and what one does in response. However, an *open* mind is not an *empty* one. It is a mind truly open to seeing and hearing what is being presented, perhaps through some of the various theoretical lenses in this book.

It makes sense that the more familiar one is with different possible ways of seeing and hearing, the more likely it should be to truly see and hear what is actually there. Of course, there are times when we simply cannot perceive the signal, like the pitch of animal sounds that are beyond the range of human hearing. More often, however, we *could* see and hear what is there, but are unable to do so because we do not *know* a frame of reference (a theory) that would make it possible. One goal of this book is to increase the number of "lenses" art therapists are able to put into their clinical "frames," to multiply the number of "listening and looking perspectives" potentially available to each clinician, so that they can receive, perceive, and conceive as well as possible.

In addition to allowing the art therapist to *see* more, different approaches allow the patient to *say* more, to make a wider variety of statements about themselves. This is powerfully demonstrated in a film which has been used extensively in the training of psychotherapists, *Three Approaches to Psychotherapy* (Shostrom, 1965). In it, a woman named Gloria is interviewed successively by three clinicians with different perspectives and technical approaches—Carl Rogers (Client-Centered), Fritz Perls (Gestalt), and Albert Ellis (Rational-Emotive).

The different personalities of the three men are, as one would expect, consonant with their theoretical views. But what is most fascinating is that each of them evokes a somewhat distinct aspect of the client. While clearly the same person throughout, Gloria expresses different facets of herself in response to each of the three interviewers. That this happens with art as well was demonstrated when both Edith Kramer and I interviewed the same child within a month at Walter Reed Army Hospital in 1979. It is clear in the two videotaped interviews that, like Gloria, this youngster revealed different facets of herself in her art and behavior with each of us.

So there is a lot to be said for having access to different ways of thinking about and doing therapy through art. Yet paradoxically, in spite of the multidimensional value of multiple lenses, there is also much to be said for the enthusiastic embrace of at least one well-known and well-digested approach.

> The notion of a general synthesis or integration usually communicates to the student the need to be cautious, take all points of view into consideration, and to avoid emotional involvement with a particular, one-sided position. ... Contrary to this conception, we recommend strongly that students should, once they have surveyed available theories of personality, adopt a vigorous and affectionate acceptance of a particular theoretical position without reservation. Let the individual be enthusiastic and imbued with the theory before beginning to examine it critically." (Hall & Lindzey, 1977, p. 705)

Not only does such an embrace of one theory make sense logically, it makes even more sense *psychologically*, in regard to each art therapist. The importance of finding a way of working that suits the individual has been noted repeatedly, and cannot be emphasized too strongly.

A person must find a theory which is sympathetic to his best talents, whether they be inter-pretive, poetic, directive or such. If he doesn't do so, he will be inept, or more likely, phony. . . . The primary question about the "rightness" of a style is whether one accepts responsibility for the consequences he evokes and is skillful in facing them . . . . Certainly, [one] should be aware of the unlikelihood of discovering *the* single [best] technique." (Polster, 1966, p. 5)

As for the search for the single best "technique" in art therapy, I think family art therapy pioneer Hanna Kwiatkowska said it best. My strong conviction is that *"the only technique of art therapy is the technique of relating to a patient through art"* (Levy et al., 1974, p. 17). Kwiatkowska felt that the numerous "technical maneuvers," which continue to explode on the art therapy scene, stemmed largely from clinicians' anxiety about what would happen if things were left more open. Whatever the cause, the reader would do well to look carefully at the approaches described in this book. Regardless of theoretical orientation, even the most prescriptive are carefully designed to promote the patient's own creative participation in the making of his or her own art.

There have always been and will always be individual art therapists who enjoy think-ing theoretically, like Aina Nucho (1987), Vija Lusebrink (1990), Diane Waller (1993), and Paolo Knill (1995), who have all devoted substantial time to that effort in recent years. Nevertheless, there has also been considerable resistance within art therapy to theoriz-ing, perhaps because those who think visually are less comfortable thinking verbally.

No doubt there are also "transferences" to theory—both positive and negative—based on experiences with therapists, teachers, or supervisors in the individual's past. If the transference is positive, the theory espoused by that person might be idealized, but if it is negative, a specific theory—or even all theories—may be viewed in an agnostic or atheistic fashion.

Whether an art therapist openly espouses a theoretical stance or insists that he or she is atheoretical, whatever is done (the "technique" employed) implies some underlying theoretical assumptions. There is always a theory beneath the practice, even if it is unacknowledged and unknown. Or, to put it another way, "Clinical judgments and activities flow organically from conscious or preconscious theoretical premises, rather than the other way around" (Deri, 1984, p. 218).

Moreover, regardless of the therapist's orientation, the patient comes to therapy "with a theory of pathogenesis of his symptoms. With his words and speech [and art] the patient conveys not only a description of what he suffers, but his own diagnoses and explanatory theories of his [problems]. . . . These explanations, the patient's theories, are not to be ignored but to be used as data, which not uncommonly go some distance toward insight" (Rangell, 1985, p. 81). Although none of the authors in this volume specifically addresses the patient's "theory," all stress that a person's associations to and ideas about their own art be taken very seriously.

In this generalization about something common to most chapters, I have been what psychoanalyst Arnold Cooper would call a "lumper." During a discussion on the rela-tion of theory to technique, Cooper referred "to the distinction between 'lumpers' and 'splitters' [and] noted that we can at any moment, and with a particular end in view, decide whether we are interested in differences in technique or in how all techniques are at bottom the same" (Richards, 1984, p. 600).

Whether "the search for common ground" is really more useful than "the examination of differences" (Richards, 1984, p. 600) is not clear to me. I am a "lumper" by inclination, tending to see commonality more than distinctions among different approaches. That is probably what has led me to see important learnings in a variety of theories and techniques, like those in this book.

In any case, I believe it would be appropriate at this point to briefly identify some commonalities, in addition to those already noted. Perhaps most important is that all the authors agree on the power of art to help and to heal. Their investigations of different theoretical worlds center on the search for an explanation of this power. In fact, one way to look at the "red thread" that runs through all of the chapters is that all reflect an attempt to answer the question: *Why and how does art heal?*

I emphasize art's role in making the unconscious conscious, Kramer stresses the sublimation possible in the making of formed expression. Wilson says that symbolization through art helps people to develop vital ego functions. Robbins notes that art is a unique form of play within the transitional space of therapy. Lachman-Chapin highlights how mirroring by the art therapist affirms the patient and their art. Edwards stresses the power of the "personified image" to give direction, and Wallace describes its vital role in "active imagination."

Betensky values the image as a vehicle for phenomenological looking and knowing. Garai feels that making art promotes self-actualization, and Rogers sees the expressive arts as "a path to wholeness." For Rhyne, art is a way of thinking which helps people move toward autonomy. For Allen, art making puts us in touch with the larger reality of the universe.

Silver says that art is another language; Rosal says that art is a way of thinking. Both see it as a tool for knowing and growing. Roth says that a child can be helped to develop by "shaping" artistic behaviors. Aach-Feldman and Kunkle-Miller state that even simple pre-art activities can help those with serious impairments to grow.

Sobol sees art in family assessment as a vivid way of illustrating underlying problems in the family system. Williams notes the power of art in systemic therapy with groups. Riley feels that art therapy is especially appropriate for systemic family work, and that it is inherently postmodern.

Ulman notes the virtues of both art as therapy and art psychotherapy, and how she uses each in her work. Wadeson shows the versatility of art therapy, and the applicability to it of the many theories that inform her approach. McNiff celebrates how the arts can free the creative spirit to access the integrating capacity of the imagination. Henley tells how the arts make academic and emotional learning both attractive and powerful.

Although unique for each, all of the contributors to this volume have found a way to integrate some of their previous training and experience with their chosen approach to art therapy. Betensky and Garai, trained as clinical psychologists, incorporated projective techniques into their work as art therapists. Both Kramer and Henley worked as art teachers. As clinicians, Kramer brought teaching into her art therapy; and Henley brought therapeutic art experiences into his classroom.

Similarly, Silver and Rosal, who had done empirical research, developed approaches characterized by precise interventions and measurable outcomes. Aach-Feldman and Kunkle-Miller drew from training in child development, special education, and rehabilitation when creating their developmental approach to art therapy. Elinor Ulman, in tracing the personal roots of three art therapy theories, makes this same point in greater depth.

In addition to finding ways to incorporate (rather than to discard or put aside) previous experiences, all of the contributors have been creative in using their chosen theories. Sometimes they have applied the ideas in a novel way, as with Roth's "reality shaping," or Rhyne's invention of "mind-state drawings" by integrating cognitive constructs with her artist self and her training as a Gestalt therapist. There is nothing Kohut wrote that would predict Lachman-Chapin's idea of drawing with the patient, though it is indeed a kind of "mirroring." She also amplified Winnicott's (1971) interactive squiggle game, as she experimented with a novel way of using her artist-self in her work as a therapist.

Aach-Feldman and Kunkle-Miller's inventiveness is evident, not only in the playful activities they created, but also in their ways of thinking about what to do with their multiply-handicapped clients. Allen's method of creating art in a group setting is a highly original form of disciplined spiritual practice. Henley's "therapeutic education" through the expressive arts is an equally unique approach to academic and emotional learning.

Another kind of independence is evident in the fact that many of the contributors to this volume have gone beyond their primary theoretical resource. Kramer, for example, long after her initial statement of the theoretical importance of sublimation for art therapy, explored its origins in ethology. Garai, though he began by referring primarily to "humanistic" psychologists, found it necessary to move beyond, citing "holistic" authors from a variety of disciplines.

In addition, all of the contributors seem to agree on at least three things: 1) the importance of the image, 2) the need to create a therapeutic space in which people can safely create, and 3) the complexity of both person and process in art therapy. As is clear in the chapters, however, which are designed to highlight and clarify distinctions, there are big differences in how each author approaches these three areas. They each evoke and use images in their own way; they are similarly unique in how they make their space safe and stimulating, and they conceptualize the complexities of people and their products in radically different ways, evident in their writing.

Indeed, some of the approaches are quite intellectual and logical, some are more emotional and intuitive, but all attempt to integrate both feeling and thought in the art therapeutic process. And, whatever the relative emphasis on art and therapy in any author's conception, all include a consideration of both. Some also make explicit their conviction that any viable theory of art therapy which might eventually evolve ought to include both elements of this hybrid discipline, as well as the special relationship between them.

"The development of a valid theory about art therapy is a more demanding task, yet perhaps the most important . . . of all. For, if we are unable to account for our effectiveness in a logical and communicable way, we will continue to be viewed as either charming romantics or hopeless airheads, depending on the bias of the perceiver" (Rubin, 1984, p. 144). Repeatedly, art therapists have suggested that the ultimate theory for our discipline "will have to be elaborated from the empirical stuff of which art therapy was originally created" (Betensky, 1975).

The years since the first edition of this book have seen the development of several attempts to articulate art-based theories of art therapy, represented in this volume by the open studio approach of Pat Allen. Similar orientations and practices, based on the properties of different art modalities, are reflected in the expressive therapies approaches of Shaun McNiff and Natalie Rogers. All three refer in one way or another to the special experience of creating and its power to enhance the development of a person as an individual, in relationship to others, to the world, and to the universe.

In contrast, the new contributions by Rosal, Henley, Sobol and Williams, and Riley include trends also affecting verbal psychotherapy. Art therapists, like other clinicians, are more likely these days to employ cognitive-behavioral methods or to make use of systemic understandings. And there is no question that all therapists are more attuned to the role of the cultural and socioeconomic environment, and of biology and heredity than in the past. Such sociocultural and physiological variables are also noted by Wadeson, and in the comments of both Anderson and Riley.

Our "medicine," however, is not chemical, but is rather closer to alchemical; that is, the special miracle of art. We still draw, as in societies from time immemorial, on the "magic power of the image," regardless of how we understand its origins or its functions. Similarly, while we are alert to the effects of trauma or cultural dislocation, we offer not a verbal "debriefing," but a way of "telling without talking," a new and potentially "corrective" kind of experience—perhaps at the level of the brain itself.

Indeed, some have suggested, like Anderson, that we will eventually be able to account for the healing power of art through research that documents changes in the brain while people are involved in creating. A new book by Frances Kaplan (2000) in fact, proposes a scientific art-based theory to account for art therapy's effectiveness, which might lessen the need to utilize other paradigms.

Art in therapy, though, is much more than the provision of a place for the inherent healing possible through an authentic creative process, however we conceptualize it. It is also art in the presence of another, whether we think of ourselves as teachers, guides, fellow travelers, companions, collaborators, containers, objects of transference, or any of the many possible ways identified in this book.

Indeed, as noted by Shirley Riley in her commentary on postmodern approaches in art therapy, one of the biggest changes in recent years, for clinicians of all theoretical stripes, is the increasingly egalitarian position of patient and therapist. While this has always been somewhat true for humanistic approaches, it is increasingly so for clinicians of all orientations who are more and more "learning from the patient" (Casement, 1991). In fact, I believe that even the more authoritarian (prescriptive) approaches, like behavioral ones, work best when the therapist truly listens, watches, respects, and takes cues from the client, not only from the theory.

But no matter how we explain what happens during the art therapy process, we have a responsibility to those whose journeys we support to have some clear notion about what is wrong and how to help. Theory is what enables any therapist to make sense of the data being received, and to be thoughtful about technique. Only with a coherent perspective on what she does can the art therapist make fully available the healing powers of art. I believe that to effectively integrate a synthesis of art and therapy requires an internalized frame of reference. Theory helps an art therapist to sharpen both thinking and clinical skills. In fact, it is only when we have truly mastered some theory of psychological functioning and of psychotherapy, when it is "in our bones," that we can use our creative intuition in the most helpful way.

I also believe that it is essential to have a solid grounding in some coherent notion of how people function and how to help them get better, before exploring any modifications or alternatives. It is similar to the need to learn to draw, paint, and model reality, before attempting alterations, abstractions, or other variations. In the same way, the enthusiastic embrace and deep understanding of one primary frame of reference provides a necessary matrix for the possible adoption and adaptation of others. One reason for a book like this is to familiarize the "becoming" art therapist with many different orientations, so that she can select intelligently from the many options available, according to what suits each individual's personality and values, as noted in the Introduction.

Moreover, as stated repeatedly, there are very good reasons for having more than one way to look at the infinitely complex phenomena of people and their art. Simply put, the more extensive any art therapist's understanding of different approaches, the more clinical lenses she has with which to see. Like a stain on a microscopic slide, a theory can enable a therapist to literally see something that would otherwise be invisible. And if she can look at a problem from a different angle, she is often able to view possible solutions from a new perspective.

It is a kind of *"reframing"* for the therapist, for whom a cup can look either half empty or half full, just as it can for the patient. That is probably why so many, like the authors of these chapters, have struggled with the difficult questions of how to understand, and do art therapy—in order to help the people they serve as much as possible through art.

It is my hope that this book—with its many "maps" of different ways to explore, to find, to create, and to help—will enable art therapists to begin their search for what suits them best. I hope, too, that it will increase the number of listening and looking "lenses" they can comfortably put into their clinical "frames." Each approach offers a potential "door" for both therapist and patient, another avenue for exporation and discovery.

Just as any theory needs to be understood and integrated through practice over time, so well-developed "technique" is not so much a collection of ideas, as it is something deeply ingrained and easily available. Elinor Ulman made this point in 1971 when she wrote that *"a little learning may be worse than none. Our understanding must be well digested if it is to inform lightning decisions"* (Ulman & Dachinger, 1975 p. 28). A good art therapist strives to have both theory and technique "in her bones" so that "relating to a patient through art" can be truly spontaneous, flexible, and artistic.

This book is meant to help all art therapists to think hard about what they do, so that they can do it even better. I hope it will also help people to be humble, to know what they don't know, and to be open to new ways of thinking, no matter how many years of experience they may have. In fact, I believe that being the best art therapist one can be is a lifetime task. Happily, it is also as wonderfully creative as the thrilling work of helping patients to find their true selves through art.

☐ References

Ault, R. (1977). Are you an artist or a therapist? A professional dilemma of art therapists. In R. H. Shoemaker, & S. E. Gonick-Barris (Eds.), *Creativity and the art therapist's identity* (pp. 53–56). Baltimore, MD: American Art Therapy Association.

Betensky, M. (November, 1975). Phenomenology: A theory of art therapy. Unpublished manuscript presented at the American Art Therapy Association Conference.

Casement, P. (1991). *Learning from the patient.* New York: Guilford Press.

Deri, S. K. (1984). *Symbolization and creativity.* New York: International Universities Press.

Frederickson, J. (1999). *Psychodynamic psychotherapy: Learning to listen from multiple perspectives.* Philadelphia: Brunner/Mazel.

Gedo, J. E., & Goldberg, A. (1973). *Models of the mind: A psychoanalytic theory.* Chicago: University of Chicago Press.

Hall, C. S., & Lindzey, G. (Eds.). (1977). *Theories of personality* (3rd ed.). New York: Wiley.

Hedges, L. E. (1983). *Listening perspectives in psychotherapy.* New York: Jason Aronson.

Kaplan, F. F. (2000). *Art, science & art therapy: Repainting the picture.* Philadelphia: Jessica Kingsley.

Knill, P. J., Barba, H. N., & Fuchs, M. N. (1995). *Minstrels of the soul: Intermodal expressive therapy.* Toronto: Palmerston Press.

Kwiatkowska, H. Y. (1974). Technique versus techniques. *American Journal of Art Therapy, 14,* 17.

Levy, B. I., Kramer, E., Kwiatkowska, H. Y., Rhyne, J., & Ulman, E. (1974). Symposium: Integration of divergent points of view in art therapy. *American Journal of Art Therapy, 14,* 12–17.

Lusebrink, V. (1990). *Imagery & visual expression in therapy.* New York: Plenum.

Moon, C. H. (2001). *Art therapy: Cultivating the artist identity in the art therapist.* Philadelphia: Jessica Kingsley.

Nucho, A. (1987). *Psychocybernetic model of art therapy.* Springfield, IL: Charles C. Thomas.

Polster, E. (1966). A contemporary psychotherapy. *Psychotherapy: Theory, Research & Practice, 3(1),* 1–6.

Rangell, L. (1985). On the theory of psychoanalysis and the relation of theory to psychoanalytic therapy. *Journal of the American Psychoanalytic Association, 33,* 59–92.

Richards, A. (1984). Panel: The relation between psychoanalytic theory and psychoanalytic technique. *Journal of the American Psychoanalytic Association, 32,* 587–602.

Robbins, A. (1981). Integrating diverse theoretical frameworks in the identification process of an art therapist. Paper presented at AATA conference.

Rothstein, A. (Ed.). (1985). *Models of the mind: Their relationships to clinical work.* New York: International Universities Press.

Rubin, J. A. (1984). *The art of art therapy.* New York: Brunner/Mazel.

Shostrom, E. (1965). *Three approaches to psychotherapy: Parts 1, 2, 3* [Film]. Corona Del Mar, CA: Psychological & Educational Films.

Stein, M. I. (Ed.). (1961). *Contemporary psychotherapies.* New York: The Free Press of Glencoe.

Ulman, E. (1961). Art therapy: Problems of definition. *Bulletin of Art Therapy, 1*(2), 10–20.

Ulman, E. & Dachinger, P. (Eds.). (1975). *Art Therapy in theory and practice.* New York: Schocken Books.

Waller, D. (1993). *Group interactive art therapy.* New York: Routledge.

Winnicott, D. W. (1971a). *Therapeutic consultations in child psychiatry.* New York: Basic Books.

Winnicott, D. W. (1971b). *Playing & reality.* New York: Basic Books.

Index

Aach-Feldman, S., 193–194, 226–240, 254, 287, 348–349
Abreaction, 17
Abstract thinking, 208, 237
Acceptance, 140
Ackerman, N., 261
Ackerman-Haswell, J. F., 214
Ackerson, J., 212
Active imagination, 82–83, 95–97, 101–107, 115, 313, 321, 348
  art and, 98
  definition, 97
  dialogue and, 98–100
Actualization, 139, 149, 152, 161
Adaptive approach, 193, 254
Adler, A., 4, 152
Adler, G., 97
Affect, 46–47, *see also* Emotions
  capacity for expression of, 228
  dissociative deadness of, 92
  interventions to promote expression of, 235
Affective disorders, 61, 64
"Age of the person," 160
Ahsen, A., 154
Akenside, M., 319
Alexander, F., 311
Allen, P. B., 119, 178–189, 259, 275, 278, 288, 344, 348–349
Altman, L. L., 2, 17
American Art Therapy Association (AATA), 263
Amplifications, 100
Anderson, F. E., 193–194, 254–255, 349–350
Anderson, H., 282
Anderson, W. T., 262
Anger, 140–141, 144
Anima/animus, 88
Anorexia, 110, 112–113
Anticipation, 141–142
Anxiety, 22
  attitude toward, 19
  denial of, 25
  drawing of, 220
  expressed through regression, 198
  life-style and, 150

reactive to the situation, 19
  symbolic play used to ventilate, 31
Aphasia, 44
Approximation, 236
  successive, 196
Aquarian conspiracy, 160
Archetypes, 83–84, 107
  creativity and, 152
  maternal figures, 159
  parental, 84
  positive/negative aspects of, 84
  self as the central, 95
  sequence of, 88
Arieti, S., 38
Arnheim, R., 123, 124, 138, 147, 193, 242, 322
Arnkoff, E., 212
Aron, L., 80
Arrington, D. B., 255
Art
  active imagination and, 98
  as a form of exhibitionism, 68–69
  as therapy, 287, 328
  as therapy or psychotherapy, 291–304
  as therapy with adults, 295–304
  as therapy with children, 30–39
  definition of, 153, 292
  derived from unconscious material, 49
  enhancing insight and, 25
  function types and, 88
  healing nature of, 316, 348
  in human development, 294–295
  in the lives of Kramer and Naumburg, 293
  incorporation into psychoanalysis, 16
  Jung's personal use of, 81–82, 180
  psychotherapy, 287
  similarities and differences over time, 132
  structure of, 124, 131, 138
  symbolic communication through, 12
  to relieve tension, 68–69
  value to society, 39
  visual display of, 127
Art materials, 109–110, 126
  pre-art materials, 228–230, 232–235
  preoperational phase and, 234
  presentation of, 231, 235
  sensorimotor phase and, 229–230